BLUEPRINT
Phonics Activities
Resource Bank

G000037945

Virginia's

Carol Cort

Stanley Thornes (Publishers) Ltd

Do you receive BLUEPRINTS NEWS?

Blueprints is an expanding series of practical teacher's ideas books and photocopiable resources for use in primary schools. Books are available for separate infant and junior age ranges for every core and foundation subject, as well as for an ever widening range of other primary teaching needs. These include **Blueprints Primary English** books and **Blueprints Resource Banks**. **Blueprints** are carefully structured around the demands of National Curriculum in England and Wales, but are used successfully by schools and teachers in Scotland, Northern Ireland and elsewhere.

Blueprints provide :

- *Total curriculum coverage*
- *Hundreds of practical ideas*
- *Books specifically for the age range you teach*
- *Flexible resources for the whole school or for individual teachers*
- *Excellent photocopiable sheets - ideal for assessment and children's work profiles*
- *Supreme value.*

Books may be bought by credit card over the telephone and information obtained on **(0242) 577944**. Alternatively, photocopy and return this **FREEPOST** form to receive **Blueprints News**, our regular update on all new and existing titles. You may also like to add the name of a friend who would be interested in being on the mailing list.

Please add my name to the **BLUEPRINTS NEWS** mailing list.

Mr/Mrs/Miss/Ms --

Home address --

--Postcode ------------------

School address --

-- Postcode ------------------

Please also send **BLUEPRINTS NEWS** to :

Mr/Mrs/Miss/Ms --

Address --

-- Postcode ------------------

To: Marketing Services Dept., Stanley Thornes Ltd, FREEPOST (GR 782), Cheltenham, GL50 1BR

Text © Carol Cort 1995
Original line illustrations by Andrew Keylock © ST(P) Ltd 1995

The right of Carol Cort to be identified as author of this work has been asserted by her in accordance with the Copyright, Designs and Patents Act 1988.

The copyright holders authorise ONLY users of **Blueprints** *Phonics Activities Resource Bank* to make photocopies or stencil duplicates of the copymasters for their own or their classes' immediate use within the teaching context. No other rights are granted without permission in writing from the publisher or under licence from the Copyright Licensing Agency Limited. Further details of such licences (for reprographic reproduction) may be obtained from the Copyright Licensing Agency Limited, of 90 Tottenham Court Road, London W1P 9HE.

Copy by any other means or for any other purpose is strictly prohibited without the prior written consent of the copyright holders. Applications for such permission should be addressed to the publishers.

First published in 1995 by:
Stanley Thornes (Publishers) Ltd
Ellenborough House
Wellington Street
CHELTENHAM GL50 1YD
England

A catalogue record for this book is available from the British Library.

ISBN 0–7487–1986-5

Typeset by Tech-Set, Gateshead, Tyne & Wear.
Printed in Great Britain

CONTENTS

Other phonic rules

Answers to word games

INTRODUCTION

The *Phonics Activities Resource Bank* is a comprehensive photocopiable compendium of 140 pages of activities and games for use alongside phonic programmes and the *Reading Activities Resource Bank*. Its aim is to develop a child's phonic ability through repetitive practice, to increase memory skills and to build self-confidence.

Most primary schools will have banks of reading equipment and activities, either bought or home-made, to support their reading and spelling programmes. This book provides a huge bank of such material ready made for use in the classroom that will save you both time and money. It allows you to prepare carefully graded, relevant activities and games at a fraction of the cost of commercially bought ones. It also means that a lost piece does not cause problems: you simply photocopy the sheet again and replace the piece.

The activities are highly versatile. They can be photocopied directly onto card or photocopied onto paper and then stuck onto card. The materials may be coloured and covered for permanent use, or quickly run off on paper for more immediate classroom use. You will find practical instructions in the next section, 'Making and using the activities.' Manufacturing the games is an ideal activity for parent helpers either at home or at school. As the cost of producing activities is minimal you can even send sheets of games home to be made up and practised with parents.

The *Phonics Activities Resource Bank* covers:

- Alphabetical order
- Alphabet sounds
- Short vowel sounds
- Initial blends
- Word endings
- Track games to provide more practice
- Vowel consonant blends
- Vowels with only one consonant between them, 'magic e' at the end
- Vowel blends
- 'ck' ending following a short vowel sound
- 'ke' ending following a long vowel sound
- 'c' or 'k' at the start of a word
- Softening of 'c' and 'g' when followed by an 'e' or 'i'.

Most of the games can be used flexibly with either individuals or groups and many have a self-correcting element so that they can be played without adult supervision. You will find general instructions for playing the games on pages 1–7.

All the games have been extensively trialled and played by real children in real classrooms. They are stimulating, fun to play – and they work. Once you have started to work with the activities we are sure that you will find this book yet another absolutely invaluable resource to return to again and again.

MAKING AND USING THE ACTIVITIES

The activities in this book can be prepared in three ways.

a) Photocopied directly onto card
b) Photocopied onto paper
c) As in b) and then glued onto card.

Preparation
1 Photocopy the sheets as required.
2 Colour the copies and then, if required, stick the paper onto card.
3 Cut out all the pieces.
4 Run a wide felt tipped pen around the edge of the cards to obtain a professional-looking finish.

    If the pen is used half on and half off the card no ruler is necessary. This technique may require some practice but it is worthwhile as considerable time can be saved. Each complete set should be edged with the same colour pen so that pieces can be returned to their correct places easily.

5 Cover all pieces, on both sides, with transparent adhesive plastic e.g. *Coverlon®*. Several cards can be covered at the same time.

6 Cut around the pieces leaving a small border. The cutting action seals the plastic sheets together. The activity is now ready for use.

Jigsaws
Copymasters 5, 8–11.
An activity for one child.

Objective of the activity
To provide self-correcting (and therefore confidence-building) material in a meaningful and repetitive way.

Preparation
a) Photocopy the required sheets and prepare as in the General Instructions.
b) Cut the jigsaws apart as shown opposite.

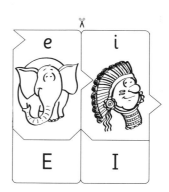

To use the activity
The child is given the jigsaw to sort into its correct alphabetical order.

Building activities
Copymasters 6–7, 76–7.
An activity for two–six children.
You will need:
One or two dice and three counters per child.

Objective of the activity
To build a child's self-confidence and memory span by providing repetitive practice of a phonetic sound.

Preparation
Each child has a set of equipment. The sets consist of the two prepared photocopied sheets and, if desired, word cards produced using the 'Find the pair' copymasters.
a) Photocopy the required number of sets.
b) Colour the copies.
c) Cut the building activity sheet numbered 2 into the component parts as shown on the base board.
d) Cover all the pieces, including the base board.
e) Velcro® pieces may be attached to the front of the base board and the back of the picture pieces using strong glue, e.g. PVA. This makes the activity easier to use.

To use the activity
1 Each child sets up his or her equipment as shown.
2 The children throw the dice in turn and the child with the highest score begins; play continues in a clockwise direction. When the dice is thrown the piece corresponding to the number thrown is collected and placed on the base board. If phonic cards are being used the first card must be read correctly before a piece can be collected.
3 The other children take their turns in the same way. If a child already has the piece corresponding to the number on the dice then he or she collects a counter instead. Three counters may be exchanged for a piece of the child's choice. The first child to fill his or her base board is the winner.

Find the pair
Copymasters 1–4, 23–4, 27–8, 31–4, 43, 67–8, 73–4, 78–9, 81–2, 87–90, 93–8, 125–6, 139–140.
An activity for two–three children.

Objective of the activity
To reinforce a phonic rule, each set being based on an individual phonic sound. The activity will improve a child's memory span and spelling.

Preparation
Each set of picture cards is immediately followed by the corresponding set of letters or words, both copymasters must be photocopied.
a) Photocopy the sheets required.
b) Colour and cut the cards as explained in the General Instructions on page 1.

At this point the cards should be marked with matching tabs so that one set can be used for several activities. Each pair must have a unique set of matching marks. By changing the colour, shape and position of the marks, several sets may be used together. (See Copymasters 43 and 85.)
c) Complete the preparation as in the General Instructions.

To use the activity
1 The cards are mixed up and then placed face down on the table in rows to form a rectangle.
2 Each child may, in turn, turn over any two cards. This needs to be done in such a way that all the children can have a good view. If the cards do not match he or she replaces them, face down, in their original positions.
3 If the cards selected are a pair, word matching picture, he or she keeps them and takes another turn. The child may do this until he or she fails to find a pair.
4 The activity continues until all the pairs have been found. The child with the most pairs is the winner.

Touch cards
Use the 'Find the pair' copymasters (see above).

Objective of the activity
To help build self-confidence by presenting phonic rules in a self-correcting (and therefore confidence-building) format.

Preparation
These cards are prepared using the 'Find the pair' cards.
a) Colour and cut out as in the General Instructions.
b) Glue each answer card onto its corresponding question card.
c) Cover the cards as usual.

There are many ways to use these cards.

Activity 1
For one child.
1 The touch cards are laid out with the words facing upwards.
2 The child points to a card, reads the word and then checks to see if he or she is right. If correct the child collects the card, if not it remains on the table and another card is chosen. The activity continues until all the cards have been collected.

Activity 2
For one child.
   The same process is repeated but this time the answers are repeated to an adult. This helps build self-confidence because the words have already been learnt.

Activity 3
An activity for two children.
   The cards are laid out on the table with the words facing upwards. The children take turns to read the words, choosing any card and checking the answer. Each child collects correctly read cards. When all the cards have been collected the child with the most is the winner.

Activity 4
An activity for two children.
1 The cards are placed in a pile, words facing upwards and the children take turns to read the words on the top card.

2 If the card is read correctly it is collected, if not it is placed in a new pile, with the pictures facing upwards, next to the original stack.

3 When the first pile is completed the wrongly read cards are turned over and the procedure is repeated until all the cards have been read correctly.

Self-correcting matching jigsaws
Copymasters as for 'Find the pair' cards.
An activity for one child.

Objective of the activity
To build self-confidence by providing a self-correcting method of phonic rules.

Preparation
Prepare as for 'Find the pair' cards.

The number of jigsaws given to a child should depend on the ability of the child. A set may be built up slowly or lengthened by joining two sets. Problem words can be carried forward and added to another set, thus providing further practice.

To use the activity
1 The cards are mixed up and then spread out face upwards.
2 The child looks at the word cards and tries to find the corresponding picture cards. The matching tabs are there to help.
3 When all the cards have been paired they should be checked and the child asked to read them.

Once a child is familiar with the answers, the cards can be used to play a game such as 'Find the pair' or 'Match the jigsaw'.

Match the jigsaw
Copymasters as for 'Find the pair'.
An activity for two children.

To use the activity
1 The cards are mixed up and half are placed face upwards on the table.
2 The second half are placed face up in a pile.
3 The first child takes the top card off the pile and he tries to match it with the cards already displayed. If it matches he takes the pair, if not the card is placed with those already on the table.
4 The second child now tries to match a card in the same way.
5 When all the cards from the pile have been used the game continues with the children collecting the pairs from the table. The winner is the child with the most cards.

Dominoes
Copymasters 15–17, 20–22, 29–30, 35, 49–50, 69, 72, 75, 80, 86, 99.
An activity for two children.

Objective of the activity
To provide repetitive practice of phonic rules. This improves not only a child's knowledge of a phonic rule but also his or her memory skills. (Phonic rules are listed on the Contents page.)

Preparation
a) Photocopy the required copymasters.
b) The phonic rule applying to each set may be highlighted or underlined on each card before cutting out the dominoes. Cut them out following the dotted lines.
c) Choose a starting card and mark it on the back.
d) Cover the cards as explained in the General Instructions.

To use the activity
1 The cards are divided equally between the two children.
2 The child with the starting card places it face upwards on the table.
3 The second child looks at his or her card and tries to find a match, word to picture or picture to word. If he or she has a suitable card it is placed to match.
4 The first child continues in the same way.
5 If the child does not have a matching card he or she misses that turn.
6 The winner is the first child to have no cards left.

Frog race track game
Copymasters 12–14.
An activity for two–three children.
You will need:
A dice and coloured counters.

Objective of the activity
To provide repetitive practice thereby building self-confidence.

Preparation
a) Photocopy the copymasters.
b) Colour and trim the copymasters and join them together.
c) Cover the track game in adhesive plastic as explained in the General Instructions.

To use the activity
1 Each child chooses a different coloured counter and places it on the start line.
2 Each player throws the dice and the one with the highest score begins by moving their counter the number of places shown on the dice.
3 Play continues with each child taking his or her turn and moving his or her counter according to the number shown on the dice.
4 The winner is the first child to reach the finish line.

Race the clock – lower and upper case
Copymasters 18 and 19.
An activity for one or two–four children.
You will need:
A stop clock. A small plastic tray would be useful for each child to store their tiles.

Objective of the activity
To provide repetitive practice of alphabetical order and to improve memory skills.

Preparation
a) Two copies of the copymaster are needed for each child.

3

b) Half the copies should be cut up into individual alphabet tiles, whilst the other half make the base boards as shown below.

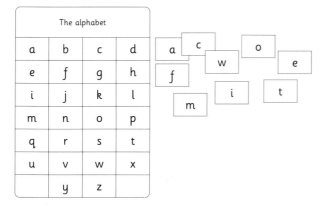

c) Colour the board. At this stage the vowels may be coloured to distinguish them from the consonants.
d) Cover all the pieces as explained in the General Instructions.

To use the activity
1 Each child has a base board and a complete set of matching alphabet letters.
2 The letters are placed face upwards on the table next to each child's base board.
3 The clock is started and each child races to place their alphabet tiles correctly on their board.
4 The first child to finish stops the clock and the time taken is recorded. The alphabet board is checked and if it has been completed correctly this child is the winner.
5 The game may be repeated with all the children trying to better the fastest time.
6 A single child may play the game by trying to improve on their own best time.

Vowel match
Copymasters 25–6.
An activity for two children.

Objective of the activity
To provide practice in recognising short vowel sounds.

Preparation
a) Photocopy the required copymasters.
b) Cut Copymaster 25 into individual tiles and Copymaster 26 into two base boards.
c) Colour and cover all the pieces as explained in the General Instructions.

To use the activity
1 Each child has a base board.
2 The picture cards are mixed and then placed face downwards in a pile.
3 The children take turns to pick up a tile and place it to match on a square on their base board.
4 If a vowel has already been covered the tile is placed in a new stack face upwards at the side of the original pile.
5 When all the original cards have been used the new pile is turned over and the game continues until one child fills their board.
6 The first child to fill their board is the winner.

Lotto
Copymasters 47–8, 83–4.
An activity for two children.

Objective of the activity
To provide practice in distinguishing between initial letter blends.

Preparing and using the activity
Follow the instructions for 'Vowel match' (above). For Copymasters 83–4, either sheet may be cut into lotto tiles.

The parachute race/Jack and the bean stalk/Humpty Dumpty
Copymasters 36–7, 38–9, 40–41 and 42 for vowel playing tiles.
An activity for two–six children.

The objective of the activity
To help a child to recognise and use short vowel sounds, thus building confidence.
You will need:
A dice.

Preparation
a) Photocopy the required copymasters. Each child needs a base board; the group of players share the vowel tiles from Copymaster 42.
b) Colour, cut out and cover all the pieces as explained in the General Instructions.

To use the activity
1 A base board is placed in front of each child.
2 The vowel letters are mixed up and then spread out face down in the centre of the table to form a 'tile bank'.
3 Each base board has a series of short words with their vowels missing.
4 Each child throws the dice, the child with the highest score begins and play continues in a clockwise direction.
5 The first child picks a vowel tile, examines it and decides whether it will fill the first space in his or her base board. If the vowel on the tile completes the word the tile is placed on the board. If the vowel does not complete a word it is returned to the tile bank.
6 The other children take their turns in the same way. The first child to fill all the spaces on their base board with the correct vowel tiles is the winner.

The game may be used by an individual child working against a timer.

Word wheels
Copymasters 44 (sl), 45 (gl), 46 (pl), 91 (ow), 112 (ew), 132 (ay).
An activity for one child or a group of children.

Objective of the activity
To reinforce phonic sound lessons thus improving a child's self-confidence.
You will need:
A brass split pin for each word wheel.

Preparation
a) Photocopy the required copymasters (see list above).
b) Colour, cut out and cover the copymaster as explained in the General Instructions.
c) Pierce a small hole through the centre of the base board and the wheel, push a split pin, from the front, through the centre of the wheel and then through the base board. The pin is then opened out and pressed flat on the back. A piece of tape should be placed over the points to prevent accidents.

To use the activity
The wheel is turned to find the words. Note that at this level every combination of letters produces a proper word.

The children should be asked to record the words they find. This can be extended and the child asked to include the words in sentences or even in a short story.

Double word wheel
Copymasters 103, 106, 108 and 110 for the word wheels; 107 and 111 for the base board; 109 for a work card.
An activity for one child or a group of children.

Objective of the activity
To provide practice in recognising words containing specific phonic sounds and to help to build self-confidence by enabling the child to correct their own work using the answer card. Note that not every combination of letters possible produces a 'proper' word.
You will need:
Two brass split pins per word wheel activity. (Small pieces of velcro are optional and can be used to produce base boards with changeable phonic letter squares and wheels.)

Preparation
a) Copy the required copymasters. For each word wheel activity you will need a base board, two wheels and a small letter square supplying the phonic sound to be practised. Note that care must be taken to ensure that the wheels are placed in their correct positions. They are labelled with a small R for right and L for left.
b) Cut out the copymasters, including the shaded squares on the lion base board.
c) Cover all the pieces as explained in the General Instructions.
d) Glue the letter square in place on the base board.
e) Pierce small holes in the centre of the wheels and at the points marked x on the base board.

To attach the word wheels and use the Leo base board: a split pin must be pushed, from the front, through the base board and then through the centre of the appropriate wheel. The pin is then opened out and pressed flat on the back. A piece of tape should be placed over the points to prevent accidents. Repeat with the second wheel. (The wheels are fixed behind the Leo base board and letters show through the cut out squares.)
To use Professor Penelope's word finder base board: push a split pin, from the front, through the word wheel and then through the base board. The pin is then opened out and pressed flat on the back. A piece of tape should be placed over the points to prevent accidents. Repeat with the second wheel. (The wheels are fixed to the front of Professor Penelope's word finder machine.)

To use the activity
The wheel is turned to find the words. Note that at this level not every combination of letters produces a proper word.

The children should be asked to record the words they find. This activity can be extended by asking the child to include the words in sentences or even in a short story.

Sliding strip word find
Copymasters 55, 57, 59 and 61 for Sam the Spaceman, Toby Tyrannosaurus, Wordal and Teddy characters; 51–4 and 63–6 for sliding letter strips; 56, 58, 60 and 62 for associated work sheets.
Copymasters 120–121 for Wanda Witch and -tch words; Copymasters 130–131 for The y to i machine.
An activity for one child.

The objective of the activity
To provide attractive, repetitive material to reinforce a phonic rule.
You will need:
Two small pieces of double-sided adhesive velcro.

Preparation
a) Photocopy the copymasters.
b) Colour the character base board.
c) Cut out the copymasters, remembering to re-cut the slots in the character base board.
d) Cover the pieces in transparent adhesive plastic as explained in the General Instructions, then re-cut the slots in the character using a single slit.
e) Attach the word base to the right or left of the slots, using the velcro strips or adhesive tape as shown below. Now thread the corresponding sliding strip through the slits from the back of the character base board. Only one word will show from the front; new words can, or course, be created by pulling the strip.

The circus race track game
Copymasters 70–71.
An activity for two–four children.

Objective of the activity
The aim of this activity is to give repetitive practice of a phonic rule chosen by the teacher. Thereby building a child's confidence in their ability to spell words following a learned rule.
You will need:
A dice and four sets of five counters, each set being a different colour. A set of word cards for each child.

Preparation
a) Photocopy the copymasters.
b) Colour. Make sure to colour one of the corner balloons to match each child's set of counters. Cut out, join and cover the sheets.
c) The question cards may be made up from any of the 'Find the pair' sets.

To use the activity

1 Each child chooses a starting arrow on the board and places their four coloured counters on the nearest balloons.

2 The children throw the dice and the child with the highest score begins.

3 The first child places his or her first counter on the arrow and then throws the dice. He or she then answers a question card and, if the answer is correct, moves forward the number shown on the dice.

4 The other children take their turns in the same way.

5 When a player's counter returns to his or her arrow it is placed within his or her balloon. The child then places the next counter on the arrow ready for his or her next turn.

6 The first child to place all their counters within their balloon is the winner.

The 'Jungle hunt track game' is produced and played in the same way. (Colour the corner flowers to match the children's counters.)

Throw the snowballs
Copymaster 92.
An activity for one child.

Objective of the activity
This activity provides practice of the 'ow' as in snow sound. The snowman image helps the child to remember the sound.
You will need:
A small piece of velcro.

Preparation
a) Photocopy Copymaster 92.
b) Colour, cut and cover all the pieces as explained in the General Instructions. Cut the copymaster to form a base board and individual 'snowballs'.
c) Stick small pieces of velcro (fluffy) onto the back of the snowballs.

To use the activity
1 The child throws the snowballs against the snowman's scarf, recording the words he or she finds.
2 The words can then be used to write sentences or to produce a short story.

Christmas tree game
Copymasters 100–102.
This game is produced and played in the same way as 'The parachute game' (see p. 4) but concentrates on the use of the vowel blends **ee**, **ea** and **ai**.

Snap!
Copymasters 113–116.
An activity for two children.

Objective of the activity
To provide repetitive practice using the **th**, **ch**, **wh**, **ph** and **sh** sounds.

Preparation
Colour, cut out and cover all the cards as explained in the General Instructions.

To use the activity
This is a pairing snap game in which only pairs are collected.
1 The cards are shuffled and dealt out between the children.
2 The first child places a card face upwards in the centre of the table and the second child places a card next to the first card.
3 If the underlined phonic sound of the two cards match, the first child to say 'Snap!' collects the two cards and places them to the side to be counted at the end of the game. The game continues with each child in turn adding a card to their central pile and shouting 'Snap!' if the top cards match.
4 At the end of each round any cards left in the central piles are re-shuffled and dealt. The game continues until all the cards have been paired.
5 The winner is the child with the most pairs.

Space fleet track game
Copymasters 117–119.
An activity for two children.

Objective of the activity
To provide practice of the **th**, **ch**, **wh**, and **sh** sounds in an exciting and repetitive activity.
You will need:
A dice.

Preparation
a) Photocopy the copymasters.
b) Colour and cut out all the pieces. Join the track using adhesive tape then cover all the pieces as explained in the General Instructions.

To use the activity
1 The letter tiles are mixed up and placed face downwards in a pile.
2 Each child throws the dice, the child with the highest score begins and play continues in a clockwise direction.
3 The first child shakes the dice and moves forward the number shown; when the pathways divide the child chooses which way to go. If he or she lands on a lettered square he or she picks up the top letter tile, if it completes the word on the lettered square the tile is placed on the track and the child collects a space ship. If the letter tile does not fit it is placed face upwards to form a 'used' pile.
4 The other children take their turns in the same way.
5 When the first pile of letter tiles has been used the 'used' stack is turned over and re-used.
6 The game continues until all the words have been completed.
7 The winner is the child with the largest space fleet.

Eskimos winter track game
Copymasters 122–124.
An activity for two children.

Objective of the activity
To provide practice in distinguishing between the **ir**, **er**, and **ur** blends (they all say er) in an exciting and repetitive activity.

Preparation and use
As for the 'Space fleet track game', though in this game the children collect fish not rockets.

Beach toys track game
Copymasters 127–129.
An activity for two–four children.

Objective of the activity
To provide practice in distinguishing between **ll**, **ss**, and **ff** in an exciting and repetitive activity.

Preparation and use
As for the 'Space fleet track game' but in this game the children collect beach toys.

Boys and girls come out to play
Copymasters 136–8.
An activity for a single child or a group of children.
You will need:
A timer.

Objective of the activity
To build self-confidence by providing repetitive practice using a learnt rule.

Preparation
a) Photocopy the copymasters, one set for each child.
b) Join the base boards, then colour, cut out and cover all the pieces as explained in the General Instructions.

To use the activity.
1 Each child's set of equipment consists of a base board, letter tiles and a rule card.
2 The timer is started and the children race to place their letters on their board to fill the spaces correctly and complete the words.
3 The first child to finish stops the timer and their answers are checked against the answer card. If all the letters have been correctly placed the child wins. If not, all boards are checked and the child with the highest number of correctly placed letter tiles is the winner.

Alphabet

Copymaster 1

a	b	c
d	e	f
g	h	i
j	k	l

Alphabet

Copymaster 3

m	n	o
p	q	r
s	t	u
v	w	x

Alphabet   Cards Y and Z are on Copymaster 17.   **Copymaster 4**

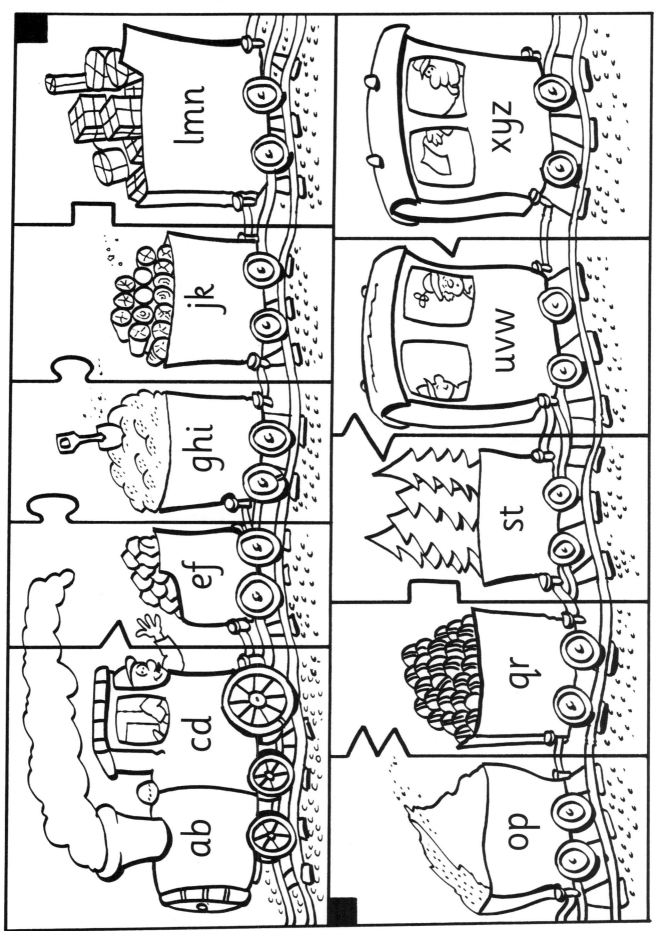

Alphabet

Build Kitty the Cat.

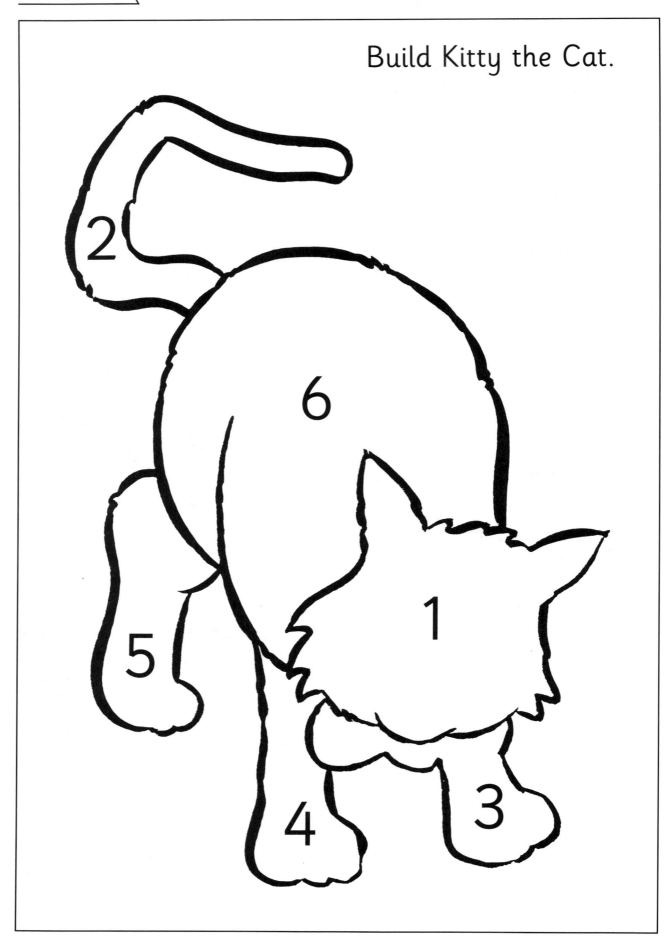

Alphabet

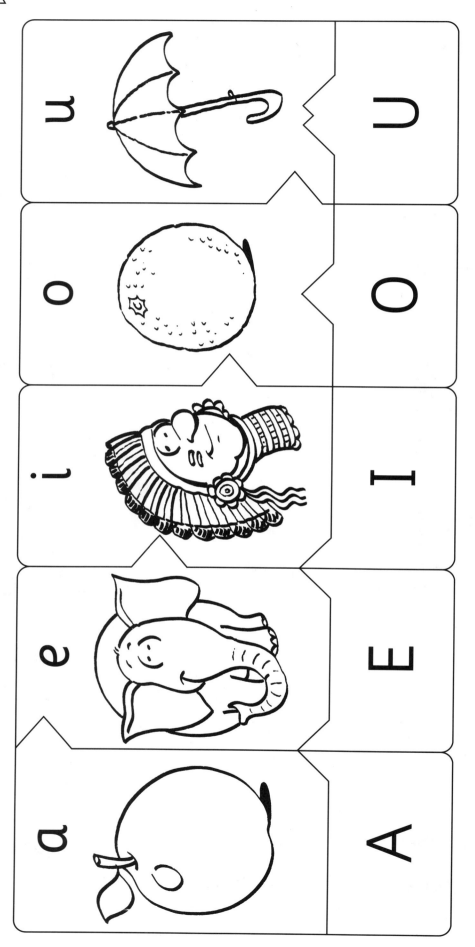

S Sam s

T Tasneem t

U Ursula u

V Vince v

W Wanda w

X Xavier x

Y Yvonne y

Z Zoe z

The alphabet

Alphabet

Copymaster 11

f	f	f
e	e	e
d	d	d
c	c	c
b	b	b
a	a	a

Start

Help the frogs hop across the pond.

	r	r	r
	q	q	q
	p	p	p
	o	o	o
	n	n	n
	m	m	m
	l	l	l
	k	k	k
	j	j	j
	i	i	i
	h	h	h
	g	g	g

Alphabet

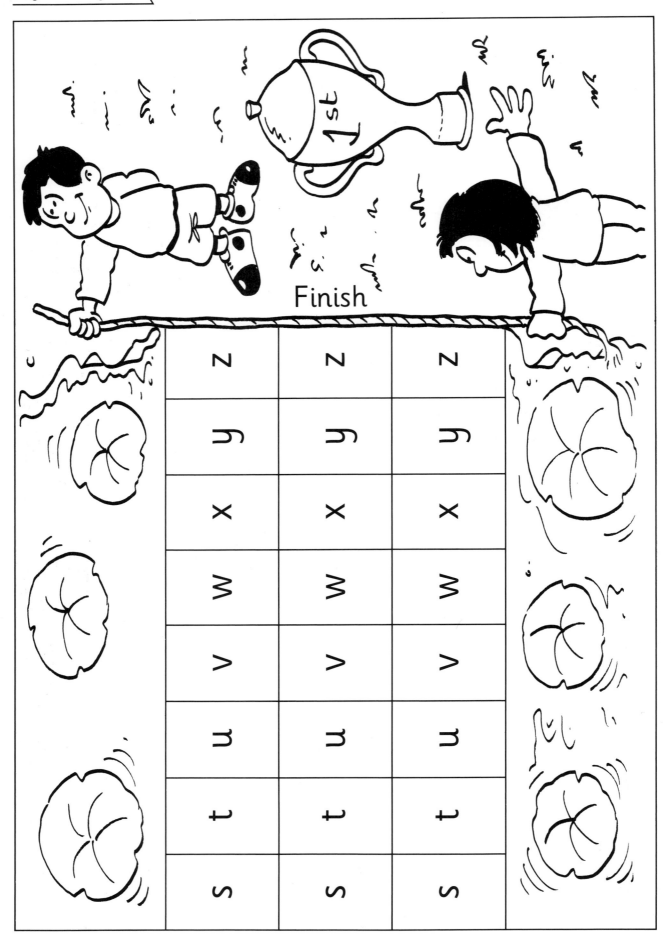

Finish

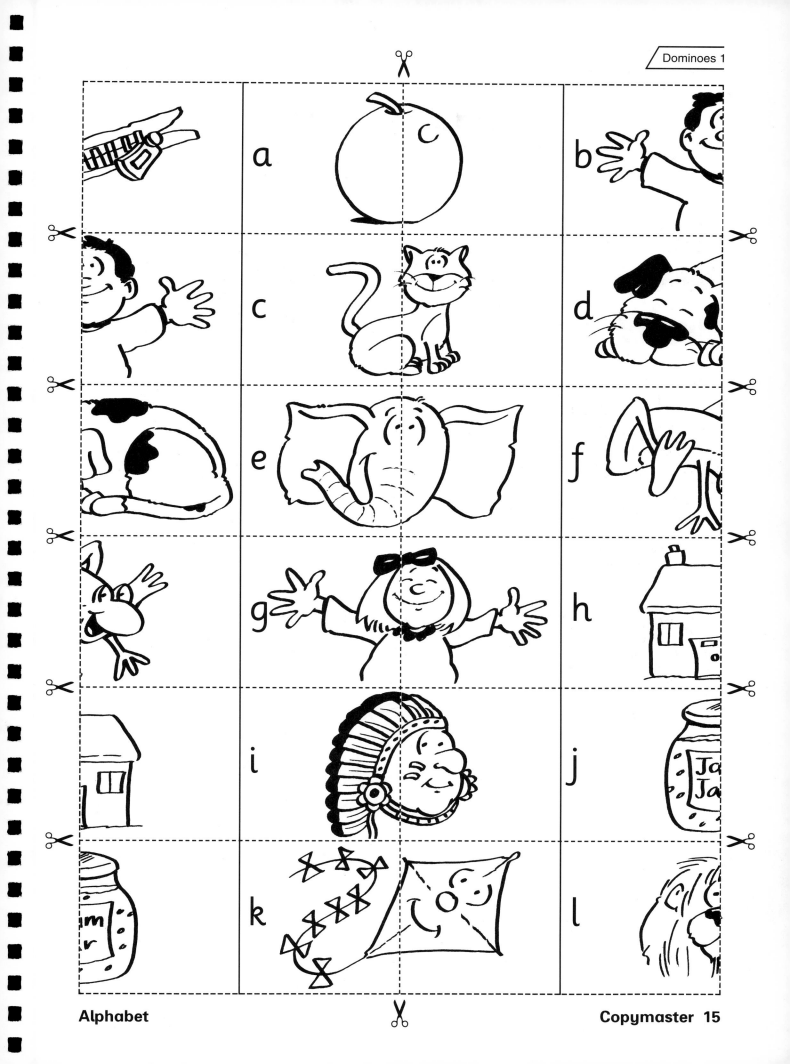

m

n

o

p

q

r

s

t

u

v

w

x

Alphabet

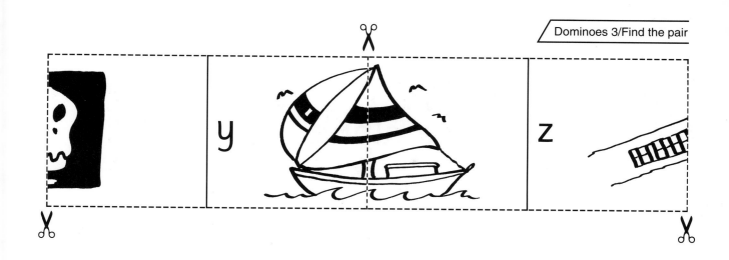

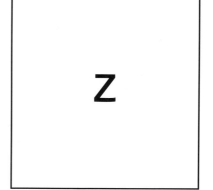

These 'Find the pair' pieces belong with Copymasters 1–4.

Alphabet

Copymaster 17

The alphabet

a	b	c	d
e	f	g	h
i	j	k	l
m	n	o	p
q	r	s	t
u	v	w	x
	y	z	

THE ALPHABET

A	B	C	D
E	F	G	H
I	J	K	L
M	N	O	P
Q	R	S	T
U	V	W	X
	Y	Z	

Z	a	A	b
B	c	C	d
D	e	E	f
F	g	G	h
H	i	I	j
J	k	K	l

L	m	M	n
N	o	O	p
P	q	Q	r
R	s	S	t
T	u	U	v
V	w	W	x

X Y Z

x y

a b c d e f g h i j k l m n o p q r s t u v w x y z

A B C D E F G H I J K L M N O P Q R S T U V W X Y Z

a b c d e f g h i j k l m n o p q r s t u v w x y z

a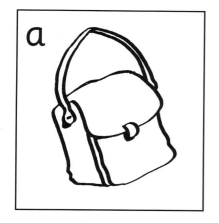

a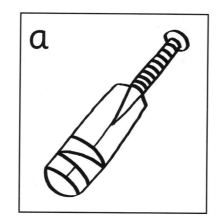

a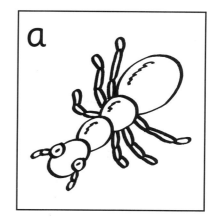

a

a

a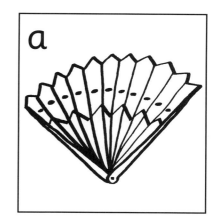

a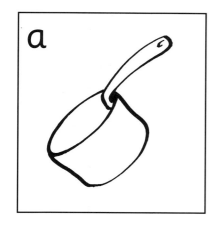

a

a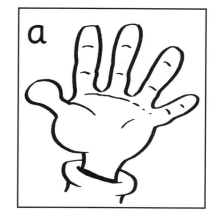

a

a

a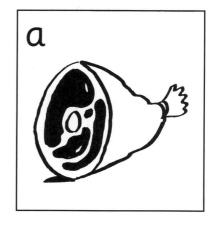

Short vowels

a	a	a
bag	bat	ant
a	a	a
jam	hat	fan
a	a	a
pan	cat	hand
a	a	a
lamp	rabbit	ham

Short vowels

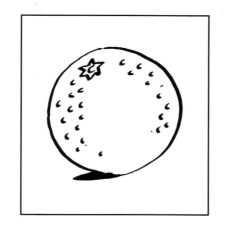

Short vowels

Copymaster 25

a	i	u
The vowels	e	o

✂ - ✂

a	i	u
The vowels	e	o

i

i

i

i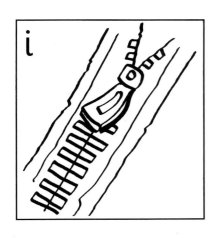

i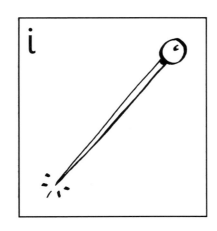

i

i

i

i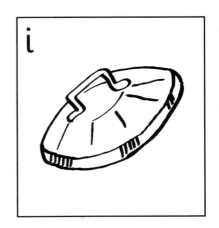

i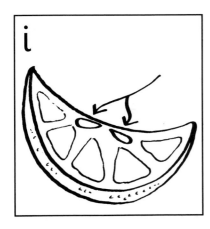

i

i

Short vowels

Copymaster 27

i	i	i
pig	tins	king

i	i	i
zip	pin	ring

i	i	i
mill	milk	lid

i	i	i
pips	bin	fish

Short vowels

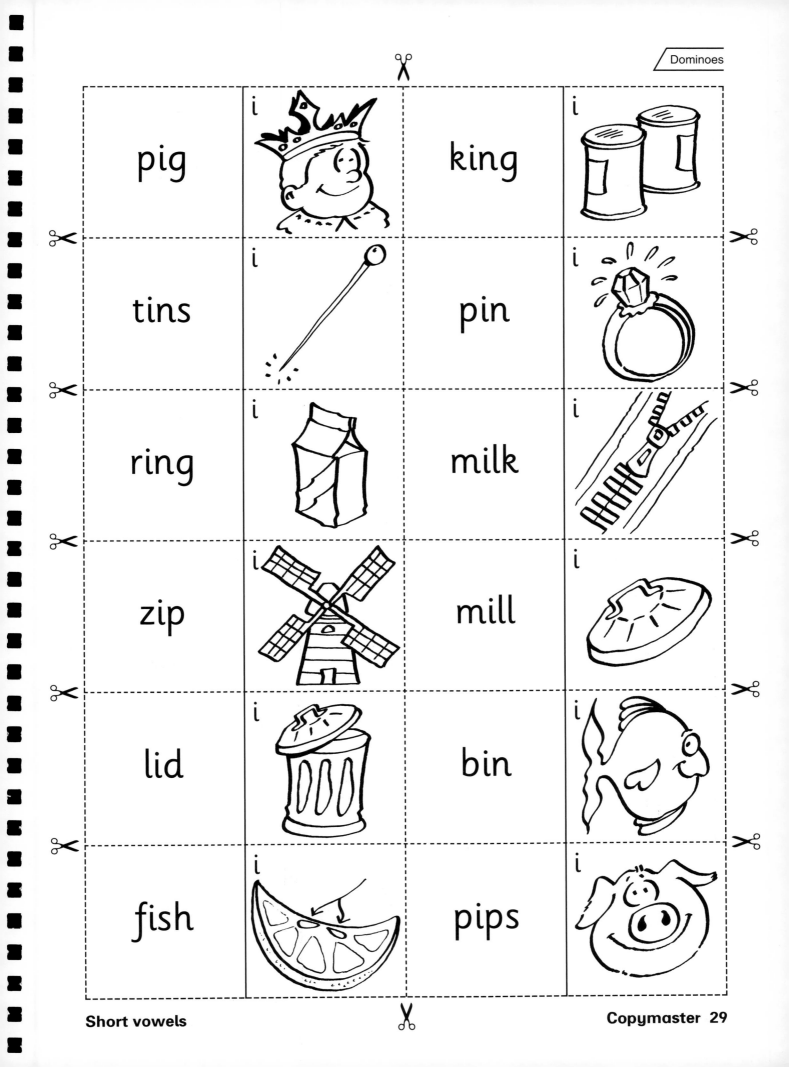

pig	i	king	i
tins	i	pin	i
ring	i	milk	i
zip	i	mill	i
lid	i	bin	i
fish	i	pips	i

net	*e*	hen	*e*
teddy	*e*	web	*e*
red	*e*	ten	*e*
bell	*e*	tent	*e*
bed	*e*	elf	*e*
leg	*e*	egg	*e*

Short vowels

Copymaster 30

e

e

e

e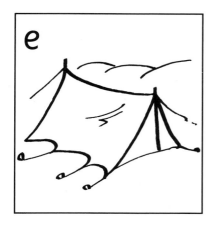

e

e

e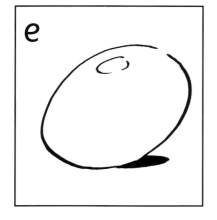

e

e

e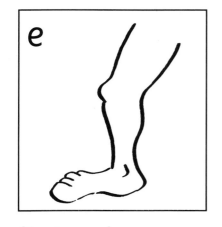

e

e

Short vowels

Copymaster 31

e bed	*e* red	*e* bell
e tent	*e* web	*e* ten
e egg	*e* hen	*e* teddy
e leg	*e* elf	*e* net

Short vowels

O

O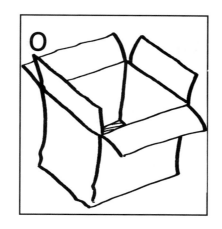

O

O

O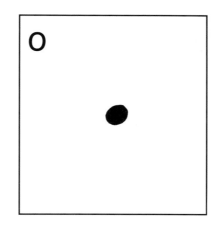

O

O

O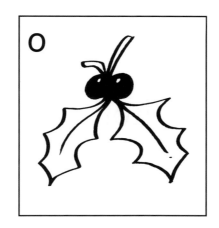

O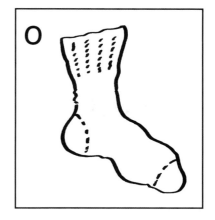

O

O

O

Short vowels

Copymaster 33

o	o	o
pot	box	frog

o	o	o
dog	dot	fox

o	o	o
cot	holly	sock

o	o	o
lock	clock	bomb

Short vowels

u 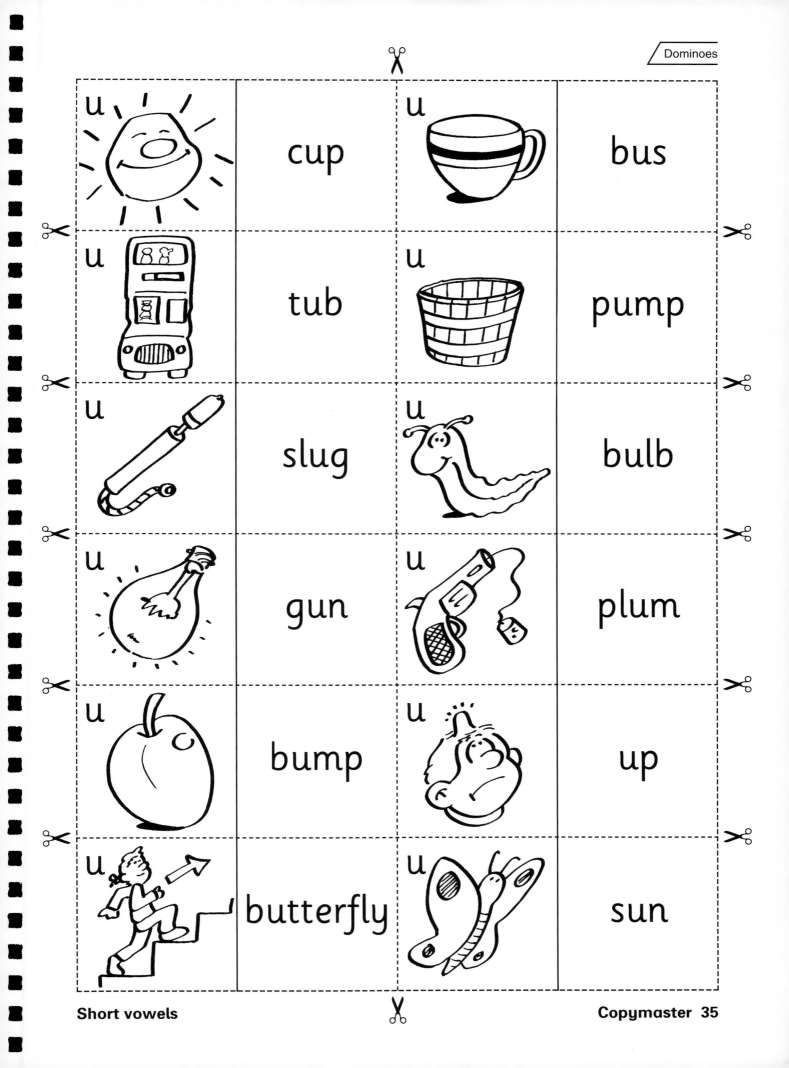	cup	u	bus
u	tub	u	pump
u	slug	u	bulb
u	gun	u	plum
u	bump	u	up
u	butterfly	u	sun

The parachute race

p _ t

c _ t

h _ t

p _ n

b _ d

Short vowels

Short vowels

Short vowels

Short vowels

Short vowels

n	n	n	n
n	n	n	n
a	e	i	o
a	e	i	o
a	e	i	o
a	e	i	o
a	e	i	o
a	e	i	o
a	e	i	o
a	e	i	o

Short vowels

Copymaster 42

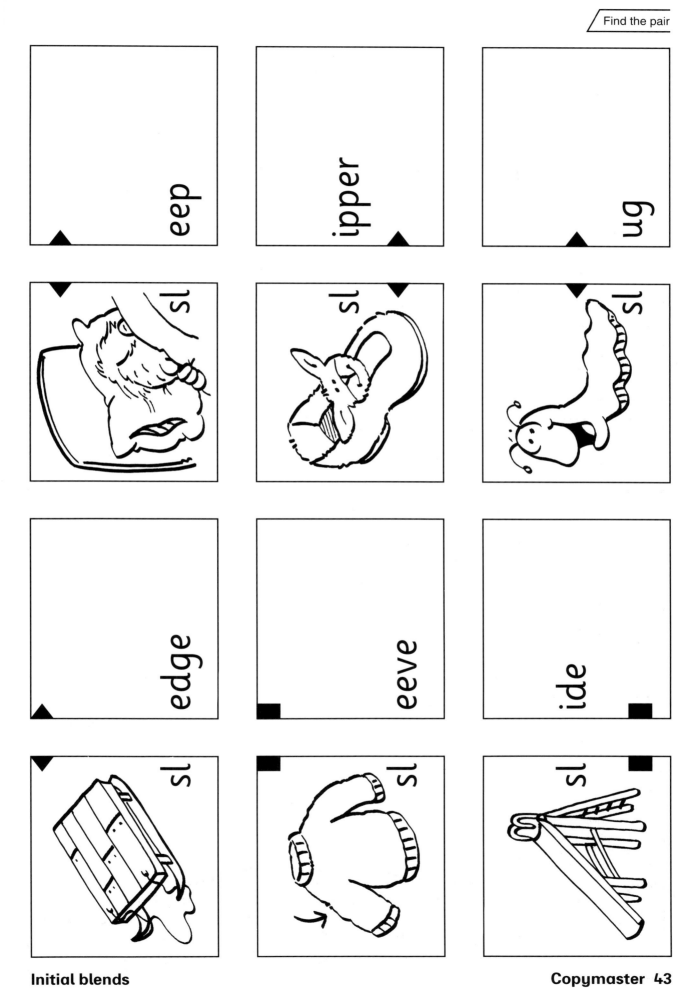

eep

ipper

ug

sl

sl

sl

edge

eeve

ide

sl

sl

sl

Initial blends

sl

Turn the wheel to find the words.

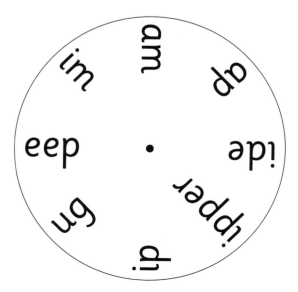

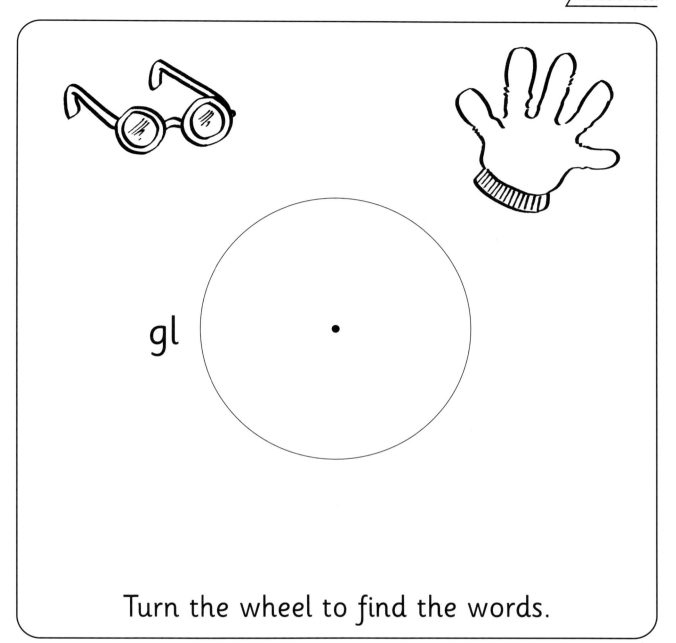

gl

Turn the wheel to find the words.

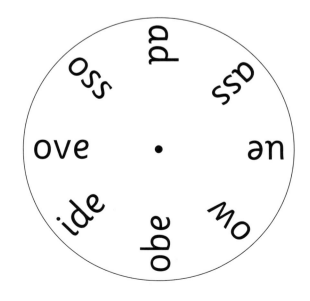

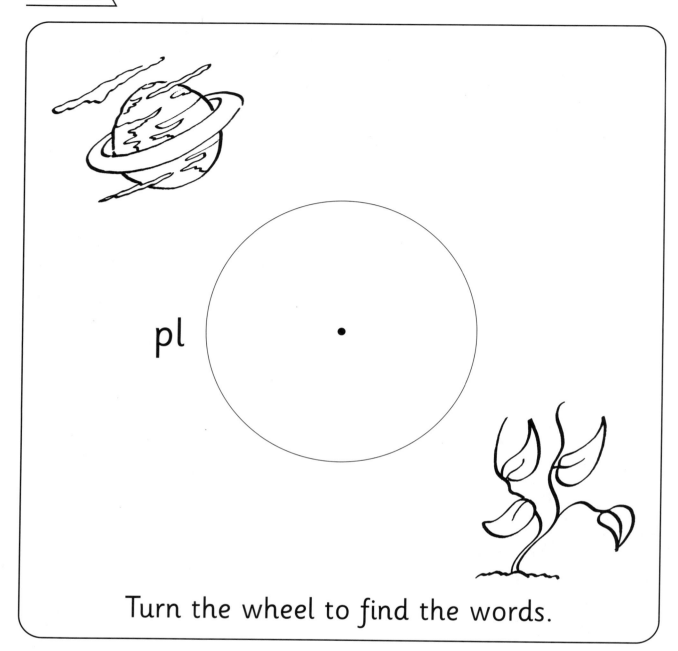

pl

Turn the wheel to find the words.

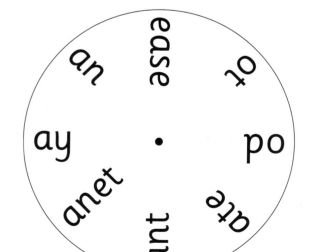

green

blue

crayons

AB

Initial blends

cr	gr	fl
st	cl	pl
bl	gl	tr

Fill the board

Initial blends

idge	 cl	own	dr
um	tr	iangle	dr
aw	dr	agon	cr
acker	fr	ame	cr
ayons	fl	ag	fr
og	cr	oss	br

ower	cl · ock	gl
ove	brown br · own	sl
ipper	tr · ain	black bl
ack	sn · owman	tr
ee	sl · eep	blue bl
ue	br · ick	fl

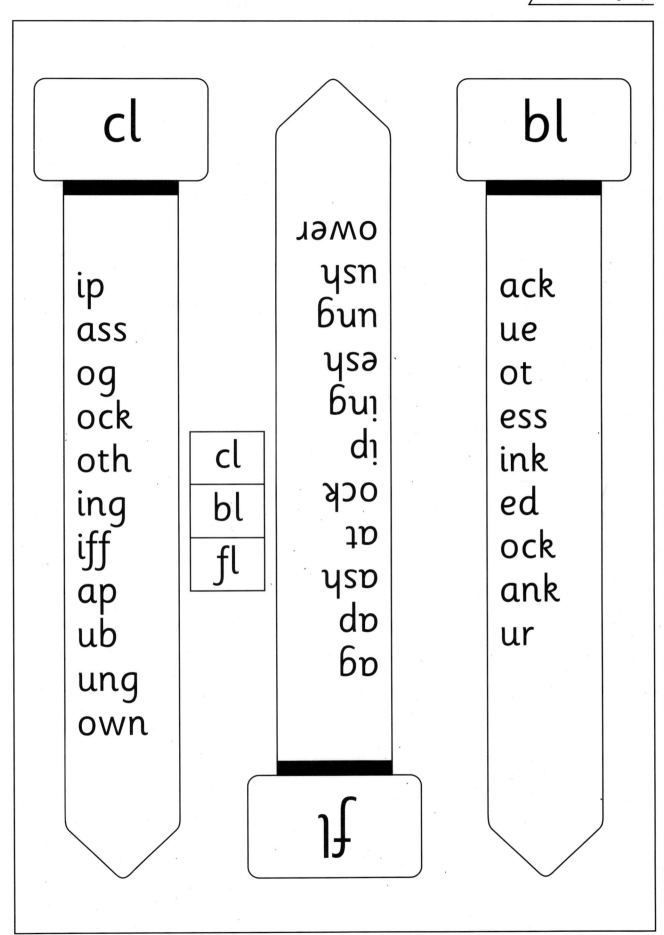

cl

ip
ass
og
ock
oth
ing
iff
ap
ub
ung
own

bl

ack
ue
ot
ess
ink
ed
ock
ank
ur

| cl |
| bl |
| fl |

ower
ush
ung
esh
ing
ip
ock
at
ash
ap
ag

fl

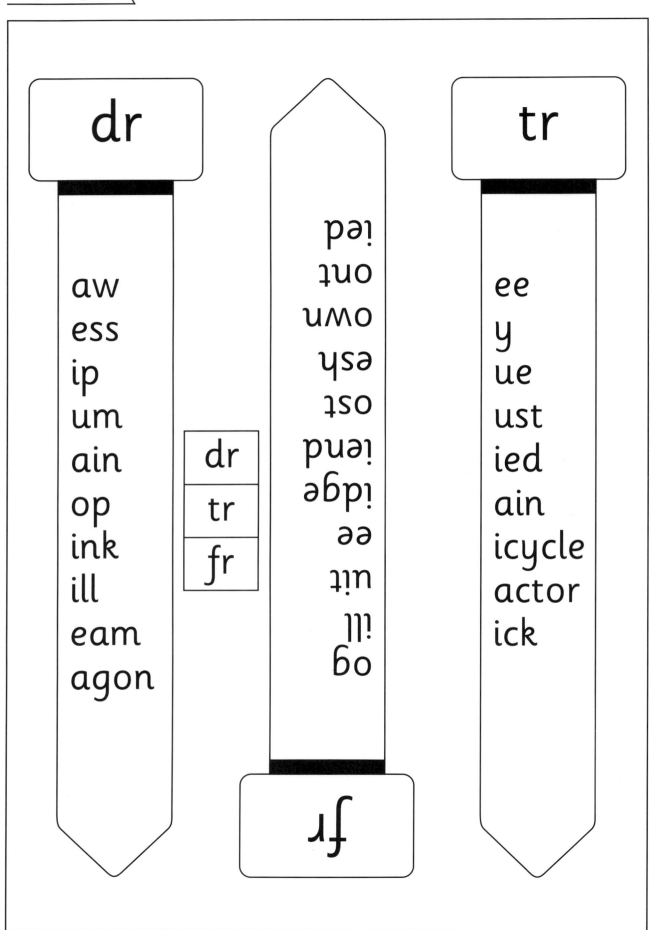

dr

aw
ess
ip
um
ain
op
ink
ill
eam
agon

dr
tr
fr

fr

ied
ont
own
esh
ost
iend
idge
ee
uit
ill
og

tr

ee
y
ue
ust
ied
ain
icycle
actor
ick

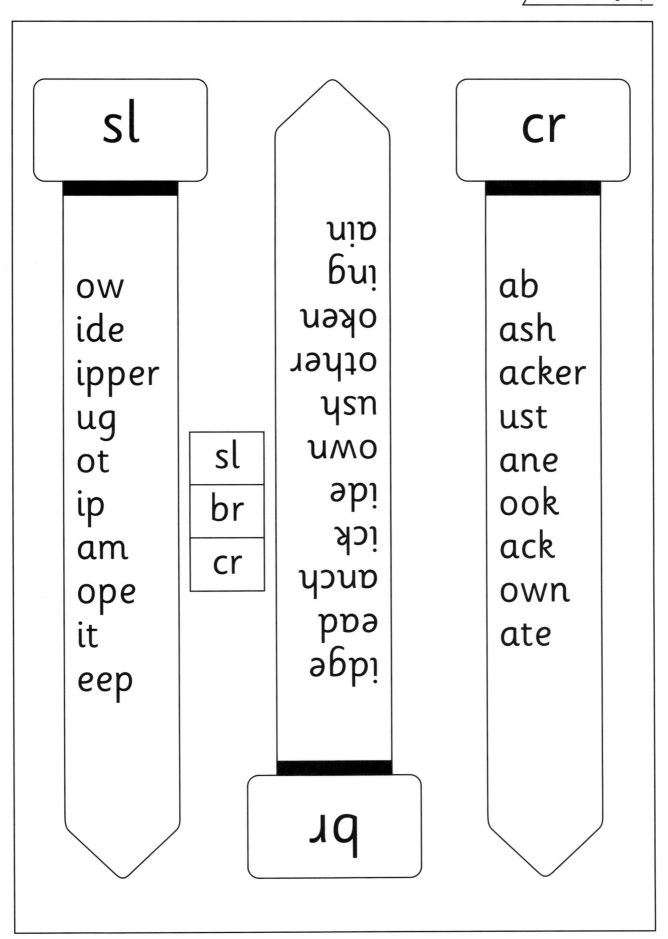

sl

ow
ide
ipper
ug
ot
ip
am
ope
it
eep

sl
br
cr

ain
ing
oken
other
ush
own
ide
ick
anch
ead
idge

br

cr

ab
ash
acker
ust
ane
ook
ack
own
ate

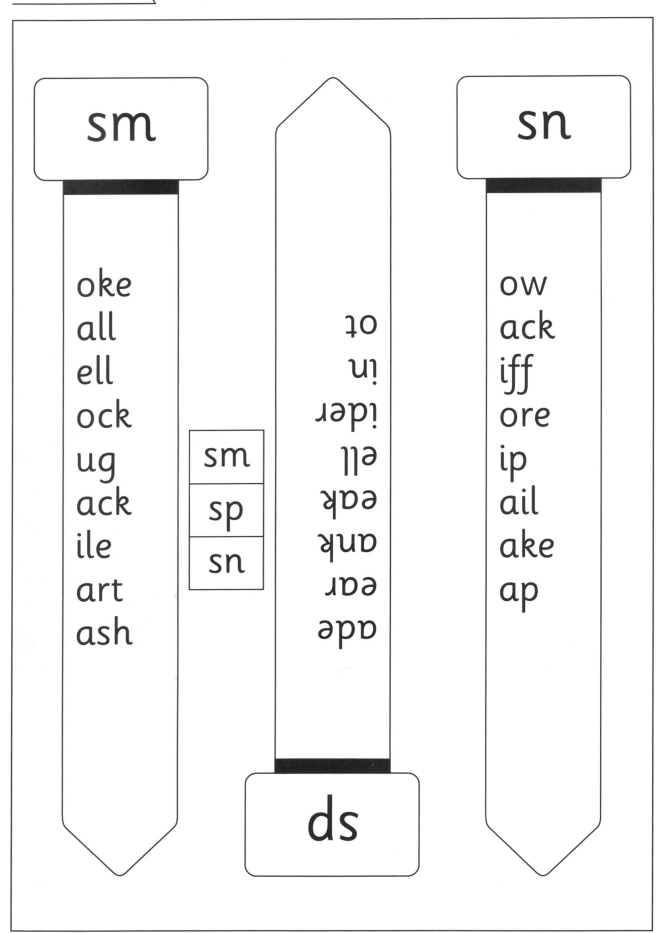

sm

oke
all
ell
ock
ug
ack
ile
art
ash

| sm |
| sp |
| sn |

sp

ot
in
ider
ell
eak
ank
ear
ade

sn

ow
ack
iff
ore
ip
ail
ake
ap

Initial blends

Name _____

Write the words on Sam's helmet.

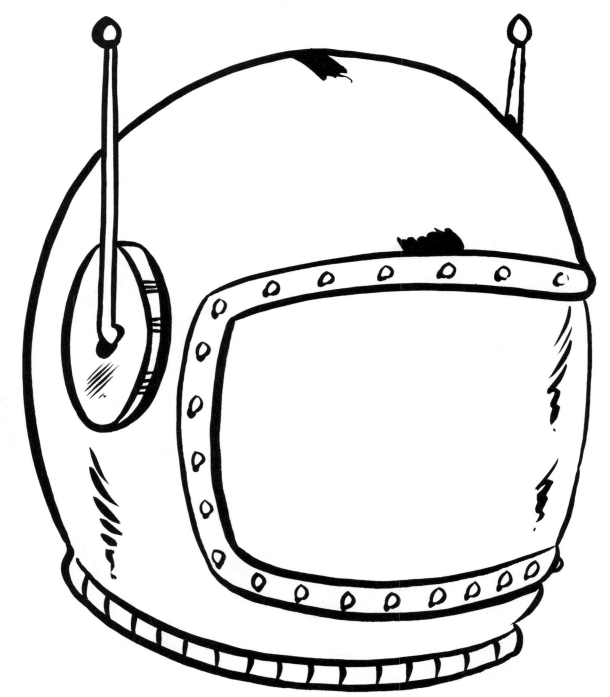

Use three of the words in sentences.

1 _____

2 _____

3 _____

Help Toby to find the words.

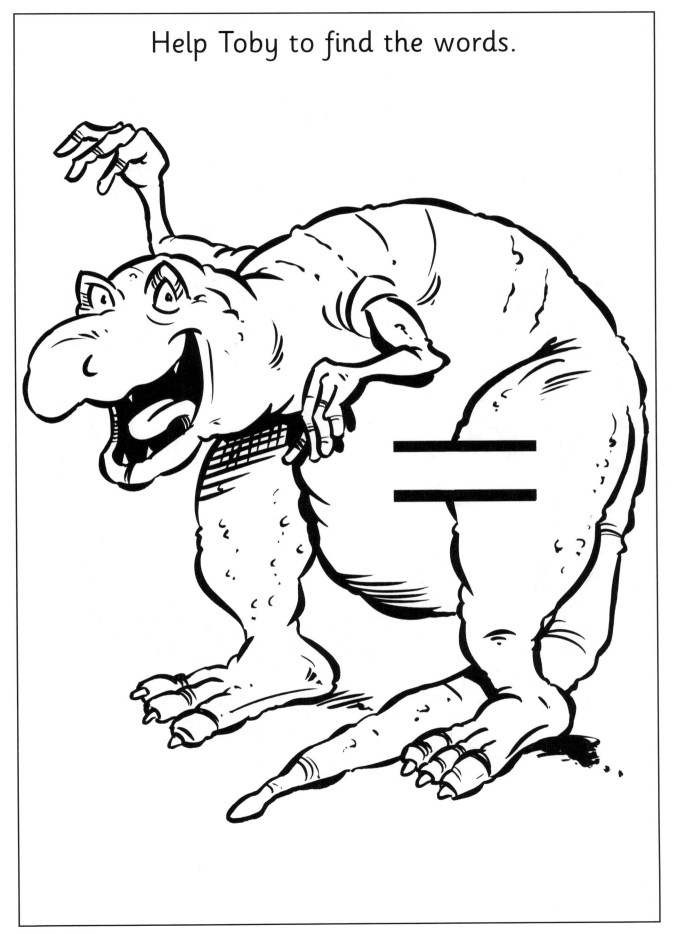

Name _____

Write the words you find on Toby.

Write three sentences using some of the words.

1 _____

2 _____

3 _____

Wordal

Name _____

t   x   a
  w   d   k   c   z
o   q   s   u
  i   g   v
  r
b   Help Wordal find his words.
  h   Write them here.
  j   p
  f
  m   e   y

Now use the words in sentences.

Remember to use capital letters and full stops.

1 _____

2 _____

3 _____

Help Teddy to find the words.

Initial blends

Find the words and write them here.

_____

_____

_____

_____

_____

_____

_____

_____

Draw a teddy bears' picnic on the back of the page.

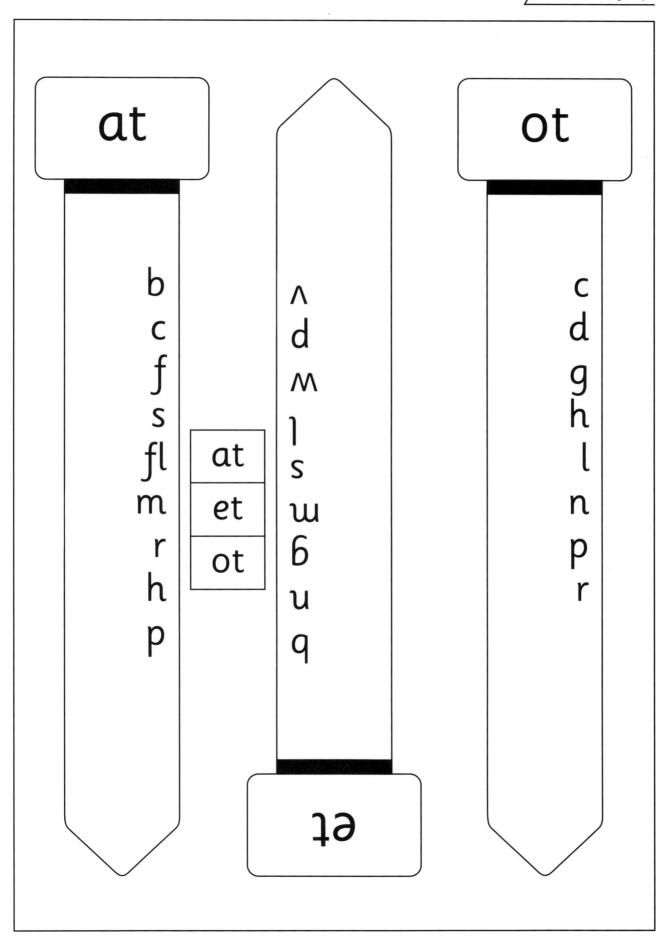

at

ot

b
c
f
s
fl
m
r
h
p

at
et
ot

c
d
g
h
l
n
p
r

et

End blends

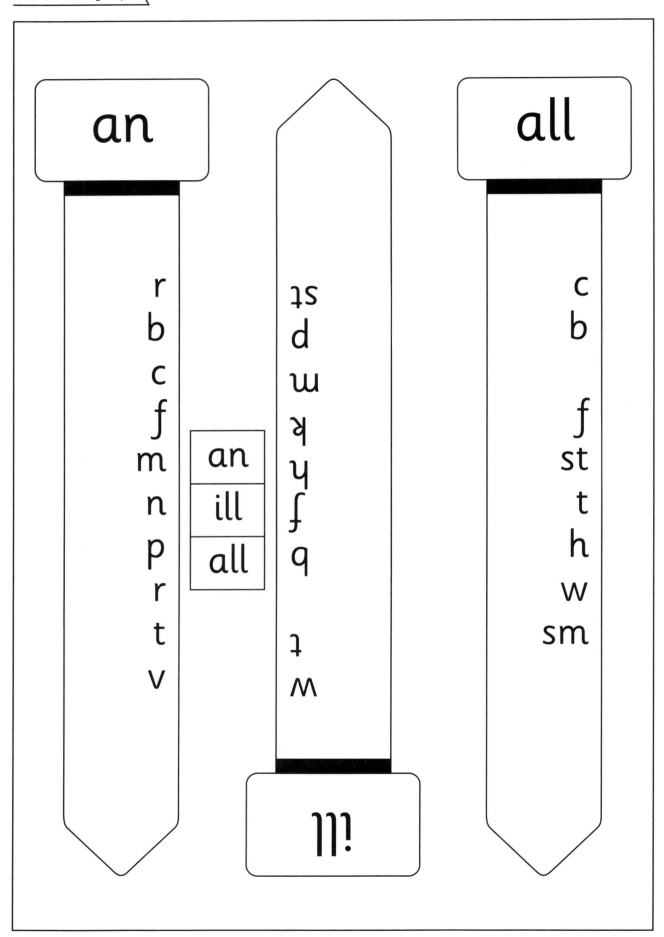

an

all

r
b
c
f
m
n
p
r
t
v

an
ill
all

st
p
m
k
h
f
b
w
t
w

ill

c
b

f
st
t
h
w
sm

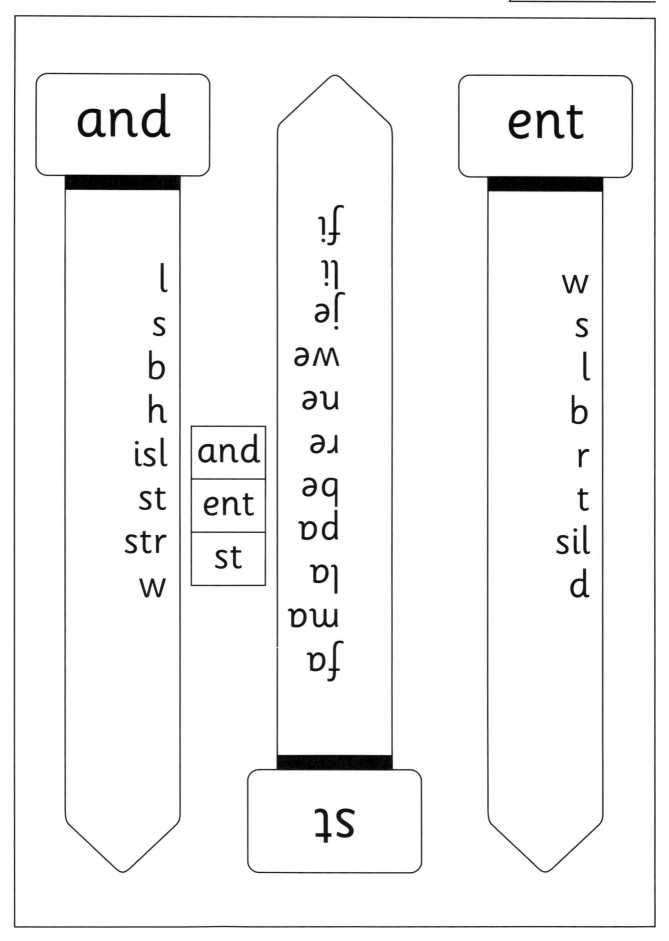

and

l
s
b
h
isl
st
str
w

and
ent
st

fi
lit
je
we
re
be
pa
la
ma
fa

st

ent

w
s
l
b
r
t
sil
d

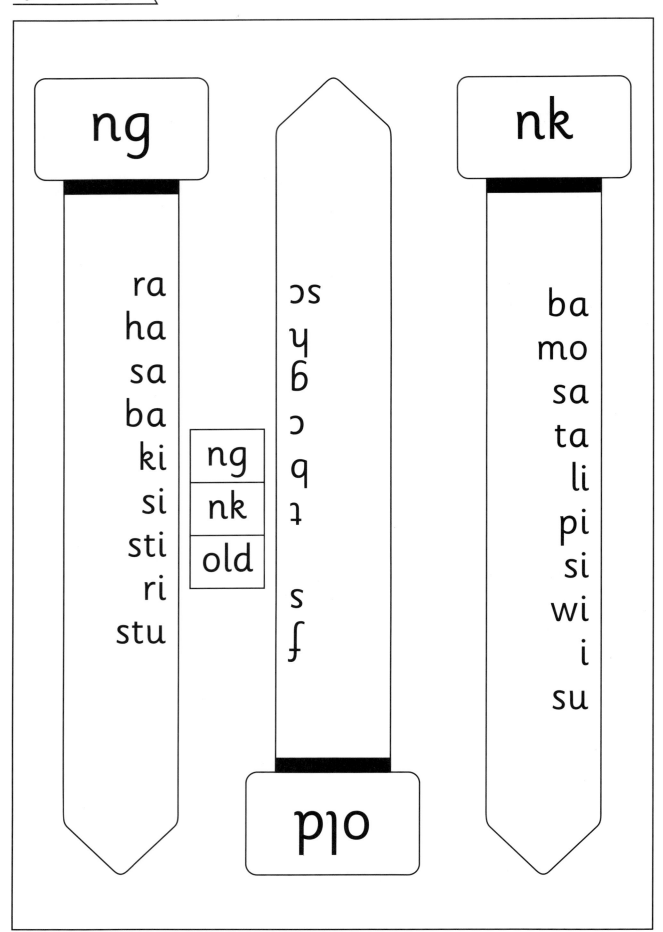

ng

nk

ra
ha
sa
ba
ki
si
sti
ri
stu

ng
nk
old

ba
mo
sa
ta
li
pi
si
wi
i
su

old

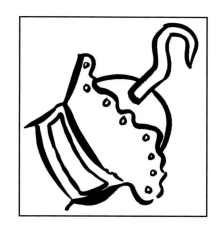

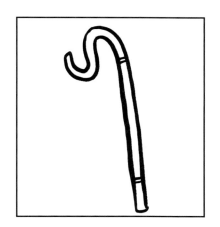
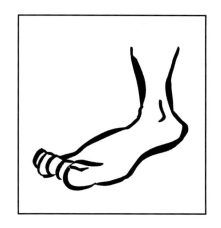

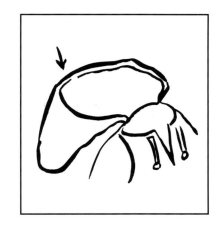

Long vowels

hook	cook	book
look	crook	foot
wool	hood	brook
rook	tooth	wood

Long vowels

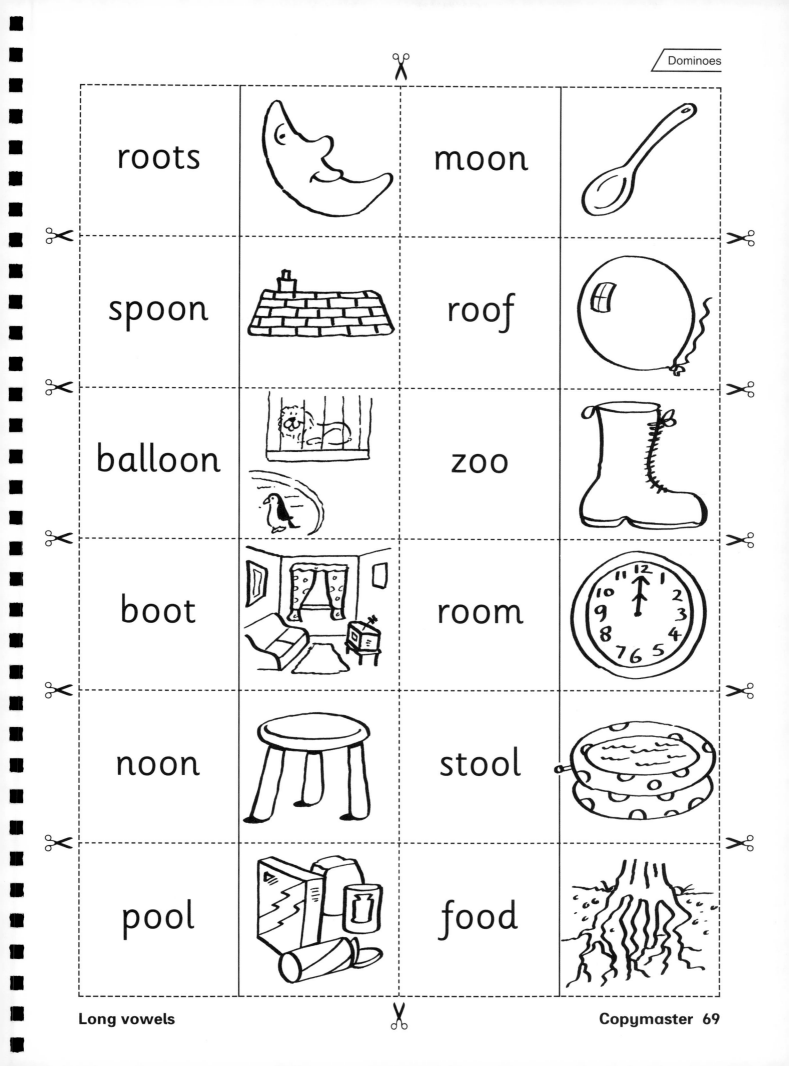

roots		moon	
spoon		roof	
balloon		zoo	
boot		room	
noon		stool	
pool		food	

Long vowels

Long vowels

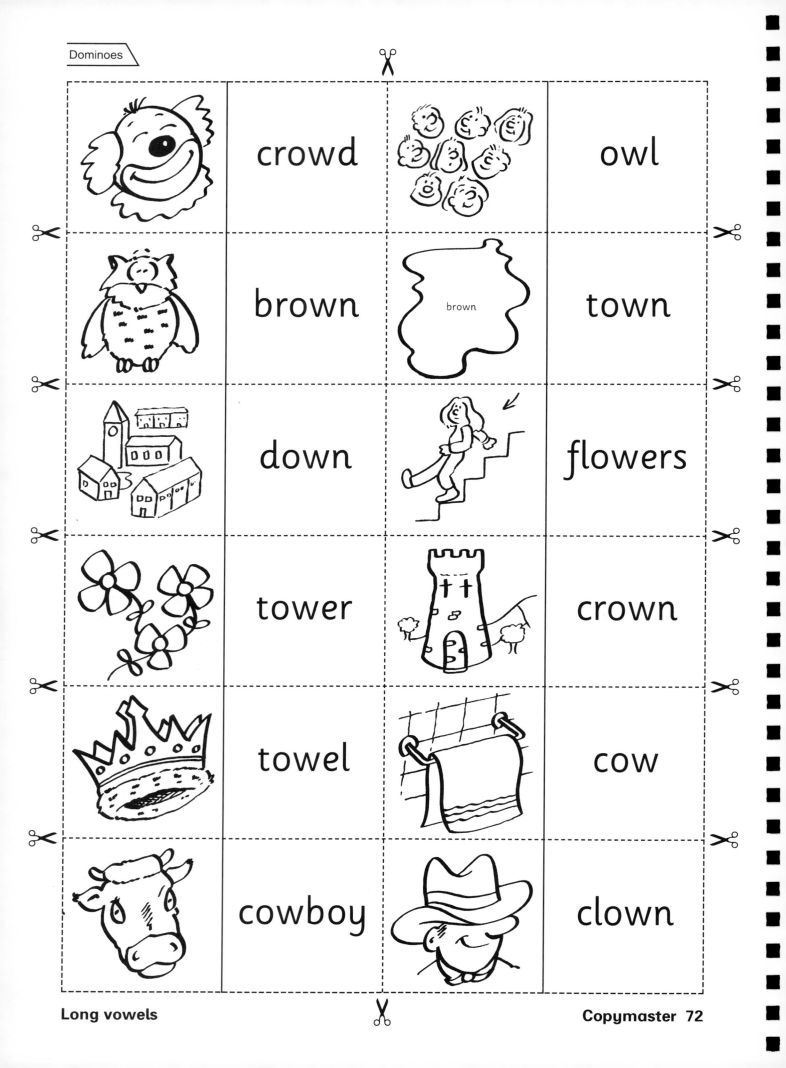

	crowd		owl
	brown		town
	down		flowers
	tower		crown
	towel		cow
	cowboy		clown

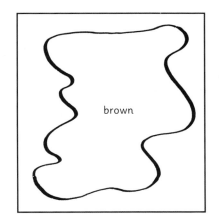

brown

Long vowels

owl	brown	town
down	flowers	tower
crown	towel	cow
cowboy	clown	crowd

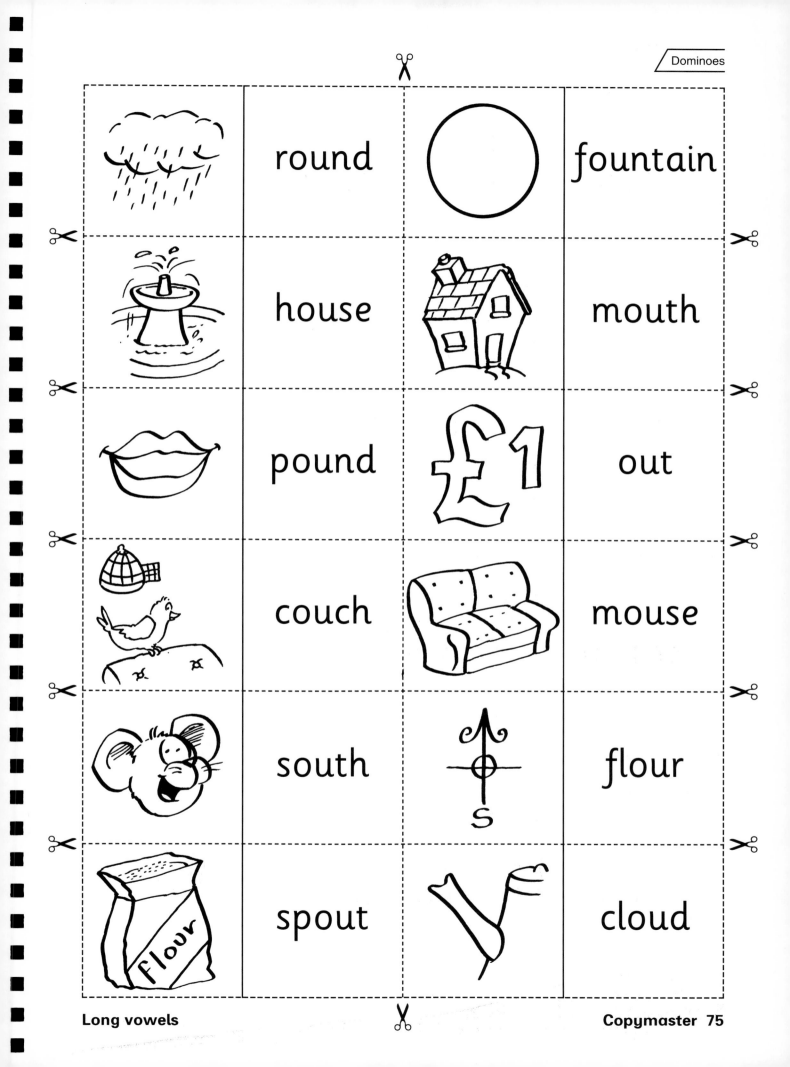

	round		fountain
	house		mouth
	pound		out
	couch		mouse
	south		flour
	spout		cloud

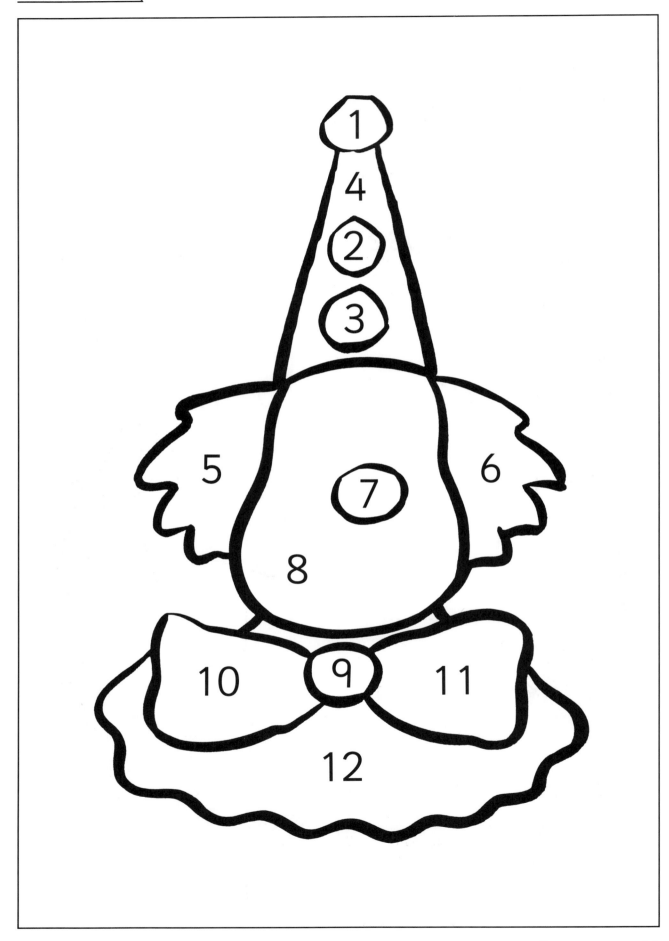

Long vowels

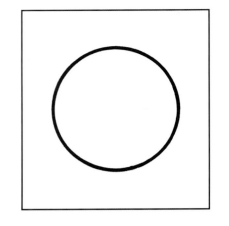

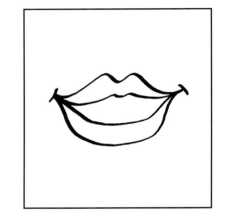

Long vowels

cloud	round	fountain
house	mouth	pound
out	couch	mouse
south	flour	spout

Long vowels

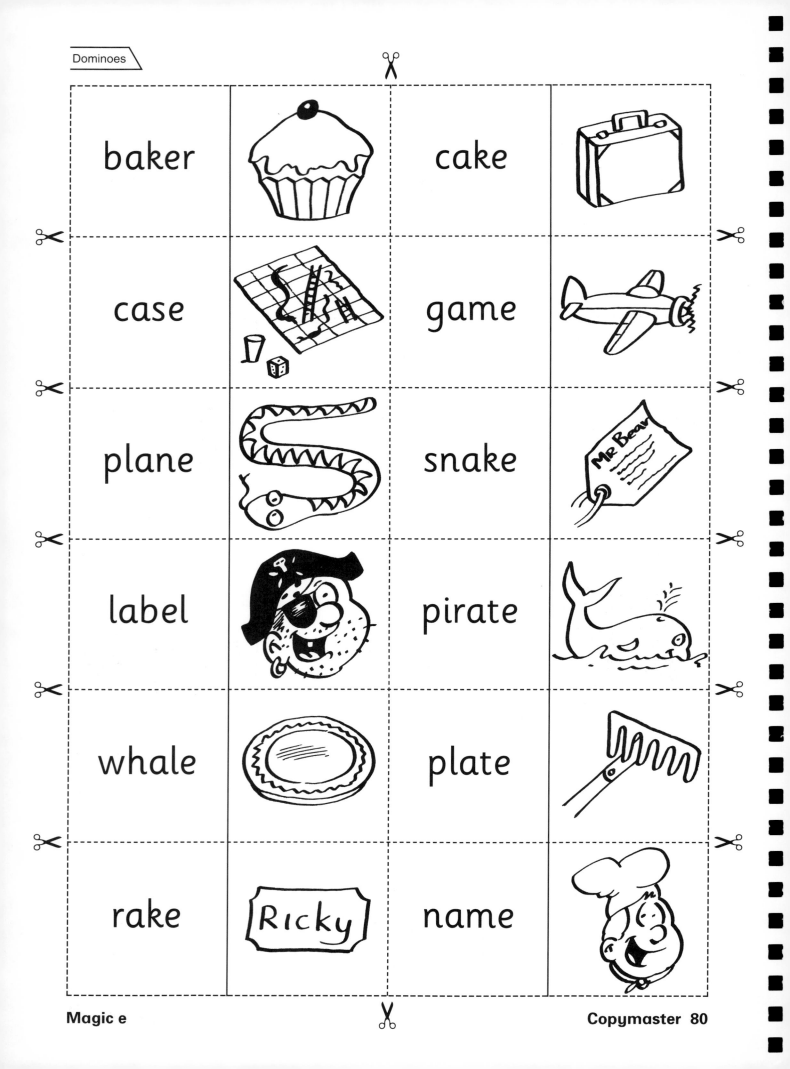

baker		cake	
case		game	
plane		snake	
label		pirate	
whale		plate	
rake	Ricky	name	

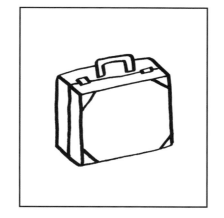

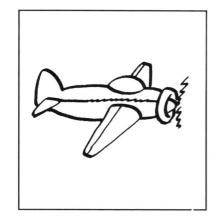

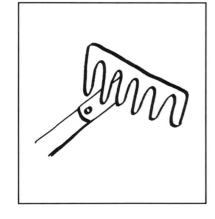
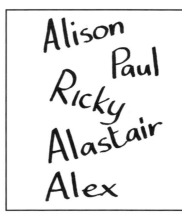

Magic e

cake	case	game
plane	snake	label
pirate	whale	plate
rake	names	baker

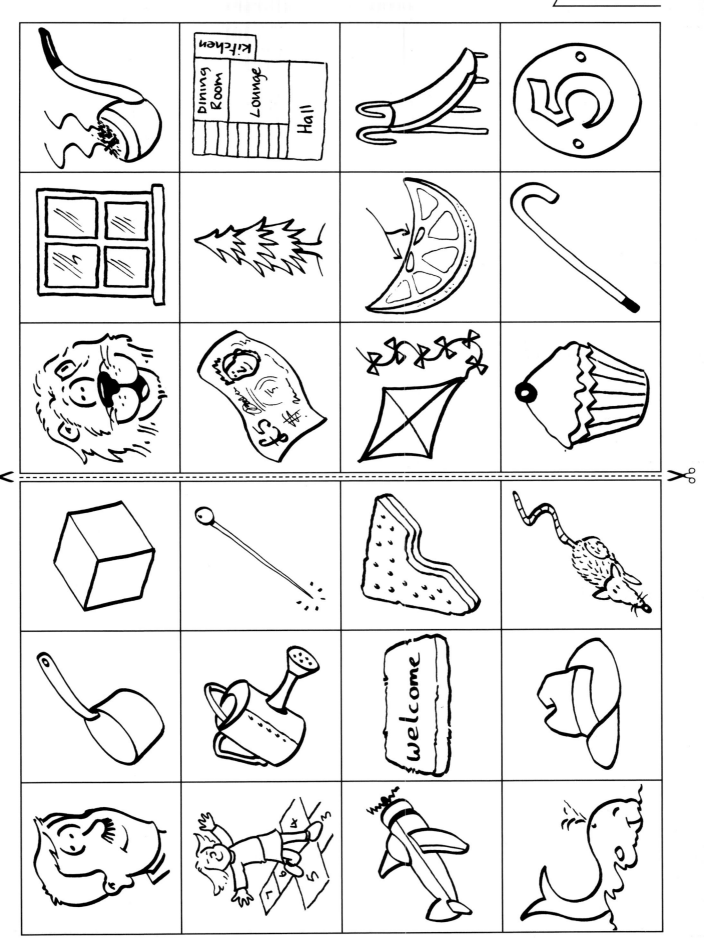

Magic e

pipe	plan	slide	five
pane	pine	pip	cane
mane	note	kite	cake

✂ - ✂

cube	pin	bite	rat
pan	can	mat	hat
man	hop	plane	whale

Magic e

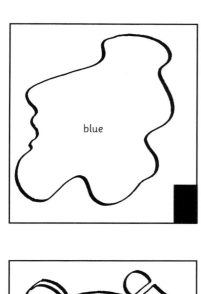

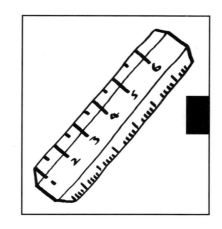

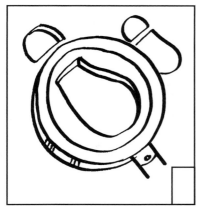

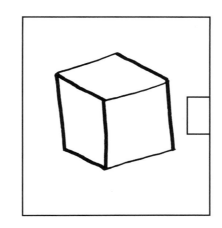

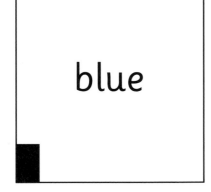

blue

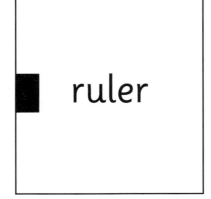

ruler

tune

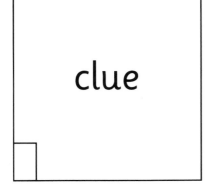

clue

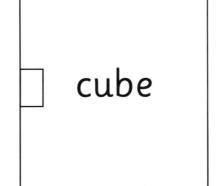

cube

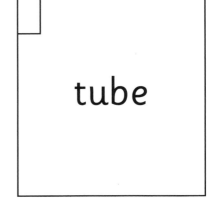

tube

Magic e

price	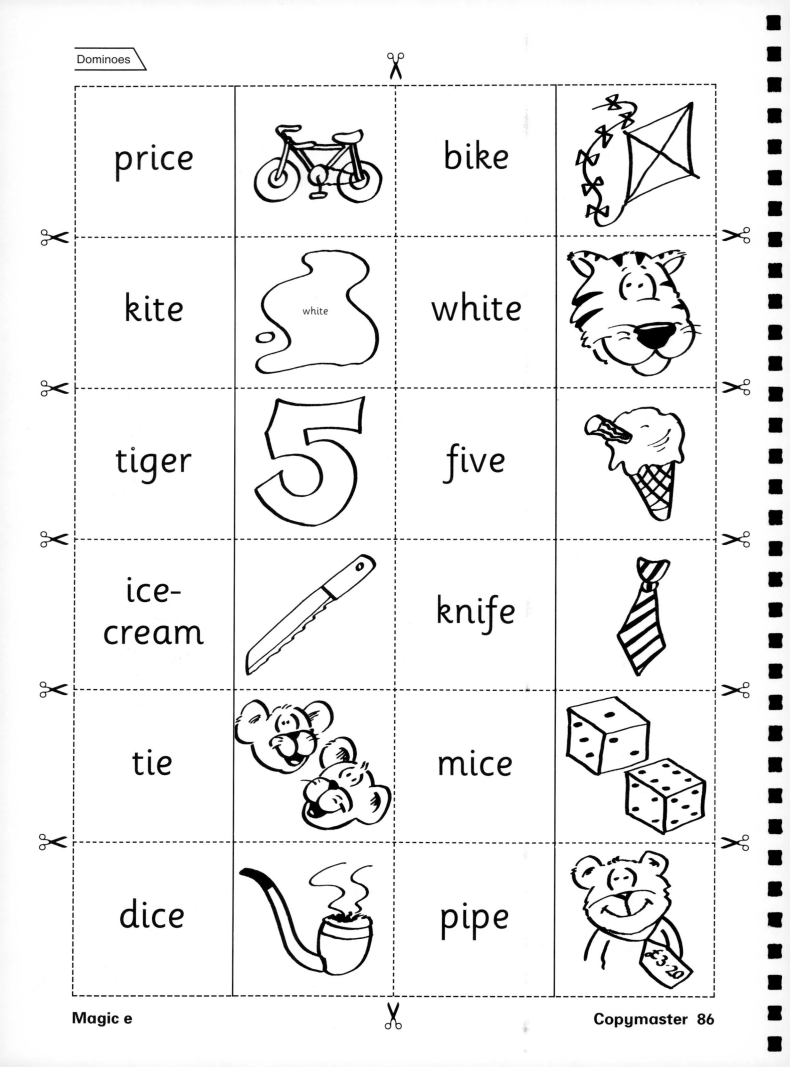	bike	
kite	white	white	
tiger	5	five	
ice-cream	knife	knife	
tie		mice	
dice	pipe	pipe	

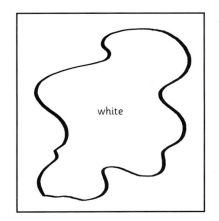

white

Magic e

bike	kite	white
tiger	five	ice-cream
knife	tie	mice
dice	pipe	price

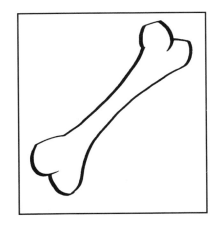  

Magic e

tadpole	rose	stove
rope	hole	nose
smoke	coke	globe
bone	telephone	cone

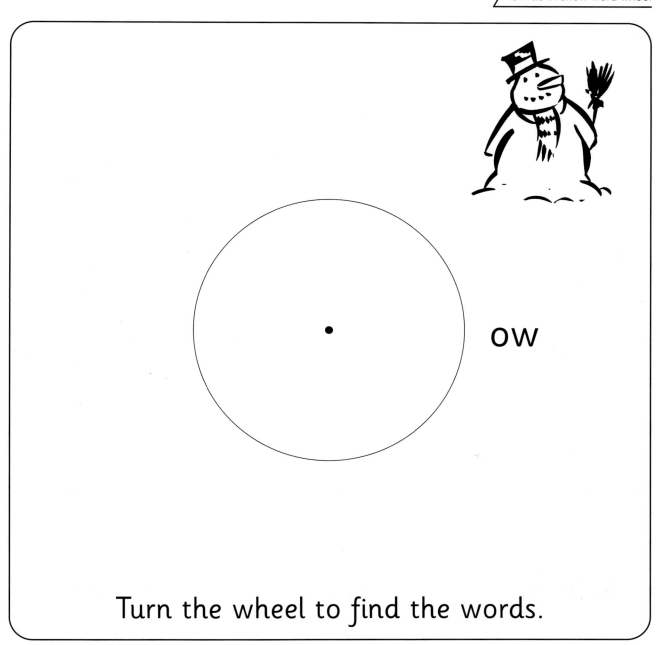

ow

Turn the wheel to find the words.

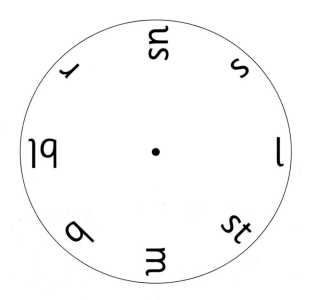

ow

m   r   s   b   sn

st   bl   l

More long vowels   **Copymaster 92**

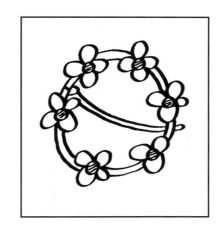

More long vowels

Copymaster 93

boat	road	toadstool
coat	goat	moat
float	broach	coach
throat	coal	goal

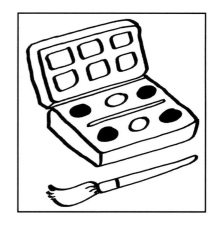

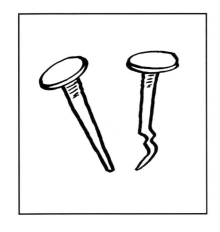

More long vowels

Copymaster 95

snail	sailor	paints
rain	train	sail
nails	tail	chain
daisy	rail	mermaid

More long vowels

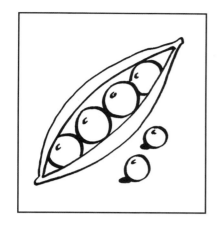  

  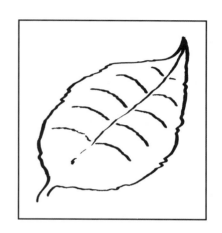

More long vowels

peas	meat	teapot
beans	sea	leaf
seal	beach	jeans
bead	lead	leak

More long vowels

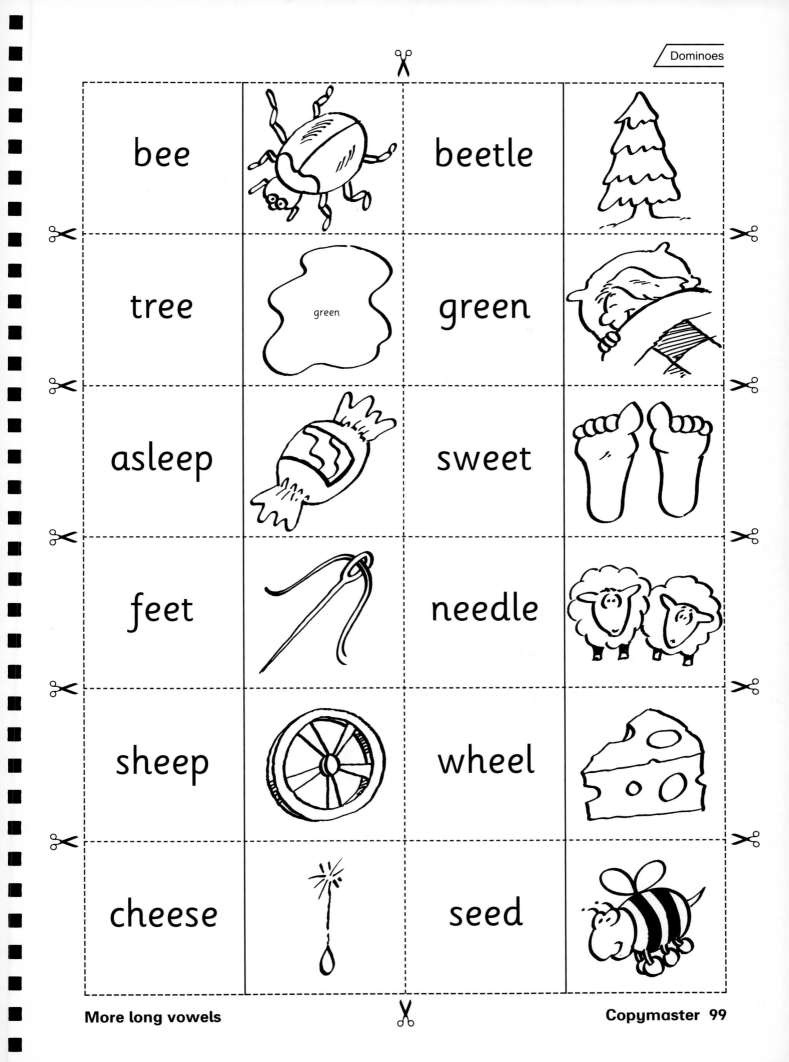

bee		beetle	
tree		green	
asleep		sweet	
feet		needle	
sheep		wheel	
cheese		seed	

More long vowels

Copymaster 99

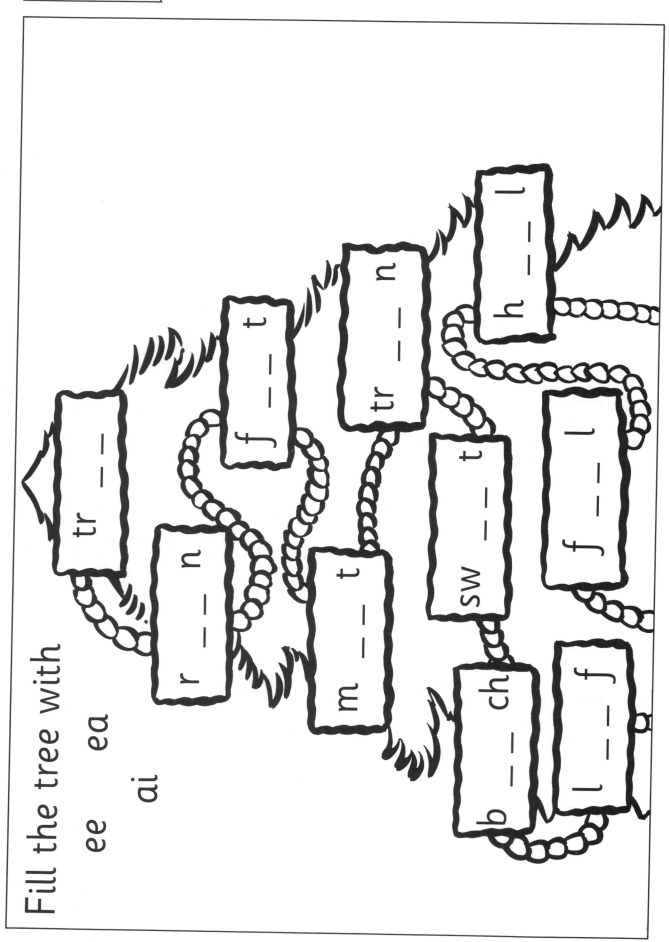

Fill the tree with

ee   ea

ai

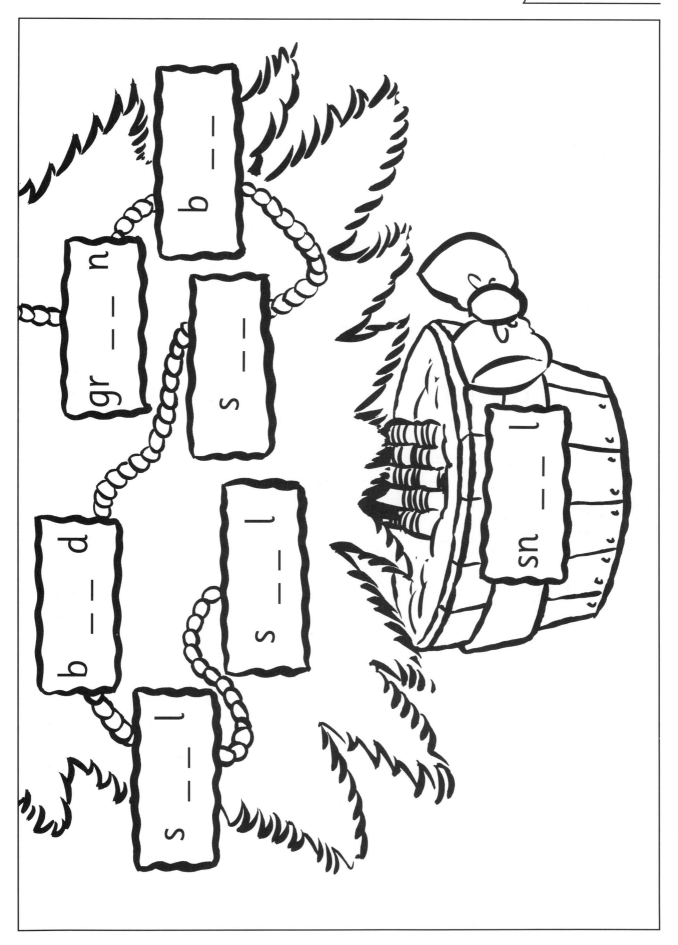

More long vowels

ea	ai	ee	ea	ai	ee	ea
ai	ee	ea	ai	ee	ea	ai
ee	ea	ai	ee	ea	ai	ee
ea	ai	ee	ea	ai	ee	ea
ea	ee	ai	ee	ai	ea	ee
ee	ai	ea	ai	ea	ee	ai

More long vowels

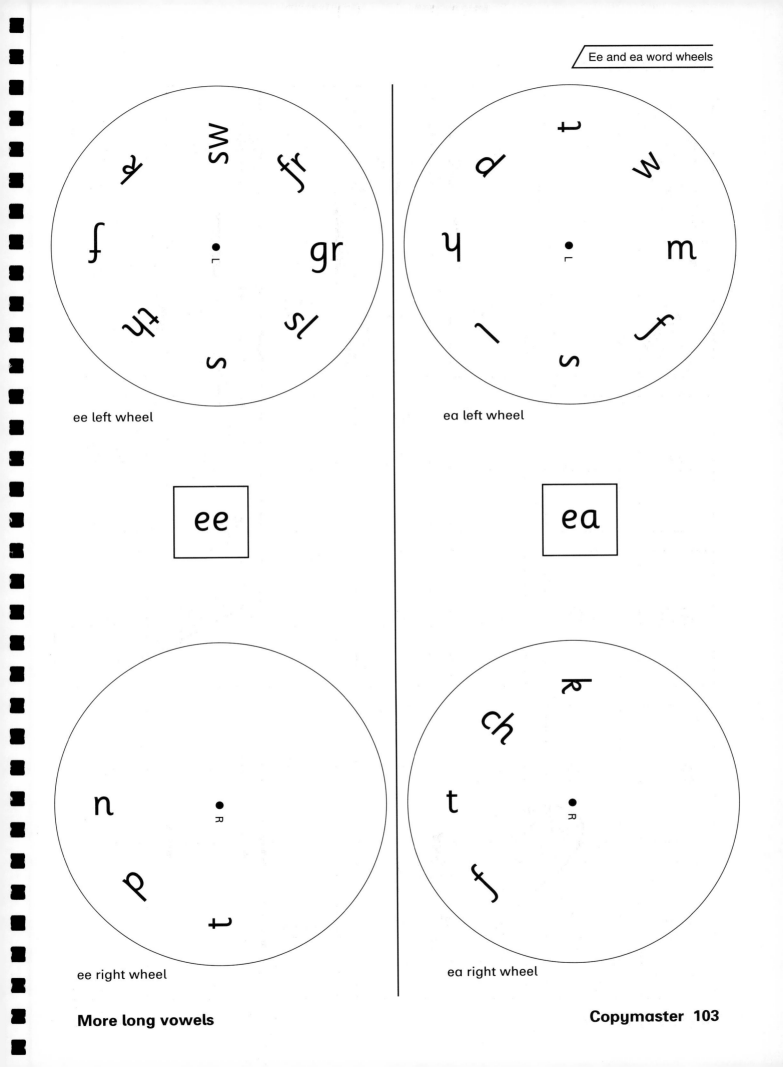

ee left wheel

ea left wheel

ee

ea

ee right wheel

ea right wheel

More long vowels

More long vowels

More long vowels

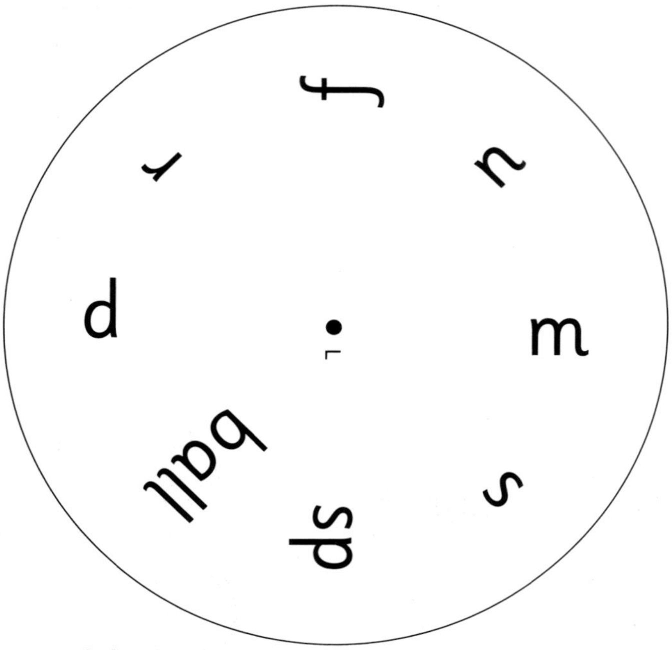

Oo and ou word wheels

oo left wheel

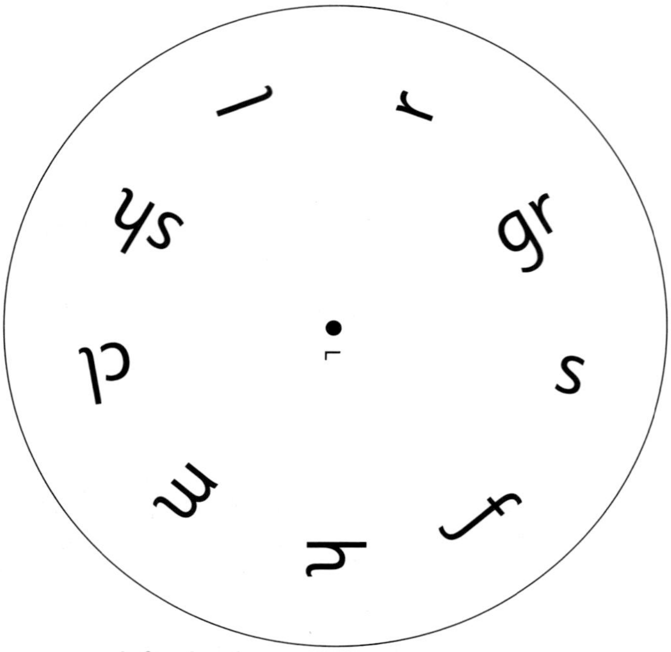

f
n
r
d
m
ball s
sp

ou left wheel

l
r
sh
gr
p
s
m
h f

oo

ou

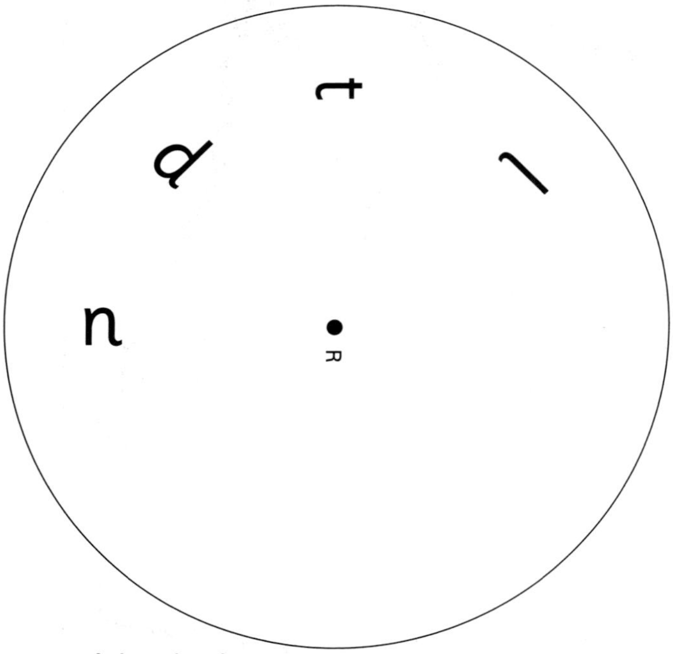

oo right wheel

t
d
l
n

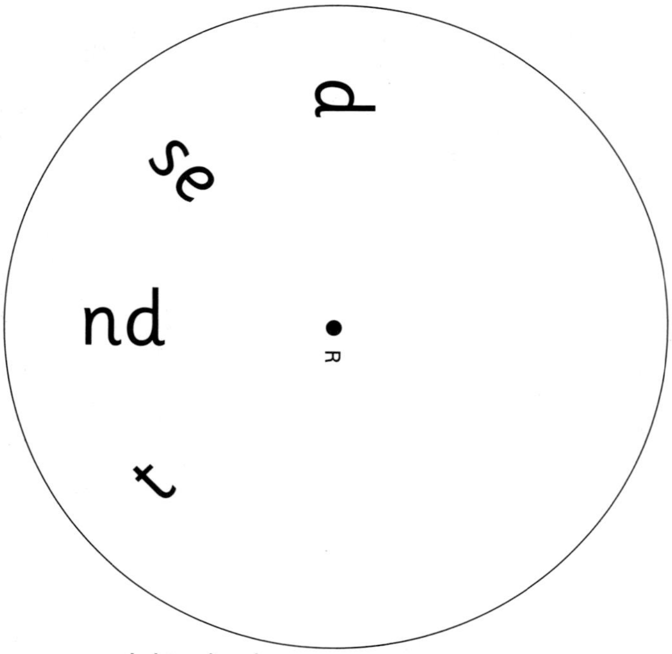

ou right wheel

d
se
nd
t

More long vowels

Copymaster 106

More long vowels

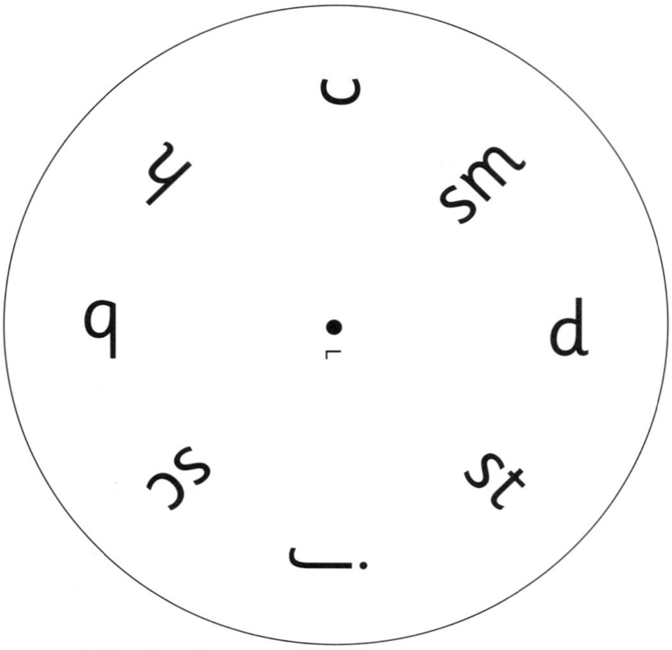

ar left wheel

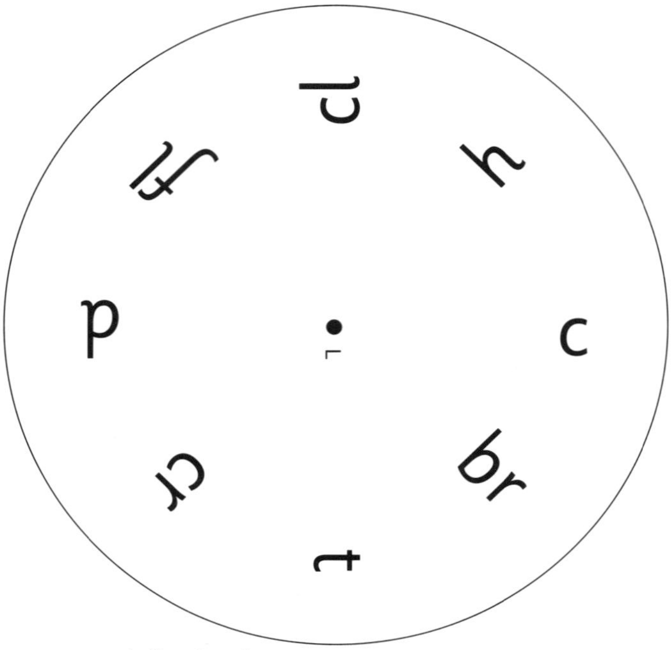

ow left wheel

ar

ow

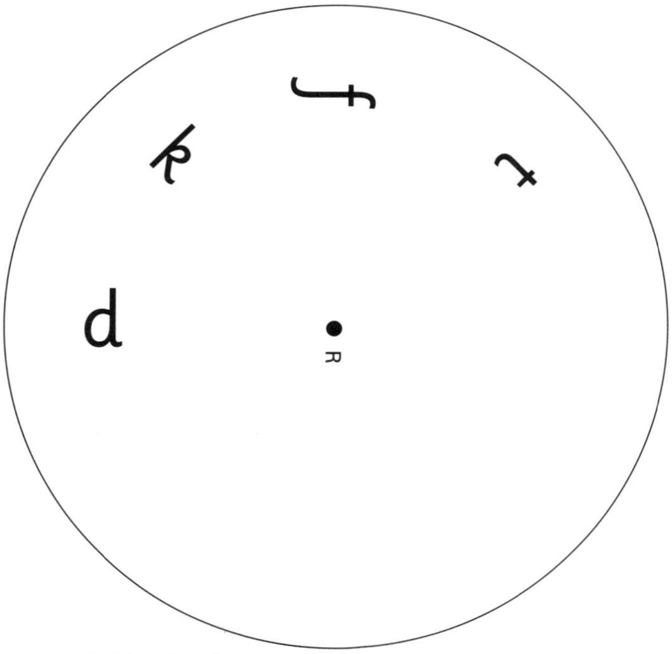

ar right wheel

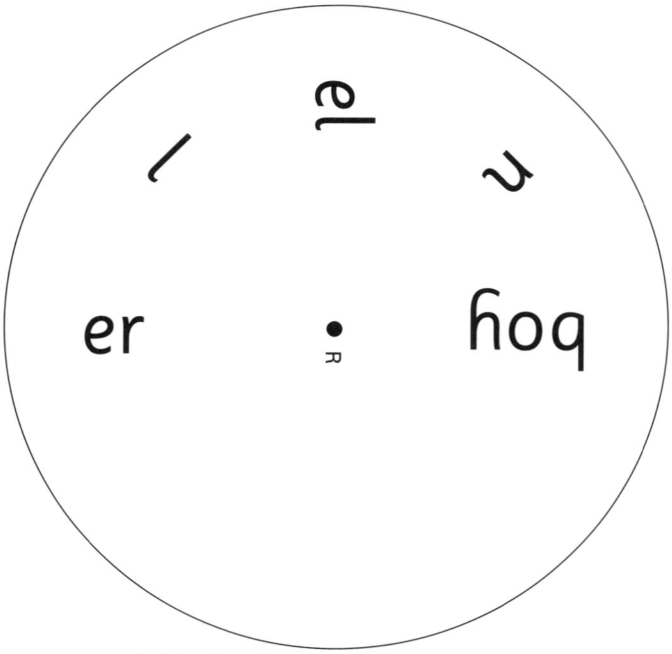

ow right wheel

More long vowels

Write the words on Leo's mane.

Write three sentences using some of the words you have found.

1 _____

2 _____

3 _____

Now draw a lion.

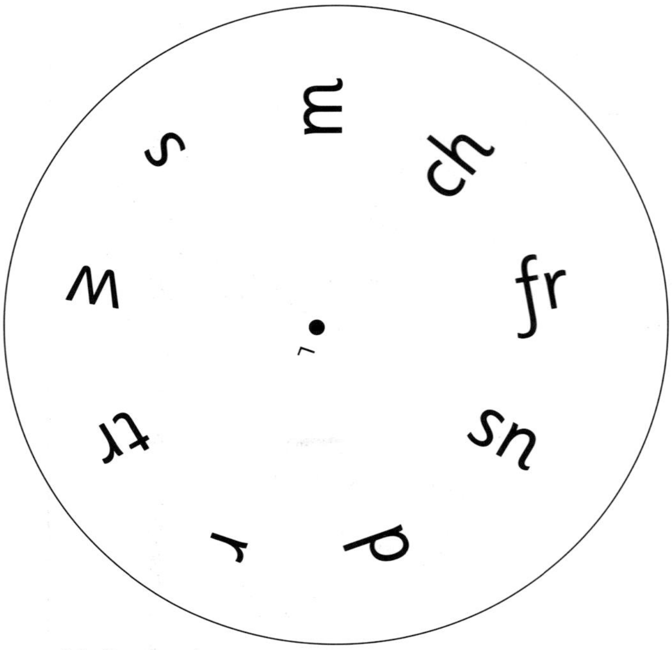

ai left wheel

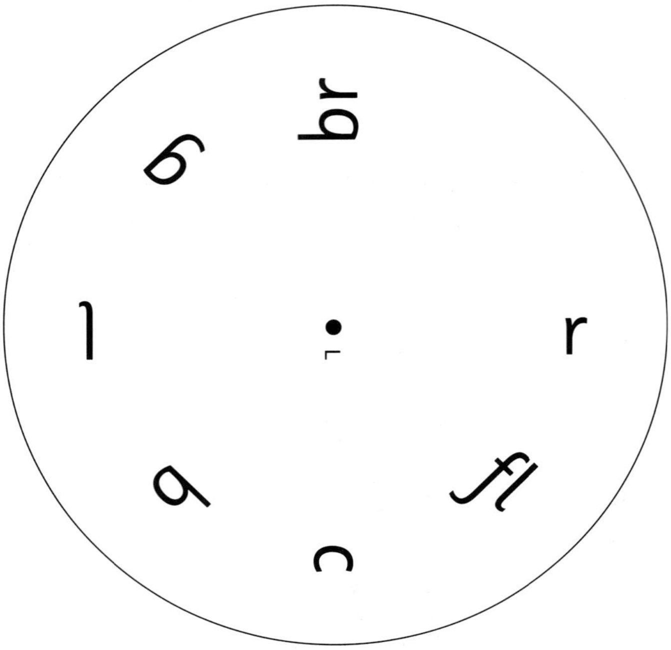

oa left wheel

ai

oa

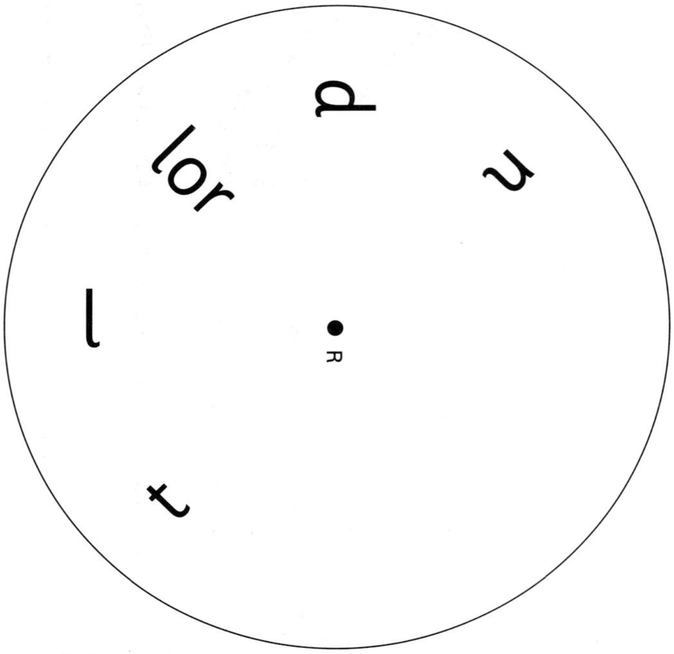

ai right wheel

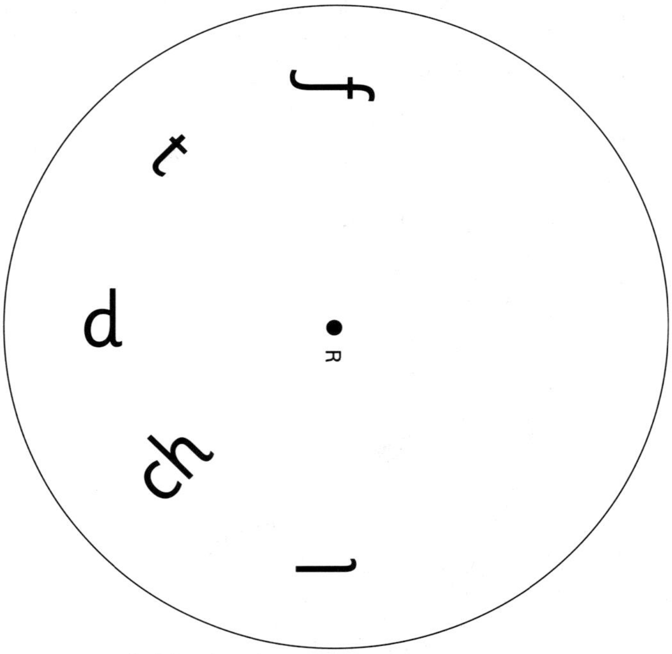

oa right wheel

More long vowels

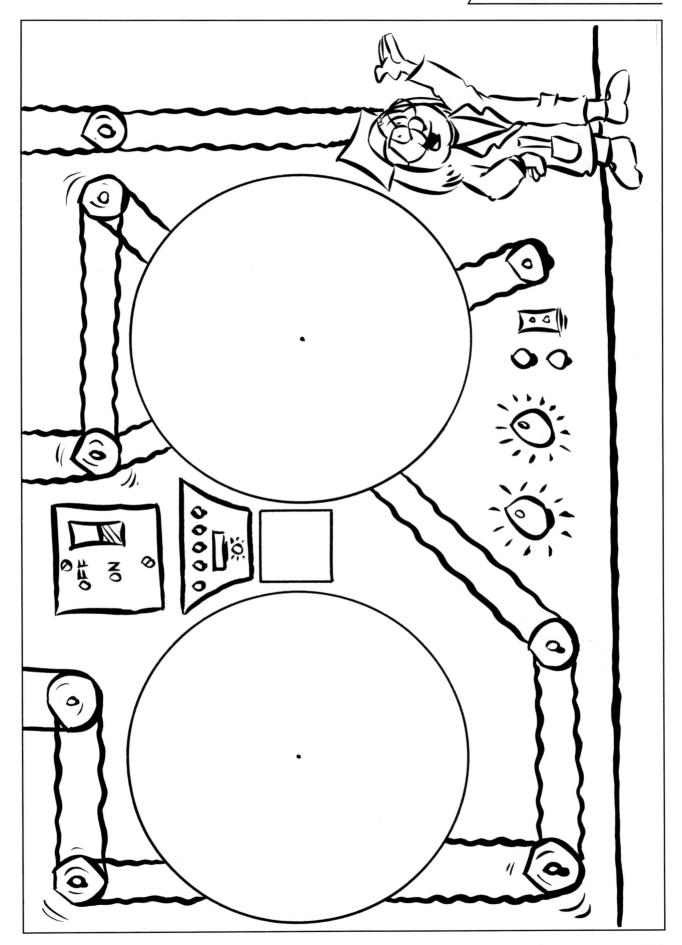

More long vowels

ew

Turn the wheel to find the words.

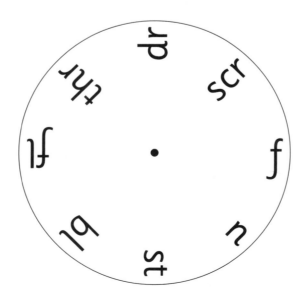

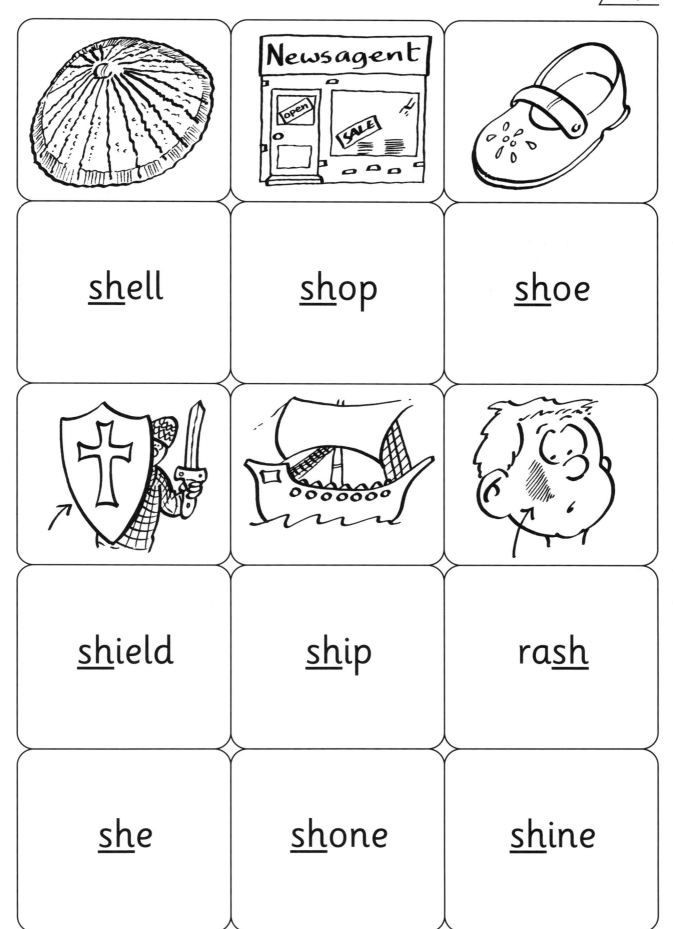

shell

shop

shoe

shield

ship

rash

she

shone

shine

More long vowels

<u>th</u>imble	<u>th</u>orn	<u>th</u>irty

<u>th</u>umb	<u>th</u>irteen	<u>th</u>ree
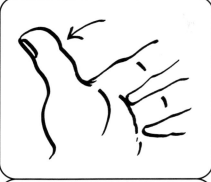	**13**	**3**
<u>the</u>	<u>th</u>en	<u>th</u>is

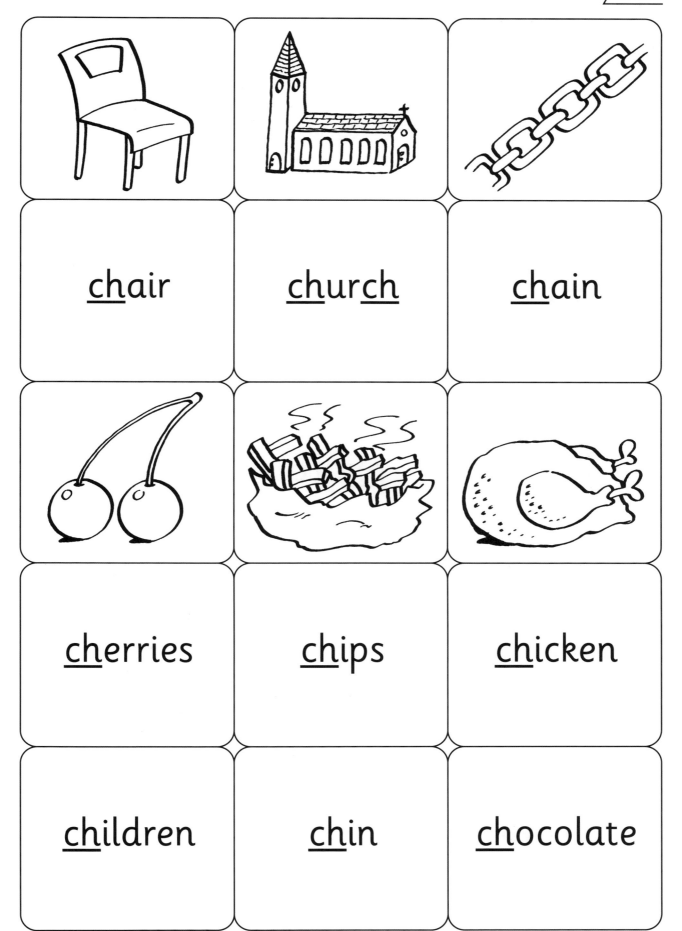

chair

chur**c**h

chain

cherries

chips

chicken

children

chin

chocolate

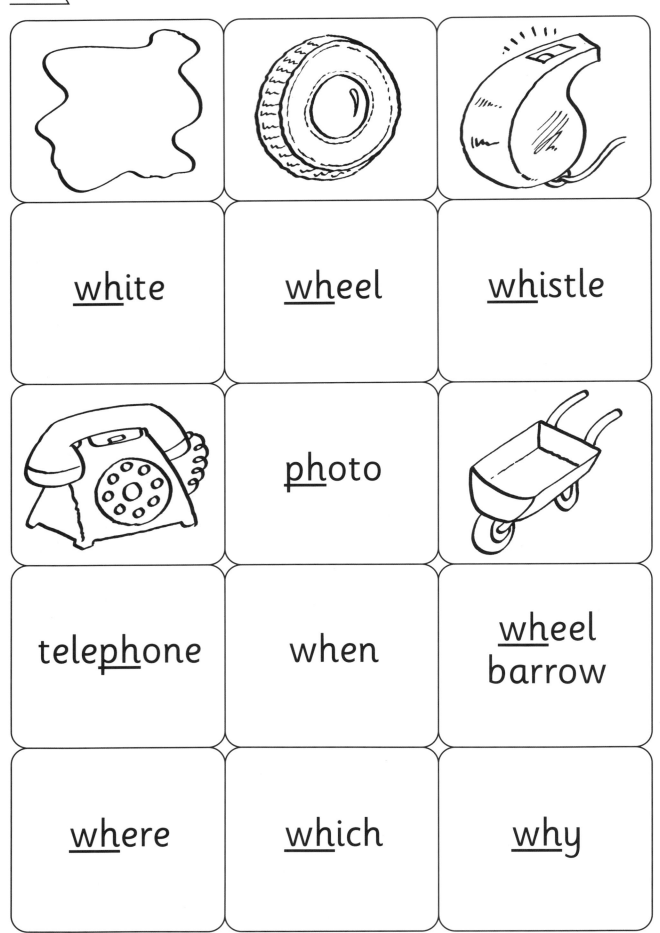

white	wheel	whistle
telephone	when	wheel barrow
where	which	why

More long vowels

ch	ch	ch	ch	ch	ch	ch
th	th	th	th	th	th	th
sh	sh	sh	sh	sh	sh	sh
wh	wh	wh	wh	wh	wh	wh

More long vowels

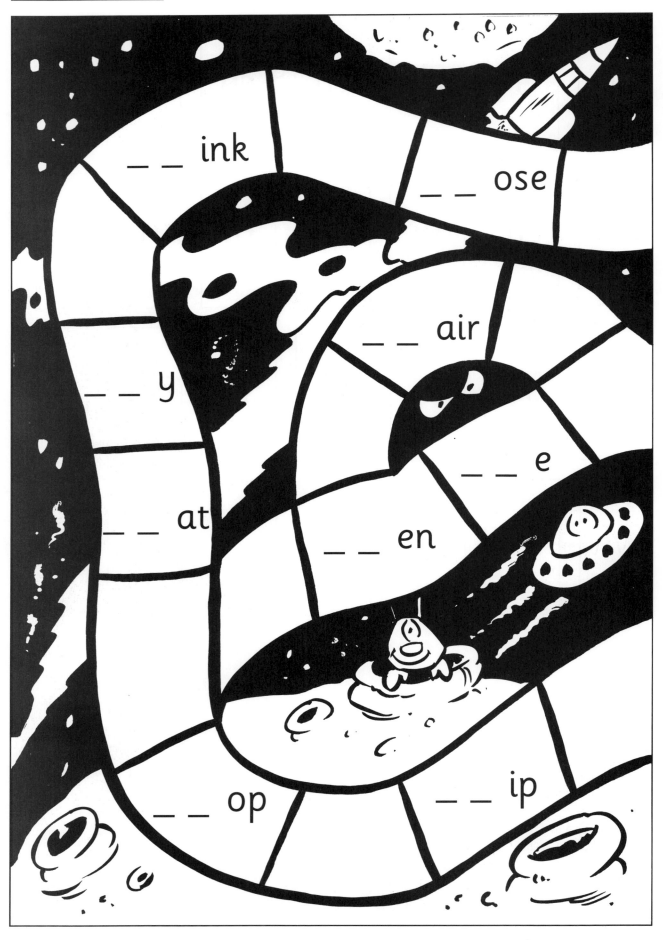

More long vowels

More long vowels

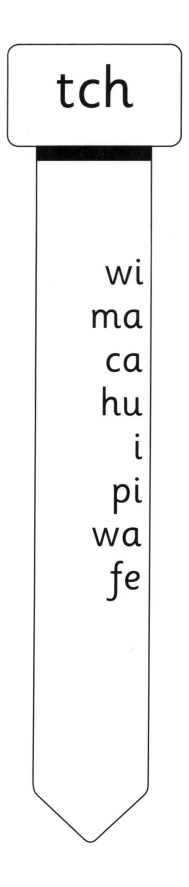

tch

wi
ma
ca
hu
i
pi
wa
fe

More long vowels

Help Wanda to find the words.

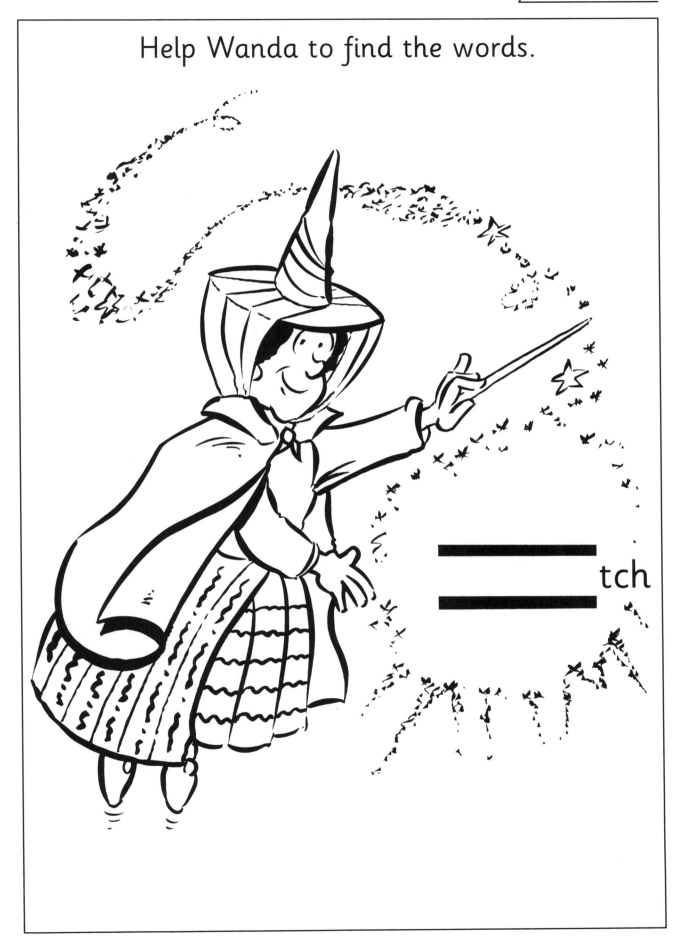

tch

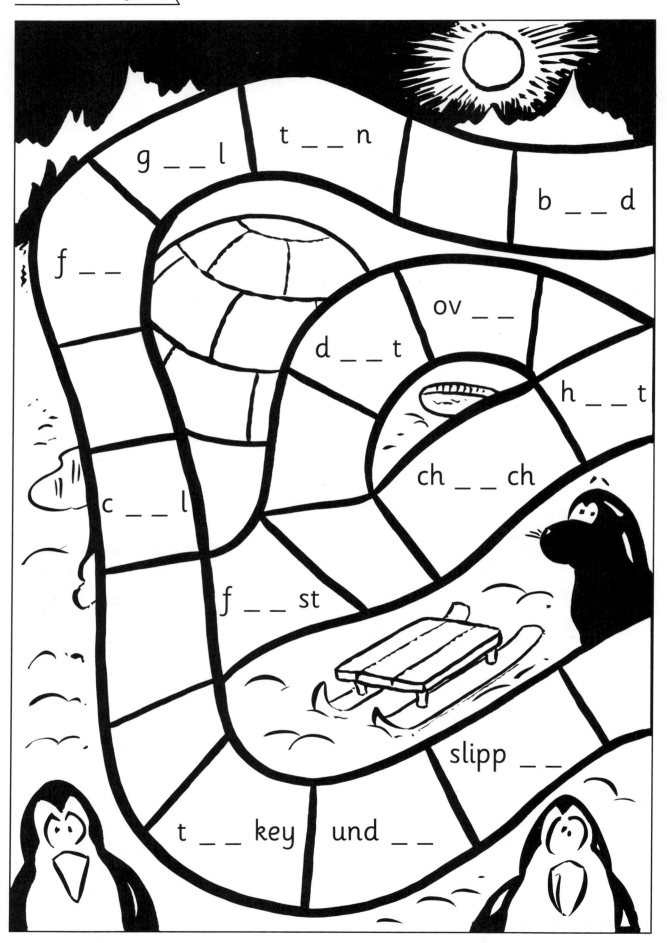

g _ _ l

t _ _ n

b _ _ d

f _ _

ov _ _

d _ _ t

h _ _ t

ch _ _ ch

c _ _ l

f _ _ st

slipp _ _

t _ _ key

und _ _

More long vowels

f _ _

sh _ _ t

st _ _

wint _ _

dinn _ _

h _ _ dle

lett _ _

b _ _ n

bett _ _   th _ _ d

h _ _ d

Start

More long vowels

er	er	er	er	er	er	er
ir	ir	ir	ir	ir	ir	ir
ur	ur	ur	ur	ur	ur	ur

More long vowels

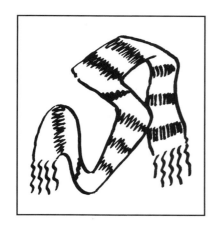

More long vowels

car	parachute	jar
scarf	farm	star
fork	torch	sport
horse	storm	cork

More long vowels

ff	ff	ff	ff	ff	ff	ff	ff
ll	ll	ll	ll	ll	ll	ll	ll
ss	ss	ss	ss	ss	ss	ss	ss

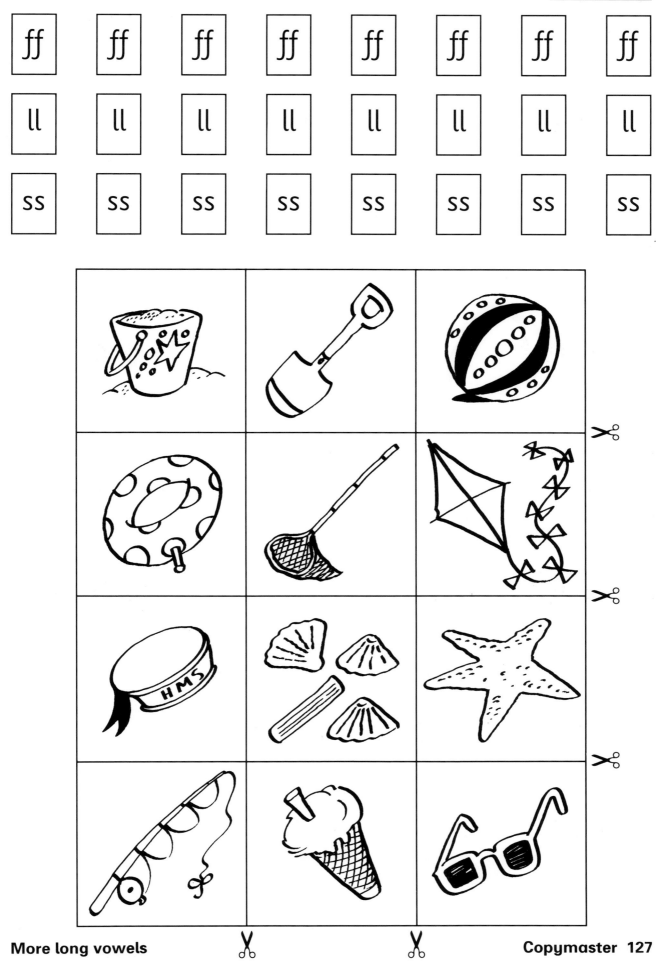

More long vowels

pu _ _

dre _ _

we _ _

ba _ _

me _ _

to _ _ ee

fa _ _

le _ _

mu _ _

sni _ _

fi _ _

do _ _

be _ _

More long vowels

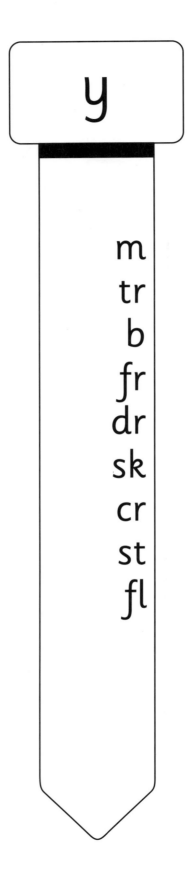

y

m
tr
b
fr
dr
sk
cr
st
fl

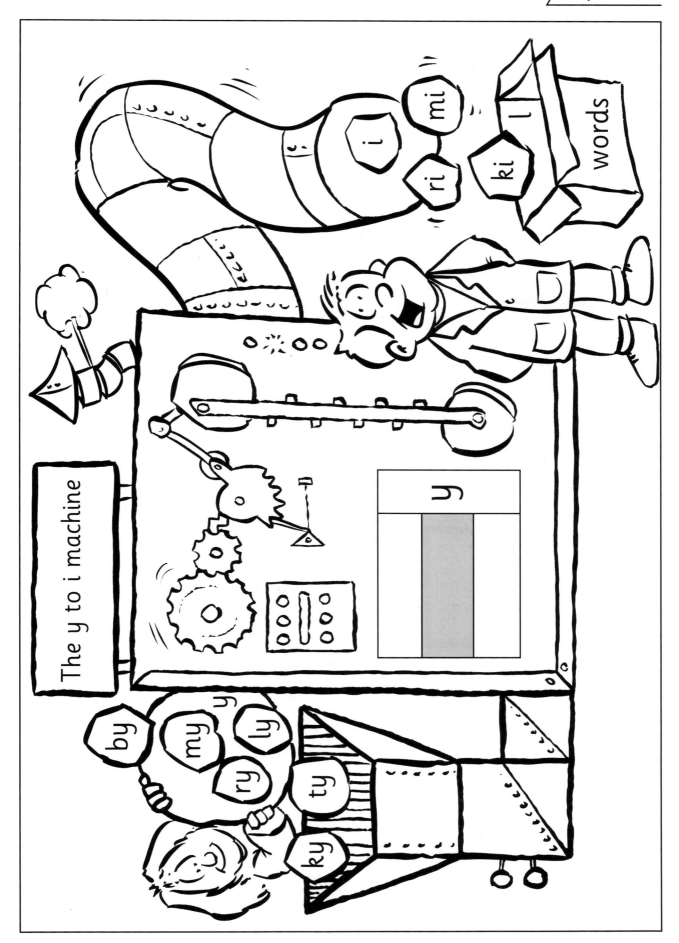

More long vowels

ay

Turn the wheel to find the words.

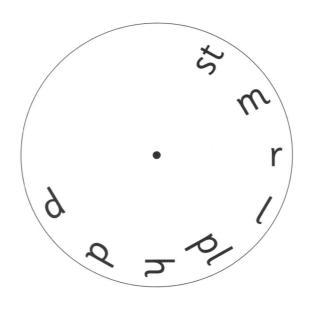

More long vowels

Short vowel sound at word ending – use ck.
Long vowel sound at word ending – use ke.

Long vowel takes -ke

Short vowel and c sound at the end of a word takes – ck.

wreck 8

quick 9

lock 2

pack 5

5 dock

2 tick

clock 9

2 tock

4 lick

chick 6

Short vowel takes -ck

Short vowel and c sound at the end of a word takes – ck.

back 8

3 pack

sick 2

duck 10

6 sack

4 neck

1 rack

quack 6

2 luck

4 tuck

Short vowel takes -ck

Boys and girls come out to play

_ arol

_ en

_ at

_ ot

_ od

_ ettle

_ itten

_ ord

_ ar

More long vowels following c or k

_ ilt

_ atie

_ ut

_ ing

_ it

_ ap

_ op

_ ennel

_ url

_ id

Vowels following c or k

c	c	c	c	k	k	k	k
c	c	c	c	k	k	k	k
c	c	c	c	k	k	k	k
c	c	c	c	k	k	k	k
c	c	c	c	k	k	k	k

c is followed by the short a, o and u.

k is followed by the short e and i.

c is followed by the short a, o and u.

k is followed by the short e and i.

Vowels following c or k

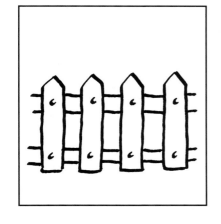

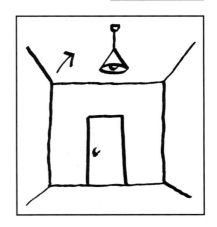

Softening of c and g

fence	parcel	ceiling
necklace	space	trace
ginger-bread man	badge	germ
large	gem	genie

Softening of c and g

ANSWERS TO WORD GAMES

Word list for Copymasters 36–37 short vowel sounds

pat pet pit pot put cat cot cut hat hit hot hut pan pen pin pun bad bed bid bud dad did dud tap tip top dig dog dug lag leg log red rid rod

Word list for Copymasters 38–39 short vowel sounds

pat pet pit pot put cat cot cut pan pen pin pun hat hit hot hut bad bed bid bud lag leg log red rid rod lad led lid dad did dud tap tip top

Word list for Copymasters 40–41 short vowel sounds

lad led lid lag leg log red rid rod dig dog dug tan ten tin ton dad did dud bad bed bid bud pan pen pin pun hat hit hot hut cat cot cut pat pet pit pot put tap tip top

Word list for Copymaster 44 words beginning with sl

slam slap slide slim slip sleep slipper slug

Word list for Copymaster 45 words beginning with gl

glad glass globe gloss glow glove glide glue

Word list for Copymaster 46 words beginning with pl

plan planet plant plate play please plod plot

Word list for Copymaster 47 words beginning with bl cl fl

bl	cl	fl
black	clip	flag
blue	class	flap
blot	clog	flash
bless	clock	flat
blink	cloth	flock
bled	cling	flip
block	cliff	fling
blank	clap	flesh
blur	club	flung
	clung	flush
	clown	flower

149

Word list for Copymaster 48 words beginning with dr fr tr

dr	fr	tr
draw	frog	tree
dress	frill	try
drip	fruit	true
drum	free	trust
drain	fridge	tried
drop	friend	train
drink	frost	tricycle
drill	fresh	tractor
dream	frown	trick
dragon	front	
	fried	

Word list for Copymaster 49 words beginning with br cr sl

br	cr	sl
bridge	crab	slow
bread	crash	slide
branch	cracker	slipper
brick	crust	slug
bride	crane	slot
brown	crook	slip
brush	crack	slam
brother	crown	slope
broken	crate	slit
bring		sleep
brain		

Word list for Copymaster 50 words beginning with sm sn sp

sm	sn	sp
smoke	snow	spade
small	snack	spear
smell	sniff	spank
smock	snore	speak
smug	snip	spell
smack	snail	spider
smile	snake	spin
smart	snap	spot
smash		

Word list for Copymaster 63 words ending in at et ot

at	et	ot
bat	bet	cot
cat	net	dot
fat	get	got
sat	met	hot
flat	set	lot
mat	let	not
rat	wet	pot
hat	pet	rot
pat	vet	

Word list for Copymaster 64 words ending in all ill an

all	ill	an
call	will	ran
ball	till	ban
all	ill	can
fall	bill	fan
stall	fill	man
tall	hill	nan
hall	kill	pan
wall	mill	ran
small	pill	tan
	still	van

Word list for Copymaster 65 words ending in and st ent

and	st	ent
land	fast	went
sand	mast	sent
band	last	lent
hand	past	bent
island	best	rent
stand	rest	tent
strand	nest	silent
wand	west	dent
	jest	
	list	
	fist	

Word list for Copymaster 66 words ending ng old nk

ng	old	nk
rang	fold	bank
hang	sold	monk
sang	old	sank
bang	told	tank
king	bold	link
sing	cold	pink
sting	gold	sink
ring	hold	wink
stung	scold	ink
		sunk

Word list for Copymaster 91 ow as in snow

mow row sow bow snow stow blow low

Word list for copymasters 100–101 ai ea or ee

ai	ea	ee
sail	seal	see
hail	leaf	bee
fail	bead	green
train	sea	heel
rain	heal	feel
grain	beach	beech
snail	sweat	sweet
	meat	meet
	feat	feet
		tree

Word lists for Copymaster 103

ee	ee	ea	ea
green	fee	meat	peak
sleep	feet	feat	peach
sleet	keen	sea	peat
see	keep	seat	teak
seen	sweep	leak	teach
seep	sweet	leaf	teat
thee	free	heat	tea
		pea	weak

Word lists for Copymaster 106

oo as in moon	oo as in moon	ou as in out	ou as in out
moo	balloon	sound	shout
mood	pool	found	loud
moon	root	hound	louse
moot	fool	house	lout
soot	foot	mouse	round
soon	food	mound	rout
spool	noon	cloud	ground
spoon		clout	grouse
			grout

Word lists for Copymaster 108

ar	ar	ow	ow
start	dark	cow	crow
stark	dart	cowboy	crown
jar	hark	cower	down
bar	hard	brow	dowel
bark	car	brown	dower
star	cart	how	flower
scar	card	howl	clown
scarf	smart	tow	flow
		town	flown
		towel	
		tower	

Word lists for Copymaster 110

ai	ai	oa	oa
frail	wail	road	loaf
snail	wait	roach	load
pain	said (not	float	goat
paid	correct sound)	coat	goad
pail	sailor	coach	goal
rain	sail	coal	broach
raid	main	boat	
rail	maid		
train	mail		
trail	chain		
trait			

Word list for Copymaster 112

blew drew few flew new screw stew threw

153

Answer list for Copymasters 118–119

ch	wh	sh	th	th
chip	who	ship	thin	think
chair	whose	shoe	that	then
chat	when	shin	thing	three
chin	why	she	there	the
chose	what	shy	those	thy
chop	where	shop	that	

Word list for Copymasters 120–121

witch match catch hutch itch pitch watch fetch

Word list for Copymasters 122–123 er ir ur all say er

er	ir	ur
herd	bird	fur
letter	fir	turkey
dinner	stir	church
winter	first	turn
over	dirt	burn
slipper	girl	curl
under	shirt	hurt
better	third	hurdle

Answer list for Copymasters 128–129 ll, ff and ss

ll	ll	ff	ss
bell	wall	sniff	brass
doll	full	muff	moss
fill	roll	toffee	miss
fall	mill	cliff	class
pull	mull	off	less
ball	well	cuff	mess
bull	still	stiff	dress
toll	call	puff	toss
		buff	fuss

Word list for Copymasters 130–131

my try by fry dry sky cry sty fly

Word list for Copymaster 132 ay words

day hay lay may pay play ray stay

Answer list for Copymasters 136–137 c or k

c	c	k	k
cat	cot	kilt	kennel
cord	cap	king	kid
curl	cop	kettle	Ken
cut	car	kitten	Katie
cod	Carol	kit	

G000037822

MORAL AND ENVIRONMENTAL ISSUES

Paul Higginson

Hodder & Stoughton

A MEMBER OF THE HODDER HEADLINE GROUP

ACKNOWLEDGEMENTS

The author would like to thank Carole Woodburn for typing the script.

The publishers would like to thank the following for their kind permission to reproduce material in this volume:

Associated Examining Board for the use of examination questions from past papers p112; British Union for the Abolition of Vivisection (BUAV)for extract from 'ugly pain' leaflet p80; examination questions from past papers p112 reproduced by permission of the University of Cambridge Local Examinations Syndicate; Central Statistics Office for extracts on pp43–5; Christian Aid for the reproduction of the cartoon on p56; HMSO for extracts from *Cleaner Seas*, and the figure from *Global Atmosphere and Air Quality*, reproduced with the permission of the Controller of Her Majesty's Stationary Office pp68–9; LIFE for the use of the logo and extracts from resource material on pp 39–40; Meat and Livestock Commission for extract from 'Technology in Meat Production and Processing' on p81; Northern Examinations and Assessment Board for use of examination questions from past papers p112; University of Oxford, Delegacy of Local Examinations for use of examination questions from past papers p112; The Vegetarian Society for extracts from the booklet on p81; The Voluntary Euthanasia Society for extract from a VES briefing on pp 40–1; newspaper article on p37 appears courtesy of the *Watford Free Observer*.

The publishers would also like to thank the following for permission to reproduce copyright photographs in this volume:

Greenpeace p67; League Against Cruel Sports Ltd. p85.

Every effort has been made to trace copyright holders of material reproduced in this book. The publishers will be glad to make suitable arrangements with any copyright holders whom it has not been possible to contact.

NB Any answers, or hints of answers, to the past papers on p112 are the responsibility of the author and have not been provided or approved by the Boards.

For Kate and Anna

Orders: please contact Bookpoint Ltd, 39 Milton Park, Abingdon, Oxon OX14 4TD. Telephone: (44) 01235 400414, Fax: (44) 01235 400454. Lines are open from 9.00–6.00, Monday to Saturday, with a 24 hour message answering service. Email address: orders@bookpoint.co.uk

British Library Cataloguing in Publication Data

Higginson, Paul
  Moral and Environmental Issues.
  (General Studies Resource Books)
  I. Title II. Series
  306. 07

ISBN 0 340 59533 7

First published 1994
Impression number 10 9 8 7 6
Year 2003 2002 2001 2000

Copyright © 1994 Paul Higginson

Printed in Great Britain for Hodder & Stoughton Educational, a division of Hodder Headline Plc, 338 Euston Road, London NW1 3BH by Hobbs the Printers Ltd, Totton, Hampshire SO40 3WX

Contents

Introduction

General Studies Resource Books are designed for groups studying A-level and sixth form General Studies, but can also be used for BTEC Courses; Key Stage 4, Years 11 to 13 and tutor groups. Book Two (*Moral and Environmental Issues*) will also prove an invaluable resource for Environmental Studies, Religious Studies and Social Science courses.

Each unit is self-contained, with resource pages which can be photocopied or transferred to OHPs, and worksheets for classroom or homework use.

AIMS

This book aims to encourage students to:

1 think critically on significant moral and environmental problems and issues in the modern world;

2 understand and evaluate a range of often conflicting arguments on each topic;

3 communicate information and viewpoints in a clear, analytical manner, supported by relevant evidence.

EXAMINATIONS

General Studies can be studied at A- and A/S-level. Courses are multi-disciplinary covering the major social, political, moral and environmental issues, as well as science and, in some cases, mathematics and a foreign language (see table p5). All examinations require good English and communication skills. The style and format of the final written papers vary but most boards include data response, short answer and comprehension questions (Nothern Examinations and Assessment Board also includes multi-choice) and all examinations require candidates to write answers to essay questions. It is also possible to take a coursework option which enables students to submit an in-depth assignment on a selected topic. As syllabus details are constantly changing, students who are taking General Studies independently from their school or college should write to the examination boards to obtain an up-to-date syllabus and past paper questions. This book can also be used as a source for Education for Citizenship, and Environmenal Education courses – two of the five cross-curricular themes identified by the Schools Curriculum and Assessment Authority.

A-Level General Studies Examination Board Details

Board	Address & Tel. No.	Coursework	Coursework Assessment	Examination Papers	Comments
Associated Examining Board (AEB)	Stag Hill House Guildford, Surrey GU2 5XJ (0483) 506506	Compulsory: two assignments (2,500–3,000 words) on prescribed titles. (20% of examination.)	Internally assessed, externally moderated.	Paper 1: 2 1/2 hrs (30%) Paper 2: 3 hrs (50%)	Coursework topics are given by board in advance, e.g. for 1994 candidates choose two of four themes: Space, Communication, Conflict and Leisure.
University of Cambridge Local Examinations Syndicate	Syndicate Buildings, 1 Hills Road Cambridge CB1 2EU (0223) 61111	6,000 word study of own choice on a single issue, or a series of short related studies. 25% of examination.	Internally assessed, externally moderated.	Syllabus 9374 (without coursework). Paper 1: 3 hrs (50%) Paper 2: 1 1/2 hrs (25%) Paper 3: 1 1/2 hrs (25%)	Syllabus 9375 (coursework option) has Paper 1: 3hrs (50%) Paper 2: 3/4 hr (12 1/2%) Paper 3: 3/4hr (12 1/2%). Papers 2 and 3 require students to answer one essay in each paper.
Northern Examinations and Assessment Board (NEAB)	Devas Street Manchester M15 6EU (061) 953 1180	Scheme 1: No coursework. Scheme 2: Personal study (or six assignments) on topic of own choice. Suggested length 4,000–7,000 words. (30% of examination.)	Internally assessed.	Scheme 1 Paper 1: 3 hrs (50%) Paper 2: 3 hrs (50%) Scheme 2 Paper 1: 2 1/2 hrs (40%) Paper 2: 2 hrs (30%)	Candidates opting for coursework (Scheme 2) sit the same two papers as Scheme 1 students but do not answer any essay questions. (Scheme 1 students answer three essay questions.)
University of Oxford Delegacy of Local Examinations	Ewart House Summertown Oxford OX2 7BZ (0865) 54291			Paper 1: 3 hrs (50%) Paper 2: 3 hrs (50%)	The syllabus covers three main areas: the arts (visual, music, performing, verbal); the organisation of society (political, economic, social and moral issues); science and technology (matter, energy, scientific thought, environmental issues).

Northern Examinations and Assessmet Board and Oxford have Mathematics/Numeracy Sections and Northern Examinations and Assessment Board has a Foreign Language Section. All of the four boards require students to answer questions on Political and Social Issues, Moral and Environmental Issues, Science and Technology.

The boards listed above also offer A/S-level General Studies, along with London, Oxford and Cambridge, Wales and Northern Ireland.

WRITING ESSAYS – TEN POINTS TO REMEMBER

1   Make a short plan jotting down key ideas, names and paragraph headings.

2   **The Introduction** – define the key words or phrases in the title, then briefly state the line or argument you intend to pursue in your essay. Tell the reader (the examiner) what you are going to write about, using the words of the title. This shows the examiner that you are answering the question set (not the question you would have liked to have been set!) and helps to keep your answer relevant.

3   **The Body** – argue your line, beginning with the most convincing point to support your argument. Remember that there will always be two or more sides to every question, so you must always deal with the counter-arguments. So, if the question asks 'Should the monarchy be abolished?' and your line is that it should, you must also deal with all the arguments which suggest that the monarchy is wonderful and should be retained.

4   Essays require a combination of evidence (information, facts, detail, statistics, examples, quotes, etc.) and analysis (this is how you use the evidence to prove something or support a line). Therefore, essays should contain supporting evidence to back up each point. The single most common error in General Studies (and most Social Science) examination papers is the superficial and sweeping statement unsubstantiated by any facts or evidence.

5   Throughout the essay make sure you keep referring to the words of the title; relate everything you write to the question which has been set.

6   Keep your writing as academic as possible. Take care not to use slang, colloquialisms, clichés and generalisations. Avoid the phrase 'I think' – just say it! ('The monarchy should be abolished' and not 'I think the monarchy should be abolished'.)

7   Take care over how your work is presented. Examiners continually complain about poor handwriting (some scripts are illegible), spelling, grammar and punctuation.

8   Usually General Studies questions seek to be topical so use recent, contemporary examples to back up your arguments. Keep up to date with current events by reading quality newspapers and watching the news each day. However, avoid the temptation to write down everything you know about a particular topic without first checking that it is relevant to the question.

9   Make comparisons when appropriate with other fields of study, other countries, other periods of history, etc. General Studies aims to encourage students to be inter-disciplinary and comparative. So compare our contemporary monarchy with other monarchies (e.g. Sweden, Spain) and republics (e.g. USA, France), and make reference to kings and queens in history.

10 **The Conclusion** – avoid the tired old phrase 'In conclusion', again just say it. Re-state your line using the words of the title: this is a good double check that you have answered the question. Too many students play safe by writing 'on the one hand this... on the other hand that'. Be confident in your argument and briefly summarise the main points again in one sentence: 'The monarchy should be abolished because...'. Some students like to finish with a final contemporary example or apt quotation which effectively proves their line.

Hodder & Stoughton   © 1994 Paul Higginson. The publishers grant permission for multiple copies of this sheet to be made in the place of purchase for use solely in that institution.

EFFECTIVE STUDY

Follow these guidelines to improve your study technique.

1 The best way of broadening your knowledge and improving your written English, outside the class, is to read and make notes at home. (Teachers and examination boards can provide relevant reading lists.) Always jot down brief notes when you are reading, otherwise the material will soon be forgotten and you will have nothing to revise from.

2 Each issue or problem will always contain two or more sides or arguments. Do not ignore viewpoints you disagree with – try to understand them as effectively as possible.

3 Examiners have indicated that they require some acquaintance with articles in the quality press and 'serious' television programmes.

4 Develop your verbal skills by actively participating in class discussion and debate. Avoid the temptation to say the first thing that comes into your head and try to think out your point in advance and present it in a logical, coherent way.

5 Keep a diary of current events. Include facts, dates, arguments, personalities involved, statistics, etc. Cut out and keep relevant articles from newspapers and journals.

6 Before you sit your examination look over the syllabus and past papers, then answer questions under timed conditions. Work out in advance how much time you must spend on each section of the paper (look at the marks awarded for each question) and then stick to this in the examination.

Hodder & Stoughton   © 1994 Paul Higginson. The publishers grant permission for multiple copies of this sheet to be made in the place of purchase for use solely in that institution.

Teacher's Notes

This book can either be used as a complete course in itself or as a resource package to supplement the teacher's existing material. The units are flexible and can be taught in a variety of ways but the emphasis throughout is on active student participation through discussion, structured worksheets, simulations and group work. The aim is to get students to look beyond their specialist fields at important aspects of the modern world, broadening and deepening their knowledge, acquiring the skills to critically evaluate complex and often conflicting points of view.

Before working through the material in a unit each lesson should ideally begin with a short brainstorming session where students provide the teacher with all the information and ideas they already have on a particular topic – anything that is relevant should be placed on the board or OHP. This allows students to make an immediate contribution while enabling the teacher to check the group's knowledge, or lack of it, on a particular topic.

When using the worksheets (for example, fox-hunting on p85) allow the students the time to think through the arguments for themselves before giving them the worksheet material.

The notes below provide brief answers to questions or exercises where specific and detailed knowledge or information is required. Guidelines are also provided on how to get the best results from the simulations and role plays.

UNIT 1 – MORALITY

Activity 1 – Influences: Parents, close family, relations, peers, older friends, teachers, television, books, the Church, the Bible or other scripture, society in general, clubs and societies, music, religious teaching, famous role-models.

Worksheet 1 – Kidney Transplants: If a consensus begins to emerge too quickly about the waiting list the teacher should disclose the patient updates to see if these change the group's attitude. Complete the additional blank card with further information on any patient if the need arises.

Worksheet 4 – Suicide: Causes of loneliness, alcoholism (suicide rate is 80 times that of the rest of the population), drug abuse, financial problems, emotional/marital problems, 'cry for help', mental illness and depression, self-sacrifice (death rather than dishonour – common in Japan as ritual suicide, hara-kiri), death of a partner/close friend, old age, disease or illness, stress.

UNIT 2 – WAR AND CONFLICT

Military Expenditure and Underdevelopment – Questions:

1 The Japanese constitution was written by the USA after the Second World War. Designed to limit Japanese militarism and calm fears of close neighbours, it has helped produce Japan's economic growth.

2 Japan relies on the US military/nuclear umbrella. There are many US bases in Japan.

Worksheet 1 – War: Answers to matching-up exercise are: Falklands 5, Roses 11, Second 7, Gulf 15, Boer 16, Crusades 12, Afghanistan 14, American 10, Napoleonic 4, American Civil 1, Cold 2, Hundred Years 9, Korean 8, Suez 13, Vietnam 6, Crimean 3.

Hodder & Stoughton   © 1994 Paul Higginson. The publishers grant permission for multiple copies of this sheet to be made in the place of purchase for use solely in that institution.

UNIT 3 – OLD AGE

The Demographic Time Bomb – Question 4: Unemployed, early retired, housewives, students, sick, disabled.

Defusing the Time Bomb – Activity 2: Note that in 1974 only 35% of pensioners had occupational pensions, today the figure is around 60%. Only 13% of pensioners rely completely on the state pension (and other benefits) for their income.

UNIT 4 – THE FAMILY

Family Types – Question 2: Examine the following: Industrial Revolution (people moved into towns to work leaving relations behind); old housing replaced by new estates often in suburbia; affluence (no economic need to all live in the same house); rise of generation gap (no desire to live with parents); high divorce rate; high number of children born to unmarried parents.

Marriage – Question 3: Reasons for women having children later: people getting married later; women wanting to establish their careers; increase in house prices; women not so worried about ticking biological clock; advances in medical science have made later pregnancies safer; women want fewer children so no need to start so early; better contraception, etc.

Worksheet 1 – Functions of the Family: Possible challenges include: child rearing – one parent families, child-minders, working mothers; sex – pre-marital and extra-marital sex is common, as is living together; education – state does the job in schools; love – emotional fulfilment often found elsewhere (with others), or through hobbies, work, etc.; behaviour – schools, television, breakdown of discipline; economic well-being – the welfare state has now taken over some aspects of this role; care of the elderly – state takes care of elderly, young are less willing to do this; social control – it can be argued that far from preserving the family, capitalism has destroyed it.

Worksheet 2 – Divorce: Explanations include: **2** In nuclear families there is less support for the family plus divorce is not so disruptive. **3** Women less economically dependent on husband, more working mothers. **4** Many divorce once children are grown up. **5** Women can survive without husband's income. **6** Reality of marriage often fails to meet romantic notions portrayed in the media. **7** Divorce becoming more acceptable. Church has less sway over people than before. **8** People can now expect to be married for 50 or 60 years if they marry in their 20s.

UNIT 5 – NORTH AND SOUTH

Debt of Underdeveloped Countries – Questions:

1 Why? – Earns foreign currency to pay off debts (80 per cent of Sudan's export earnings go on debt repayment) by providing raw materials to North. Results – food is not grown, peasants cannot feed themselves, little public spending/services/welfare.

2 Supply and demand – as more tea has been produced in the world a glut has occurred and the price has fallen (although lower raw material costs have not been passed on to the Western consumer, they have simply increased multinational companies' profits).

3 Why? – Multi-national companies' control of the industry, plus demand for cheap tea and big company profits in West.

6 Debt default or moratorium, fixed interest rates, index-link the price of raw materials to manufactured goods, abolish tariff barriers and quotas, force multi-national companies to plough profits back into Southern countries.

Child Sponsorship – Question 4: Criteria might include: a) helping all the community regardless of race, politics or religious belief; b) involving local people fully; c) helping to tackle the underlying causes of poverty not just the symptoms; d) spending the bare minimum on administration; e) helping the poor to help themselves rather than relying on expert outsiders.

Hodder & Stoughton

© 1994 Paul Higginson. The publishers grant permission for multiple copies of this sheet to be made in the place of purchase for use solely in that institution.

3 Examples include; South Africa, some oil-rich Middle-Eastern countries, some parts of South-East Asia like Hong Kong, Malaysia, Taiwan, etc.

4 Poorest countries of world in terms of GNP per capita in US dollars (1987) are Ethiopia (130), Zaire (150), Bangladesh (160), Nepal (160), Laos (170), Mozambique (170), Tanzania (180). Richest are Switzerland (21,330), USA (18,530), Norway (17,190), United Arab Emirates (15,830), Japan (15,760). The UK is the 17th richest (10,420).

5 Major wars and conflicts have taken place in the following countries since 1945; El Salvador, Nicaragua, Colombia, Peru, Bolivia, Chile, Argentina, Morocco, Algeria, Libya, Chad, Sudan, Ethiopia, Nigeria, Angola, Uganda, Somalia, Mozambique, Yemen, Israel, Egypt, Lebanon, Syria, Iran, Iraq, Jordan, Kuwait, India, Pakistan, Bangladesh, Sri Lanka, Cambodia, Vietnam, Korea, Philippines, Indonesia, Rwanda, Hungary, Czechoslovakia, Yugoslavia. Only the last three are in the North.

Worksheet 2 – Rich and Poor: The full list of figures is: **1** 30%, 70%; **2** two thirds, one third; **3** 70%, 30%; **4** $14,000, less than $500; **5** 3,200, 1,600; **6** 150 million, 300 million; **7** 74, 55; **8** less than 1%, 70%; **9** 99%, 50%; **10** less than 1%, 35%; **11** nil, 15,000; **12** 10%, 90%; **13** 15%, 80%; **14** 90%, 10%; **15** 10, 81; **16** 25%, less than 1%.

UNIT 6 – POLLUTION
Pesticides and Fertilisers – Questions:

4 Factors include: expense; threat to living standards and jobs; lack of agreement amongst scientific community (some scientists claim that nature can cope with a certain amount of pollution); the need to do more research and tests before taking decisions; the lack of interest in green issues amongst many voters (i.e. it is not as important a political priority as the need to raise living standards or reduce unemployment) – some politicians claim that green issues are merely a temporary fad that voters will soon tire of; a lack of international agreement from other countries (no use just one country acting alone); a high proportion of the money given to the UN and international agencies gets wasted on administration.

5 Pests quickly become immune to pesticides. Their natural enemies (predators), however, are contaminated and decline, creating an imbalance in nature. Therefore, while pesticides work for a short time, in the longer term they create more pests.

6 Possible steps; see Unit 11, Worksheet 1.

UNIT 7 – GLOBAL WARMING, THE OZONE LAYER AND DEFORESTATION
Worksheet 1 – Global Cooling: Practical suggestions might include those listed below.

1 Use up other energy sources; nuclear, wind, solar, etc.

2 Better home insulation, producing buildings and designing factories/industrial systems that use less energy, turning down thermostats, using energy-efficient light bulbs, lagging hot water cylinders, etc.

3 Reducing number of cars by subsidising public transport, increasing taxes on petrol and cars, making cars more energy-efficient, banning cars from city centres, taxing larger cars that consume more fuel, using unleaded petrol.

4 Writing off or renegotiating the debt of Underdeveloped Countries. Introducing a UN fund to help poor nations pay for renewable energy sources.

5 Banning all export of wood from tropical rainforests. Giving tax incentives and aid to plant millions of new trees. Land reform in Underdeveloped Countries.

Hodder & Stoughton © 1994 Paul Higginson. The publishers grant permission for multiple copies of this sheet to be made in the place of purchase for use solely in that institution.

6 Introduce a World Carbon Tax scheme; big taxes on large producers of emissions (like USA, Canada and Australia – the top three users), very small taxes on the small producers like India and Nigeria.

7 Producing aerosols, fridges, etc. without CFCs. Devising alternatives. The Montreal Protocol agreed to phase out CFCs by 1997.

8 Raising awareness through education, putting pressure on governments (through voting behaviour, pressure groups, etc.).

9 Consumers rejecting excess packaging on goods and demanding environmentally-friendly products.

Worksheet 2 – Deforestation:

1 …to absorb carbon-dioxide and produce oxygen, helping to prevent global warming; to conserve the soil and maintain its fertility, thereby preventing erosion; to store water and provide a habitat for wildlife.

2 …air pollution (acid rain) and increased building.

3 …huge profits in the timber trade; clearance for agriculture (needs of growing population for more land); conversion of land into reservoirs. Note that half of all forests in Underdeveloped Countries have been lost since 1900, and tropical forests are disappearing at a rate of 7 per cent per annum. The logging industry has destroyed half of Malaysia's forests since 1960. In Brazil 60 per cent of recent forest destruction has been caused by large-scale cattle ranching programmes.

4 …the desperate need for more land. In Latin America 7 per cent of population owns 93 per cent of farming land so peasant farmers invade the forests in order to make a living.

5 …eroded, and rivers silt up.

6 …desertification. A land area twice the size of Belgium is lost every year. UN estimates that 30 per cent of the world's land surface could become desert.

7 …trees are the key to biological diversity and provide fodder for animals and food, fruits, fibres, firewood and timber for man.

8 …the UN *Tropical Forest Action Plan* (much criticised by some environmentalists) aims to invest $8,000million in: a) increasing the supply of firewood; b) promoting agro-forestry and education; c) reforesting upland watersheds; d) conserving tropical forests.

9 …recycling, especially newspapers, less packaging and wrappings on goods. The USA wastes four times as much paper as is used by all Underdeveloped Countries combined. Each US citizen throws away the equivalent of three trees per annum.

UNIT 8 – ANIMAL RIGHTS AND CONSERVATION

Zoos – Question 3 : The impression is often that animals are there for our benefit, as exhibits to please and entertain. People want to be noticed and recognised, not ignored. Zoo visitors often get annoyed if animals hide out of sight, refuse to move around or fail to behave in certain ways.

Biological Diversity – Questions:

1 Yes, this periwinkle has been used to treat children with leukaemia. Before this plant was discovered only 1 in 5 children survived, now it is 4 in 5.

2 Pests and diseases take about ten years to develop ways to combat the existing defences of crops. Therefore, new resistance has to be provided, and the only way to do this is through inbreeding with other strains.

Hodder & Stoughton   © 1994 Paul Higginson. The publishers grant permission for multiple copies of this sheet to be made in the place of purchase for use solely in that institution.

3 Destruction of the natural habitat is by far and away the single most important reason. The other reasons are very much secondary factors.

4 Prevention: set up reserves to protect animals and plant species; establish gene banks (to keep seeds); end the destruction of the natural habitat; stop the trade in wildlife as well as over-hunting and over-fishing by concerted international action.

Worksheet 1 – Rights and Wrongs: Consider the following examples for each category:

2 pigs, cats, dogs, locusts, horses, whales, blackbird paté;

3 snake, fish, tortoise, worm, robin, canary, St Bernard dog;

4 smoking beagles, rabbits testing shampoo in eyes, mice in cancer research, rats, chimps in AIDS research;

5 fur coats, leather jackets, sheepskin coats, woollen sweaters, Eskimos wearing fur coats;

6 elephants logging in India, guide dogs for blind, horses pulling carts, oxen ploughing fields, donkeys carrying loads, bomb-disposal sniffer dogs, pit ponies;

7 ivory earrings, stuffed head on wall, leather wallet, crocodile handbag, perfume;

8 zoos, safari parks, animals kept alone/in groups, dolphinaria, aquaria;

9 use of fly killer, spraying aphids on roses with insecticide, giving rabbits myxomatosis, use of mousetrap, shooting foxes, rat poison, leg-traps;

10 circus acts, performing seals, dancing bears in India, talking parrots;

11 free-range chickens, battery farms, artificial insemination of livestock, fish farms, factory fishing (hoovering up fish), Jewish and Muslim methods of slaughter (cutting the throat);

12 animal 'actors' in films performing stunts, chimpanzees in adverts;

13 cat is going blind, stray dog, pit pony too old to work, zoo is closing down, bird is in pain, cow no longer providing milk, culling seals or red deer to keep numbers down;

14 rabbits testing shampoo, detergents etc.

UNIT 9 – POPULATION

Can the World Feed Itself? – Activity 1: Possible reforms include:

1 reducing consumption in the North;

2 redistributing land ownership in the South;

3 protecting the rainforests;

4 ending desertification;

5 increasing food production in rural areas (and ending production of cash crops for export);

6 writing off the debt of Underdeveloped Countries.

The answer to the question 'does the world have enough food?' is yes it does. The 1986 harvest, if distributed equitably could have fed 6 billion people (projected population in the year 2000). However, this is not to say that the world **can** feed itself – this requires structural change in society.

Rapid Urbanisation – Questions:

1 This UN figure assumes certain levels of increased economic growth, use of contraception, ageing populations, therefore less fertile adults.

Hodder & Stoughton

© 1994 Paul Higginson. The publishers grant permission for multiple copies of this sheet to be made in the place of purchase for use solely in that institution.

2 Greater strain on health and welfare, fewer workers (and taxpayers) supporting growing number of pensioners (who live longer due to medical advances, etc.).

3 The flaw in the Worldwatch argument is that the North experienced great social alienation during industrialisation but this did not stop the 'transition'. Why should the South be any different?

4 Wrong (but famine has increased dramatically in the 1980s and 1990s).

5 Factors include history, climate, natural resources, natural disasters, geography and geographical location, employment opportunities, infrastructure, etc.

Worksheet 2 – North-South factfile:

1 Families have more children than they would otherwise have, because of the uncertainty and insecurity of knowing that not all will survive to adulthood. UNICEF estimates that preventing 7 million babies dying each year will lead to the prevention of between 12 to 20 million births by the year 2000.

3 Problem could be solved by clean water, adequate food, breastfeeding, immunisation, basic health care and education.

4 Most common methods of contraception (with % figures for use in rich/poor countries in brackets): sterilisation (14 rich/47 poor), pill (23/23), IUD (7/9), condom (24/6), other (32/15). 'Others' includes: withdrawal, abstinence, douches, abortion, and traditional folk methods such as herbal potions. Low usage is caused by: lack of education; expensive to buy; difficult to obtain; social, cultural and religious reasons; and most importantly the poor often want as many children as possible for economic reasons.

5 Generally on religious grounds (e.g. Catholic or Muslim).

6 More people in the fertile age range at any one time.

7 The best way to reduce population growth in Underdeveloped Countries is to reduce poverty. If the North continues to refuse to share the world's wealth and resources then the South will not be able to develop, hence population growth will continue.

UNIT 10 – ENERGY

World Energy – Questions:

2 Middle-East oil shocks – world oil prices rocketed.

4 Subsidies and tax incentives could be given to companies producing renewable energy. Tax incentives could also be provided for individuals installing solar panels, cavity-insulating their homes, installing loft insulation, and lagging tanks and pipes, etc.

Britain's Energy Problems – Questions:

2 Department of Energy estimates that our energy consumption will probably increase by about 15 per cent in the next 20 years. Future variables include: How much will energy conservation reduce demand? Will increased technology lead to more fuel-efficient cars, light bulbs, electrical appliances, etc.? Will the population increase or decrease? How much more industrialisation can we expect and will new industries be more energy efficient? Will new products like dishwashers become commonplace, thereby increasing energy demand? Will cost or scarcity of energy force demand down? Will environmental or safety factors lead to cuts in demand?

5 Wind power and tidal power could be very useful. Little room for expansion of hydropower (most good sites already in use). Nuclear power is debatable!

6 More energy required in winter, and during the day (especially at meal-times – 6 o'clock sees

Hodder & Stoughton

© 1994 Paul Higginson. The publishers grant permission for multiple copies of this sheet to be made in the place of purchase for use solely in that institution.

a huge surge in demand). Therefore, energy sources which are constant are more efficient than those which depend on, say, the tide or levels of sunshine.

Activity – Criteria include: safety; cost of energy produced; level of production (constant or weather-dependent); effect on environment and capacity to pollute; building costs; running costs; job creation (can be a plus or a minus, i.e. more jobs created lead to higher wages costs i.e. more expensive for consumer); amount of energy that can be supplied; aesthetic effect (visually and with regard to noise); able to supply energy to all parts of the country.

UNIT 11 – ENVIRONMENT AND DEVELOPMENT

Worksheet 2 – Environment Quiz: 1b, 2c, 3c, 4c, 5b, 6a, 7b, 8a (television uses twice as much electricity as a fridge-freezer or washing machine), 9c, 10a, 11b, 12c, 13c, 14b, 15a (it is actually a fraction of 1%).

Worksheet 3 – The Last 20 Years: 1992 figures are: population 5.47 and 79; global warming 23; ozone layer 3; motor vehicles 600; rainforests 170,000; nuclear energy 428 and 31; water 60; fisheries 90; arms spending 1,000; urbanisation 46 and 13; refugees 16; UK aid 0.28; health 65; food 2.2; debt 1,400 and 30; biodiversity 1,000; AIDS 10.

Hodder & Stoughton

© 1994 Paul Higginson. The publishers grant permission for multiple copies of this sheet to be made in the place of purchase for use solely in that institution.

1 Morality

Morality is concerned with right and wrong. People behave in different ways when confronted with moral choices, and have a set of personal beliefs or values which helps them to determine their ethical standpoint.

How do we decide what is right and wrong? Part of the answer lies in the way we have been socialised, especially in our early childhood, by parents, close family, television and other influential factors.

■ Activity 1

Make list of all the major influences that have affected your personal set of beliefs. Prioritise them in order of significance and give an example of how each can affect a person. Discuss the results in the group. Each person develops a personal moral code as he or she grows older which continually develops and changes. For example, a person may consider that swearing or eating meat is moral but later they may come to view it as immoral. Different people will inevitably come to different conclusions and hold different beliefs. Moreover these beliefs will vary according to factors such as class, age, religion, culture, race or region.

■ Activity 2

Write down an example of a change in your personal morality, i.e. something that you now believe is wrong which you once thought was right (or vice-versa). What influenced you into changing your mind?

■ Activity 3

Examine the actions below and place a cross next to those you think are morally wrong. Think of reasons to support your view in each case.

1 Taking things from work or school without paying for them.
2 Earning money and claiming dole without informing the Social Security Office.
3 Taking time off when you are supposed to be at work.
4 Using an employer's telephone without permission.
5 Using cannabis.
6 Having sexual relations with a person who is married to someone else.
7 Printing photographs of topless 'Page Three' girls in newspapers.
8 Living together before marriage.
9 Killing animals for food.
10 Showing scenes of sex and violence on television.

Discuss and compare the results in groups of three. Find out why others have different views to you.

❖ Discussion

In a recent survey only 16 per cent of under 24s thought 'Page Three' girls were wrong, compared with 43 per cent of pensioners. Pensioners were far more likely to feel that most of the above actions were wrong. Does this mean that moral standards are falling? Do you feel that you are more, or less moral in your behaviour than your parents and grandparents?

Hodder & Stoughton

© 1994 Paul Higginson. The publishers grant permission for multiple copies of this sheet to be made in the place of purchase for use solely in that institution.

MORAL THEORIES

Many philosophers, religious leaders and moral theologians have analysed ethical dilemmas and constructed systems to try to help individuals to better determine what is right and wrong. In Western moral philosophy two distinct approaches have emerged.

1 Morality is a predetermined set of laws or rules which is applied to each situation (known as Deontology).

2 The morality of an action is determined by the goodness or badness of the consequences (Teleology or Consequentialism).

■ Activity 4

How might the two approaches (Deontology and Teleology) produce different perspectives on the following ethical dilemmas?

1   The assassination of Hitler (or any tyrant);
2   stealing food;
3   lying to a friend;
4   dropping the A-bomb on Japan in the Second World War;
5   smacking a child who is misbehaving;
6   homosexual activity between consenting adults.

CHRISTIAN MORALITY

Christians believe that God has given humans 'The Law' based on the Ten Commandments. However, Jesus brought a new commandment 'love one another; as I have loved you'. He was not overly concerned with rules and regulations but wanted men to change their behaviour from within, thereby transforming 'hearts of stone into hearts of flesh'. The Gospel is essentially a law of love. Nevertheless, like most religious faiths, Christianity teaches that God has given man a set of universal, eternal moral principles.

HUMANISM

Humanists do not believe in a god, or gods. Therefore morality does not spring from any supernatural power but from calculating the potential consequences of our behaviour. Actions which hurt or exploit others are wrong, actions which make people happier or have loving consequences are right. Humanist moral philosophy can be summed up as 'treat others in the way you would like them to treat you' – a view shared by most world religions.

HEDONISM

This moral theory states that whatever leads to pleasure is good and whatever results in pain is bad. Pleasure and pain are not just confined to the physical, however, but include enjoyment or distress of any kind (spiritual, emotional and mental). In fact, Epicurus the Greek philosopher who first outlined hedonism believed that too much physical pleasure can lead to pain and therefore cease to be pleasurable.

UTILITARIANISM

Utilitarianism is a theory found in the writings of Jeremy Bentham (1748–1832) and John Stuart Mill (1806–73). It suggests that our morality should be based on trying to achieve the greatest good for the greatest number of people. This would mean that there are no absolute moral laws, valid for all time and all people, but the morality of actions is judged by their consequences.

SITUATION ETHICS

Situation ethics rejects any general, absolute ethical code and states that morality will depend on the situation in each particular case. Actions should be based on doing what is most loving, not on rules. This position has been criticised for leading to antinomianism (*nomos* is the Greek word for law), which does not accept that God has given man a detailed set of absolute moral laws.

Hodder & Stoughton

© 1994 Paul Higginson. The publishers grant permission for multiple copies of this sheet to be made in the place of purchase for use solely in that institution.

MARXISM

Most Marxist thinkers reject the idea of an absolute, eternal moral code. Engels felt that all moral theories were merely a result of the economic stage which society had reached at that particular time. Lenin stated that whatever destroyed capitalist exploitation and created a classless Communist society was good.

❏ ■ Questions and Activities

1 Separate the six theories above into those which are Deontological and those which are Teleological.

2 Can there be any objective set of universal moral laws valid for all time and all peoples and every situation? List the arguments for and against.

3 Apply the theories above to the six ethical dilemmas posed in Activity 4 and note what differences emerge.

4 Construct a table listing the flaws or problems that might occur with each theory, e.g. Hedonism – pursuit of pleasure for one person may lead to pain for another.

5 Examine the Ten Commandments below and try to interpret what each means. Do you think they are relevant to the world today? Are some more important than others?

   1 I am the Lord your God.
   2 You shall have no other gods before me.
   3 You shall not take the name of the Lord your God in vain.
   4 Keep the Sabbath day holy.
   5 Honour your father and mother.
   6 You shall not kill.
   7 You shall not commit adultery.
   8 You shall not steal.
   9 You shall not lie.
   10 You shall not covet (desire) what does not belong to you.

(Exodus 20: 2–17)

❖ Discussion

Debate these topics:

1 'Does the end always justify the means?'
2 'Is there such a thing as the lesser of two evils?'
3 'The problem with Consequentialism is that it is impossible to forecast the results accurately.'
4 'Christian morality is based on the fear of punishment: if you do good you go to heaven, if you do evil you go to hell.'

MAKING CHOICES

There are, then, a number of factors we may take into consideration before we make moral choices:
1 rules and laws (religious or civil);
2 predicted consequences of our actions;
3 love of others;
4 conscience (deep-seated inner feelings which instinctively tell us when something is wrong, and can make us feel guilty);
5 experience of similar situations – learning from our, or other people's, past behaviour.

The worksheets for this unit all present a number of issues that require moral choices to be made.

Hodder & Stoughton © 1994 Paul Higginson. The publishers grant permission for multiple copies of this sheet to be made in the place of purchase for use solely in that institution.

Kidney Transplants

SITUATION

After a car accident two good kidneys have become available for transplant at the local hospital. There is a waiting list of patients who are all desperate for a life-saving transplant operation. Only one person can be selected but it is necessary to prioritise all the patients in case other kidneys become available. Note that in most Developed Countries only about 1 in 4 patients who need a kidney transplant gets one.

ROLE-PLAY

Three members of the class are Senior Consultants at the hospital – they must make the final decision. The rest of the class divides into small groups of five junior doctors – each group must prioritise the patients in order of importance and then present its recommendations to the Consultants, who will make the final choice.

PATIENTS

1 Dr Sean White — 65-year-old doctor on the verge of making a significant research breakthrough in the fight against AIDS. Unmarried, no children. Very wealthy.

2 Hilary Whicker — 30-year-old single mother of four young children. Divorced. Living on income support.

3 Marie Vandome — 18-year-old A-level student. Single, only child. Parents would be devastated if she died.

4 Trevor Parker — Aged 25. Shop-worker. Married with two small children. Two police convictions for assault in his late teens.

5 Liz Cooper — Aged 35. Single. Only child – cares for mother who has a poor heart, and father who is disabled and in a wheelchair.

6 Sir Stephen Mansfield — Very popular MP, has raised money for local charities and is spearheading a campaign to open a much-needed new wing at the hospital next year. Aged 55, married, three children over 18. Has been tipped as a possible future Prime Minister.

7 Paul Andrews — Six years old. Has two older brothers and a sister – all healthy.

Hodder & Stoughton

© 1994 *Paul Higginson. The publishers grant permission for multiple copies of this sheet to be made in the place of purchase for use solely in that institution.*

Patient Updates

These cards contain previously undisclosed information on the patients and can be distribution by the teacher to groups where necessary.

Dr Sean White Has recently written to one of the Consultants promising a large donation to the hospital if the transplant operation goes ahead.	**Hilary Whicker** She is an alcoholic.
Marie Vandome She is the favourite niece of one of the Senior Hospital Consultants. She is the first person on the list chronologically (she has been waiting for three years).	**Trevor Parker** Became a Christian at the age of 20 and has recently been accepted to train as a Church of England minister.
Liz Cooper She is pregnant and plans to marry her boyfriend in three months.	**Sir Stephen Mansfield** Has smoked 40 cigarettes a day for the last 35 years and refuses to give up. Attempted to commit suicide in his late 30s.
Paul Andrews Suffers from Down's Syndrome.	**Additional card**

Hodder & Stoughton

© 1994 Paul Higginson. The publishers grant permission for multiple copies of this sheet to be made in the place of purchase for use solely in that institution.

Worksheet 2
Abortion

THE LAW

Abortion is the termination of a pregnancy before birth; this can happen naturally (a miscarriage) or deliberately (a 'procured' abortion). In Britain the 1967 Abortion Act and the 1990 Human Fertilisation and Embryology Act allow abortion subject to certain conditions.

1   The mother's life is at risk.

2   The mother's physical or mental health is at risk.

3   Another child could put at risk the physical or mental health of any existing children.

4   There is a risk that the child could suffer from serious physical or mental handicap.

5   Abortion can be performed up to the twenty-fourth week of pregnancy, but there is no time limit if there is a danger of grave permanent injury or death to the woman or serious handicap for the child.

Normally two doctors must certify that an abortion is necessary and that one of the above conditions applies but in the case of condition 5, only one doctor is required. The Acts do not apply to Northern Ireland.

STATISTICS

1   Abortion is the most performed operation in Britain and the second most frequent on the NHS. In 1990 there were 173,900 abortions, 13.6 per 1000 women aged between 14 and 49.

2   Eighty-eight per cent of abortions take place before the twelfth week of pregnancy; 1 per cent occur after 20 weeks.

3   Sixty-seven per cent of abortions are to single women.

4   Two per cent of women having abortions (3,422) are under 16, 54 per cent of the total are under 24.

5   Just under half of all abortions are carried out on the NHS.

6   Grounds for abortion in 1990 were:

   •   risk to mother's life   0.2 per cent;

   •   risk to mother's physical/mental health   90 per cent;

   •   risk to health of existing children   9 per cent;

   •   risk of fetal abnormality   0.8 per cent.

7   In 1990, 16 women a day came to England and Wales from Northern Ireland and the Irish Republic to have abortions.

Hodder & Stoughton

© 1994 Paul Higginson. The publishers grant permission for multiple copies of this sheet to be made in the place of purchase for use solely in that institution.

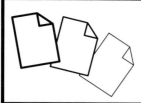

ARGUMENTS

Complete the table below with the main arguments for and against abortion.

For	Against
As the foetus is not capable of surviving on its own outside the mother's womb it is not a human life but only has the potential for life.	All life begins at the moment of conception – abortion, therefore, is murder.

❖ Discussion

1   Babies born at 24 weeks have survived – should abortion be permitted at this stage?

2   Should the healthy foetus have more rights than the handicapped?

3   Is abortion acceptable in rape cases?

4   'The woman should be the one to decide what happens with her own body.' Do you agree?

5   Will stricter abortion laws lead to an increase in dangerous back-street abortions?

6   'Adoption is a better solution than abortion.' Do you agree?

Hodder & Stoughton

© 1994 Paul Higginson. The publishers grant permission for multiple copies of this sheet to be made in the place of purchase for use solely in that institution.

Test-Tube Babies and Medical Ethics

In-vitro fertilisation is the joining together of a sperm and an egg in a glass Petri dish (*in vitro*), thereby creating an embryo which is then transferred to the womb. If this process is successful the embryo will grow in the normal way until birth occurs nine months later. In 1990 around 8,000 women tried IVF in Britain; this resulted in around 1,500 pregnancies, but fewer than 1,000 test-tube babies were born. There are currently around 50 licensed test-tube clinics and of these only two are fully funded by the NHS; the rest charge about £3,000 for a course of treatment.

Study the facts below and decide which of the current practices you feel are ethical.

1   Around 10 per cent of British couples are infertile and IVF is a way of helping them to have a family.
2   About 12 per cent of women who undergo IVF will have a baby.
3   Eggs are often donated to women who are unable to produce their own. In Britain donors are not paid (unlike in the USA) and there is a huge waiting list for women needing egg donation (there is a shortage of donors).
4   In the first days after fertilisation abnormal embryos can be discarded, thereby eliminating many genetic abnormalities.
5   Embryos that are not implanted in the woman are either frozen for possible future use, discarded, or used in embryo research, which is permitted in the first 14 days after fertilisation (this has led to advances in research into miscarriage, contraception, infertility and the prevention of genetic disease).
6   It is possible to determine the sex of an embryo and therefore select the sex of an IVF baby.
7   Sperm banks help women conceive through artificial insemination (AI). Sperm from an anonymous donor are injected into the uterus at ovulation. This treatment is available to single women.
8   Surrogate motherhood (womb-leasing) involves a woman carrying a child for an infertile couple (using AI with sperm from the male partner), and handing over the baby after birth.
9   The 1990 Human Fertilisation and Embryology Act enables children to have access to a limited range of information about their conception (at 18), in order that they do not marry anyone with same the genetic parent as themselves.
10 The Act also states that frozen embryos can be stored for a maximum of 10 years, after which ownership goes to the licensed storage authority.

Read the viewpoints below from two opposing pressure groups.

'IVF has enabled childless couples to have children, and brought happiness to thousands. Moreover, embryo research has led to tremendous medical advances in the areas of infertility, miscarriage, contraception and genetic disease. Development of IVF may make it possible to be sure from the outset that a pregnancy carries no genetic abnormality.' Progress

'Embryos are human beings and all IVF embryos should be inserted in the mother's womb. Freezing, discarding or experimenting on embryos (human vivisection) is unacceptable because it is incompatible with their dignity and rights as human beings. No human being should be the subject of experimentation which is not for his/her own benefit. The end does not justify the means.' LIFE

❖ Discussion

1   What are your views on IVF, embryo research and surrogate motherhood?
2   The Catholic Church has stated that AI with donor sperm is like 'mechanical adultery'. Do you agree?
3   Do all couples have a right to have children, and should infertility treatment be freely available on the NHS?
4   Should embryos be created purely for scientific research?
5   How far is it ethical for humans to interfere with nature in these ways?

Hodder & Stoughton

© 1994 Paul Higginson. The publishers grant permission for multiple copies of this sheet to be made in the place of purchase for use solely in that institution.

Worksheet 4
Suicide

STATISTICS

- 200,000 people attempt suicide in Britain every year. About 4,000 succeed. The suicide rate trebled between 1958 and 1988.
- Someone commits suicide somewhere in the world every minute.
- Men are three times more likely to commit suicide than women.
- Suicide is the third most common cause of death among the under 25s (after accidents and cancer). The Samaritans report that as many as 1 in 100 girls aged 15 to 19 attempts suicide by taking an overdose each year.
- There are four times as many suicides in the UK as in the Republic of Ireland (and Germany has ten times as many as Ireland).
- Suicide was a crime in the UK until 1963, and it is still a crime to help someone to commit suicide (punishable by a maximum of 14 years' imprisonment).

■ Activity

List the possible causes of suicide and prioritise those you feel are the most significant.

❏ Questions

1 Why has the suicide rate trebled in the last 30 years?
2 Why are men more likely to commit suicide than women?
3 Why are young women more likely to attempt suicide than young men (85 per cent of young suicide attempts are female)?
4 Why do you think the suicide rate varies so much between different countries?
5 Should it still be a crime to help a person commit suicide?

TWO VIEWS

Read the newspaper articles below.

'In some cultures suicide is perfectly honourable. In Japan it is very common to commit suicide after a humiliation or failure so that dishonour is not brought upon oneself or the family. Ritual suicide is known as hara-kiri. In World War Two kamikaze pilots sacrificed their lives for their country by flying planes loaded with explosives into enemy ships. On Scott's journey from the South Pole Captain Oates, who was suffering from frostbite, walked out to die in a blizzard so that he would not continue to slow the rest of the party down. It is a fundamental human right to be able to choose to die and indeed there are circumstances (incurable illness or unremitting pain) when people should be allowed to help others to end their lives.'

'Suicide is "that most selfish of acts". It leaves those left behind with the sorrow of bereavement and the guilt that comes with wondering if they could have prevented the act. All religions condemn suicide. For Muslims it involves running away from life's responsibilities. Hindus believe that God is within the human body so to commit suicide is an attempt to destroy God. Buddhists (and Hindus) who believe in reincarnation argue that it is an attempt to escape from one's destiny. Christians proclaim that all life belongs to God and only God can take life away from man. However, Christians accept the idea of self-sacrifice – Jesus said that man has no greater love than to lay down his life for his friends (as Jesus himself did).'

❖ Discussion

These two views on suicide clearly illustrate the differences between Deontological and Teleological morality. Which extract do you most agree with and why? Discuss this in groups.

Hodder & Stoughton © 1994 Paul Higginson. The publishers grant permission for multiple copies of this sheet to be made in the place of purchase for use solely in that institution.

2 War and Conflict

Politics has been defined as the art of solving problems and disagreements without the use of force. When politics fails, force is often used to settle an argument. Physical conflicts are an everyday occurrence, not just in international relations but in our streets, homes, schools and places of work.

War is the most destructive form of physical force and has been defined as violence by at least one regular armed group using weapons, for at least one hour. Using this definition, there have been approximately 120 wars since 1945.

WHAT CAUSES WAR?

There have been thousands of wars in history, each one caused by a number of different factors. It is important not to confuse the spark or trigger which can begin a war with the longer term, deep-seated causes which often build up for years beforehand. For example, the assassination of Archduke Ferdinand at Sarajevo in 1914 was the spark for the First World War, but the underlying causes include the rivalry between the major powers in the Balkans and in Africa (for new imperial colonies), the arms race and naval competition between Britain and Germany, economic discontent (especially in Germany), and the splitting of Europe into two rival hostile camps through diplomatic intrigue and alliances. Historians disagree on the weight that should be attached to each factor and some support the notion that the powers simply stumbled into war as a result of miscalculation and misconception.

The table below lists a number of common causes of war and appropriate examples.

Cause	Example
1 Politics/ideology	Communism v Capitalism
2 Religion	Protestant v Catholic, Muslim v Christian
3 Nationalism	getting rid of a foreign ruler
4 Ethnicity/race	Serb v Croat
5 Lust for power/expansion	seizing territory of other nations
6 Revenge	defeat in a previous war
7 Economics	providing better resources for own people
8 Injustice	righting an oppressive situation/overthrowing a dictator
9 Fear	defence against a threatening militaristic enemy
10 A powerful individual or group	a dictator who seeks to rule others by force

Use the information above to complete Worksheet 1.

Hodder & Stoughton

© 1994 Paul Higginson. The publishers grant permission for multiple copies of this sheet to be made in the place of purchase for use solely in that institution.

❖ Discussion

Do you agree or disagree with the following viewpoints? Provide examples to support your views.

1 *'Wars are caused by power-hungry individuals. If Hitler had not existed, the Second World War would not have taken place.'*

2 *'People's greed, their desire for material wealth, land and possessions – this is the root of all war.'*

3 *'War, conflict and violence are a part of human nature. Humans are naturally aggressive animals – hence war can never be eliminated.'*

NUCLEAR WEAPONS

KEY DATES

1945   US scientists from the Manhattan Project produce the world's first atomic device after three years of research. It was dropped on Japan at Hiroshima (80,000 dead) and Nagasaki (35,000 dead).

1949   The Soviet Union acquires the bomb, later it is joined by Britain (1952), France (1960) and China (1964).

1952   The Hydrogen (thermo-nuclear) bomb was first tested by the USA – it was far more destructive than the A-bomb.

1962   The Cuban missile crisis. The closest the world has come to superpower nuclear war.

1968   The Nuclear Non-Proliferation Treaty is signed. It tried and failed to limit the spread of weapons.

1974   SALT 1 (Strategic Arms Limitation Talks) limited US and Soviet weapons.

1983   The USA begins the Star Wars project: an ambitious space-based defensive system that could destroy offensive nuclear weapons before they reach their target.

1987   The INF treaty (Intermediate Nuclear Forces) is signed by Gorbachev and Reagan. Its aim is the reduction of land-based missiles.

1991   START 1 (Strategic Arms Reduction Talks) lead to superpower arsenals being cut by 30 per cent.

1993   START 2, the USA and Russia cut weapons by two-thirds.

NUCLEAR POWERS

The 'nuclear club' consists of the USA, Russia, Britain, France and China. However, when the USSR broke up, some of the new nations created (like the Ukraine) were left with nuclear weapons. Other countries such as India, South Africa, Israel and Pakistan either already have nuclear capability or the potential to create nuclear weapons very quickly if the need arises; India has exploded an A-bomb and Israel is reported to have nuclear warheads and launchers. A number of other nations (Brazil, Argentina, Libya, Egypt, Taiwan and South Korea) are very close to possessing weapons and only the Gulf War prevented Iraq from achieving a nuclear capability.

Hodder & Stoughton

© 1994 Paul Higginson. The publishers grant permission for multiple copies of this sheet to be made in the place of purchase for use solely in that institution.

TERMINOLOGY

MAD	Mutually Assured Destruction – both superpowers can absorb a first strike attack and respond with a huge counter-attack. This theory, therefore, deters both sides from offensive action.
Conventional Forces	Non-nuclear weapons such as tanks and planes.
CND	Campaign for Nuclear Disarmament. Pressure group which aims to get one side to give up its nuclear weapons (unilateral disarmament).
ICBM	Intercontinental Ballistic Missile
SDI	Strategic Defence Initiative, commonly known as Star Wars.
Flexible Response	US strategy of building smaller more accurate nuclear weapons, which could destroy purely military targets and be difficult to intercept (e.g. Cruise and Pershing missiles). Makes the battlefield use of nuclear weapons a possibility.
Trident	Britain's submarine-based nuclear missile system (replacing the Polaris system).
NATO	North Atlantic Treaty Organisation. Established in 1949 – a military alliance of Western states intended to deter attack by Communist powers (who later formed the Warsaw Pact).

❏ Questions

1 'Nuclear weapons cannot be disinvented or abolished, only controlled.' Do you agree with this statement?

2 What arguments can you think of to support unilateralism?

3 What dangers arise when more and more countries possess nuclear weapons?

4 'If nuclear war occurs it will begin in the Middle East or in Underdeveloped Countries.' What is the reasoning behind this viewpoint and do you agree?

5 What particular problems arise from nuclear disarmament in the countries of the former Soviet Union?

6 Japan, Germany, Italy and most other countries do not possess nuclear weapons yet Britain is committed to maintaining its independent nuclear capability. List the pros and cons of the British position.

7 What are the advantages and disadvantages of the Flexible Response strategy?

8 'Bacteriological and chemical weapons present a far greater threat to humanity than nuclear weapons.' Explain the reasoning behind this statement.

THE JUST WAR THEORY

This theory was developed by Augustine and Thomas Aquinas as a Christian response to war and violence. It consists of four conditions which are necessary for a war to be justified in the eyes of the Church (thereby enabling Christians to participate).

1 War must be waged by a legitimate authority on behalf of the people and only as a last resort when diplomacy has failed.

2 War must have a serious cause which can justify all the resulting death and destruction.

3 War must have a just, lasting and realistic peace as the ultimate aim.

4 The methods used must be just: non-combatants must be protected and excessive force should not be used against the enemy.

Hodder & Stoughton   © 1994 Paul Higginson. The publishers grant permission for multiple copies of this sheet to be made in the place of purchase for use solely in that institution.

1 Give examples to clarify each condition, for example, the first means that individual citizens cannot wage war.

2 Choose a recent modern war, such as the Gulf War or the Falklands War, and apply Aquinas' theory to decide whether it was a 'just war'.

3 How do nuclear weapons make the fourth condition difficult to fulfil?

4 Are nuclear weapons intrinsically unjust and immoral?

MILITARY EXPENDITURE AND UNDERDEVELOPMENT

KEY STATISTICS

1 Every year over $1,000 billion is spent on arms.

2 Half of Britain's scientists and engineers work on military research.

3 Fifteen million children die each year from disease and starvation.

4 Over 1 billion people do not have safe drinking water.

5 The country with the highest rate of growth in the world (Japan) spends less than any other major developed nation on the military (1 per cent of GNP).

THE PATHWAY TO POVERTY

More than 60 countries in Underdeveloped Countries are ruled by military dictatorships. These nations often follow a similar pathway:

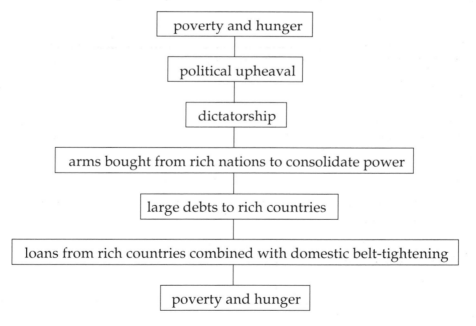

ARMS SELLERS

The world's largest arms exporters are the USA, Russia, Britain and France. Two-thirds of Britain's annual arms exports (around £6 billion worth) go to Underdeveloped Countries, in fact many of the weapons used by Saddam Hussein in the Gulf War against US and British troops were manufactured in the UK.

Hodder & Stoughton

© 1994 Paul Higginson. The publishers grant permission for multiple copies of this sheet to be made in the place of purchase for use solely in that institution.

ARMS SPENDERS

League table of spenders as a % of Gross National Product

Rank	Name	% of GNP
1	Iraq	30
2	Oman	25
3	Israel	24
4	Iran	20
5	South Yemen	17
6	Saudi Arabia	17
7	North Yemen	14
8	Syria	14
9	Jordan	11
10	Russia	11
19	China	8
28	USA	6
36	UK	5
92	New Zealand	2

The USA spends the most: the annual US military budget is more than the annual amount spent on education and health in all the Underdeveloped Countries put together. For the price of one jet fighter, 40,000 village pharmacies could be set up.

❏ Questions

1. Japan's constitution limits military spending to 1 per cent of GNP. Why is this and what have been the results for Japan and its neighbours?
2. Japan has only a small defence force – who would protect the country if it were attacked?
3. Why do Underdeveloped Countries spend so much on arms?
4. What benefits are there for the Developed Countries in selling arms to Underdeveloped Countries?
5. 'If we don't sell them arms somebody else will, so we may as well get the jobs and the profits for Britain.' Do you agree with this statement?
6. Why does the arms spending as a percentage of GNP provide a more useful league table than simply the amount spent?
7. What do the top nine countries in the league table have in common?
8. List the arguments for and against switching arms spending to health and education.

❖ Discussion

Debate these statements:

1. 'Selling red poppies helps to glorify war – only white poppies should be sold.'
2. 'Young people should not be allowed to play with guns as they glamorise warfare and teach children to be aggressive.'
3. 'All those who take up the sword will die by the sword.' (Matthew 26:52)

✿ Further study

Invite a member of the armed forces into class to talk about his or her role (contact your local Army Recruitment Office). Do the same with a member of the Peace Pledge Union or Quaker Peace and Service (their addresses are in the Additional Information, p109).

Hodder & Stoughton

© 1994 Paul Higginson. *The publishers grant permission for multiple copies of this sheet to be made in the place of purchase for use solely in that institution.*

Worksheet 1

War

Match up the war with the description by putting a number in the appropriate box on the left. When you have completed this, fill in the 'causes' box with what you think was the most significant cause (or causes) of this war (taken from the table in the main text, p24, numbered 1 to 10). For example, if you feel that the main causes of the Falklands War were religion and injustice write 2, 8 in the box on the right.

War	Causes		Description
Falklands 1982	☐	1	Dispute over slavery helped to begin struggle of North v South: 600,000 killed in first modern war in history.
of the Roses 1455–85	☐	2	Superpower rivalry that stopped short of direct military conflict largely because of the fear of nuclear war.
Second World 1939–45	☐	3	Anglo-French forces defeat Russians in order to capture port of Sebastopol.
Gulf 1990–1	☐	4	French dictator inspires rise and fall of European Empire. Final defeat at Waterloo.
Boer 1899–1902	☐	5	Britain retakes South Atlantic islands (also called Malvinas) after initial seizure by Argentina.
Crusades 1096–1252	☐	6	Major defeat for USA in South-East Asia against Nationalist/Communist guerilla army, 1.3 million killed.
Afghanistan 1979–89	☐	7	After defeat in earlier war, Germany tries and fails to build an Empire (Third Reich). Fifty million people die world-wide.
American Independence 1775–83	☐	8	UN forces repel invasion of South by North. Country divided at 38th parallel.
Napoleonic 1803–15	☐	9	English claim on French Crown and territory defeated after lengthy struggle.
American Civil 1861–5	☐	10	Major European colonial power removed by well-organised nationalist force.
Cold 1945–85	☐	11	Struggle for English Crown between two factions (York and Lancaster).
Hundred Years 1337-1453	☐	12	Christian knights attempted to defeat Muslims for control of Jerusalem and the Holy Land.
Korean 1950–3	☐	13	Dispute over control of canal leads to short war and eventual withdrawal of British and French troops and arrival of UN peacekeepers.
Suez Crisis 1956	☐	14	Muslim fundamentalists defeat Soviet invaders after protracted guerilla war.
Vietnam 1964–75	☐	15	Multi-national force (mainly US) drives out invaders in small Middle-Eastern kingdom.
Crimean 1854–6	☐	16	British forces counter effective nationalist guerilla army in South Africa by use of concentration camps (where 20,000 died).

Hodder & Stoughton

© 1994 Paul Higginson. The publishers grant permission for multiple copies of this sheet to be made in the place of purchase for use solely in that institution.

Worksheet 2

Is Peace Possible?

Here are some ideas for helping to promote peace and end war. Against each point write down a possible counter-argument in the box opposite, providing specific examples if you can.

Proposals for Peace	Counter-Arguments
1 Peace through strength. Policy of USA and UK during the Cold War; deter others from waging war by maintaining strong forces (there has been no use of nuclear weapons since 1945).	
2 Multilateral disarmament. All powers ease tension by agreeing to reduce weapons together. 1993 US-Russian START agreement (Strategic Arms Reduction Talks) has cut nuclear weapons by two-thirds and saved billions of dollars.	
3 Unilateral disarmament. One country takes the lead by deciding to stop holding or manufacturing nuclear weapons, whatever other countries decide.	
4 Strong United Nations. Can provide peace-keeping forces (e.g. Bosnia, Lebanon, Cyprus) enforce sanctions against aggressors (e.g. Iraq, Serbia) or solve problem through diplomacy.	
5 Economic development and justice for poorer countries. Wars are caused by people's desire for wealth and land. Create social justice and economic opportunity and war will disappear.	
6 Political reforms and the introduction of democracy. Political instability and ideological rivalry can be overcome through a common world-wide democratic system.	
7 Non-violence. Gandhi and Martin Luther King believed that problems could be solved by non-violent protest and passive resistance.	
8 World government. Overcome nationalism and selfish national interests by joining the human race together in a world government.	
9 Superpower World Policeman. Strong power can intervene to correct injustice, and put down dictators e.g. the USA in Grenada, Panama, Kuwait, Somalia.	

❏ Questions

1 Share your counter-arguments with the group.
2 Can you think of any other proposals which might help to end war?
3 Place a tick next to the peace proposal you feel is the most practical and stands the best chance of success.
4 Examine one current war in the world and decide which of the above proposals might help bring peace to this situation.

Hodder & Stoughton

© 1994 Paul Higginson. The publishers grant permission for multiple copies of this sheet to be made in the place of purchase for use solely in that institution.

Worksheet 3
Pacifism

Pacifists believe that force and violence are wrong, refuse to enter the armed services and fight, and argue that the abolition of war is possible. In previous wars conscientious objectors who refused to fight were imprisoned as traitors. Examine the arguments for and against pacifism, placing a tick next to those statements you agree with.

<table>
<tr><th>For</th><th>Against</th></tr>
<tr><td>

1 Wars inevitably lead to death, injury, destruction and misery.
2 All the major religions of the world instruct us to love our neighbour, and Christianity teaches us to 'turn the other cheek'. Jesus practised non-violence when he told Peter to put away his sword in the Garden at Gethsemene.
3 Dispute and disagreements can and should be settled by negotiation and compromise.
4 Wars are costly, not just in terms of lives lost but in the waste of the world's resources. Just one day's world-wide military spending would save all the 15 million children who die each year from disease and starvation. Our energies, technology and money should be put into saving lives not killing others.
5 Violence always leads to more violence and rarely (if ever) achieves the results intended. Little is ever accomplished by war.
6 Passive resistance as practised by Gandhi, Martin Luther King and Archbishop Tutu is far more effective and less destructive in the long run. Goodness can overcome evil.
7 War brings out the worst in humankind and lays bare the dark side of human nature – torture, cruelty, rape, destruction, genocide (as in the Nazi Holocaust).
8 In the nuclear age, war could lead to the destruction of the planet in a nuclear holocaust. Any injustice or political system is worth enduring if it means survival ('Better Red than Dead').
9 The people who end up getting killed in wars are always poor, ordinary, working people – 'cannon fodder'. The generals and politicians who often start conflicts never find themselves in the front line.

</td><td>

1 Aggression must never be rewarded by inaction. Dictators and madmen must be defeated. To do nothing often leads to even greater death and misery. 'For evil to triumph all that is required is for the good person to do nothing.'
2 Religion teaches us to protect the weak and innocent. Jesus said a man can have no greater love than to lay down his life for his friend.
3 The Muslim Koran says that it is right to fight in self defence 'but do not begin hostilities'. When attacked, everyone has the right and duty to defend themselves.
4 When talking fails, war must be used to right injustice, especially when a small country is the victim of a stronger, aggressive nation.
5 Passive resistance would not have stopped the Holocaust – only armed force saved the world from the tyranny of Hitler.
6 All people should be expected to fight for their country when their families and freedom are threatened.
7 Man can reveal the highest virtues in war: self-sacrifice, loyalty, courage, comradeship, mercy and endurance.
8 The results of war are often very positive – peace, liberty, fairness, the overthrow of tyrants, long-term stability, and economic prosperity.
9 'If my mother were attacked, I'd defend her in the most effective way possible. Pacifism is fine in theory, but doesn't work in practice.'

</td></tr>
</table>

■ Activity: examine the evidence

If Britain were to go to war would you be prepared to fight 'for Queen and Country', and kill others in order to achieve certain objectives? In order to help you answer this question, examine the following recent wars and conflicts to see whether the above ideas on pacifism are true or false:

Saddam and the Gulf War; the Falklands War; the Vietnam War; the First and Second World Wars; Gandhi and the independence movement in India; the struggle for black majority rule in South Africa; dropping the A-bombs on Japan; the conflict in the former Yugoslavia.

Discuss in the group, or better still hold a full-scale debate on the issue of pacifism and fighting 'for Queen and Country'.

Hodder & Stoughton

© 1994 Paul Higginson. *The publishers grant permission for multiple copies of this sheet to be made in the place of purchase for use solely in that institution.*

3 Old Age

AN AGEING POPULATION

The number of old people is increasing. In the last 100 years we have moved from a very youthful population to a situation where we now have a large number of elderly people.

	Under 20 years	20-60 years	Over 60 years
1890	50%	45%	5%
1990	30%	50%	20%

This is essentially because people are living longer, as the following life expectancy figures for the UK show.

	1901	1931	1951	1971	1991
Males	48	58	66	69	73
Females	52	62	71	75	79

Life expectancy means the average life-span that new born babies will have if the death rates in their year of birth continue in the future. The death rate in the UK in 1992 was 11 deaths per 1,000 population.

Some people are living to a very old age. The number of people over 100 years of age has been steadily increasing.

	1951	1961	1981	1991
100 years or older	271	479	2,410	3,500

❑ Questions

1 Why are people living longer?

2 The death rate for men in unskilled jobs is 2.3 times that for men in the professions. Suggest possible explanations for this.

3 Why do women live on average six years longer than men?

4 What problems might arise from a rapidly ageing population?

THE DEMOGRAPHIC TIME BOMB

After a period of high birth rates in the 1960s, there followed a period of low birth rates in the 1970s. The main consequence of this will be a 25 per cent reduction in the number of 16- to 19-year-olds between 1988 and 1995. This will lead to a shortage of young people entering the labour market and may lead to a reduction in youth unemployment. This trend will be exacerbated by the government's desire to increase the number of young people staying on at school after 16 by expanding further and higher education places. The shortfall in young people may also enable the elderly, or married women to increase their job prospects by filling the gap left by the shrinking 16- to 19-year-old group. Tesco has recently pioneered schemes to recruit the over-55s.

Hodder & Stoughton

© 1994 Paul Higginson. The publishers grant permission for multiple copies of this sheet to be made in the place of purchase for use solely in that institution.

As the number of people of working age decreases it becomes increasingly difficult to provide for children and the elderly. In 1992 there were 36 million people of working age but of these 11 million were not employed. Therefore, 25 million workers (43 per cent of the population) must pay the tax and provide the economic growth which are required to support 57 per cent. The pension, social services and health needs of the elderly are set to take up an ever-increasing share of government spending in the future. By the year 2031, 1 in 5 of the population will be over retirement age (12 million compared to 8.8 million in 1992). A person over 75 costs the Welfare State seven times more than the average person of working age.

❏ Questions

1 Why is the government so concerned to increase the staying on rate at school? How is it achieving this?

2 What other factors will determine whether youth unemployment is reduced?

3 List the potential advantages and disadvantages for an employer in recruiting the over-55s as opposed to 16- to 19-year-olds.

4 What groups make up the 11 million people aged 16 to 65 who do not work?

5 In what ways should the government plan for the year 2031? List three proposals that could be implemented to help alleviate some of the potential problems in store.

■ Activity

Study the newspaper article below and answer the questions.

Defusing the Time Bomb

'The demographic time bomb, a smaller proportion of younger workers supporting a larger number of dependents (mainly the elderly), is fast becoming a major issue in Britain. As the average age of the population rises, a huge burden will be placed on the Welfare State. At present many old people are in financial difficulties; the basic state pension for a single person is £56 per week (1993) and those who require care in a residential or nursing home will only receive major financial support from the state if their assets (including their home) amount to no more than £8,000. There are two ways of dealing with the problems associated with the large increase in the number of old people: huge tax increases, or people taking responsibility for providing for their old age themselves (rather than relying on the Welfare State). Tax increases are unpopular with the voters and governments are unlikely to pursue this line. The alternative, which many in the Conservative Party would like to see implemented, is for everyone to begin providing for old age when they first begin to work – taking out private pension plans, life assurance, private medical insurance and care insurance that will pay out if long-term home or residential care is needed. The basic state pension would then wither away; most people would rely on private pension plans and the state would merely target benefits ('a safety net') on those who were unable to make their own private provision. In other words, taxpayers' money could be targeted at those in greatest need.

The danger, however, is the creation of a two-tier system – affluent private pensioners and a poor underclass dependent on a second class welfare system.'

1 Do you think that the state pension will exist by the time you retire? State the reasons for your answer.

2 Find out the difference between a state pension, an occupational pension and a private personal pension.

3 The average cost of care in an old peoples' home is £300 per week. Many single people have to sell their homes to pay for this care (but if they live with a partner or relative who is also over 60 then the home is not taken into consideration when calculating their assets). Do you agree with this or should the state provide (regardless of a person's assets)?

4 Why are so many people against paying much higher taxes to help fund the welfare state?

5 List the pros and cons of the privatisation philosophy outlined in this article.

6 'Well-off pensioners should not get a state pension.' Do you agree?

Hodder & Stoughton

© 1994 Paul Higginson. *The publishers grant permission for multiple copies of this sheet to be made in the place of purchase for use solely in that institution.*

AGEISM

Ageism refers to discrimination against a person simply because of his or her age. It is often hidden or institutionalised, for example in government policies towards benefits or employers' attitudes towards work. Surveys have shown that a majority of the non-elderly, stereotype the over-65s as lonely, frustrated, unhealthy, poor and afraid of crime, whereas only a small minority of the over-65s felt they had experienced problems in these areas or viewed themselves in this light.

Although a poor image of the elderly exists in Britain, in other cultures the old have more power and status than the young. In traditional rural societies age brings greater respect and authority, not less. In Britain, the rigidities of the retirement age (65 for men, 60 for women) have meant that many who are physically and mentally capable of useful employment are being pushed out of the labour market. Forced retirement is resented by many old people as it can lead to increased poverty and boredom through unwanted idleness.

CASE-STUDY – AGEISM AND WORK

In 1991 the Institute of Personnel Management helped to launch a campaign to help end ageism in employment.

Research has shown that older workers are far less likely to be hired by employers because they are perceived as being less flexible and dynamic compared to younger workers. They are seen to be suitable only for low skilled jobs with little responsibility. Many advertised jobs actually bar the over-50s from applying, and research on job-interviews has revealed a distinct prejudice against older workers. Many women suffer from ageism when they attempt to return to work after raising children.

Moreover, older workers are often the first to be made redundant in periods of recession, and many are given incentives to take voluntary early retirement. However, many stores like Tesco have adopted a policy of positive discrimination in favour of the over-50s, actively recruiting older workers whom they argue are reliable, hard-working and relate well to customers.

❏ Questions

1   Is it possible to talk about ageism in the same way as racism or sexism? List examples of ageist attitudes and behaviour, especially in advertising and the media.

2   What is the difference between individual ageism and institutionalised ageism?

3   Why might other cultures give greater respect and authority to the old?

4   In the USA and Canada there is no compulsory retirement from work (except for special cases like airline pilots and the police). Should Britain adopt a similar stance?

5   Many in Britain would like to see a common non-sexist retirement age of 63. Would you support such an idea? Give reasons for your answer.

6   List the possible pros and cons for a company considering employing older workers.

7   Why have employers and the government encouraged early retirement?

Hodder & Stoughton

© 1994 Paul Higginson. The publishers grant permission for multiple copies of this sheet to be made in the place of purchase for use solely in that institution.

Theories on Age

Academics and gerontologists (who study old age) have put forward various theories to help explain the sociological processes of ageing.

1 DISENGAGEMENT

As people age they must be disengaged or removed from significant positions in society so that when they die this does not disrupt the smoother workings of the community. For old people to achieve contentment they must accept this state of affairs gracefully and allow younger more efficient people to replace them.

2 ACTIVITY

Old people must keep active and try to hold on to a middle-aged lifestyle and values for as long as possible. They should be encouraged to make a positive contribution to society in old age.

3 LABELLING

Society stereotypes the elderly as sick, dependent, miserable, and so on. Old people then actually take on the labels which society has allotted to them. In other words, if we label old people as dependent and put them in homes, they will act out this role.

4 SEGREGATION

The elderly are increasingly living together in homes and sheltered accommodation away from their families and often in the same geographical area (for example, small towns on the south coast). They are becoming separate and different from the rest of society.

■ Activities

1 Which of the above theories do you feel offer valid explanations? Give reasons in support of, and against, each theory.

2 Debate the topic: 'Old people live longer, better lives than ever before'.

✪ Further study

Write off for information from pressure groups like Age Concern and Help the Aged (addresses in Additional Information on p109) or invite a speaker from such a group to address the class.

Hodder & Stoughton   © 1994 Paul Higginson. The publishers grant permission for multiple copies of this sheet to be made in the place of purchase for use solely in that institution.

Challenging the Stereotype

Below are some common stereotypical statements about old age. Challenge these ideas by putting forward a positive non-ageist view in the right hand column.

Stereotype	Challenge
1 Old people are not as efficient in the workplace as the young.	Companies like B&Q and Tesco have actively recruited the over-55s because they are reliable, hard-working, conscientious and polite to customers.
2 People live longer – they are becoming a greater burden on the taxpayer.	Longer life is a great social benefit for all. We must ensure that the old are well-provided for in financial terms (e.g. by increasing pensions).
3 Most old people are lonely, depressed and bored.	
4 The elderly are inflexible (difficult to retrain) and unproductive.	
5 Once people stop working they go downhill.	
6 Public money should be spent on the young rather than the old.	
7 Old people are different from the rest of society.	
8 It is better to keep the elderly together in homes where they can entertain each other.	
9 We can best help the elderly by giving them special privileges like bus-passes, Christmas pension bonuses, free butter, cut-price admission tickets, etc.	
10 Early retirement helps to provide job opportunities for younger workers.	
11 The elderly are a problem.	

Hodder & Stoughton

© 1994 Paul Higginson. The publishers grant permission for multiple copies of this sheet to be made in the place of purchase for use solely in that institution.

'Granny-Dumping'

Read this newspaper article then discuss the questions which follow in groups of three.

ELDERLY DUMPED LIKE UNWANTED PETS

... 'care in the community' is fuelling the growing national scandal of 'granny-dumping' as families resort to horrific ways of getting someone else to look after elderly parents

As the Government puts care back into the community the problem of 'granny-dumping' is on the increase.

At one General Hospital, doctors are finding more and more families struggling to cope with an elderly relative are just abandoning them like unwanted Christmas pets.

A care for the elderly consultant said that although the problem wasn't a major one it was something she was concerned about. She said: 'We work very closely with social services and we are usually able to do something before the family gets too desperate.

'But as more families struggle through the recession and as the Government puts the emphasis back on to families to look after relatives, I am worried the problem could increase.'

Although the General hasn't had anyone dumped in casualty, as has happened at hospitals in other parts of the country, it has had several elderly patients left in its wards after treatment by families who don't want them back.

The consultant said: 'It is a very sad situation. The people we are talking about are the generation who fought in the world wars for us and they are a generation who have real community spirit. They have probably given 40 to 50 years of contributions to the NHS and now, when it is their turn to reap the rewards, there is nothing left.'

Although many of the elderly people dumped by relatives have dementia problems, others are quite lucid but have basic problems such as incontinence which families find hard to cope with.

The consultant said: 'Many of these people know their family doesn't want them and they often try to make excuses for them. But deep down the elderly relatives are very hurt and sad and in some cases they just don't want to live any more and be a burden to anyone. They feel uncared for.'

But the consultant does not blame the families for the growing problem. She said: 'We all understand just how desperate someone must be to desert an elderly relative. It's not the way our society works but sometimes people get so desperate they just turn to anything and as a hospital our doors are always open.

'At the end of the day I would rather they came to us with their problems than just leave their relative uncared for.'

The consultant said the way we finance care for our elderly is really the main cause of the problem. She said: 'The money available to look after elderly people is not sufficient especially since the numbers of old people are constantly on the increase.

'In the last census in 1991 there were 36,500 people aged 65 years and over living in Hertfordshire, that number is rising yet we still have only 80 long-term NHS places available.'

The consultant advises elderly people to hang on to their own homes whenever possible as they will be able to return there and have the back up of home help, district nurses and Meals-on-Wheels if needed.

For those who have become dependent on families, life is much more of a struggle.

The consultant said: 'If the family really can't cope with an elderly relative we have to look at what kind of needs that person has.

'The social services can provide residential care which is partly paid for by the person's pension and attendance allowance.

'If nursing is needed there are different homes but the more help needed the higher the cost.'

One option many elderly people are now faced with is spending their life savings on private nursing homes which the consultant says makes more difficulties between families.

She said: 'The older generation have usually been saving money which they intend to leave to their children. Now they feel guilty using this to look after themselves and some children get angry that their inheritance is being spent.'

She added: 'I hope people will read this and realise the many problems old people face and we can put an end to this problem. After all we will all be old one day.'

(The names of the hospital and the consultant involved have been removed.)

Hodder & Stoughton

© *1994 Paul Higginson. The publishers grant permission for multiple copies of this sheet to be made in the place of purchase for use solely in that institution.*

Worksheet 2: continued

❏ **Questions**

1 What is 'granny-dumping' and what reasons are given in the article for the increase in this phenomenon? List these reasons in order of importance.

2 The consultant in the newspaper article on p37 feels that finance is the main cause of the problem. Do you agree?

3 The government is putting care back 'in the community'. Discuss the implication of such a policy.

4 What problems arise from an old person needing long-term care in a nursing home and why does this cause friction in families?

5 In what ways can the problem of granny-dumping be overcome?

6 By 2025 the proportion of divorced old people will have increased four-fold in comparison with today's figures. How will this exacerbate the problem outlined in the article?

7 In what ways might sheltered-accommodation (which provides separate housing but has support and services on hand if necessary) be one way forward?

Hodder & Stoughton   © 1994 Paul Higginson. The publishers grant permission for multiple copies of this sheet to be made in the place of purchase for use solely in that institution.

Voluntary Euthanasia

One of the most controversial moral issues connected with old age is voluntary euthanasia. In 1993 a Bill was introduced into Parliament which would allow voluntary euthanasia in Britain. Those in favour, such as the Voluntary Euthanasia Society, argue that 'people should have the right to choose to die'. Groups opposed, like LIFE, define euthanasia as 'the intentional killing by act or omission, of a person, supposedly in his or her interest, who is felt to have a life not worth living'. This is an issue that applies to the adult incurably ill, (for example those with AIDS/HIV illnesses) or those in great pain, and these can obviously be of any age, although the majority are elderly. Under present legislation, anyone (including a doctor) who assists another to end his or her life can be charged with attempted murder (this happened in 1992 to Dr Nigel Cox, who was tried and acquitted of attempted murder for assisting a patient to end her life). In Holland, doctors are allowed to practise euthanasia, free from prosecution, as long as they follow strict guidelines.

A distinction must be made between doctors giving strong pain-killers to a patient, which as a side effect cause earlier death, and the desire of a person to be given drugs whose sole purpose is to bring about death. Euthanasia only applies in the latter case.

The case for voluntary euthanasia is that it quickly and mercifully ends a patient's (and his/her family's) suffering and allows death with dignity. It is a basic human right to be able to choose when and how to die, as long as this is a decision that has been made well in advance in a rational state of mind.

Those opposed argue that many old people or those in an anxious state of mind who feel they are a nuisance to others could be forced into euthanasia. Life can only be taken away by God and euthanasia is the 'thin end of the wedge', which if permitted will devalue life and break down the trust between doctor and patient. The Hospice Movement could be expanded to enable everyone to die with dignity.

■ Activity

What is your view of voluntary euthanasia? Examine the following two extracts.

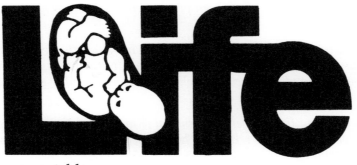

'Why Euthanasia is unacceptable.

Euthanasia will undermine the advances made in good palliative and hospice care. "Mercy killing" will directly lead to the dehumanisation of the dying, especially for those in terminal conditions associated with AIDS/HIV illnesses…

People of good will everywhere should instinctively oppose direct killing by medical personnel. Recent history has shown the horrors that can follow when the doctors (and/or nurses) are encouraged to dehumanise and end the lives of the elderly, the handicapped, the unwanted, and the unproductive. We must reject all euthanasia proposals. We do not want or need doctors who are licensed to kill. What we need is good medical practitioners, since good doctors do not kill patients: they kill pain and alleviate suffering.

Hodder & Stoughton

© *1994 Paul Higginson. The publishers grant permission for multiple copies of this sheet to be made in the place of purchase for use solely in that institution.*

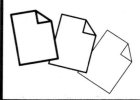

Euthanasia is not withholding or discontinuing heroic, unnecessary, futile or experimental treatments from the patient. Euthanasia is an action or omission (including the withholding of food and fluids) designed specifically to kill. To withhold food and fluids is to condemn the patient to death through starvation and dehydration. That is not death with dignity. It is brutal agonising death by design and neglect.

It is hard to watch loved-ones suffer pain and death. However that does not give us the right to kill them. Even when the sick are incurable they are never untreatable. Whatever their condition they should always be given appropriate loving care. Even in the most serious of situations patients should always be shown respect, made comfortable, fed (as appropriate to the condition) and should be given all reasonable medical treatments. No drugs or other medical treatments should ever be administered (or withheld) if the prime purpose is to bring about premature death.

That does not however mean that those who oppose euthanasia believe that we should 'strive officiously to keep alive' someone who has a condition incompatible with independent living. That would be equally indefensible. As patients and the next of kin we already have the legal right to refuse those types of treatment which only prolong a burdensome and precarious existence. We do not therefore need legalised euthanasia, nor do we need "advanced directives" ("living wills")'   **LIFE**

'The Case for Voluntary Euthanasia

Aim: To change the law so that it ceases to be a crime for a doctor to respond to an incurably ill patient's persistent request for help to die provided he/she acts within the published guidelines.

The case for legalising voluntary euthanasia

- *Seventy-nine per cent of British people think this option should be legally available at the end of life, according to a new 1993 NOP [National Opinion Poll survey].*

- *A 1987 Poll showed that nearly half of all GPs might consider practising VE if it were legal.*

- *Powerful anecdotal evidence shows that many doctors do this for suffering patients already, despite risks of prosecution. Few doctors have ever been prosecuted… , and they have always been treated with great sympathy.*

- *Modern medical technology and knowledge have actually increased the need for active help to die. Early treatment for killer diseases can keep patients alive for years, but paradoxically can mean a more painful death in the end. Also, more and more people are living longer but dying of long drawn-out degenerative diseases.*

- *Not everyone dies well. About five per cent of terminal pain is uncontrollable, even in hospices. Many other distressing symptoms cannot be relieved. The founder of the hospice movement has written that hospice care can be unavailing.*

- *At the moment, doctors can legally practice 'passive' euthanasia – withholding or withdrawing treatment, or providing pain relief in such high doses that death is hastened. This has exactly the same moral and practical result as actively giving a lethal injection on request.*

- *When the alternatives are, death with dignity and peace, or death accompanied by prolonged pain and distress, common sense as well as compassion supports the demand that the choice should belong to the individual.*

- *A few miles away across the North Sea, Dutch people have had this choice available to them for many years. Dutch people and Parliament are satisfied with their system.*

Hodder & Stoughton
© 1994 Paul Higginson. The publishers grant permission for multiple copies of this sheet to be made in the place of purchase for use solely in that institution.

Worksheet 3: continued

Some common objections and their rebuttals

- **Religious objections** – *only God can give and take away life.*

  Most opposition to the decriminalisation of voluntary euthanasia arises from religious groups, but they do not speak for all religious viewpoints. There are many deeply religious advocates of VE, including VES vice-president Lord Soper. In the Netherlands, Catholic or Dutch Reformed clergymen may be present at VE deaths. In any case, religious arguments cannot apply to anyone who does not share that belief.

- **The "slippery slope"** – *voluntary will soon lead to involuntary.*

  This argument has been used against every social reform, but there is no evidence for it at all. Voluntary euthanasia as an individual choice is entirely distinct from murdering people who are judged (by others) to have no worth. The VES would NOT support legislation for involuntary euthanasia. Skiers will be vividly aware that being on a slippery slope does not mean going downwards out of control.

- **Fear of abuse** – *the impossibility of framing watertight laws.*

  No-one knows how much abuse there is because active euthanasia is practised outside the law. If it were brought into the open and strictly controlled, there would be less chance of abuse. At present, doctors allow patients to die, for example by witholding treatment, or not resuscitating. But no-one suggests they do so because they 'want the bed free', or out of conspiracy with greedy relatives!

- **Hospices** – *palliative care means VE is not necessary.*

  While hospices do a wonderful job for many people, others would not want that slow way of dying. Also, a minority of people cannot be kept comfortable even in hospices.

- **A right to die could become a duty to die.**

  The many people involved in a voluntary euthanasia decision would be likely to judge accurately the sincerity of a patient's wishes. If anything, relatives usually 'bully' the patient to struggle on.

- **Miracle cures and wrong diagnosis.**

  A patient in hope of a miracle cure would not ask for VE. A doctor who thought one imminent would not do it. A second opinion on the patient's condition will be sought anyway.'

❏ Questions

1 What is the difference between voluntary and involuntary euthanasia?

2 'Only God can take human life.' Do you agree?

3 If euthanasia were to be legalised, what guidelines do you feel would be necessary to prevent abuse?

4 What are the alternatives to euthanasia?

5 List the pros and cons of an 'advanced directive' or 'living will' (i.e. a document specifying what treatment a person wants if he or she becomes terminally ill, with a named proxy to ensure such wishes are carried out).

6 It has recently been reported that terminally ill patients admitted to one particular hospital can opt to be left alone if their heart stops beating. They can choose not to have doctors try to resuscitate them. Do you think this is morally acceptable?

Hodder & Stoughton

© 1994 Paul Higginson. *The publishers grant permission for multiple copies of this sheet to be made in the place of purchase for use solely in that institution.*

4 The Family

Although society has changed through time, and varies according to region and culture, the basic unit of social arrangement is the family. This is essentially because the family satisfies certain basic needs by fulfilling a number of important functions. However in Western society in recent years the traditional functions of the family have been challenged (see Worksheet 1).

FAMILY TYPES

1 **Nuclear** – Consists of just an adult couple and their children.

2 **Extended** – The basic nuclear group has been extended to include grandparents, aunts, uncles and cousins who either live together or very close to each other (with a lot of contact between them).

3 **Reconstituted** – A married couple, where one or both has been married before, and the children are stepbrothers and stepsisters.

4 **Modern or Symmetrical** – Nuclear, but both parents work and household chores are evenly shared.

5 **Single-parent** – One parent, usually the mother, and children.

❏ Questions

1 Two hundred years ago most people in Britain lived in an extended family. Why was this?

2 Why has the extended family declined and the nuclear family increased?

3 What differences in family type exist between Developed and Underdeveloped Countries, and between different ethnic groups in Britain?

MARRIAGE

Ninety per cent of all people will marry at some point in their lives. Marriage is more popular in Britain than in any other EC country: in 1988 there were 7 marriages per 1,000 of the eligible population (compared to just 5 in France). However, the recent trend is for people to marry later in life: the average age for first marriages is 27 for men and 25 for women (much higher than in previous years). Nearly two-fifths of weddings now involve a divorce and in one-eighth of weddings both partners are divorcees. Within marriage, women are having their children much later in life: the average age of mothers having their first child has steadily increased and is now 27 (as opposed to 22 outside marriage).

❏ Questions

1 Why does marriage remain so popular?

2 Suggest reasons to explain why people are marrying later in life.

3 Give three reasons why women are having children later in life.

❂ Further study

1 Find out the views of the various religious faiths on marriage.

2 In some cultures marriages are arranged. Outline the pros and cons of such arranged marriages.

Hodder & Stoughton   © 1994 Paul Higginson. The publishers grant permission for multiple copies of this sheet to be made in the place of purchase for use solely in that institution.

COHABITATION

Cohabitation is defined as living together as husband and wife without having married legally. Between 1979 and 1989 the number of couples cohabiting trebled. About a quarter of single people aged 25 to 29 are cohabiting and the average period of cohabitation for single people is about one year and nine months.

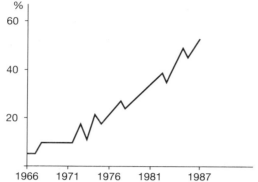

Proportion of married women in Britain who cohabited with their future husband before marriage (Office of Population Censuses & Surveys)

In the 1980s most couples who cohabited, lived together before getting married, not instead of getting married. However, in the 1990s the statistics for births outside marriage (28 per cent) suggest that living together could now be replacing marriage. The largest numbers cohabiting are in East Anglia and the South East; they get fewer the further the region is from London. The numbers in Scotland and Wales are around half the levels for the South East.

❏ Questions

1　Outline the possible reasons for increased cohabitation.

2　List the arguments for and against the idea of a trial marriage.

3　Do you think that cohabitation will eventually replace marriage? Explain your answer.

4　Why do more people cohabit in the South East and in big cities than in Scotland, Wales and rural areas?

DIVORCE

Divorce can be obtained if there is an 'irretrievable breakdown of marriage'. The divorce rate in England and Wales has risen by 600 per cent in the last 30 years. It is now estimated that two out of five marriages will ultimately end in divorce.

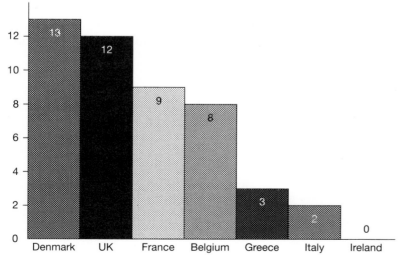

Divorces in Europe per 1,000 marriages (1990)

Hodder & Stoughton

© 1994 Paul Higginson. The publishers grant permission for multiple copies of this sheet to be made in the place of purchase for use solely in that institution.

Some Sociologists have isolated factors which make divorce more likely.

- marrying under 21 years old;
- partners are from different ethnic groups;
- partners have different sexuality;
- marrying because of pregnancy;
- infertility problems;
- partners have different religions;

- economic or housing problems;
- partners are from different social classes;
- occupation (sales reps, armed forces, etc.);
- parents are divorced;
- unemployment;
- low social class.

Divorce petitions filed (1,000s) in England and Wales (1961–89)

	1961	1971	1981	1985	1989
By husband	14	44	47	52	50
By wife	18	67	123	139	135

❑ Questions

1 Suggest reasons for the different divorce rates in European countries.

2 Look at the list of factors which make divorce more likely. Are some groups of people more susceptible to divorce? Examine the list and place an asterisk next to the three you consider as the most significant. Are there any groups you feel should not be in the list? Are there any that could be added?

3 List the reasons that might explain why more women than men petition for divorce.

4 When did the rate appear to level off? Suggest reasons for this.

❖ Discussion

Do you agree or disagree with the following comments?

1 'The easier you make divorce the more you encourage it. It should be made more difficult to get a divorce.'

2 'If couples have young children they should stay together even if they feel their marriage is over.'

3 'The rising divorce rate is a symptom of lower moral values in society and suggests a rejection of family life.'

Hodder & Stoughton   © 1994 Paul Higginson. The publishers grant permission for multiple copies of this sheet to be made in the place of purchase for use solely in that institution.

HOUSEHOLDS IN BRITAIN

The typical stereotype of the British family usually consists of a married couple with 2.4 children. How does this compare with the reality?

		% of population in each category			
		1961	**1971**	**1981**	**1989**
1	living alone (pensioner)	7	12	14	16
2	living alone	4	6	8	10
3	two or more unrelated adults	5	4	5	3
4	married couple (no children)	26	27	26	27
	(1 to 2 children)	30	26	25	21
	(3+ children)	8	9	6	5
	(non dependent children only)	10	8	8	9
5	Single parent with children	6	7	9	9
6	Two or more families	3	1	1	1

❏ Questions

1 What percentage of households in 1989 consisted of a married couple with young children? Compare this with 1961, and suggest reasons for the change.

2 How many one-person households are there? How has this changed since 1961?

3 Suggest reasons for the sharp rise of single-person households.

4 Suggest reasons for the rise of single-parent families.

THE ONE-PARENT FAMILY

In 1990, 19 per cent of all families with dependent children in Britain were headed by lone parents. In 1971 the figure was 8 per cent. The types of single-parent families are outlined below:

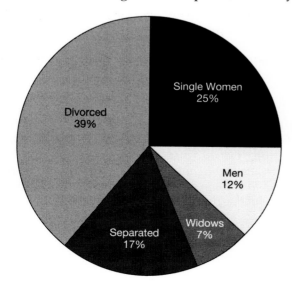

Hodder & Stoughton

© 1994 Paul Higginson. The publishers grant permission for multiple copies of this sheet to be made in the place of purchase for use solely in that institution.

In 1991 the Department of Social Security produced the following statistics on lone parents.

1 There are 1.15 million one-parent families in Britain.

2 Sixty-two per cent of children of single mothers never see their fathers.

3 Ninety-four per cent of such families depend on social security for most of their income.

4 Sixty per cent describe themselves as 'hard pressed' for money.

5 Sixty-one per cent have never received any maintenance payments from their former partner.

■ Activity

Analyse the consequences for: a) children; b) parents; c) the state; of the rise in one-parent families and examine the controversy surrounding the work of the government's Child Support Agency.

The Family Studies Centre (December 1991) has used information from the National Child Development Study to compare living with a single parent with living in a reconstituted family (i.e. parents who divorced and subsequently married other partners). Those with reconstituted or stepfamilies were:

1 twice as likely as those with single parents to leave home due to friction;

2 twice as likely to marry by the age of 20;

3 almost twice as likely to become a parent by the age of 20;

4 less likely to continue in education after 16, and less likely to do well in terms of work and career.

■ Activity

List the reasons why children in stepfamilies might be at a greater disadvantage than those in single-parent families.

TWO ALTERNATIVES TO THE FAMILY

Study the following newspaper extracts, which describe alternatives to the family unit.

KIBBUTZ

'There are nearly 300 Kibbutzim in Israel, with a total population of around 150,000. Although couples get married in a kibbutz, their first loyalty is always to the community. Often children are not brought up with their parents but in a separate children's house with others of the same age. This allows mothers to return to work soon after having their babies. Jobs are shared out equally (there are no jobs reserved solely for men or women), and there are no wages – each Kibbutz supplies its members with the housing, food and clothing they need. In recent years the original ideas have been modified and the nuclear family is re-emerging as the basis of communal life.'

FEMINIST

'The traditional family unit is the cause of female disadvantage in Western society. Women are socialised into becoming housewives and mothers ('a woman's place is in the home') so that they can look after men. Many women are locked into unhappy marriages; some suffer violence and abuse. If women can break out of their traditional role as childbearer and child rearer then they will gain true equality with men. In the United States professional surrogate mothers are now paid to become pregnant and bear someone else's child. Through sperm banks, women can choose to have a child without having a husband.'

❑ Questions

1 List the advantages and disadvantages of living on a kibbutz.

Hodder & Stoughton   © 1994 Paul Higginson. The publishers grant permission for multiple copies of this sheet to be made in the place of purchase for use solely in that institution.

2   In his book *The Children of the Dream* (Thames & Hudson, 1969) Bruno Bettelheim pointed out that although kibbutz children are rarely neglected and grow up to be stable caring adults they find deep, intimate personal relationships very difficult. Why do you think this is so?

3   What are the main differences between life on a kibbutz and life in a British nuclear family?

4   Do you agree with the view that 'The family is the cause of female disadvantage'? Explain your answer, and if you disagree, say what you feel is the cause of female inequality?

5   What are the pros and cons of surrogate motherhood and the use of sperm banks for reproduction?

6   'I'm not trying to suggest that single parents are incapable of rearing children. However, I do believe that children need the support and experience of two parents.' (Kenneth Baker, Chairman of the Conservative Party, May 1990.) Do you agree?

❖ **Discussion** - Is the Family in Decline?

This could be either a topic for a debate or an essay. Construct your arguments around the following points (see the main text for detailed statistics).

Yes	No
the rise in births outside marriage	but most are registered by both parents
the increase in number not marrying	but 90 per cent still do
more cohabitation	but people usually marry eventually
the divorce rate has soared	but fewer people trapped in unhappy marriages (therefore free to re-marry?)
the rise in single-parent families	but perhaps they are happier than families forced to stay together? (many live with grandparents in a kind of extended family)
one-fifth of women will never have a baby and women are having fewer children, later in life, therefore the population is not being replaced	but support for the conventional family amongst the British is still strong

Hodder & Stoughton   © 1994 Paul Higginson. The publishers grant permission for multiple copies of this sheet to be made in the place of purchase for use solely in that institution.

Functions of the Family

Complete the table below showing the functions of the family with the appropriate recent challenge to the family in Western society.

Function	Description	Challenge
Procreation	To avoid extinction society must replace those who die with new members.	In many Western countries deaths now outstrip births. Contraception.
Child rearing	Usually by two parents and often including grandparents and extended family.	
Sex	Enables couples to have a socially acceptable sexual relationship.	
Education	Family passes on skills and knowledge to child.	
Love	Provides emotional support and fulfils the psychological need for close, loving relationships.	
Behaviour	Acceptable behaviour patterns and discipline are learnt by children in the family through socialisation.	
Economic well-being	Parents are responsible for children until they are 18.	
Care of elderly	Younger family members care for the elderly members.	
Social control	The Marxist idea that the family is a capitalist tool to produce obedient citizens who will work for a low wage.	

❏ Questions

1   In what ways has the Welfare State and the rise in living standards weakened the family?

2   What is the most important function that still remains with the family?

3   How many of our beliefs (religious, political, moral, etc.) come from the family?

4   The psychologist R D Laing suggests that the family is a place where people feel lonely, repressed and suffer emotional damage. Do you agree?

Hodder & Stoughton

© 1994 Paul Higginson. The publishers grant permission for multiple copies of this sheet to be made in the place of purchase for use solely in that institution.

Worksheet 2
Divorce

In 1960, for every 1,000 married people in England and Wales there were two divorces. Today there are 13 – the second highest number in Europe. In groups of three, complete the table below, listing the possible reasons for the increased divorce rate.

Factor	Explanation
1 Legal changes.	Divorce Acts and the 1984 Matrimonial Proceedings Act have made divorce easier to obtain.
2 Change in family type from extended to nuclear.	
3 Changed role of women – greater equality and independence.	
4 Fewer children (most born in first seven years of marriage).	
5 Rise in living standards and growth of Welfare State.	
6 High (romanticised?) expectations of marriage.	
7 Changes in social and religious attitudes.	
8 Greater life expectancy.	

■ Activity

Prioritise these factors in order of importance from 1 to 8.

Hodder & Stoughton

© 1994 Paul Higginson. The publishers grant permission for multiple copies of this sheet to be made in the place of purchase for use solely in that institution.

Conceptions and Births

Conceptions outside marriage (England and Wales) – eventual outcome
(*Population Trends*, Autumn 1991)

% leading to	1979	1989
Births outside marriage	37	53
Births inside marriage	23	10
Abortion	40	36

❏ Questions

1 Suggest reasons for the increase in births outside marriage.

2 Suggest reasons for the decreased proportion of conceptions resulting in abortions. Why might women in such a situation opt for an abortion?

3 In 1989 conceptions outside marriage were 42 per cent of all conceptions (up from 26 per cent in 1979). Suggest reasons for this trend.

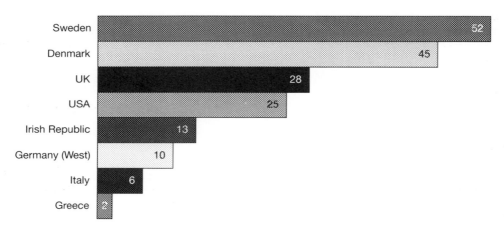

Births outside marriage (as a percentage of all births)
(*Population Trends*, Autumn 1991)

❏ Questions

1 Why are the figures so high in the Scandinavian countries?

2 Why are there so few births outside marriage in Italy and Greece?

3 In 1971 only 8 per cent of births were outside marriage in England and Wales. Some see the huge increase to 28 per cent in 1991 as unwelcome, others see the figures in a positive light. Suggest reasons to support both viewpoints.

4 Seventy-three per cent of births outside marriage in 1990 were registered jointly by the mother and father, compared to 47 per cent in 1971 (*Social Trends*, 1991). What are the implications of these statistics?

Hodder & Stoughton

© 1994 Paul Higginson. *The publishers grant permission for multiple copies of this sheet to be made in the place of purchase for use solely in that institution.*

5 North and South

In 1980 an important report on world poverty was published by a group of academics and international politicians led by Willy Brandt (the former West German Chancellor). Entitled *North–South. A programme for Survival*, the report divided the world into two camps: the rich, developed, North and the poor, underdeveloped, South. Living standards in the North are forty times higher than in the South, where 450 million people do not have enough to eat and 15,000 people, mostly children, die each day from hunger.

THE CAUSES OF POVERTY

1 DROUGHT

Many countries (e.g. Sudan, Ethiopia) regularly suffer from a lack of water. When the rains fail to come the crops fail. Global warming and holes in the ozone layer could cause severe climatic changes in the South.

2 TRADING INEQUALITIES

The countries of the North often exploit those in the South by paying low prices for the South's exports of raw materials, while blocking Southern manufactured goods with high tariff barriers. Old-style colonialism has been replaced by the economic colonialism of multi-national companies, which often use cheap labour in poor countries.

3 POPULATION GROWTH

Those countries with the least food have the highest birth rate. By 2025, 86 per cent of the world's population will be in the South (79 per cent at present).

4 ARMS SPENDING

The North/South report estimates that 40,000 village pharmacies could be established for the cost of a single jet fighter.

5 DESERTIFICATION

Desertification occurs as a result of climate change, drought, the chopping down of forests and the mismanagement of the land. In 1980 Africa lost arable land equivalent to one-third of the area of France. $4 billion each year for 20 years would reverse this trend (annual arms spending is around $1,000 billion).

6 WAR

Ninety-five per cent of the wars and conflicts that take place in the world occur in Southern countries. The result is death, destruction and over 10 million refugees.

7 DEBT

Most poor countries owe vast sums of money to the Northern countries, which lend money to the South at high rates of interest.

8 LACK OF AID

The UN suggests that Northern countries should provide 0.7 per cent of their gross national product (GNP) as aid, but most rich countries (including the UK) pay less than half this amount. Moreover, strings are often attached to aid money so that the donor countries benefit (e.g. aid must be spent on buying Northern armaments).

Hodder & Stoughton
© 1994 Paul Higginson. The publishers grant permission for multiple copies of this sheet to be made in the place of purchase for use solely in that institution.

9 INEQUALITY WITHIN THE POOR COUNTRIES

Within the countries of the South there are huge differences between rich and poor. On average less than 10 per cent of the population owns 50 per cent of the land. Often a rich élite enjoys a lavish lifestyle while many go hungry.

10 UNHELPFUL AID

Many economists warn against too much food aid which might discourage local production and self-sufficiency. Aid must liberate, rather than result in dependency. 'Give a man a fish and you feed him for a day; teach him how to fish and you feed him for life.'

11 THE ROLE OF WOMEN

In some Southern countries education is not available to women; a valuable human resource is being wasted.

12 UNEMPLOYMENT

Lack of work means a lack of money. Most poor countries cannot afford a welfare state to provide basic necessities for the unemployed.

13 LACK OF RESOURCES

Only 30 per cent of the earth's land surface can be used for crop growth and most of this is in the North. Moreover many Southern crops are lost through pests (50 per cent in India) and much livestock is killed by disease.

14 COLONIAL LEGACY

The economies of many Southern ex-colonies still revolve around European needs. They often concentrate on one crop (such as coffee, tea or cocoa). If there is a crop failure or a slump in world prices the economy is plunged into serious difficulty.

15 THE GREED OF THE NORTH

People and politicians in the North are unwilling to accept a lower standard of living in order to help the South. Most Western democratic political parties are committed to increasing the wealth of the Northern countries, but few are prepared to accept the sacrifices that are required to achieve a more just distribution of the world's resources.

16 THE SPREAD OF AIDS

About 5 million people in Africa are HIV positive (1 million have already died). The virus affects the most crucial economic group, those aged between 16 and 45 years old. It was estimated that the economic growth rate in most African countries would be 3 per cent per annum after the year 2000, now it is expected to decline by 0.8 per cent, principally because of AIDS.

■ Activities

1 In groups of three select what you consider to be the five most important causes of poverty and rank them in order of importance. Compare and discuss them with the rest of the class.

2 It has been suggested that the causes of poverty can be divided into **three** types: a) caused by the North; b) caused by the South; c) caused by nature. Try classifying the 16 factors above in this way; what problems arise from such an exercise?

DEBT OF UNDERDEVELOPED COUNTRIES

One of the most important problems in the North-South relationship is the ever-increasing debt crisis. In 1990 the South paid $43 billion in interest repayments to the rich nations. This is three times more than the aid given to the poorer countries, i.e. for every £1 given in aid £3 is repaid to the North in debt repayment. The total debt of the Underdeveloped Countries is now approximately $1,400,000,000,000 ($1.4 trillion). In order to repay these loans poor countries must cut public spending on such things as health, education and food subsidies. The UN has estimated that 1.5 million people have died as a result of cutbacks demanded by the banks of

Hodder & Stoughton

© 1994 Paul Higginson. The publishers grant permission for multiple copies of this sheet to be made in the place of purchase for use solely in that institution.

Developed Countries to meet debt repayment conditions. The crisis has its roots in the inequality of trade between rich and poor nations. The North exploits the South by buying cheap raw materials and selling expensive manufactured goods, as is shown in the diagram below.

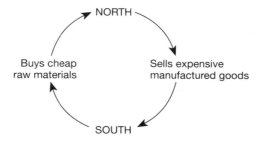

The gap between rich and poor countries is widening. Manufactured goods become more expensive while raw materials get cheaper. Between 1986 and 1989 the prices paid for Indian tea fell by 20 per cent, while the cost of the oil, tractors and machinery India imports from the North rose by a similar amount.

In the mid-1970s Northern banks started to lend money to Underdeveloped Countries. Initially the interest rate was 6 per cent but by the early 1980s this had risen to 22 per cent. Many countries were forced to borrow more money just to pay off the interest on old debts.

In 1982 Mexico halted all repayments on its debts and other poor countries followed. The International Monetary Fund and other banks agreed to restructure these loans but insisted that the Southern countries cut back on public spending. By 1988 the banks were setting aside money for bad debts (£3.5 billion by British banks in 1988). This did not mean, however, that the debt was written off; banks were simply setting money aside in case loans were not repaid in the future.

❏ Questions

1 In Sudan large areas of the country have been given over to growing cotton. Why is this and what have been the results?

2 The more efficient the Underdeveloped Countries become by producing more raw materials, the less money it receives. Why is this?

3 The diagram below shows how much of the cost of your cup of tea goes to the tea producers. Only 17 per cent stays in India. Once the landowner has taken his cut there is little left for the growers and pickers (about 70p a day for the picker). Why has this situation arisen? Suggest a fairer distribution of the 'cuppa'.

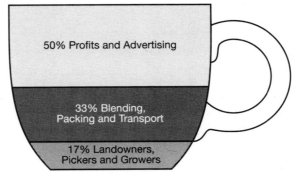

4 The Old Testament and the Koran state that charging interest on loans is against the will of God. Do you agree that charging interest is bad? Give reasons for your answer.

5 The poor countries want their debts to be wiped out by the setting up of a New International Economic Order (NIEO). Split the class into two: one group, representing the Northern countries, argues against this idea, the other (the South) puts forward arguments in favour.

6 In what ways can the problem of trading inequality between North and South be overcome?

Hodder & Stoughton   © 1994 Paul Higginson. The publishers grant permission for multiple copies of this sheet to be made in the place of purchase for use solely in that institution.

SOLUTIONS

Listed below are a number of possible solutions to the problem of North-South inequality. Fill in the boxes with detailed, practical examples of how such solutions might be implemented.

Possible Solutions	Detail
1 Increase aid.	All countries to meet 0.7 per cent of GNP target. No strings to be attached, and aid to be targeted on self-help projects.
2 Cut population growth.	
3 Reduce war and conflict in Underdeveloped Countries.	
4 Stop climate change.	
5 Solve the debt crisis.	
6 Reduce arms spending.	
7 End the inequalities between rich and poor within Southern countries.	
8 Reduce unemployment.	
9 Get the North to accept a lower standard of living.	
10 End food shortages.	
11 Decrease the spread of AIDS.	
12 Better education (especially for women).	
13 End trading inequality.	
14 Allow easier movement of people from South to North.	

■ Activity

For each solution and detailed example above, write down an argument against. For 1 this argument could be that Britain cannot afford to increase its aid budget without raising taxes or making cuts in British public services (both of which would be unpopular with voters). Moreover, ending strings-attached aid, which is often linked to the purchase of weapons, would lead to unemployment in British factories.

Hodder & Stoughton

© 1994 Paul Higginson. The publishers grant permission for multiple copies of this sheet to be made in the place of purchase for use solely in that institution.

AID

There are four main types of aid: food, money, education, and technology. It is given in **three** ways.

1   International organisations (such as the EC and the UN) give multilateral aid from donations made by rich countries.

2   Bilateral aid is when one country gives to another. Seventy-five per cent of Britain's bilateral aid has strings attached, and is tied to the purchase of British goods and services. Britain spends 0.3 per cent of its GNP on official aid (the Netherlands gives 1 per cent).

3   Voluntary charities donate money received from the public, and from the government.

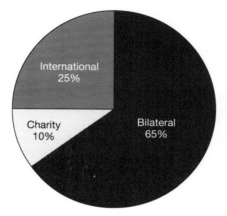

Types of British Aid

CASE STUDY – CHILD SPONSORSHIP

Child sponsorship is a popular way of giving aid. Over one million people in the North each give an average of £12 a month to sponsor a child in a country of their choice in the South. There are many possible advantages of this kind of sponsorship. The sponsor receives regular contact with an individual in the South and receives letters, photographs, drawings and information from the child. It builds links in a personal, direct way across the North–South divide and provides much-needed cash for the poor. Those who give in this way have good intentions, but consider the extract below.

'Helping just one child in a community can be very divisive, creating bitterness and inequality. Even within families, what happens when only one child is sponsored and the others are not? Whole communities (including the elderly) should be supported by providing aid for everyone. A paternalistic relationship can develop with the donor, and letters from the rich to the poor can lead to feelings of inferiority in the child or produce false dreams of a lifestyle he or she can never achieve. If the sponsorship ends for some reason the child can feel great rejection and disappointment as well as renewed material hardship. Providing case histories and photos of the children and keeping correspondence flowing is expensive and between one quarter and one third of the money donated is spent on administrative costs. Finally, such programmes are especially damaging if they are linked to the child accepting a particular religious belief.'

❏ Questions

1   What arguments might the child sponsorship charities use to combat the above viewpoints?

2   What arguments would you use to try and persuade someone in Britain to vote for a government that would increase the overseas aid budget to the UN target of 0.7 per cent of GNP?

3   Some economists and politicians in the North have argued against aid on the grounds that it actually worsens the long term position of people in the South. What justification might there be for this viewpoint and how would you argue against it?

4   Look at 'Aid Blunders!' on p56 (taken from Christian Aid's *Aid Matters*). In the light of these blunders and the extract on child sponsorship, outline the kinds of aid which you think are most likely to be effective. List the criteria you would use to judge whether aid was helpful or harmful.

Hodder & Stoughton

© 1994 Paul Higginson. The publishers grant permission for multiple copies of this sheet to be made in the place of purchase for use solely in that institution.

1 Donors may place conditions on the use of money given
2 Donors can insist on unsuitable aid
3 Aid can help the individual, but neglect the community.
4 Much aid is in the form of loans.
5 Highly skilled personnel can be expensive.
6 Charities can be too influenced by their supporters.
7 Aid doesn't always help the poor.
8 Aid can treat symptoms and ignore causes, especially if powerful interests are threatened.
9 Aid can undermine local producers.

© Christian Aid

Copyright © Christian Aid

PERSONAL ACTION

What can an individual in Britain do to help solve the injustice and inequality of the North-South divide? Complete the following sentences with ideas for personal action.

1 Give money and time to charities like…
2 Vote for a party committed to North-South justice like…
3 Change my eating habits by…
4 Cut down on waste by recycling things like…
5 Join a pressure group such as…
6 Educate myself about the issues involved by…
7 Try to increase awareness amongst my family and friends by…
8 Buy goods in shops like…
9 Put pressure on politicians by…
10 Raise money in the school or community by…
11 Adopt a simpler lifestyle by…

CONCLUSION

The Brandt Report concluded that unless the North responds to the needs and aspirations of the South then the problems of war, violence, economic recession and poverty will increasingly spill over into, and affect the countries of the North. In other words it is in the interests of the North to co-operate with the South: we live in an interdependent world and we ignore the widening gap between rich and poor at our peril.

■ Activities

1 Invite a speaker from a voluntary organisation working in Underdeveloped Countries (e.g. Christian Aid, Oxfam or CAFOD) to visit the group and discuss North-South issues (for addresses see Additional Information p109).
2 Send off for further information from the aid charities on the debt trap, trade, aid and the arms trade.
3 Organise a debate on the following theme: 'Aid is a sticking plaster. Only radical long-term political and economic change will solve the problems of North-South inequality.'

Hodder & Stoughton

© 1994 Paul Higginson. The publishers grant permission for multiple copies of this sheet to be made in the place of purchase for use solely in that institution.

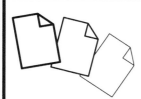

Divided World

1 Label the map with the following: India, Africa, North America, Western Europe, South Africa, China, Japan, South America, Middle East, Central America, Australia.

2 Using shading or colour, mark the Developed Countries (Western) and the Developing Countries (of the old Communist Eastern bloc).

3 The poorer Underdeveloped Countries are often referred to as 'the South'. Which countries or areas are clearly in the South but not suffering from poverty or underdevelopment? Why are these countries not poor?

4 Which countries in the world suffer the greatest poverty and hardship? Mark them on the map and suggest reasons for their problems.

5 List some of the wars and conflict situations in the world since 1945. How many have been in the South and what conclusion can be drawn from this information?

Hodder & Stoughton   © 1994 Paul Higginson. The publishers grant permission for multiple copies of this sheet to be made in the place of purchase for use solely in that institution.

Worksheet 2

Rich and Poor

Test your knowledge of the gap between North and South by completing the boxes below in pencil.

	North	South
1 population of the world	30%	70%
2 proportion of the world's food		
3 consumption of the world's resources		
4 average Gross National Product per head of population	$14,000	
5 adult calorie intake per person per day (the average person needs 2,600)		1,600
6 unemployment	150 million	
7 life expectancy	74	
8 proportion of the population with no access to organised health care		70%
9 literacy rate (reading and writing)	99%	
10 percentage of population regularly suffering from lack of food	less than 1%	
11 deaths from lack of food per day	nil	
12 proportion of population increase (1 million people every five days!)		
13 percentage of average person's personal income spent on food		80%
14 ownership of world's manufacturing industry (percentage)		
15 infant mortality rate (number of infants in every 1,000 of population who die before they are 1 year old)	10	
16 percentage of population which is overweight		less than 1%

1   Place a tick next to the three points above which most surprised you.

2   All of these factors are linked, e.g. 15 is linked to 8. Think of other connections – what is linked to 9?

3   Write a short paragraph outlining what you think is the single most important change that needs to occur in order to rectify the huge imbalance between rich and poor. When you have finished, compare with others in the group.

Hodder & Stoughton   © 1994 Paul Higginson. The publishers grant permission for multiple copies of this sheet to be made in the place of purchase for use solely in that institution.

Worksheet 3

The Debt Trap

Southland is a poor, underdeveloped country in Africa, regularly plagued by drought and famine, and controlled by a military dictator. The International Monetary Fund has offered to lend the government £200 million (at an interest rate of 10 per cent). The class divides into nine groups of Southland civil servants in different departments. Using the information below each group must present its proposals to the military dictator (the teacher) who chairs the meeting. Through consultation and discussion decide if, or how, you are going to spend the loan. N.B. The dictator will always have the last word though he will attempt to reach agreement and consensus.

1 **Defence Ministry** – Southland is always in danger of attack from hostile neighbours. Buy five multi-role combat aircraft from the UK at special discounted price of £20 million each. Total cost £100 million.

2 **Health Ministry** – Build, staff and run ten new hospitals (total cost £100 million). Build a network of village pharmacies throughout the country (£40 million). Ensure clean water by digging wells, laying pipes, etc. (£25 million).

3 **Education** – Provide free primary education for all (£50 million). Construct a university (£10 million).

4 **Industry** – Give grants to companies to start up small businesses and create a small manufacturing industrial base (£200 million).

5 **Agriculture** – Provide farmers with cheap loans to buy new machinery and tools (tractors, harvesters). Total cost £100 million.

6 **Housing** – Tear down shanty towns in the city and build new homes, thereby providing thousands of new jobs (£100 million).

7 **Transport** – Connect the main population centres by building new roads (£20 million).

8 **Personal advisors** – spend £5 million on a new prestige palace for the dictator and another £5 million on an international conference centre for hosting foreign dignitaries. Increase the pay and resources of the police, secret police and armed forces in order to keep them loyal to the government and suppress opposition (£10 million).

9 **Treasury** – Refuse the loan. The country cannot afford to repay £20 million per annum without making severe spending cutbacks in future years. The people will benefit in the short term, but in the long term they will be saddled with a huge debt.

Hodder & Stoughton

© 1994 Paul Higginson. The publishers grant permission for multiple copies of this sheet to be made in the place of purchase for use solely in that institution.

6 Pollution

Unit 7 will deal with two major threats to our environment caused by pollution of the atmosphere – global warming and the destruction of the ozone layer. This unit will deal with other forms of pollution, beginning with one of the industrialised world's most serious problems – acid rain.

WHAT IS ACID RAIN?

When fossil fuels like coal and oil are used in industrial production, cars, power stations, and so on, the waste gases (mainly sulphur and nitrogen emissions) are discharged into the air. These gases then combine with water vapour, sunlight and oxygen and are transformed into weak acid droplets which fall to earth as dry particles or as rain or snow.

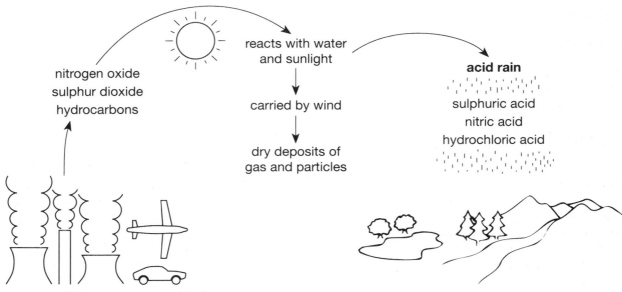

nitrogen oxide
sulphur dioxide
hydrocarbons

reacts with water and sunlight

carried by wind

dry deposits of gas and particles

acid rain

sulphuric acid
nitric acid
hydrochloric acid

ENVIRONMENTAL DAMAGE

1 **Water** – Acid rain has increased the acidity of lakes, streams and soil. In Sweden 22,000 lakes are acidified and 18,000 are so bad that they are unable to support fish. In southern Norway 80 per cent of lakes and rivers are either dead or critical.

2 **Trees** – A UN study found that in Germany acid rain had contributed towards leaf damage and needle loss in over half the country's forests, and in Britain 64 per cent of all trees have been affected.

3 **Soil** – Acid rain releases metals into the soil. Scientists are not yet sure if plants take up these metals into their stems and leaves but if so this would seriously contaminate vegetables and livestock.

4 **Buildings** – In Greece acid rain is helping to destroy the Parthenon, which has suffered more damage in the last 25 years than in the previous 2,400. The beautiful historic cities of Europe such as Krakow and Cologne are finding their buildings disintegrating under the onslaught of pollution.

5 **Health** – Many doctors are concerned that air, water and food affected by acid rain can contribute to respiratory and digestive illness.

Hodder & Stoughton

© 1994 Paul Higginson. The publishers grant permission for multiple copies of this sheet to be made in the place of purchase for use solely in that institution.

TRANSBOUNDARY POLLUTION

Acid rain can be carried many miles by strong winds – in this way Scandinavia suffers heavily from its industrialised neighbours like Britain. Every year 130 million metric tons of sulphur dioxide are emitted over Europe and North America and the rainfall is regularly one hundred times more acidic than the natural level (in the USA rain as acidic as battery acid once fell on West Virginia). Underdeveloped Countries such as China, India and Brazil are also now badly affected.

SOLUTIONS

1 In the 1960s and 1970s the answer to air pollution was to build taller chimneys and disperse the pollutants at a higher level. While this helped preserve the immediate environment it simply meant that pollution was exported to other regions.

2 In the 1980s Sweden began adding lime to 5,500 lakes in order to neutralise the acid and bring them back to life. This cost $25 million. However, this is merely treating the symptoms of the problem rather than addressing the causes.

3 The EC countries have agreed to cuts in the emissions that cause acid rain. From 1993 all new cars have to be fitted with catalytic converters that reduce pollution. However these measures have been criticised by environmentalists as too little, too late and they warn that the spread of acid rain will continue.

■ **Activity**

Split into groups of three. Explain to each other the problem of acid rain. One group then prepares a two-minute presentation to the rest of the class on the essential facts of acid rain. **Do not use these sheets!**

GROUND LEVEL OZONE AND SMOG

Another damaging pollutant is ground-level ozone. Different from the high ozone layer in the atmosphere, this is a kind of smog produced by the action of strong sunlight on nitrogen oxides and volatile organic compounds. It occurs during hot, dry spells and causes damage to trees, crops and humans (especially those with respiratory ailments). When combined with other pollutants such as hydrocarbons and carbon monoxide it provides a deadly smog cocktail which contaminates big cities the world over. Lead-free petrol is reducing the lead levels in the atmosphere which have contributed in the past to damage to the human brain and nervous system.

POLLUTION OF RIVERS AND LAKES

Industrial and agricultural waste pours into our rivers and lakes, polluting our water with toxins and chemicals. In the industrialised Developed Countries water quality legislation has not succeeded in curing diffuse pollution, i.e. pesticide and fertiliser run-off from farm land and urban stormwater run-off containing sewage, chemicals, heavy metals and other pollutants. Lakes in particular can quickly become eutrophic, overdosed with nutrients such as fertilisers which kill marine life and adversely affect water quality. Nitrates in drinking water can cause both cancer and birth defects and in 1990 1.7 million Britons were drinking water containing nitrates above the recommended WHO (World Health Organisation) levels. In Eastern Europe and Underdeveloped Countries the problems were much more severe as environmental protection takes second place to the dash for industrial growth. Asia's major rivers are little more than open sewers, which carry untreated sewage and industrial waste out to sea.

Some of the most dangerous pollutants are polychlorinated biphenyls (PCBs), used in light fittings, some lipstick, and cooling systems. PCBs enter the food chain by passing into the fat of smaller animals before working their way up to the higher mammals, including humans.

Hodder & Stoughton
© 1994 Paul Higginson. The publishers grant permission for multiple copies of this sheet to be made in the place of purchase for use solely in that institution.

SEA-POLLUTION

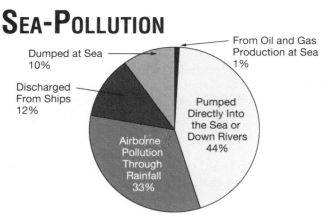

This graph shows the ways in which the sea becomes polluted

Some enclosed seas like the Aral Sea in Kazakhstan are completely dead through pollution, while the Mediterranean and the Black Sea are in a critical state. Huge slicks of toxic algae caused by an excess of nutrients from pollutants have become commonplace. These toxic blooms of algae starve the bottom of the sea of oxygen, killing marine life and contaminating seafood. In Britain more than 25 per cent of all beaches fail to come up to EC safety standards, often because of contamination from raw sewage discharged into the sea from coastal towns. Oil pollution from shipping and accidents like the Exxon Valdez and the Shetland disaster create enormous environmental problems, and even low levels of oil will severely affect plankton and larvae. The dumping of industrial waste and sewage at sea still continues despite various international agreements to phase it out.

TOXIC WASTE

It is estimated that 430 million metric tons of toxic waste are produced each year (260 million in the USA), most of it from the chemical industry. Before the 1970s hazardous waste was dumped into landfills, rivers, lakes, seas or discharged into the air. The clean-up of these toxic dumps is costing billions of dollars ($100 billion in the USA alone). Most countries now try to concentrate and contain the waste in deep holes in the ground, whereas the UK still dilutes and disperses waste with ordinary domestic rubbish in landfill sites all over the country. Some countries such as Japan now recycle more than 50 per cent of their waste, but the only long term solution to the problem lies in reducing the production of hazardous waste in the first place.

PESTICIDES AND FERTILISERS

New agrochemicals have increased crop yields yet they are causing great environmental concern because of the contamination of drinking water through run-off from agricultural land. About 30,000 people die each year from pesticide poisoning in Underdeveloped Countries, and the US National Research Council has shown that 20,000 Americans may die from cancer caused by pesticide-contaminated food and water. A WHO study in 1987 stated that human breast milk is now contaminated with pesticides and recommended that breastfeeding should be avoided in certain parts of the world.

❏ Questions

1 Write one-sentence definitions of; a) transboundary pollution, b) eutrophy.

2 Which of the problems mentioned in this unit do you regard as the most serious, and why?

3 In what way is pollution connected to; a) the poverty of Underdeveloped Countries, b) the greed of Developed Countries?

4 List the factors which many politicians say are preventing them from taking decisive action on the above issues.

5 Pesticide producers say that without pesticides the world would starve. Why is this largely a false claim?

6 What steps can you take as a consumer to help combat pollution?

Hodder & Stoughton

© 1994 Paul Higginson. The publishers grant permission for multiple copies of this sheet to be made in the place of purchase for use solely in that institution.

✪ Further study

1 Write two newspaper front pages for publication in 2050, one assuming that no steps were taken to control pollution, the other assuming that the world community united to act decisively. Describe the world as it is in 2050; in the worst-case scenario describe the consequences of inaction, in the best-case report outline the successful initiatives taken to protect the environment. Report on such things as energy usage, agricultural methods and land use, pollution control, the developing world, recycling, waste disposal, forestry policy, etc.

2 Invite a member of one of the environmental groups listed in the back of this book (Additional Information p109) to talk to the class.

3 Write to your local council for information on the ways that they try to protect the local environment.

Hodder & Stoughton

© 1994 Paul Higginson. The publishers grant permission for multiple copies of this sheet to be made in the place of purchase for use solely in that institution.

Worksheet 1
UN Conference

The class divides into Environment Ministries from 13 different countries who meet together in an international conference organised by the UN to discuss how to combat pollution. Here are some useful statistics on each country.

India
Every day each person in Bombay breathes pollution equivalent to smoking ten cigarettes – rapid industrialisation has taken place without regard for proper environmental standards. Seventy per cent of surface water is polluted. Out of 3,100 towns only 200 have sewage treatment facilities.

Greece
Great buildings are being destroyed by acid rain. Deaths in Athens rise by up to six times on days of heavy pollution.

Brazil
Two-thirds of all farmers have suffered acute poisoning from pesticides.

Poland
One of the most polluted countries on earth – industrialisation under communism without environmental protection has led to immense health problems and crumbling buildings. Those living in Katowice Province have a 47 per cent higher rate of respiratory ailments and 30 per cent more cancers than others in Poland.

Sweden
Thirty-eight per cent of trees, and a quarter of all lakes are affected by acid rain.

Mexico
In Mexico City smog levels exceed WHO standards 84 per cent of the time. In January 1989 it was so bad that children were given a month off school.

China
Those living in cities are four to six times more likely to die of lung cancer than those living in the country. Fifty-four out of 78 monitored rivers are seriously polluted with sewage and industrial waste.

UK
Sulphur dioxide levels in London exceed WHO safety standards. Has 4,800 toxic tips, 1,300 of them threatening groundwater supplies. In 1990 1.7 million Britons were drinking water with nitrate levels above the WHO recommendation. Almost 300 UK water supplies contain pesticides above levels permitted under EC law. Huge oil pollution from Shetland tanker disaster in 1993.

Italy
Pollution in cities is so bad that traffic is now banned from centre of Rome and Florence during the day. Huge annual algae plagues in the Adriatic caused by fertiliser nutrients washed into the sea.

Bangladesh
If global warming continues 18 per cent of the country will be under water by 2050.

USA
Ozone depletion helps to cause skin cancer, which kills 12,000 people a year. Has 10,000 hazardous waste dumps needing immediate clean up (cost $100 billion).

Malaysia
Forty major rivers are biologically dead due to industrial and agricultural waste.

Ethiopia
Global warming is causing climate change, disrupting rainfall patterns, leading to drought.

■ Activities

1 Draw up a list of the major problems and prioritise them in order of importance.

2 Suggest solutions. Remember that different countries have different priorities – no one wants to sacrifice growth in living standards, especially in Underdeveloped Countries, and no one wants to shoulder the expense of combatting pollution.

3 Write a joint communique to present to the UN outlining specific agreed proposals on combatting international pollution – what arguments would you use to persuade the various governments involved that urgent action was needed?

Hodder & Stoughton

© 1994 Paul Higginson. The publishers grant permission for multiple copies of this sheet to be made in the place of purchase for use solely in that institution.

Greenpeace V Government

THE GREENPEACE VIEW

Study the following extracts recently published by Greenpeace, a pressure group campaigning for greater environmental protection, in their *Greenpeace Campaign Report*.

In June of this year, as Greenpeace UK and the rock band U2 mounted their Stop Sellafield campaign which threatened the company with a mass protest at its gates, German Greenpeace activists were collecting samples of sand and mud from the beaches and rivers close to the Sellafield nuclear facility.

Analysis at universities in Germany and Britain found the samples contained high levels of radioactive caesium, americium and plutonium – sufficiently high for much of the coastal region of north-west England to be classified as nuclear waste according to safety standards required by German nuclear law.

Greenpeace reveals Britain's top 50 polluters… Greenpeace dumps barrels and skips of toxic effluent onto the doorstep of the Department of the Environment in London.

In October Greenpeace UK operated a Toxic Trade Patrol at major ports which regularly transit toxic cargoes. The UK is a major importer and exporter of toxic waste, including exports to the Third World.

A Greenpeace delegation meets with Secretary of State for the Environment Michael Howard to discuss, amongst other issues, toxic pollution of the North East Atlantic. Greenpeace climbs Eiffel Tower to hang a banner saying 'NON to legal pollution of the seas' as North East Atlantic Environment Ministers meet in Paris to negotiate a new Convention for the seas.

In a new study, specially commissioned by Greenpeace, scientists report that pollution from exhaust fumes may be as much as eighteen times higher for car drivers and their passengers compared to the air outside. While cyclists and pedestrians walking along the kerb are exposed to dangerous pollution levels, it is the vehicle drivers themselves who are the most exposed.

Meanwhile, the Government refused to acknowledge the severity of the health impacts caused by motor vehicles. Although the Department of the Environment is extending its pollution monitoring network, it is totally inadequate and will not even cover all major population areas. Meanwhile the Department of Transport continues to be wedded to the 'Great Car Economy' and has no policies to combat the expected increase in numbers of vehicles using the roads.

Greenpeace names top Welsh and Severn polluters. A public meeting was held in Aberystwyth, highlighting the threats to Cardigan Bay, home to bottlenose dolphins, from pollution and the development of the oil industry.

Greenpeace was given leave by the High Court on October 24th to carry out a Judicial Review on the National Rivers Authority, challenging whether it is carrying out its statutory duty to protect Britain's rivers and seas from pollution. A Judicial Review is a legal procedure where people affected by the decisions of public bodies, like the NRA, can challenge their decisions in court.

Reproduced by kind permission of Greenpeace

Hodder & Stoughton

© 1994 Paul Higginson. *The publishers grant permission for multiple copies of this sheet to be made in the place of purchase for use solely in that institution.*

Worksheet 2: continued

> **Death in small doses** Organochlorines, a major class of deadly toxic chemicals, targeted by Greenpeace during its 'No Legal Pollution' campaign, have been found to cause physical deformities, radical changes in sexual characteristics and reproductive failures in marine wildlife, particularly affecting top predators such as dolphins and seals. Now, new research shows alarmingly high levels of these chemicals in polar bears in Norway – and scientists believe that pregnancy rates in the bears have dropped dramatically this year. Human impacts have included reduced sperm counts in males, and learning difficulties in children contaminated through their mothers' breast milk.
>
> Organochlorines are a group of thousands of chemicals derived from the chlorine industry. Many are virtually non degradable in the marine environment and bioaccumulate in living creatures, including fish and concentrate as they pass up the food chain to marine mammals at the top.

Greenpeace has forced Britain to change direction regarding its policy on toxic discharge to the marine environment and on its policy on dumping radioactive waste at sea. After a successful campaign and with documents leaked to Greenpeace outlining the Government position on toxic pollution, signatories of the new Convention for the Protection of the Marine Environment of the North East Atlantic, meeting in Paris in September, managed to isolate the UK with its weak stance on toxic substances entering the seas. They also forced Environment Minister David McLean to back down on the UK's refusal to sign any agreement which included an outright ban on radioactive waste dumping at sea. The right to use its rivers and surrounding seas as a free conduit for industrial wastes has been the cornerstone of Britain's antiquated approach to industrial effluent management. Britain has also fought tooth and nail to retain the option to discard large radioactive structures, such as defunct nuclear submarines, into the sea.

Such policies have not only earned Britain the title of Dirty Man of Europe, but as the North East Atlantic's largest marine polluter, with around 12,000 industrial discharge pipes, they have been responsible for the catastrophic decline in the environmental quality of these seas over the past two decades.

An increasing number of scientists have been expressing concern over the North East Atlantic marine environment. Dr Susan Mayer, Director of Science at Greenpeace UK has warned that marine biologists think the oceans may be nearing breaking point, due in large part to the onslaught of persistent and bioaccumulative toxins entering the seas from industrial sources. 'There have been mass die-offs of seals and dolphins, outbreaks of cancer in fish, and dramatic declines in some populations of sea-birds'. The announcement that Britain had agreed to sign the new 'Clean Seas' convention in Paris was greeted with enthusiasm by Greenpeace campaigners. They could now celebrate a real victory after an intense campaign designed to dislodge the British Government from its view that the seas and rivers could endlessly cope with increasing burdens of toxic industrial waste streams.

Greenpeace's 'No Legal Pollution' campaign, nick-named the Waterbabies' Revenge, involved a six week tour of Britain's rivers and estuaries by the Greenpeace ship MV *Solo*, and region by region exposés of the country's top polluting companies. In terms of information management and logistics the campaign was the most complex Greenpeace UK had ever undertaken.

The campaign set out, specifically, to highlight the UK Government system of 'legal pollution'. Through the acquisition of 'consents to discharge', from the National River Authority (NRA) companies have been able to pour billions of litres of toxic effluent, completely legally, into Britain's rivers and the sea. Only if a company exceeded its 'consent' would it be open to prosecution, but in practice, prosecutions were few and far between.

All this is now set to change. The days of legal pollution and the 'consent system' are numbered. Britain, along with the other signatories of the North East Atlantic Convention has until the year 2000 to clean up its act. And Greenpeace is pledged to hold all the signatories to their commitment.

Reproduced by kind permission of Greenpeace

Hodder & Stoughton   © 1994   Paul Higginson. The publishers grant permission for multiple copies of this sheet to be made in the place of purchase for use solely in that institution.

Cumbria September 11th. 22 Greenpeace activists were arrested and 3 Greenpeace inflatables impounded following the action to block the Albright and Wilson discharge pipeline at Whitehaven in Cumbria. The pipeline is the largest single source of toxic heavy metals and phosphates into British coastal waters. Albright and Wilson are alleging £50,000 of damage was caused to their discharge pipeline by the protesters. The company had earlier been found guilty and fined £2,000 for pollution offences following a prosecution brought by Greenpeace. The action followed Albright and Wilson's refusal to close the pipeline and clean up their plant after being found guilty. Albright and Wilson are also suing Greenpeace for damages, alleged to be £250,000, for lost production caused by the action.

Reproduced by kind permission of Greenpeace

Hodder & Stoughton

© 1994 Paul Higginson. The publishers grant permission for multiple copies of this sheet to be made in the place of purchase for use solely in that institution.

THE GOVERNMENT VIEW

Examine the following extracts from recent booklets published by the Department of the Environment (*Cleaner Seas* and *Global Atmosphere and Air Quality*).

WASTE ENTERING THE SEA

Industrial waste may contain a range of contaminant substances from dilute acids to complex organic chemicals, and may only be discharged where a consent is given by the National Rivers Authority (NRA) in England and Wales, by the Department of the Environment in Northern Ireland or, in Scotland, by a river purification authority. The consent is based as far as possible on the ability of the receiving water to take the waste in question without serious adverse environmental effects. The NRA may also impose legally enforceable conditions including strict limits on particular substances. The discharge of toxic chemical waste outside these conditions is likely to be an offence

• Substances entering the sea as a result of human activities are a tiny proportion of its constituent materials, but they may still have an effect on marine life. However, scientific examination of the evidence for the North Sea and other UK coastal waters suggests that effects on marine life appear to be primarily the result of factors such as natural changes in the population of species and direct human impacts such as fishing rather than of contaminants in the sea.

• The most important source of such contaminants is rivers and coastal discharges making up about 40% of inputs to the North Sea. But in most cases dispersion of materials is such that effects cannot be detected more than a few miles from the coast or river mouth.

RADIOACTIVITY

In the seas around the UK, man-made radiation represents generally only about 2% of the normal background radiation from the Earth's surface, the sun and other natural sources. Discharges from the largest source of man-made emissions, the reprocessing plant at Sellafield, are now some 3% of what they were in 1979. New plant is planned for 1992 and discharges of the most radiologically significant nuclides are expected to remain at about 1986 levels.

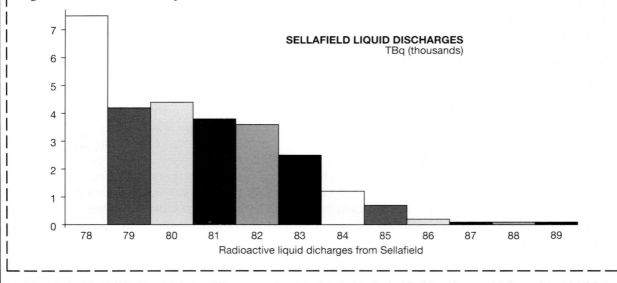

SELLAFIELD LIQUID DISCHARGES
TBq (thousands)

Radioactive liquid discharges from Sellafield

Hodder & Stoughton

© 1994 Paul Higginson. The publishers grant permission for multiple copies of this sheet to be made in the place of purchase for use solely in that institution.

VEHICLE EMISSIONS
The UK response

Since 1970 a series of increasingly stringent regulations on petrol vehicles have been implemented by the Government to bring CO emission limit values down by 50% and those for hydrocarbons and NOx down by over 30%. Smoke regulations on heavy diesels have been enforced to ensure that HGVs are properly maintained. The police have powers to test offending vehicles by the roadside.

New regulations to limit carbon monoxide and hydrocarbon emissions from in-service cars came into operation on 1st November 1991.

These limits are subject to enforcement at roadside spot checks and during the MOT test for cars over three years old.

Since 1990, all new vehicles have had to be capable of running on unleaded fuel. By the end of 1992, all new cars will require catalytic convertors to meet more stringent exhaust standards; these will have to use unleaded petrol as lead damages the catalyst. Unleaded petrol is now on sale at virtually all filling stations in the UK. The Government has introduced successive tax incentives in favour of unleaded fuel to encourage its wider use and adoption by motorists; it now accounts for over 43% of the UK market.

❑ Questions

1. Explain the meaning of;
   a) organochlorines,
   b) nondegradable,
   c) bioaccumulate,
   d) radioactive waste,
   e) legal pollution,
   f) Sellafield,
   g) the 'Great Car Economy',
   h) judicial review,
   i) toxic waste.

2. What methods does Greenpeace use in its campaign? List 10 tactics then prioritise them in order of effectiveness.

3. Can you detect any elements of bias in either the Greenpeace or government reports?

4. Do you agree with direct action by Greenpeace which breaks the law (e.g. blocking the outflow)? Is there any justification for this, and what are the advantages and disadvantages of using such tactics to achieve their aims?

5. Greenpeace says the government has been cautious in its reaction to environmental problems. Do you think this is true, and what reasons might the government give to explain its approach? (The Department of the Environment publishes free booklets explaining its position on environmental issues – address is in Additional Information p109.)

Hodder & Stoughton   © *1994 Paul Higginson. The publishers grant permission for multiple copies of this sheet to be made in the place of purchase for use solely in that institution.*

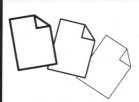

Worksheet 3
Pollution Checklist

Complete the table using the information provided in the main text and the other worksheets.

Type	Description	Causes	Results
Acid rain			
Ground level ozone			
Diffuse freshwater pollution			
Toxic algae			
Oil at sea			
Organochlorines and sea discharges			
Toxic waste			
Agrochemicals			

Hodder & Stoughton

© *1994 Paul Higginson. The publishers grant permission for multiple copies of this sheet to be made in the place of purchase for use solely in that institution.*

7 Global Warming, the Ozone Layer and Deforestation

Climate can be defined as a description of the long-term pattern or behaviour of the weather. Throughout the earth's history the climate has undergone great fluctuation, causing warm periods and ice ages. Some scientists predict that another ice age will begin in about 5,000 years, a result of small natural changes in the earth's orbit which result in the world receiving less solar energy from the sun. Other scientists have argued that other natural phenomena cause climate change, like volcanic activity or a natural fluctuation in the sun's power.

In recent years there has been an increase in the earth's average temperature.

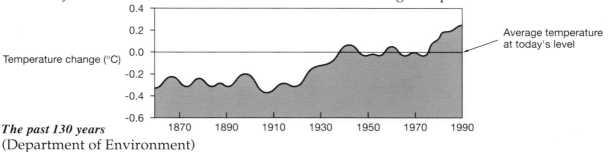

Temperature change (°C)

Average temperature at today's level

The past 130 years
(Department of Environment)

One of the main factors contributing to this global warming is the greenhouse effect.

WHAT IS THE GREENHOUSE EFFECT?

The earth is surrounded by a layer of natural gases (the greenhouse gases) which act like a greenhouse. They allow in solar energy and then stop some of the heat from escaping. Without these gases the earth would be frozen and lifeless, so they serve a vital purpose.

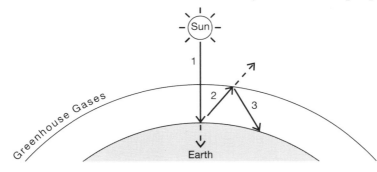

1 Sunlight enters the atmosphere unimpeded. About one-third is absorbed and heats the earth.
2 The earth radiates infra-red energy back into the atmosphere. This is absorbed by the gases. About 30 per cent escapes back into space.
3 Some heat is then sent back to earth by the greenhouse gases, which act as a blanket keeping the heat in.

Some of the greenhouse gases are natural (like water-vapour and carbon dioxide), some occur naturally but are also man-made (carbon dioxide, methane, nitrous oxide and ozone) and some are totally man-made (CFCs – chlorofluorocarbons).

Since the Industrial Revolution the production of carbon dioxide (CO_2) has increased dramatically and now accounts for about 60 per cent of the total man-made greenhouse gases.

Hodder & Stoughton © 1994 Paul Higginson. The publishers grant permission for multiple copies of this sheet to be made in the place of purchase for use solely in that institution.

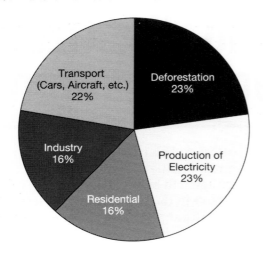

Contribution to carbon dioxide emissions from human activities

Some gases are more effective at causing global warming than others. CFCs are the most powerful (7,000 times stronger than carbon dioxide), and have a lifetime of around 100 years in the atmosphere. At present, CFC levels are increasing by 4 per cent per annum.

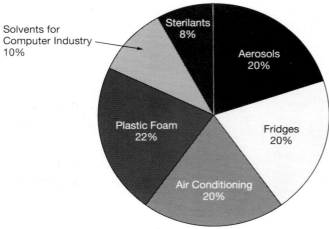

Where do CFCs come from?

Who produces the greenhouse gases? These graphs show where the main man-made gases come from.

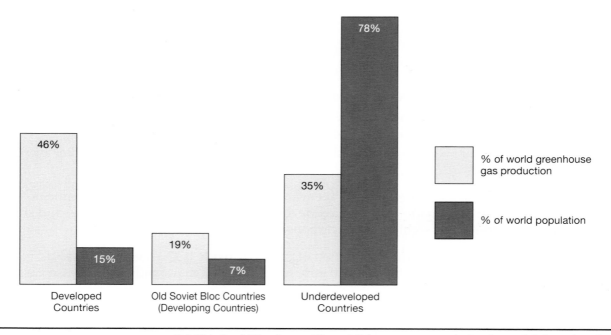

Hodder & Stoughton

© 1994 Paul Higginson. The publishers grant permission for multiple copies of this sheet to be made in the place of purchase for use solely in that institution.

The USA produces 5 tons of carbon emissions per person per annum. Nigeria produces 0.1 tons (the UK produces 2.8 tons). If we do not curb the emissions of greenhouse gases then most scientists predict that global warming will continue.

- In the last 100 years the earth has warmed by 0.5°C;

- The temperature in 1993 was 0.4°C higher than the average temperature from 1950 to 1980;

- The warmest seven years in the period 1900–90 were (in order) 1990, 1988, 1987, 1983, 1981, 1980 and 1976.

The earth's temperature will probably rise by 3°C by 2050. If this occurs it will almost certainly result in dramatic climate change. The difference in temperature between today's levels and an ice age is approximately 6°C. A rise of 3°C would make the world hotter than at any time for the last 2 million years.

THE FUTURE

Measuring and predicting the greenhouse effect is a complex matter. Bodies such as the Intergovernmental Panel on Climate Change (IPCC) have produced predictions by studying the following factors:

- the level of emissions of greenhouse gases based on changes in population, energy demand, industrial development, agricultural production and deforestation;

- the ways in which the greenhouse gases enter and leave the atmosphere;

- the annual average global temperatures in the last 100 years;

- the knock-on effects (often called 'feedbacks') of increased greenhouse gases such as the fact that a warmer atmosphere holds more water vapour, itself a greenhouse gas which leads to a further increase in temperature.

This graph shows the temperature rises predicted in the next century if no action is taken to decrease the greenhouse gases. It is impossible to predict the temperature rise with any great certainty but the best estimate puts the increase at around 3°C by 2050.

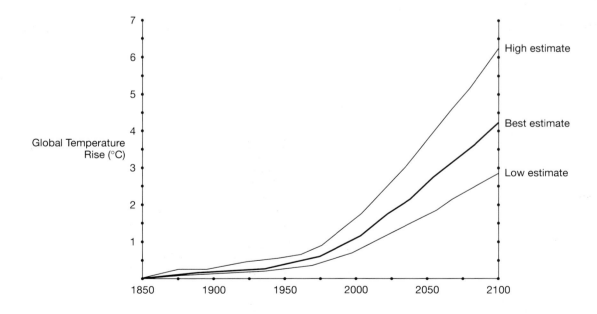

(Department of Environment)

Hodder & Stoughton

© 1994 Paul Higginson. The publishers grant permission for multiple copies of this sheet to be made in the place of purchase for use solely in that institution.

Global warming may affect our environment in many ways.

1 There may be a rise in the sea level, caused by the melting of polar ice sheets and glaciers and thermal expansion of the seas. Predictions range from 10 centimetres to 50 centimetres by 2050. (A 50 centimetre rise would permanently flood 12 per cent of Bangladesh and cause Egypt to lose 20 per cent of its arable land.) This would affect tides and the frequency and power of storms, resulting in the flooding and erosion of coastlines. Three thousand Pacific islands would disappear.

2 There may be changes in vegetation. Many native species could die and others (including weeds and pests) would be introduced as a result of migration or invasion. In Britain new crops like maize could be grown, but others may die out (potatoes are difficult to grow in warm climates because of their vulnerability to pests). Vast forests in Canada, Scandinavia and the old USSR could die. The wheat fields of the US mid-west could lose one-third of their harvest. Developing countries like Ethiopia, Somalia and parts of Asia will be hardest hit by desertification.

3 As trees and plants die out (with every 1°C rise in temperature, species will have to move approximately 100 kilometres polewards to survive) then so will the animals that depend on them.

4 Rainfall may be affected, leading to longer and more extensive droughts. This would have consequences for river flow and ground water storage. Tropical countries will experience more devastating storms and hurricanes.

WHAT IS BEING DONE?

EC countries have agreed to try to stabilise Community carbon dioxide emissions at 1990 levels by the year 2000. This could be achieved by energy efficiency and the greater use of renewable energy sources. The UN has proposed a world-wide action plan to reduce global warming with financial and technical assistance for Underdeveloped Countries to meet the requirements. In 1991 the EC proposed an energy tax of $10 per barrel of oil, and Germany, not content with merely stabilising emissions, announced the aim of a 30 per cent reduction by 2005. However, overall progress has been hindered by a number of powerful countries who argue that imposing carbon dioxide targets is interfering with national sovereignty. The USA, responsible for about a quarter of the world's carbon dioxide emissions, still refuses to accept that global warming is a major international problem and is unwilling to accept the reductions in US living standards that may follow on from a cut in CO_2 emissions.

THE OZONE LAYER

Ozone is a form of oxygen with three atoms instead of the usual two. The ozone layer is between 15 and 50 kilometres above the earth and forms a protective filter around the planet, absorbing ultraviolet (UV) radiation from the sun. Excessive UV radiation can have a damaging effect on the environment (including fish and marine life, crops, plants and trees) and human health, causing cataracts, skin cancer and suppressing the immune system, making it more difficult to fight off illness. In the USA alone, skin cancer causes 12,000 deaths per annum and at least 12 million people are blinded by cataracts every year.

Hodder & Stoughton

© 1994 Paul Higginson. The publishers grant permission for multiple copies of this sheet to be made in the place of purchase for use solely in that institution.

OZONE LAYER DEPLETION

Between 1979 and 1990, 3 per cent of the ozone layer was lost. In the spring of 1985 a huge hole in the ozone layer over the Antarctic was discovered (covering an area the size of the USA and as deep as Mount Everest). Recent satellite data has shown that there has been an 8 per cent decrease in ozone in the northern hemisphere each spring (this is double the original predictions). Chlorofluorocarbons (or CFCs) are the main cause of ozone depletion. These are man-made gases used as propellants in aerosols, in the production of foams (for use in furniture and packaging), and as coolants in refrigerators and air conditioning. They can last for up to 100 years in the atmosphere releasing chlorine, which changes the ozone into ordinary oxygen. The chlorine is regenerated and consequently takes part in many chemical reactions, helping to destroy thousands of molecules of ozone. The ozone hole which opens up over Antarctica every southern spring has not yet been matched by a similar hole over the Arctic, although many scientists expect this to happen very soon. Outside the polar regions the northern hemisphere is suffering 20 per cent depletion over Europe, North America, the old Soviet Union, Northern China, and Japan. In 1987 and again in 1990 most of the world's nations agreed the Montreal Protocol, which arranged to phase out CFCs by the year 2000, but many countries have since agreed an earlier phase out (1995 for the USA and the UK). A unique fund was created to help Underdeveloped Countries to afford the more expensive alternatives to CFCs. By 1989 the UK's consumption of CFCs was half that of 1986 and today fewer than 10 per cent of aerosols contain CFCs.

Depletion of the ozone layer will continue to worsen, and is expected to peak around the turn of the century. It will take over a century to fully recover. However, the crisis shows how quickly the international community can act to phase out dangerous chemicals when the environment is threatened.

INDIVIDUAL ACTION

1 Only buy fridges or freezers which display CFC-free stickers.

2 Take your old fridge to a CFC recovery scheme (organised by some companies and local councils).

3 Only buy furniture or insulation material that is CFC free.

4 Don't buy halon fire extinguishers.

5 Only use environmentally friendly aerosols.

6 Discuss this comment from a leading manufacturer 'We don't make CFCs for fun but because people need them.'

POSTSCRIPT

In spring 1992 the Canadian government issued daily bulletins monitoring UV radiation and advised people to wear sunglasses, cover up bare arms and legs and not allow children outside without sun-block cream.

The UN Environment Programme estimates that a sustained 20 per cent loss of ozone would result in an additional 600,000 skin cancers and 3 million more eye cataracts a year world-wide.

Hodder & Stoughton   © 1994 Paul Higginson. The publishers grant permission for multiple copies of this sheet to be made in the place of purchase for use solely in that institution.

Worksheet 1

Global Cooling

On the left are ideas which may lead to a reduction in global warming. For each point come up with a practical suggestion on how each goal might be achieved.

Goal	Practical Implementation
1 Reduce the carbon dioxide emissions from coal-burning power stations.	
2 Save energy in industry and the home.	
3 Reduce the carbon dioxide produced by cars.	
4 Enable Underdeveloped Countries to take steps to cut down on their emissions.	
5 Stop deforestation and increase forest land (the average tree absorbs 4 kilograms of CO_2 per annum).	
6 Prevent rich countries from producing greenhouse gases.	
7 Reduce the production and usage of CFCs.	
8 Reduce the obsession in Developed Countries with economic growth at any cost.	
9 Persuade consumers, companies and governments to reject the throwaway society.	

■ **Activity**

Which of the above would be most difficult to achieve and why?

Hodder & Stoughton

© 1994 Paul Higginson. The publishers grant permission for multiple copies of this sheet to be made in the place of purchase for use solely in that institution.

Worksheet 2
Deforestation

Carbon dioxide is the main greenhouse gas and one of the major factors contributing to the rise in carbon dioxide emissions is deforestation. Complete the boxes below in groups of three.

1   Functions of trees are…

2   In Developed Countries trees are dying because of…

3   In Underdeveloped Countries big business chops down trees because of…

4   Landless peasants chop down trees because of…

5   Stripped of trees, the soil becomes…

6   The result is d _ _ _ _ _ _ _ _ _ _ _ _ _ _

8   Possible solutions include…

7   This has significant consequences for animals and man: …

9   Wood-waste in rich countries could be cut by…

❖ **Discussion**

1   'Hamburgers come from cows. An American cow costs four times more than a Costa Rican cow. Therefore, forests are cut down in Costa Rica and grass is planted so cows can graze. Each hectare of land produces 1,600 burgers a year, all consumed in the affluent North. Over-grazing often leaves the land barren, leading farmers to cultivate more forest land, chopping down more trees. Costa Rican beef production doubled from 1959 to 1979 – however, beef consumption by native Costa Ricans fell in the same period by 40 per cent.'

2   Tropical forests cover 6 per cent of the world's surface but support 66 per cent of the world's plant and animal species.

Hodder & Stoughton

© 1994 Paul Higginson. The publishers grant permission for multiple copies of this sheet to be made in the place of purchase for use solely in that institution.

Worksheet 3
Test Yourself

Write short answers to the following questions.

1 Briefly explain the greenhouse effect (outlining why it is called the greenhouse effect).

2 What are the greenhouse gases and why have they increased in recent years?

3 List the three most important causes of increased carbon dioxide emissions.

4 What are CFCs and where do they come from?

5 How are predictions made about the extent of the greenhouse effect?

6 Outline the major consequences for the planet if global warming continues at the current rate.

7 Describe five ways in which global warming could be reduced.

8 What is being done to reduce global warming and why is progress so slow?

9 What is the ozone layer and what causes depletion?

10 What are the consequences of depletion of the ozone layer?

11 Briefly explain the Montreal Protocol.

12 Why is deforestation occurring?

13 What are the results of deforestation?

❖ **Discussion**

Debate this topic: 'This house believes that VAT on fuel is a good thing. The government should heavily tax all sources of energy in order to discourage excessive consumption, thereby reducing global warming. The revenue raised should then be used to invest in energy efficiency schemes for low-income households, and to help Underdeveloped Countries to conserve energy.'

Hodder & Stoughton

© 1994 Paul Higginson. The publishers grant permission for multiple copies of this sheet to be made in the place of purchase for use solely in that institution.

8 Animal Rights and Conservation

In recent years animal rights and conservation have become major ethical and environmental issues. Humans clearly have rights, but do animals and plants? What responsibilities do humans have towards the animal and plant kingdoms?

ANIMAL RIGHTS, FOR AND AGAINST

Study the arguments, ticking the ones you agree with.

For	Against
1 Animals feel pain, fear, pleasure, etc. and are very similar to humans in the way they mate, rear young, eat and think. Chimpanzees have 99 per cent of the genetic structure of humans.	Humans are superior to animals. They can reason, philosophise, worship God, use complex language systems, and are capable of real love – animals simply act on instinct.
2 God has given the earth to all his creatures – all living things have rights.	God created humans to have dominion over his creation – humans are different to animals because they have immortal souls.
3 It is morally wrong to exploit animals or cause them suffering.	Animals kill and exploit each other for food so why shouldn't we – it's the law of nature.
4 All living things are linked together in a complex ecological and environmental chain. If we destroy our wildlife we risk our own destruction by disturbing this delicate and finely-balanced system.	We must protect our environment but people must always come first. Human rights and poverty in Underdeveloped Countries are more important than animal rights.
5 All animals have rights and should not be discriminated against.	Where do you draw the line? What about rats, flies, amoebae and plants?

Discuss your views in the group. Perhaps you have ticked boxes on both sides. Is it possible to reconcile these two viewpoints?

ANIMAL RESEARCH

World-wide an estimated 200 million animals a year are used in laboratory experiments, and 3.5 million are killed each year in British laboratories. They are injected with diseases or drugs, exposed to radiation and toxic chemicals (often without anaesthetic). There are two main types of research. Almost all cosmetic and household products are tested first on animals. Standard international tests include the LD50 test (Lethal Dose 50 per cent toxity test) where animals are fed a product until half of them die (most detergents are tested in this way). The Draize eye test involves dropping products (like shampoo) into the eyes of rabbits for seven days and recording the results. As rabbits cannot blink this is an effective way of measuring damage to the eye. Pain-killers are rarely used in such tests.

In medical research animals have made a significant contribution to developing new drugs, medicines and surgical techniques; dog experiments were responsible for advances in kidney transplants and open-heart surgery, monkey research led to a vaccine against rubella and life support machines for premature babies, and rabbits were used to develop chemotherapy for leukaemia. Animals are currently being used in research into AIDS and heart disease. The ethical dilemma of using animals in research is summed up on p80.

Hodder & Stoughton

© 1994 Paul Higginson. The publishers grant permission for multiple copies of this sheet to be made in the place of purchase for use solely in that institution.

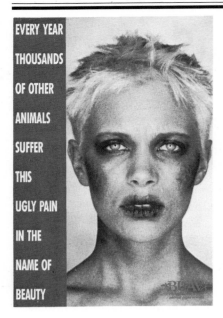

EVERY YEAR THOUSANDS OF OTHER ANIMALS SUFFER THIS UGLY PAIN IN THE NAME OF BEAUTY

For

1 Although the animals do suffer, this is outweighed by the benefits to mankind (thousands of people owe their lives to the medical advances made through research). Human suffering is more important than animal suffering.
2 There is no alternative to animal testing (other than testing on humans and this is morally unacceptable). For most purposes computer predictions or cells in culture cannot replace a whole animal.
3 Some of the research will benefit animals too as vets are able to use the drugs and techniques developed.

Against

1 It is unethical to inflict such pain and suffering on animals (even if it does lead to improvements in human health).
2 Tests can be misleading – Thalidomide and Opren passed animal safety tests but had disastrous side-effects on humans.
3 Other ways of testing should be used (computer simulation and test-tube research).
4 Much laboratory research concerns non-essential goods like cosmetics, detergents and pesticides. We know enough about these products already and further research is unnecessary.

❖ **Discussion**

'Scientists must abandon laboratories and factories of death', Pope John Paul II. Do you agree?

Zoos

A fierce argument is raging over whether zoos are cruel prisons for animals or important ways of conserving endangered species. Which of these points of view do you find most convincing?

'Most zoos take animals out of their natural environment and confine them in small spaces. The animals quickly become lethargic and unfit, they are often alone, have little opportunity or inclination to breed and are often given food they are not used to in the wild. Animals in zoos often display signs of anxiety, depression or 'psychosis' including pacing up and down, swaying from side to side and self-mutilation. They are robbed of dignity and demeaned, reduced to mere objects to entertain and amuse a gawping public.'

'Many zoos now have captive breeding and animal research programmes, helping to conserve threatened species and re-introducing animals back to the wild. They help educate the public, enable humans to see wild animals, provide pleasure, and encourage people to take an interest in conservation issues. Most modern zoos now try to recreate the animals' natural habitat, with social groups of animals placed in large enclosures.'

Hodder & Stoughton

© 1994 Paul Higginson. The publishers grant permission for multiple copies of this sheet to be made in the place of purchase for use solely in that institution.

1 If you have visited a zoo recently describe the condition of the animals. Were they exhibiting any signs of stress or anxiety or did they appear fairly contented?

2 When people visit zoos what impressions do they get of animals? Do zoos really educate and give people a true understanding of animals or do they merely entertain?

3 Anthropologists who visit zoos and observe the human visitors frequently report that people demand that the animals take notice of them by banging on the cages, teasing or waving. Why do people do this?

4 Establish a set of criteria that could be used for establishing whether a zoo was good or bad.

FACTORY FARMING

In an average lifespan a British meat-eater will consume 550 poultry, 36 pigs, 36 sheep and 8 cattle. Ninety per cent of all chicken and 55 per cent of all pig meat in Britain comes from factory farms. Below are descriptions of two such farms from a booklet produced by the Vegetarian Society.

Batteries for shorter life. Battery hens know no daylight and are crammed together so tightly, it's both difficult and painful to move. The birds' feet are grossly deformed due to the wire mesh of the cages' base. A huge build up of filth ensues. Increasingly desperate, the hens will begin to peck each other. But the farmers have an answer to this: cutting the beaks off every chick. Problem solved.

Broiler chickens – popular when roasted – fare no better. Up to 100,000 are jammed into a single room building. The floor of wood chips becomes a carpet of faeces. Here, bacteria, flies and rats flourish; even maggots are sometimes seen feeding on the birds. And the birds are forced to feed on the remains of each other.

Before being served on a plate, a sow is served on a rape rack. A metal-barred stall, with barely inches to move, is where 400,000 sows spend their entire four months' pregnancy. Half are tightly tethered and forced to lie in their own excreta. The sows are kept over a slatted concrete floor which creates almost inevitable spinal problems.

After giving birth in a small crate often on a perforated metal floor, the animal, pathetically trying to follow instinct, will attempt to 'build' a nest with non-existent materials. Her piglets are ripped away at five weeks old. Then it's back to the Rape Rack and forced insemination.

In an horrific irony, 'clapped out' sows which spend their lives as baby machines, very often end up as baby food for humans.

The Meat and Livestock Commission claims that the kinds of farm described above are rare in Britain, as government regulations are designed to ensure that factory farming is humane and controlled. It argues that the introduction of technology into animal production in the twentieth century has benefitted animals and consumers in a variety of ways:

The understanding of the principles of nutrition has led to better feed formulation, both in terms of whole diets to be fed to housed animals and of the supplementation of the rations of animals grazing, feeding on conserved grass, grains or arable by-products.

In parallel to the development of drugs for humans, drugs have been developed to facilitate the control and cure of animal diseases which have in the past caused many deaths and condemned many other animals to distressed and unproductive lives.

Animal breeding has become increasingly focused onto traits of economic significance and ways have been introduced to test and to measure the performance of potential breeding animals to provide a basis for objective selection – so speeding up the rate of genetic improvement.

Housing, built especially for animal production, has become increasingly sophisticated to provide better protection, temperature control and proper ventilation, and to allow the efficient feeding of animals and the disposal and utilization of their waste products with progressively less and less human labour.

A range of products has been developed to stimulate growth and to enhance the leanness of animals as consumer preference swung from fatty meat to a demand for lean meat.

Hodder & Stoughton © 1994 Paul Higginson. The publishers grant permission for multiple copies of this sheet to be made in the place of purchase for use solely in that institution.

Questions

1 Some meat and eggs are not produced in factory farms. Although such produce tastes better it tends to be much more expensive. Would you be prepared to pay more for food not produced in factory farms?

2 Food poisoning scares are now quite common. Government statistics show that there are up to two million salmonella infections per year in England and Wales (35 per cent caused by chicken and egg infection). BSE or 'mad cow disease' is probably caused by the recycling of sheep remains into animal feed. Why are such problems increasing and what are the possible solutions?

3 Do you agree that technology has benefitted animals and consumers? State reasons for your answer.

GENETIC ENGINEERING

Genes are essentially chemical messengers which make each of us similar to our species but individually different. They determine our appearance and behaviour and are passed from one generation to the next. Genetic engineering is the science of manipulating genes within or between organisms.

By passing genes from one species to another, scientists are able to develop bigger animals that grow faster, produce more meat and are more resistant to disease. Moreover scientists are developing and patenting new genetic life forms (designer animals) which can be used in medical research.

Questions

1 Researchers are trying to develop the 'perfect' carp (twice as big as usual) and the 'perfect' chicken (without feathers). What do you think of this?

2 Genetic engineering has led to new super crops, which produce more food and are less prone to disease. Is this acceptable?

3 Is genetic engineering going too far? Are humans playing at being God, or are they merely helping the process of evolution?

4 Is it morally acceptable for animal genes to be injected into humans for medical purposes (and vice versa)?

DISSECTION IN SCHOOLS AND COLLEGES

In Britain some examination boards require whole-animal dissection for A-Level Biology and Zoology (although it is no longer compulsory, and alternative papers can be set for those opposed to dissection).

Pros	Cons
• Some skills cannot be taught from books or models – they require practical application, a hands-on approach.	• It is better to study living animals.
• Students learn better by studying the real thing – it makes the subject more interesting.	• Dissection treats animals as disposable objects (thousands are bred solely for this purpose) thereby undermining student respect for life.
• It's important that we understand how animals' internal structures function – dissection is the best way to achieve this.	• We can learn just as much about biology from models, books and computer programs.

Hodder & Stoughton   © 1994 Paul Higginson. The publishers grant permission for multiple copies of this sheet to be made in the place of purchase for use solely in that institution.

1 Discuss the arguments outlined above. Can you add any other pros and cons to the list?

2 Is dissection essential for a student at university who is studying to become a vet?

3 Medical students have to dissect humans as part of their training. Is this acceptable? Give reasons for your answer.

BIOLOGICAL DIVERSITY

Biodiversity is the variety of biological forms within an environment. It is essential to conserve and protect the richness of the world's plant and animal species, most of which are found in Underdeveloped Countries. Only about 1.7 million species have been identified but scientists estimate that there are between five and forty million (including approximately half a million flowering plants). This diversity needs to be conserved for a variety of reasons.

1 Many plant and animal species provide us with food and materials for industry. Crop diversity is crucial in case our current staples like wheat and maize become diseased. We are also continually discovering new foods.

2 Half of all medicines come from plants – morphine comes from poppies, Amazonian trees provide quinine. Disappearing species mean a loss of potential cures.

3 All species, including humans, are part of a complex chain, relying and depending on each other. The loss of one plant can result in the loss of up to 30 animals and insects which rely upon it. If enough links in the chain are broken our own survival may be at stake.

4 When species disappear the world inevitably becomes a less beautiful, less interesting place.

However, the world is moving towards uniformity rather than diversity. Species are being lost at a rate of almost three a day – by 2050 half of all species alive today could be extinct. In recent years over 90 per cent of Brazilian coastal forest has disappeared due to industrial and agricultural development. The population of the African elephant has halved in ten years largely because of poaching. Half the tropical rainforests have disappeared and the rest are being destroyed at a phenomenal rate (an area the size of England every year). The sea's equivalent of the rainforests are the coral reefs, which contain one-third of all the world's fish species and are between 5,000 and 10,000 years old. These too are fast disappearing. There are four reasons for this huge decline in animal and plant life:

- pollution;

- destruction of the natural habitat because of industrial or agricultural development;

- over-hunting and over-fishing;

- trade in wildlife (now worth over $1,500 million per annum).

❑ Questions

1 Does it really matter whether the Madagascan rosy periwinkle survives or not? Explain your answer.

2 Crops must be inbred with other strains, often wild ones, every ten years or so. Why?

3 Which of the above four reasons for species loss do you think is the most damaging? Explain your answer.

4 Many biologists see this enormous loss of species as the greatest threat to mankind's survival in the world today. Why is this, and what can be done to prevent it?

Hodder & Stoughton   © 1994 Paul Higginson. The publishers grant permission for multiple copies of this sheet to be made in the place of purchase for use solely in that institution.

Worksheet 1
Rights and Wrongs

Listed below are ten things that humans do to animals. In the spaces list as many examples as you can, deciding whether you feel such examples are acceptable or unacceptable. In no. 1, for example, where would you put horse racing, fox-hunting, fishing, greyhound racing, grouse-shooting, cock-fighting, stag-hunting and bull-fighting?

	Acceptable	Unacceptable
1 animals in sport		
2 use as food		
3 pets		
4 medical experiments		
5 use in clothing		
6 working animals		
7 use as an ornament		
8 animals in captivity		
9 method of pest control		
10 entertainment		
11 farm animals		
12 use in advertising and the media		
13 putting animals down		
14 testing household products		

Discuss your findings in groups. What criteria did you use to enable you to decide whether something was acceptable or unacceptable?

Hodder & Stoughton

© 1994 Paul Higginson. The publishers grant permission for multiple copies of this sheet to be made in the place of purchase for use solely in that institution.

Fox-hunting

Read each point below, tick the arguments you find the most convincing, then share your views with the group.

For	Against
1 There is no deliberate cruelty in fox-hunting; the kill is either outright or the fox gets away. Foxes look cuddly but they do not have human feelings. Townspeople get sentimental about foxes (but not rats!).	It is cruel. The terrified fox is forced to run until exhausted and is then ripped apart by hounds. As close relatives of the dog, foxes can feel fear and pain in the same way.
2 Fox-hunting farmers help to conserve the countryside and the habitat most suited to wildlife, acting as a brake on commercial land management.	Landowners and farmers plant hedgerows and woodland for important reasons (shelter, screening, landscaping, wildlife conservation). The abolition of hunting would not lead to a wholesale destruction of hedgerows and copses.
3 Over 200,000 people enjoy hunting – it is a broad-based popular activity.	Public opinion is on the whole opposed to it.
4 It provides employment for about 1,000 people.	If something is cruel and unethical it should be abolished whatever the cost in jobs.
5 Foxes are a pest to farmers and game rearers. In a survey financed by the League Against Cruel Sports 30 per cent of farmers experienced significant losses from foxes in the preceding 12 months.	Ministry of Agriculture studies have shown that foxes pose little threat to lambs. There is a threat to free-range poultry, but this can be overcome by strong or electrified fencing. The fox's natural diet is actually helpful to most farmers (rabbits, voles, rats and scavenged carcasses of animals and birds).
6 If hunting were abolished it would still be necessary to control foxes by other methods (gassing, trapping, snaring and shooting). In such instances death is not necessarily instantaneous (unlike hunting).	Some studies have shown that attempts to artificially control foxes may be counter-productive: nature may simply compensate for any losses by increasing the number of cubs that vixens produce. A Bristol University survey said 'fox-hunts play no significant role in the control of fox populations'.
7 Hunts are not primarily about a bloodthirsty 'kill', but rather the working of the hounds and the horses, and the thrill of the chase.	Drag hunting, in which the hunt follows a specially laid trail, allows all the excitement without the need for a live animal.

Hodder & Stoughton

© 1994 Paul Higginson. *The publishers grant permission for multiple copies of this sheet to be made in the place of purchase for use solely in that institution.*

Vegetarianism

A vegetarian is someone who does not eat fish, flesh or fowl. One person in 17 in the UK is vegetarian (6 per cent of the population) and over 40 per cent of the population are cutting back on meat consumption (naming health as the main reason). One in 14 women is a vegetarian compared to 1 in 24 men. One in 8 women aged 16 to 24 is a vegetarian, along with 11 per cent of the student population. It is a growing movement – 28,000 people give up meat each week. The statements below are based on information provided by the Vegetarian Society and the Meat and Livestock Commission. Some of the arguments contradict each other – so who is right? Tick the statements you support and place a cross next to those you disagree with.

1. Meat contains many more chemicals and pesticides than plant food. It can also contain cancer-causing substances. A vegetarian diet can reduce cancer rates by 30 per cent.
2. Humans are biologically omnivores – designed to eat a whole range of foods including meat. They have the teeth of an omnivore and the gut is certainly not that of a vegetarian. Humans have eaten meat for thousands of years.
3. The world's cattle consume a quantity of feed equal to the calorific needs of nearly double the human population of the planet. Yet 500 million people in the world are severely malnourished.
4. In 1990–1 there was a world grain surplus of some 333 million tonnes. If these grain stocks are not fed to the world's starving this is a political problem unconnected with meat eating.
5. All the protein, vitamins and minerals the body needs can be obtained through vegetables, cereals, fruit, nuts and beans (which contain no unwanted saturated fat).
6. Meat has many obvious nutritional benefits as part of a balanced diet. It is an excellent source of protein, B vitamins and minerals such as iron and zinc. Fat can be trimmed or otherwise removed. The fat content of lean beef is low, only 4.4 per cent, compared to Edam cheese (25 per cent and chocolate 30 per cent).
7. Vegetarians have a 30 per cent less incidence of heart disease (the biggest killer in Britain).
8. Britain has the highest rate of heart disease in the EC but the second lowest meat consumption per head. France has the highest meat consumption rate and lowest heart disease rate.
9. There are 1,000 cases of food poisoning recorded every week. Of these 95 per cent are meat and poultry-related. Unreported cases are estimated to be much higher.
10. Food poisoning occurs because people fail to observe the required standards of hygiene when preparing meat. It's the caterer – not the meat – that's to blame.
11. To satisfy the insatiable meat demands of the West, 40 per cent of the world's cereal harvest goes to feed livestock. It actually takes 10 pounds of grain to produce just 1 pound of beef.
12. Even after grain is fed to animals we still have a surplus of grain in this country. Whether it could or should go to help food aid is another matter – such decisions are reached by politicians and governments.
13. Modern factory farming and slaughterhouse techniques are systematic production lines of misery and prolonged death for animals.
14. All farm animals should have the best kind of treatment possible. Intensive farming, at first hailed as providing livestock with shelter and ready access to food and water, should be phased out. Animals, however, are here to be utilised by man.
15. In Britain the biggest polluters of water are not chemical manufacturers but meat producers. Animal sewage (slurry) is over a hundred times more polluting than human sewage. Moreover, half the world's rainforests have already been destroyed to provide land for meat production (adding to global warming).
16. Environmental problems must be tackled by governments. Polluters must be stopped and deforestation (caused by the poverty of Underdeveloped Countries) controlled by international political agreements.

Hodder & Stoughton

© 1994 Paul Higginson. The publishers grant permission for multiple copies of this sheet to be made in the place of purchase for use solely in that institution.

9 Population

The population of the world is now 5.5 billion. Each year another 95 million people are added: about 250,000 per day or three every second. Every 11 years the population grows by another billion and if present trends continue the world population will reach 14 billion by 2100. However, the UN expects the population to stabilise at around 10.2 billion in the middle of the next century. Over 90 per cent of all births occur in developing Southern countries, which will experience a 25 per cent increase in the next 10 years. In the industrialised world, however, the population will grow by only 5 per cent during this period. This fact has led many to talk of a population explosion in Underdeveloped Countries which may lead to mass hunger and starvation.

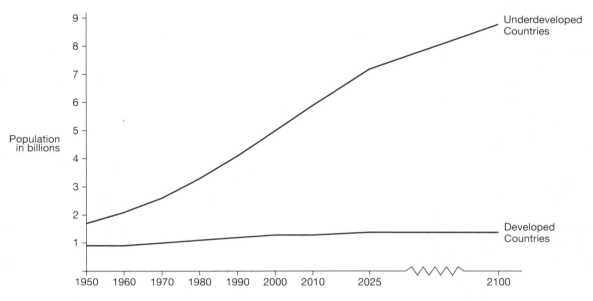

World population growth

To calculate the world's population, add together Underdeveloped and Developed World figures (for example, in 1990 the world's population was 5.3 billion).

THE DEMOGRAPHIC TRANSITION AND THE NORTH

Until the seventeenth century the population in the North grew very slowly because there were only slightly more births than deaths. The subsequent rise in population was not due to an increase in births but rather a decrease in deaths as infant mortality rates fell and life-expectancy rose. There were **three** reasons for this.

1 Better and more food led to improved health.
2 Clean water and better drainage systems lessened the spread of disease.
3 Public health was improved by the wealth produced by industrialisation, which led to cheaper and more available medicine, washable clothing, cheap soap, etc.

Initially, therefore, the population grew rapidly and it almost doubled in Britain in the 40 years from 1811 to 1851. However, as people began to realise that most of their children would survive, the birth rate began to fall. It became expensive to feed, clothe and educate a child, particularly when they stayed on longer at school, and were therefore not contributing to the family income by working. It is estimated that the cost of supporting a child to the age of 18 is over £80,000 in the UK. Eventually birth and death rates levelled out again, the UK population is now stable at about 56 million, and in Sweden and Denmark the population is in decline. This phenomenon of population rise and decline is known as the 'demographic transition'.

Hodder & Stoughton   © *1994 Paul Higginson. The publishers grant permission for multiple copies of this sheet to be made in the place of purchase for use solely in that institution.*

Southern Population Growth

Most Underdeveloped Countries are growing at a rate of between 2 and 4 per cent per annum. Kenya's population will double in 17 years. Reasons for this growth are:

1 reduction in death rates from diseases such as smallpox and malaria;

2 a high birth rate; six to eight children per family as opposed to two in the North. Children are an economic resource from the age of 7 when most will start working. (In Bangladesh boys already earn more than they consume by the age of 10). Moreover, if infant mortality rates are high, it makes sense for people to have a lot of children to ensure that enough survive to provide security for their parents in old age. Hence in Africa 45 per cent of the population is under 15 years old.

However, these countries are the ones least able to cope with rapid population growth and the result is that economic growth and development can be slowed down, unemployment rises, health care is adversely affected and education suffers.

It has been argued that only when people have financial security will the birth rate decline but this demographic transition has been challenged by the Worldwatch Institute, which claims that in Underdeveloped Countries social alienation, not economic worries, leads to large families: economic development breaks up traditional community life and the extended family by driving people into big cities, destroying their natural environment and causing them to worry about their old age.

Can the World Feed Itself?

Two views have emerged in answer to this question. Which do you agree with?

'There is a limited amount of food, resources and jobs in the world and more people means less for everyone. Unless the population can be reduced the only way of maintaining the balance between resources and population is through famine, epidemics and war.'

'Society needs to be structured differently; there is plenty of food for all, it is just that the poor do not have the same access to these resources as the rich. Population growth will slow once the world's resources are shared out more equitably with people in the South.'

■ Activities

1 Suggest reforms that might result in the structural changes described in the second extract.

2 The average person in the North eats 30 to 40 per cent more than he or she needs, while the average person in the South gets 10 per cent less than he or she needs. How and why has this situation come about?

Rapid Urbanisation

In 1800 only 5 per cent of the world's total population lived in towns. By 1990 this figure had risen to 40 per cent and by 2010 it will be over 50 per cent. Where there are roads, housing, employment, social services, adequate food and sanitation, etc., a high density population does not necessarily decrease the quality of life. The Netherlands has over 400 people per square kilometre, Japan has 340, and both are highly urbanised and very wealthy, yet Somalia, a rural country, has less than 10 people per square kilometre and is one of the world's poorest.

The most rapid urbanisation is taking place in Underdeveloped Countries: Mexico City, Sao Paulo and Calcutta have doubled their populations in less than 20 years bringing the infrastructure of these cities to breaking point. Poor conditions in the countryside lead people to this mass exodus to the cities in the hope of improving their social and economic position. For the many people living in overcrowded slums with poor sewage systems and sanitation, there is little hope of employment or improvement. Overcrowding can also lead to crime, violence and other social problems. Most of the resources (and aid) in a poor country tend to be concentrated in the cities and towns and the only way to counteract the migration is to direct more resources to rural areas to try and convince people to remain where they are.

Hodder & Stoughton

© 1994 Paul Higginson. The publishers grant permission for multiple copies of this sheet to be made in the place of purchase for use solely in that institution.

❏ Questions

1 Suggest reasons why the world's population will probably peak at around ten billion.

2 Britain's population is ageing, i.e. the number of old people is rising dramatically. Why is this, and what problems does it pose for the rest of society (and for younger people)?

3 Do you believe that the demographic transition will occur in Underdeveloped Countries in the way it has done in the North? Can you see any flaws in the Worldwatch argument?

4 Thomas Malthus (1766-1834), a wealthy English landowner, believed that food supply can only increase by the same amount every few years (for example from 2 to 4 to 6 to 8), whereas the population will multiply by the same proportion every few years (for example from 2 to 4 to 16 to 32). Therefore, the population will eventually overtake food supply and the result will be starvation. Has Malthus been proved right or wrong? Explain your answer.

5 'High density urban populations are not necessarily poor.' What factors determine whether or not they are?

6 What problems does rapid urbanisation pose for Underdeveloped Countries?

7 The Roman Catholic Church opposes artificial birth control on moral grounds because it feels that it is frustrating God's purpose for the sex act i.e. sex is for procreation as well as a way of deepening a relationship. Therefore all sex must be open to the possibility of conception. What do you think about this viewpoint and what relevance does it have to the situation in Underdeveloped Countries?

8 China has slowed down its population growth by introducing tough one-child per family legislation. What implications does this have on; a) civil liberties, b) child socialisation in the family? Do you agree with such a policy?

9 Some politicians have argued that only certain people should be allowed to have children (such as university graduates or those with a high IQ). Think of arguments for and against this proposal.

10 Many cities in Underdeveloped Countries will double their populations in the next 20 years. List the changes that would take place in your village, town or city if its population were to double.

Hodder & Stoughton © 1994 Paul Higginson. The publishers grant permission for multiple copies of this sheet to be made in the place of purchase for use solely in that institution.

Slowing Population Growth

The North-South Report of 1980 said that 'whether a hopelessly overcrowded planet in the next century can be averted depends on what is done now to hasten the stabilisation of population'. Below are some ideas to slow down population growth – which would you propose to the UN as most effective and morally acceptable? Rank them in order of importance by numbering from 1 to 13 in the boxes.

1 Pass laws which only allow parents to have one child, as in China (if parents have more than one they lose various benefits).

2 Encourage people to marry later.

3 Sterilisation programmes (voluntary or compulsory). Food and money could be used as an incentive, as in India.

4 Increase old age pensions and benefits so that children are not needed as an insurance policy.

5 Improve family planning services so contraception is available for all.

6 Improve living standards so that the economic incentive to have more children disappears.

7 Extend abortion facilities (at present 1 in 4 pregnancies is aborted).

8 Promote women's equality – provide alternatives to childbearing through education and employment.

9 Improve agricultural technology, removing the need for families to produce children as cheap labour.

10 Improve health care so that all children survive into adulthood and parents can plan their family size more precisely.

11 Improve education – this generally leads to better jobs and smaller families.

12 Pay money to people who use contraception (as in Thailand and Bangladesh).

13 Remove child benefits and allowances.

• Compare your ranking with the rest of the group and produce a class ranking.

• Which ideas do you feel are morally unacceptable and why?

Hodder & Stoughton

© 1994 Paul Higginson. The publishers grant permission for multiple copies of this sheet to be made in the place of purchase for use solely in that institution.

Analyse the following differences between rich Northern and poor Southern countries.

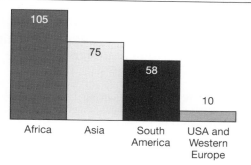

Infant mortality, i.e. the number of infant deaths per 1,000 live births

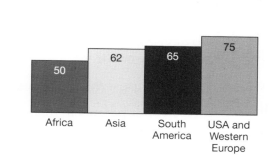

Life expectancy

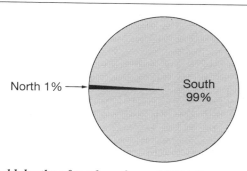

World deaths of mothers from childbirth

Percentage of women using modern contraception

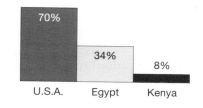

Percentage of people under 15 in total population

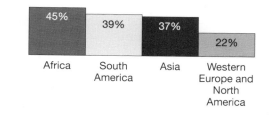

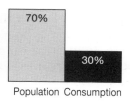

Consumption of world's resources compared to population

❑ Questions

1. Why do high infant mortality rates lead to population growth?
2. Why is life expectancy so much greater in the North than the South?
3. Why do most deaths of women in childbirth occur in the South? In what ways could this problem be tackled?
4. List the different types of modern contraceptives. What reasons might there be for such low usage in Underdeveloped Countries?
5. Some countries ban or restrict access to contraception (e.g. Saudi Arabia, Libya, Malta, Ireland). Why is this?
6. Why do countries with a high percentage of young people experience rapid population growth?
7. The North has a disproportionate share of the world's resources. In what ways might this lead to further population growth in the South?

Hodder & Stoughton

© *1994 Paul Higginson. The publishers grant permission for multiple copies of this sheet to be made in the place of purchase for use solely in that institution.*

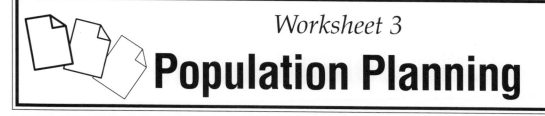

Population Planning

WHY HAVE CHILDREN?

If people want to have children then all the best contraceptive advice in the world will achieve little. In order to devise a realistic population programme it is essential to understand why people in the South have children.

1   It makes economic sense – children work and bring in money for the family.

2   Children can look after parents in their old age. As traditional extended families break up due to development, parents become more insecure about their future.

3   High infant mortality means that in Ethiopia, for example, a woman must have ten children to be 95 per cent certain of having a surviving adult son.

4   Many women fear infertility, which results in early and frequent childbearing.

5   Contraception is often avoided out of fear of side-effects.

6   Contraception may be expensive, difficult to obtain or banned.

You are given £100,000 by the UN to devise and organise a population programme in Ethiopia. In groups of three decide how you will spend the money and write a short leaflet or A4 sheet which will be distributed to get across your message.

COPING WITH POPULATION GROWTH

Imagine you are the local government of Mexico City. Your population is currently 20 million people (the largest city in the world). By 2013 this population will have nearly doubled. How are you going to plan for this growth? Under various headings such as Housing, Employment, Crime, Education, Energy, Health, Pollution, and Food, list the consequences of rapid population growth, then draw up plans to try and cope with these consequences. One final point to consider: how are your plans going to be paid for – where will the money come from?

Hodder & Stoughton

© 1994 Paul Higginson. The publishers grant permission for multiple copies of this sheet to be made in the place of purchase for use solely in that institution.

10 Energy

Energy, mainly in the form of electricity, is vital to industrial development; world consumption increases every year. However, many questions hang over the way we produce electricity in ever-larger quantities. Should we continue to burn coal, oil and gas, thereby gradually damaging our environment, should we opt for nuclear power, which poses potentially catastrophic risks? Or should we look to renewable energy sources such as solar or wind power which are safe but which may not be able to produce sufficient quantities of energy to meet world demands at current levels?

WORLD ENERGY

It is difficult to quantify world energy consumption but this graph gives an approximate breakdown.

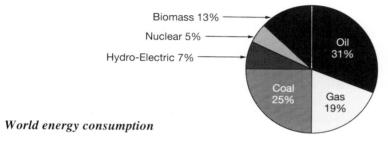

Biomass 13%
Nuclear 5%
Hydro-Electric 7%
Oil 31%
Coal 25%
Gas 19%

World energy consumption

The countries of the North use far more energy than those in the South. The USA has just 6 per cent of the global population yet consumes 30 per cent of the energy. India, with 20 per cent of the population, uses just 2 per cent of the world's energy. The average American consumes twice as much energy as the average Briton and 150 times more than the average Bangladeshi.

Northern countries rely in the main on electricity generation, but many Southern countries use biomass – vegetable matter used as an energy source (such as wood, straw and animal dung). In Ethiopia and Nepal 90 per cent of all energy consumed is biomass and 40 per cent of all Southern energy needs are met in this way. Many tractors in Africa are now being converted so they can use sunflower oil instead of diesel.

FOSSIL FUEL ENERGY

Coal, oil and natural gas are the major fossil fuels, and they provide the main fuel source for the generation of electricity. When these fossil fuels are burnt the heat produced turns the blades of a steam turbine which generates electricity. However, by-products of the process such as sulphur dioxide and carbon dioxide pass into the atmosphere and cause acid rain and global warming. Another problem with fossil fuels is that supplies are limited; estimates vary but world coal supplies will probably only last another 200 years, oil and gas another 100 years.

NUCLEAR ENERGY

Eleven per cent of electricity in Western Europe is now produced by nuclear power (three-quarters of all France's electricity is nuclear). Uranium is packed into fuel rods, which are put into the core of a nuclear reactor. Nuclear fission occurs when the nuclei of the uranium break apart when struck by neutrons. A chain reaction of neutrons bombarding and splitting other nuclei produces a huge amount of energy. This heats a coolant which is then channelled away to produce the steam required for electricity generation. One ton of uranium produces the same energy as 25,000 tons of coal. Britain's first reactor was the Magnox, but new improved types are the advanced gas cooled reactor (AGR) and the pressurised water reactor (PWR).

Hodder & Stoughton

© 1994 Paul Higginson. The publishers grant permission for multiple copies of this sheet to be made in the place of purchase for use solely in that institution.

RENEWABLE ENERGY

The sun warms the earth and drives the wind and waves. The amount of solar energy received by the earth each year is the equivalent of the planet's entire stock of fossil fuel reserves. Therefore if ways could be found to harness the sun's power then all the world's energy needs could be met. Current renewable energy sources are hydropower, wave, wind, solar and geothermal power.

HYDROPOWER

Hydropower is already used to produce one-fifth of the world's electricity. Power is obtained by damming a river, which provides a steady flow of water, which in turn rotates a turbine, thereby generating electricity.

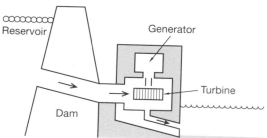

A cut-away view of a hydropower station

The potential for exploitation of hydropower in Underdeveloped Countries is immense. China plans to produce most of its electricity in this way by the year 2000, and the World Energy Conference has said that hydro output could conceivably rise fourteen-fold. However, although this form of energy production does not pollute the atmosphere, there are drawbacks. Giant dams flood land (in Brazil it is often rainforest) and displace people from their homes (several million in China). Water pressures can cause earthquakes and dry up water supplies downstream. Moreover, in the tropics dam-reservoirs are an ideal breeding ground for the carriers of malaria and river-blindness.

TIDAL AND WAVE POWER

A tidal power station at the mouth of the River Rance in France channels tidal waters into 24 tunnels, each housing a turbine generator which can operate whatever the direction of the tide. The plant provides electricity for about one million consumers. In Britain it has been estimated that the Severn Estuary could provide 5 per cent of our total electricity needs. Clearly tidal power can only be harnessed in certain areas, and large plants can damage wildlife habitats and alter sea levels down the coast. Wave power, still in its infancy, relies on the movement of floating rafts or ducks. The main problem has been to devise structures which can resist the damaging force of the waves without continual maintenance. Most countries are now involved in developing wave technology.

WIND POWER

Windmills have been used for centuries for grinding corn, but modern variants, in the main three-bladed propeller turbines, are now used to provide electricity. Fifty thousand are now in operation and 90 per cent of these are in California, which hopes to get 8 per cent of its energy from the wind by the year 2000. Wind farms are usually located on hills and coasts (but could be placed at sea) and are ideal for supplying power to remote locations; two huge turbines now provide much of the energy requirement on the Orkney Islands. The Department of Energy has estimated that wind power could meet about a fifth of the annual demand for electricity in the UK by 2020. The only disadvantages are the ugliness of huge wind farms blighting the countryside and coastline and the loud noise generated by the turning blades.

SOLAR POWER

One of the simplest sources of power is sunshine – direct solar energy. Ninety per cent of homes in Cyprus have solar panels to heat water and the world's largest solar power station in California has nearly 2,000 mirrors reflecting sunlight into a central collector. Solar (or

Hodder & Stoughton © 1994 Paul Higginson. *The publishers grant permission for multiple copies of this sheet to be made in the place of purchase for use solely in that institution.*

'photovoltaic') cells are becoming cheaper and more efficient and are ideal for producing electricity in remote locations. Solar power is clearly more suited to sunny regions of the world, and is currently more expensive than other forms of energy production.

GEOTHERMAL POWER

All of the energy the world may ever need is located in the top five miles of the earth's crust. Slow radioactive decay of elements within the earth produces great heat and when this is collected using water pumped down boreholes the steam produced can drive turbines on the surface. Tests in Cornwall have shown that geothermal power could eventually provide energy for the UK equivalent to 10 billion tons of coal. However, most geothermal energy is widely dispersed and can only be successfully harnessed in a few suitable locations where there is a high concentration and easy accessibility (as in Iceland, which heats most of its homes in this way). Moreover, geothermal drilling has been linked to an increase in earthquakes.

RUBBISH

In Sweden refuse incinerators burn about half the country's domestic refuse, thereby heating local homes. Decomposing rubbish dumped in the ground produces methane gas which is extracted to provide energy at more than 30 sites in the USA.

❏ Questions

1   Why is there such a huge discrepancy in energy consumption between North and South?

2   During the 1970s Western oil consumption fell back dramatically. Why was this?

3   What is the difference between renewable and non-renewable energy?

4   What kind of incentives and encouragement should governments give to promote renewable energy?

5   Which of the renewable sources would be best suited for Britain and why?

CHERNOBYL AND ITS AFTERMATH

On 26 April 1986, the world's worst nuclear accident occurred at Chernobyl in the USSR (now the Ukraine). Operators made a mistake when testing a reactor and in order to correct this they overrode a series of safety systems designed to prevent an accident. The result was a split-second surge in power which blew aside a 1,000 tonne steel lid, releasing enormous quantities of radiation. Thirty-five people died from the blast and the subsequent radiation, and 135,000 people were permanently evacuated from a 30 kilometre radius around the plant. In 1989 a further 100,000 people were removed because of fears concerning deformities amongst livestock and huge increases in cancers among the human population. Estimates of the numbers who will die of cancer from Chernobyl-related radioactive exposure range from 9,500 (UK Atomic Energy Authority) to a final toll of one million predicted by some US experts.

In Britain, wind currents and heavy rains after the explosion led to high levels of radiation in North Wales, Cumbria and Scotland and millions of sheep were deemed unfit for human consumption.

Recent data from the Ukraine reveals that 7 million people are still living in areas of high contamination, and general health problems and infant deaths have multiplied. The genetic consequences are not yet known.

Chernobyl marked the end of the global love affair with nuclear power as the easy answer to the world's energy crisis. Public opposition to building new plants rose from 44 per cent to 82 per cent in West Germany and from 65 per cent to 83 per cent in the UK. The USA slowed down its nuclear programme, the UK has cancelled all plans for new power stations after the new Sizewell plant is completed, and many countries abandoned proposals to begin operating nuclear plants. Although nuclear output is still rising as plants are completed and come on stream, few new power stations are being built. As old plants are closed and not replaced, the nuclear power industry may eventually come to a slow and expensive end.

Hodder & Stoughton

© 1994 Paul Higginson. The publishers grant permission for multiple copies of this sheet to be made in the place of purchase for use solely in that institution.

BRITAIN'S ENERGY PROBLEMS

Britain's energy comes from five sources.

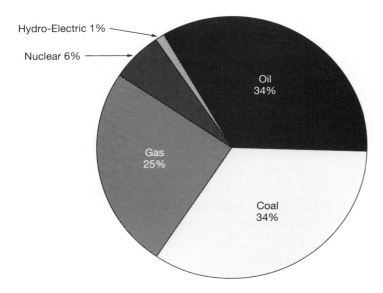

Our coal supplies will last for another 300 years, but gas and oil reserves will only last about another 75 to 100 years. These fossil fuels damage the environment so what alternatives might be used in the UK?

Nuclear power is a possibility but is it safe? The nuclear industry has produced figures which show the sources of radiation exposure for the UK population.

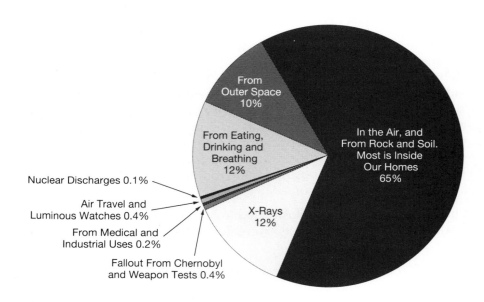

British Nuclear Fuels Limited (BNFL) claims, therefore, that 87 per cent of radiation is from natural sources and less than 0.1 per cent comes from the nuclear power industry.

However, opponents of nuclear energy claim that this is missing the point – although current nuclear discharge may be small in the UK it would only take one accident to produce the most catastrophic loss of life and lasting damage to the planet (BNFL says such an accident is impossible). Worksheet 1 examines the cases for and against nuclear power.

Hodder & Stoughton

© 1994 Paul Higginson. The publishers grant permission for multiple copies of this sheet to be made in the place of purchase for use solely in that institution.

Power is generally rated in megawatts (MW). All of the following would produce the same amount of energy – around 1,000 MW.

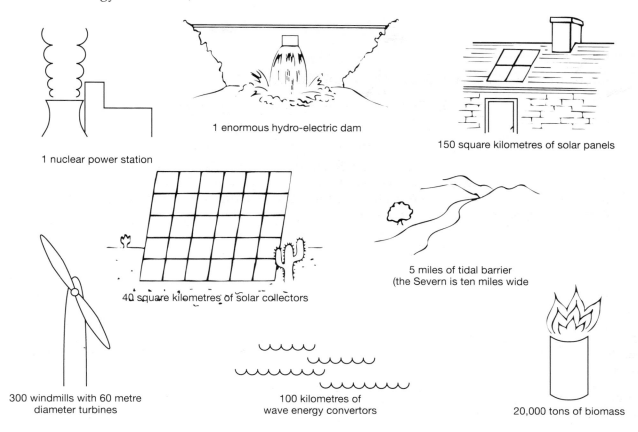

1 nuclear power station

1 enormous hydro-electric dam

150 square kilometres of solar panels

40 square kilometres of solar collectors

5 miles of tidal barrier
(the Severn is ten miles wide

300 windmills with 60 metre
diameter turbines

100 kilometres of
wave energy convertors

20,000 tons of biomass

❏ **Questions**

1 Make a list of all the ways in which you have used energy so far today. Which of these consumed the most energy?

2 Will Britain continue to use energy at its present rate? What are the variables which will affect future consumption levels?

3 BNFL argues that Sellafield has the experience and the technology to reprocess nuclear waste far more safely than most other countries, while making large profits for Britain. Should the UK take on the role of world reprocessor?

4 Many councils have set up nuclear-free zones in their areas. Why is this?

5 Which of the alternatives above is most practical for Britain?

6 What are the variations (daily and seasonal) in UK energy consumption? What consequences might this fluctuation have on our choice of future energy sources?

■ **Activity**

Role play a meeting at the Department of Energy to discuss Britain's future energy needs. Firstly draw up a list of five or six criteria to use in selecting an energy source, for example safety risks. Then 11 members of the class select an energy source each from the list on Worksheet 3 (leave out biomass and have one each for coal, gas, and oil) and present the pros and cons of each to the rest of the class (comprising Department of Energy civil servants).

The civil servants must then brief the Minister (the Teacher) and recommend a course of action.

Hodder & Stoughton

© 1994 Paul Higginson. The publishers grant permission for multiple copies of this sheet to be made in the place of purchase for use solely in that institution.

Worksheet 1
Nuclear Power in the UK

Examine the arguments for and against nuclear power.

Against	For
RADIATION	
Sellafield in Cumbria has discharged radioactive waste into the Irish Sea which returns to land. It is thought that local children may be ten times more likely to get leukaemia than others. The genes of Sellafield workers may be damaged by radiation. Discharges were particularly bad in the 1970s, but have reduced since; however when Sellafield 2 (or THORP) begins reprocessing discharges will increase by 2000 per cent (returning to the levels of the 1970s).	The average person receives 2000 times more radiation from natural sources than from nuclear power. The average radiation dose in the UK from Chernobyl is approximately equivalent to that received on a return flight from London to New York. Moreover the nuclear industry is eight times less dangerous than coal mining. There is also no contribution to acid rain/global warming which fossil-fuel power plants generate.
EXPENSE	
When the cost of construction, maintenance, decommissioning and waste disposal is evaluated nuclear energy is three times more expensive than fossil-fuel energy. Heavy government subsidies have masked this cost, but when the UK government privatised the electricity industry the true costs came to light.	Nuclear power stations have low running costs once set up, and a much lower wage bill. They reduce the UK's dependence on foreign sources such as Middle-Eastern oil, which caused recession and economic problems in the West in the 1970s. One nuclear power station provides the same power as 300 wind turbines, 150 square kilometres of solar panels or 10 UK hydrostations.
NUCLEAR WASTE	
Intensively radioactive waste is produced which is then stored and cooled. No one has yet found a publicly acceptable way of disposing of this waste. Britain reprocesses other countries' waste, which is usually transported by rail – risking collision, derailment or terrorist hijack.	At least 97 per cent of the spent fuel can be reprocessed and used again. The remainder is waste. High level liquid waste has until recently been stored in double-walled stainless steel tanks, now it is vitrified (made solid) and stored in stainless steel flasks. Low level liquid waste is treated and discharged into the sea, solid waste is stored in a concrete lined vault. Spent fuel is transported (much from other countries) in specially designed steel flasks weighing 50 to 100 tonnes, tested to international standards to withstand transport accidents.
ACCIDENTS	
There have been many minor accidents at nuclear plants and four major ones: a fire at Sellafield in 1957, Kyshtym in the USSR in 1957, Three Mile Island in the USA in 1979, and the Chernobyl disaster in the Ukraine in 1986. Some scientists now predict a major nuclear accident will occur approximately every 10 years.	Chernobyl, an accident caused by human error, could not happen here. All UK reactors have safety back-up systems (which cannot be manually over-ruled) automatically shutting down the reactor if a serious problem occurs.

Hodder & Stoughton

© 1994 Paul Higginson. The publishers grant permission for multiple copies of this sheet to be made in the place of purchase for use solely in that institution.

Worksheet 1: continued

Against	For
EMPLOYMENT	
Other energy sources such as coal mining provide far more jobs.	16,000 people are employed by BNFL – it is one of the largest employers in North-West England. A further 50,000 jobs are supported in construction and manufacturing industries.
WAR AND TERRORISM	
Power plants would be targets for conventional weapons in times of war. Terrorists could blackmail governments by hijacking plants or nuclear waste. Moreover, many countries see obtaining nuclear power as a first step towards producing nuclear weapons.	Power stations and transport flasks are very well guarded. Nuclear weapons production is controlled by the UN and through international treaties, and plutonium stocks are carefully monitored.
DECOMMISSIONING	
Plants only last 30 years because their core materials deteriorate. No large plant has yet been dismantled and decommissioned. High level waste will have to be disposed of and this will be very expensive.	Studies have shown that everything can be removed from the plant except the core and shielding. These could perhaps be removed by remote-controlled handling equipment.
ENERGY DIVERSIFICATION	
Britain should diversify into safe renewable energy sources such as wind, tidal and solar power.	Britain's energy needs will continue to rise. The oil shocks of the 1970s, the miners' strikes and the depletion of non-renewable energy stocks prove that it is foolish to rely on just one source of energy. Nuclear power should be part of a diversified energy programme. The world has enough uranium, the fuel used in nuclear power, to last another 1,000 years.

■ Activities

1 Place a tick next to the arguments you agree with, then discuss both sides in small groups.

2 Hold a debate on the issue.

3 Obtain further information from BNFL and Greenpeace (addresses in Additional Information, p109).

Hodder & Stoughton

© 1994 Paul Higginson. The publishers grant permission for multiple copies of this sheet to be made in the place of purchase for use solely in that institution.

Worksheet 2
Coal Not Dole

In late 1992 the UK government announced that it was to close 31 coal mines in Britain with the loss of 30,000 jobs. The government argued that the UK did not need as much British coal for electricity generation because other sources such as gas and imports of foreign coal were cheaper. In the so-called 'Dash for Gas', many gas-fired power stations have been built, and they produce cheaper electricity than do coal-fired stations. The Government initially argued that market forces should determine policy; if there is no market for coal then pits have to close. However, many MPs opposed the plan arguing that it was uneconomic to close highly efficient pits (amongst the most productive in Europe). In 1993 a House of Commons Select Committee suggested a compromise solution.

1   Close half the pits or sell them to the private sector. Keep the rest open.

2   Pay a £500 million taxpayers' subsidy to British Coal over five years in order to make coal less expensive and therefore more competitive. An idea to raise the subsidy through a 6 per cent levy on all electricity bills was rejected.

3   Some of the subsidy could come from the £1.2 billion a year levy on power bills which is to be used by Nuclear Electric in the future to decommission old nuclear power stations.

4   Slow down the 'Dash for Gas', increase exports and reduce some foreign coal imports. An idea to close some nuclear plants was rejected.

■ Activity

Hold a debate on this issue using some of the following arguments.

Close the Pits

- The market should decide;
- coal is very expensive to produce;
- coal burning pollutes the atmosphere;
- no one wants to buy British coal;
- public subsidies are unfair – if an industry cannot stand on its own two feet then it has to go;
- coal mining, especially open-cast mining, destroys the rural landscape;
- why pick on coal to subsidise, what about other industries going bust (like construction or truck manufacturing)? – before too long the taxpayer would be subsidising no end of inefficient businesses;
- in the long term the subsidy would be better spent on retraining the miners for new jobs;
- coal mining is eventually going to disappear in the UK anyway so let's take the tough decisions now.

Keep them Open

- The Government already pays a massive subsidy to nuclear power so there is no level playing field when it comes to energy prices;
- whole communities are built around certain pits and to close down a mine kills off the town or village, resulting in mass unemployment;
- it will be costly to pay redundancy and dole money;
- there will be other high social costs to pay such as the disillusionment amongst the young who can't find work, and increasing crime rates;
- many others would have to be laid off in businesses and industries related to coal production, like the rail workers who transport coal;
- the UK should maintain a diversified energy programme which retains a large coal element;
- British Coal, if it continues to raise productivity, might be able to stand on its own feet without subsidy in five years' time
- Britain has coal reserves that could last another 300 years.

Hodder & Stoughton

© 1994 Paul Higginson. The publishers grant permission for multiple copies of this sheet to be made in the place of purchase for use solely in that institution.

Worksheet 3

Energy Sources

Fill in the boxes for each of the energy sources listed below.

Source	Brief Description	Advantages	Disadvantages
1 Fossil fuels			
2 Nuclear			
3 Biomass			
4 Hydro			
5 Tidal			
6 Wave			
7 Wind			
8 Solar			
9 Geothermal			
10 Rubbish			

Hodder & Stoughton   © 1994 Paul Higginson. The publishers grant permission for multiple copies of this sheet to be made in the place of purchase for use solely in that institution.

11 Environment and Development

This unit will examine a number of issues that have not been covered so far in this book, as well as providing an overview of the whole area of the environment and development.

CAR CRISIS

Transport is the movement of people and goods by various means. Most people in the world still rely on their own feet, bicycles, animal-pulled carts and public transport (buses and trains). However, the trend – particularly in the UK – is towards a 'great car economy', an automobile-centred transport system. Each year, 2.5 million new cars are produced in Britain to add to the 20 million currently in use. Although some old cars are taken off the road the number of cars is growing by half a million every year. In Britain there is one car for every 2.7 people (in China it is one car for every 1,374, in the USA for every 1.8). Twenty-three per cent of British households own two or more cars. Only 1 per cent of people in Underdeveloped Countries owns a car (compared with 40 per cent in the West) and governments there are planning to catch up: China is to invest $10 billion in the car industry and wants to be producing a million cars per annum by the year 2000. A number of problems arise from this increasing emphasis on the motor-car.

1 Pollution. Cars generate all the major air pollutants (carbon monoxide, nitrogen oxide, lead etc.) which damage health and contribute to the greenhouse effect and acid rain.

2 More cars mean more roads, which use up more of the countryside. Even with new roads traffic congestion in our major cities often brings urban life to a standstill and costs industry millions of pounds per annum in time wasted. In the London rush hour traffic speed averages about 13 kilometres per hour.

3 Private cars are not very fuel-efficient and waste vast amounts of fossil-fuel resources.

4 About a quarter of our urban areas consist of roads and places to park.

5 Every year around a quarter of a million people die in car accidents (around 4,500 in the UK).

6 Because so much attention is focused on the private car, public transport is downgraded, leading to a vicious circle – because buses and trains are often unreliable, infrequent, dirty, expensive and underfunded people become even more determined to use a car. Often this leaves only the poor and elderly as the main users of public transport (especially women – men drive cars twice as often as women).

❑ ■ Questions and Activities

1 'The growth of the "great car economy" is caused by public choice and government policy.' Explain this statement.

2 List the benefits to the general public and the UK as a whole of increased car ownership and usage.

3 Why are many people so reluctant to use public transport?

4 In what ways have developments like out-of-town hypermarkets, increased leisure time, and the growth of suburbia increased car usage?

5 Research ways in which the problem of a car-centred transport system might be overcome using the following headings: electric cars; alternative fuels; better funded, subsidised public transport; government promotion of cycling (and walking). Refer to Dutch government policy, increasing taxes on motorists (fuel and road taxes), catalytic converters and town planning.

Hodder & Stoughton   © 1994 Paul Higginson. The publishers grant permission for multiple copies of this sheet to be made in the place of purchase for use solely in that institution.

6 'People complain about a car-based economy, but they are not prepared to stop using their cars. In a democracy the government should promote freedom of choice and respond to what the people want – and they want their cars.' How true is this statement and are there any flaws in the argument?

DESERTIFICATION AND SOIL EROSION

Desertification leads to 6 million hectares of new desert every year, and 21 million hectares of land that is so diminished it is no longer worth farming. One-seventh of the world's population is affected and by the year 2000 this could have grown to one-fifth if the current process continues.

How is a desert defined? It is an area where agriculture or livestock farming is impossible without huge imports of water, fodder or fertiliser. This therefore applies equally to cold rocky mountain ranges as well as hot sandy deserts. What causes desertification?

1 Global warming and climate change (longer, more frequent drought).

2 Poor soils, over-cultivated and exhausted by the spread of mechanised farming and intensive agriculture. Pressures on poor farmers have meant that land is not allowed to lie fallow for long enough.

3 Deforestation and cutting down of trees for firewood. Forest loss has turned parts of Ethiopia from fertile agricultural land to barren desert.

4 Poor irrigation techniques result in alkalisation or salinisation, which sterilises the land (the old Soviet Union has 7 million hectares in this condition).

5 Impoverishment of land by livestock through over-grazing.

An inch of soil takes 200 years to accumulate but it can turn to dust and be blown away in months. Around a quarter of the world's surface is now at risk.

However, desertification can be reversed and land reclaimed for farming. In China a large forest has been planted to hold back the desert and protect agricultural land.

■ Activity

Suggest ways in which desertification and soil erosion could be reversed. What problem might the world community face when trying to implement such solutions?

TOURISM

By the year 2000 tourism will be the world's largest economic activity. Nearly a third of all Britons go abroad on holiday each year. Many poorer countries depend almost entirely on tourism to generate much needed foreign currency and provide jobs, and most governments go to great lengths to encourage foreign visitors. Holidays to Underdeveloped Countries are becoming increasingly popular with Westerners who have become bored with package holidays to traditional tourist resorts.

☻ Further study

1 Construct a table to highlight the advantages and problems associated with increased tourism using the following headings: impact on the physical environment; impact on wildlife; impact on people; impact on culture.

2 In some African countries special game reserves have been created for tourists, which have helped to preserve species. Are there any potential problems in this kind of 'green' tourism?

3 'Global tourism means the export of "hamburger" culture to Underdeveloped Countries'. Is this true and does it matter?

4 Write a short paragraph describing the feelings and thoughts of a person living in an Underdeveloped Country watching tourists from Developed Countries on holiday.

Hodder & Stoughton   © 1994 Paul Higginson. The publishers grant permission for multiple copies of this sheet to be made in the place of purchase for use solely in that institution.

HEALTH

About 30 per cent of the world's people are ill at any one time and most of them are in Underdeveloped Countries. The big killers are diseases that have largely disappeared as major problems in Developed Countries (diarrhoea, pneumonia, measles, tetanus, etc.). Poverty is the main reason for poor health. The poor cannot buy medical treatment when they get sick, and their sickness means they cannot work effectively and earn enough to pay for treatment to get better. There are also fewer doctors to go round in Underdeveloped Countries; there is one doctor for every 25,000 people in Africa compared to one for every 500 in the West. In Developed Countries much ill-health is caused by a surplus of wealth and food. Every year heart disease and illnesses associated with obesity claim the lives of around 2.5 million people in Developed Countries (World Health Organisation [WHO] figures).

World-wide environmental damage causes increased health problems for everyone. Four current health problems are:

1 Pollution of our atmosphere. For example, the depletion of the ozone layer, which can cause skin cancer.

2 Carcinogenic chemicals and low-level radiation contribute to the 6 million new cancer cases each year (WHO figures).

3 Tobacco smoking and pollution cause lung cancer (the most common cancer in Developed Countries). As smoking declines in these countries the tobacco companies are now targeting those in the poorer countries.

4 Food scares abound in the UK, from salmonella to BSE ('mad-cow disease'). Attention has been focused on food additives and preservatives, as well as the poor quality of our drinking water.

❑ Questions

1 Why is poverty the major cause of ill-health in Underdeveloped Countries?

2 List the ways in which a more affluent lifestyle can lead to health problems.

3 Is it morally acceptable for tobacco companies to advertise cigarettes? Should governments increase the tax on cigarettes to make them more expensive and thereby reduce consumption?

4 List what you have eaten and drunk today (or yesterday). How much of this was processed (biscuits and cakes, crisps, sugary breakfast cereals, fizzy drinks, etc. which have been bought) and how much was fresh (vegetables, fruit, meat, fish)? Examine the labels on the processed food you eat and write down how much sugar, salt, preservatives, colourings and flavourings are contained in each. For example, tomato ketchup and ice-cream both contain 23 per cent sugar. Compare your findings with the group.

5 In small groups make a list of all the ways that the health of people in Britain could be improved.

Hodder & Stoughton

© 1994 Paul Higginson. The publishers grant permission for multiple copies of this sheet to be made in the place of purchase for use solely in that institution.

Worksheet 1
Green Checklist

Are you environmentally friendly? Place a tick next to all the things below that you already do and put a question mark next to everything you intend to do in the future (you may not be able to afford to do everything now).

1   Use recycled paper. ☐
2   Use unleaded petrol. ☐
3   Stop using CFC-propelled aerosols. ☐
4   Turn down the heating at home. ☐
5   Give money to charities working in Underdeveloped Countries. ☐
6   Recycle paper. ☐
7   Get rid of lead water pipes if you have them. ☐
8   Recycle glass. ☐
9   Stop buying things you don't really need. ☐
10 Turn off lights when they are not in use. ☐
11 Buy free range eggs. ☐
12 Have a compost heap. ☐
13 Avoid over-packaged goods. ☐
14 Recycle aluminium cans. ☐
15 Don't drop litter. ☐
16 Use environmentally-friendly detergents, bleaches and washing-up liquid. ☐
17 Smoke less or give up altogether. ☐
18 Use refill containers in supermarkets when possible. ☐
19 Re-use plastic bags and envelopes. ☐
20 Buy organically-grown produce. ☐
21 Shop in charity shops and jumble sales. ☐

22 Read the labels on goods. ☐
23 Give old things to charity shops and jumble sales. ☐
24 Clear up after your dog has fouled the street or park. ☐
25 Belong to an organisation campaigning on green issues. ☐
26 Lobby politicians to take green issues seriously. ☐
27 Save stamps and tin foil for charity. ☐
28 Use your car less and walk or cycle more. ☐
29 Put plants and trees in your garden to attract wildlife. ☐
30 Fit solar panels in your home. ☐
31 Take showers instead of baths. ☐
32 Eat more simply. ☐
33 Use rainwater in the garden. ☐
34 Don't pick wild flowers. ☐
35 Eat less food containing preservatives, colourings and flavourings. ☐
36 Cut down on meat consumption. ☐
37 Insulate your home to stop heat loss. ☐
38 Cut down on the use of chemicals in the garden and avoid peat. ☐
39 Use public transport more. ☐
40 Buy a car with a catalytic converter. ☐

❏ Questions
1   Is there anything that can be added to the list?
2   What problems can arise in trying to do the above things?

Hodder & Stoughton   © 1994 Paul Higginson. The publishers grant permission for multiple copies of this sheet to be made in the place of purchase for use solely in that institution.

Worksheet 2

Environment Quiz

How much do you know about environmental and developmental issues?

1 What is the world's population:

   a) 4.4 billion; b) 5.4 billion; c) 6.4 billion?

2 How many people in the world lack adequate drinking water:

   a) 2 thousand; b) 2 million; c) 2 billion?

3 How much is the debt of the Underdeveloped Countries:

   a) $1.4 million; b) $1.4 billion; c) $1.4 trillion?

4 How much rainforest is destroyed each year? An area the size of:

   a) London; b) Yorkshire; c) England?

5 What is the life expectancy in most African countries:

   a) 40; b) 50; c) 60?

6 How many of the world's fisheries are heavily exploited and over-fished (according to the UN Food and Agriculture Organisation):

   a) 90%; b) 75%; c) 50%?

7 What proportion of newspapers is recycled in the UK:

   a) 10%; b) 20%; c) 30%?

8 Which domestic appliance uses most energy:

   a) television; b) fridge-freezer; c) washing-machine?

9 How many rush hour cars does the average double-decker bus replace:

   a) 10; b) 16; c) 22 ?

10 How many people were prosecuted for littering in London in 1988:

   a) 1; b) 500; c) 3,000?

11 How much of British domestic rubbish is packaging:

   a) a quarter; b) a third; c) a half?

12 In 1972, 47 per cent of the population smoked. What proportion smoked in 1992:

   a) 54%; b) 43%; c) 32%?

13 How many vegetarians can be fed from the land needed to feed one meat eater:

   a) 7; b) 26; c) 61?

14 How many trees does the average Briton use a year:

   a) 1; b) 2; c) 5?

15 How much of our drinkable tap water is actually drunk:

   a) 1%; b) 10%; c) 30%?

Hodder & Stoughton

© 1994 Paul Higginson. The publishers grant permission for multiple copies of this sheet to be made in the place of purchase for use solely in that institution.

Worksheet 3
The Last 20 Years

1992 was the year of the Earth Summit in Rio de Janeiro. If we compare statistics from 1972 and 1992 we can evaluate the planet's environmental progress, or lack of it, in the last 20 years. Write in your estimates of the figures for 1992 (in pencil) – your teacher will give you the answers.

Issue	1972	1992
population	3.84 billion, 72% living in Underdeveloped Countries	___ billion, ___ % in Underdeveloped Countries
global warming	16 bn tons of carbon dioxide released into the air	___ billion tons released
ozone layer	ozone-depleting chlorine concentration was 1.4 parts per billion	___ parts per billion
motor vehicles	250 motor vehicles	___ motor vehicles
tropical rainforests	one-third already destroyed a further 100 square kilometres going per annum	___ square kilometres now lost every year
nuclear energy	100 nuclear power stations in 15 countries	___ plants in ___ countries
water	16 per cent of people in rural areas in the South had access to safe drinking water	___ per cent had access to safe water in rural areas
fisheries	56 million tonnes of fish caught per annum	___ million tonnes caught per annum
arms spending	$700 billion spent (at today's prices) by the world on arms	___ billion spent per annum
urbanisation	38 per cent of population is urban. Three cities have populations exceeding 10 million.	___ per cent of population is urban, ___ cities have 10 million-plus population
refugees	three million people are displaced by war and violence	___ million people are now refugees
UK aid	0.48 per cent of British GNP was given as official development assistance	___ per cent of GNP was given as aid
health	the under-5 mortality rate in the Developing World was 145 per 1,000 live births	the under-5 mortality rate is now ___ per 1,000
food	grain production (which provides half the world's calories) stood at 1.2 billion metric tons	___ billion metric tons of grain produced
debt mountain	South owed little to North. Each year South received an inflow of around $20 billion	Debt is now ___ billion. Annual repayment is___billion from South to North
biodiversity	considerable species loss (no accurate figure available)	___ plant and animal species are lost every year
AIDS	no AIDS cases	___ million people estimated with HIV

■ Activities
1. After you have received the correct figures, place a tick next to areas where there has been an improvement and a cross next to those where there has been a decline.
2. Which of these statistics surprises you the most? Give reasons for your answer.
3. Why do you think that environmental progress has been so difficult to achieve.

Hodder & Stoughton

© 1994 Paul Higginson. The publishers grant permission for multiple copies of this sheet to be made in the place of purchase for use solely in that institution.

Worksheet 4
Model Earth Summit

At the 1992 Earth Summit in Rio two international treaties were signed, on biodiversity and global warming. Imagine that you will be at the next Earth Summit – which issues would you want to highlight? Divide into groups of two or three. Select a country for the group to represent from the following list: USA, UK, Brazil, China, India, Ethiopia, Poland, Russia, Australia, Mexico, Somalia, Saudi Arabia, Japan, Iran, Philippines, Pakistan, Cuba.

Each country now selects one of the issues on Worksheet 3 which it feels should be addressed at the Summit. Using the information provided in the relevant units of this book, and through your own research, draw up a short presentation paper for the Summit (no more than two sides of A4 paper). It should include the following details:

- what the problem is (include relevant statistics) and how it was caused;

- what is being done about it at present;

- what will happen if the issue is not tackled;

- solutions to discuss (there should be a mixture of solutions ranging from the 'easy to implement' category to the 'difficult but desirable' category);

- ways of paying for the solutions;

- why this issue is so important and an international treaty is so necessary.

AT THE SUMMIT

A student Chairperson presides over the Summit and chairs discussion and debate. Each country presents its papers to the Summit (these could be photocopied in advance) and outlines its proposals (using appropriate visual aids where necessary). Only two or three treaties can be signed so once the presentations are over delegates need to vote to decide which issues should be discussed further. Delegates then debate the most popular issues in depth. The proposed solutions are read out again and the various countries, through discussion and compromise, agree a draft treaty containing an action plan for change. Remember that the final treaty must be acceptable to all member countries or it cannot be signed, for example if the USA or the UK feels that the proposed solutions are too expensive for them, then there will have to be negotiations to reach a compromise. A treaty that is not signed by all the global community simply will not work – there must be international agreement from all nations. Once agreement has been reached move on to the next issue.

❂ Further study

Once the treaties have been agreed in principle the Chairperson and his or her secretariat can draw up the final versions and these can then be signed and displayed on the school or college notice board. If this is going to be a whole school or year group event you could involve the local press on the day of the simulation and ask them to publish your final treaties.

Hodder & Stoughton

© 1994 Paul Higginson. The publishers grant permission for multiple copies of this sheet to be made in the place of purchase for use solely in that institution.

Additional Information

USEFUL ADDRESSES

Acid Rain Information Centre, Department of Environment and Geography, Manchester Metropolitan University, John Dalton Extension, Room E310, Chester Street, Manchester.

Age Concern England, 1268 London Road, London SW16 4ER (produces useful fact sheets).

Animal Aid, 7 Castle Street, Tonbridge, Kent TN9 1BH.

Animals in Medicines Research Information Centre (AMRIC), 12 Whitehall, London SW1A 2DY (pro animal research).

Association for the Conservation of Energy, 9 Sherlock Mews, London W1M 3RH.

British Field Sports Society, 59 Kennington Road, London SE1 7PZ.

British Humanist Association, 14 Lambs Conduit Passage, London WC1R 4RH.

British Nuclear Fuels Ltd. (BNFL), Visitors' Centre, Sellafield, Seascale, Cumbria CA20 1PG; 09467-27027.

British Union for the Abolition of Vivisection (BUAV), 16a Crane Grove, London N7 8LB.

British Wind Energy Association, 4 Hamilton Place, London W1V 0BQ.

Campaign Against the Arms Trade, 11 Goodwin Street, London N4 2HQ.

Campaign for Nuclear Disarmament (CND), 162 Holloway Road, London N7 8DQ.

Catholic Fund for Overseas Development (CAFOD), Development Education Department, 2 Romero Close, Stockwell Road, London SW9 9TY.

Centre for World Development Education (CWDE), 128 Buckingham Palace Road, London SW1W 9SH.

Christian Aid, PO Box 100, London SW9 8BH.

Compassion in World Farming, 20 Lavant Street, Petersfield, Hampshire GU32 3EW.

Council for Education in World Citizenship, Mews House, Seymour Mews, London W1H 9PE.

Department of Energy, House C, Millbank, Westminster, London.

Department of the Environment, 2 Marsham Street, London SW1P 3EB (publishes pamphlets on global warming, the ozone layer, etc.).

Department of Transport, 2 Marsham Street, London SW1P 3EB.

Friends of the Earth, 26-28 Underwood Street, London N1 7JQ.

Green Party, 10 Station Parade, Balham High Street, London SW12 9AZ.

Greenpeace, Canonbury Villas, Islington, London N1 2RP, 071-354 5100.

Help the Aged, St James Walk, London EC1R 0BE (produces excellent fact sheets).

Human Fertilisation and Embryology Authority, Paxton House, 30 Artillery Lane, London E1 7LS.

International Institute for Environment and Development (IIED), 3 Endsleigh Street, London WC1H 0DD.

International Whaling Commission, The Red House, Station Road, Histon, Cambridge CB4 4NP.

League Against Cruel Sports, Sparling House, 83-87 Union Street, London SE1 1SG.

LIFE, Life House, Newbold Terrace, Royal Leamington Spa, CV32 4EA (anti-abortion, anti-euthanasia).

Meat and Livestock Commission, PO Box 44, Winterhill House, Snowdon Drive, Milton Keynes MK6 1AX.

Hodder & Stoughton *© 1994 Paul Higginson. The publishers grant permission for multiple copies of this sheet to be made in the place of purchase for use solely in that institution.*

Ministry of Agriculture, Fisheries and Food Information Division, 3 Whitehall Place, London SW1A 4JU.

National Abortion Campaign, The Print House, 18 Ashwin Street, London E8 3DL.

National Anti-Vivisection Society, 261 Goldhawk Road, London W12 9PE.

Oxfam, 274 Banbury Road, Oxford OX2 7DZ.

Peace Pledge Union, 6 Endsleigh Street, London WC1H 0DX.

Population Concern, 231 Tottenham Court Road, London W1P 0HY.

Progress, 27-35 Mortimer Street, London W1N 7RJ (pro embryo research).

Quaker Peace and Service, Friends House, Euston Road, London NW1 2BJ.

Relate, 76a New Cavendish Street, London W1M 7LB.

Research Defence Society, Grosvenor Gardens House, Grosvenor Gardens, London SW1W 0BS (pro animal research).

Royal Society for the Prevention of Cruelty to Animals (RSPCA), Causeway, Horsham, West Sussex RH12 1HG.

Samaritans, 17 Uxbridge Road, Slough SL1 1SN.

Society for the Protection of Unborn Babies Educational Trust (SPUC), 7 Tufton Street, Westminster, London SW1 3QN (LIFE, NAC and SPUC all provide education kits for teachers on abortion, embryo research, IVF etc.).

Transport 2000, Walkden House, 10 Melton Street, London NW1 2EJ.

United Nations Environmental Programme (UNEP), c/o IIED, 3 Endsleigh Street, London WC1H 0DD (information on the ozone layer).

United Nations Information Centre, 20 Buckingham Gate, London SW1E 6LB.

Vegetarian Society, Parkdale, Dunham Road, Altrincham, Cheshire WA14 4QG.

Voluntary Euthanasia Society, 13 Prince of Wales Terrace, London W8 5PG.

World Wide Fund for Nature, UK (WWF), Panda House, Weyside Park, Godalming, Surrey GU7 7RX.

Zoo Check, Cherry Tree Cottage, Coldharbour, Dorking, Surrey RH5 6HA.

As most of the above groups rely mainly on donations for survival it is important that if you do request information you enclose a large stamped addressed envelope.

FURTHER READING

Animal Aid, *Why Animal Rights*, Animal Aid.

Blunden J and Reddish A (eds), *Energy, Resources and Environment*, Hodder & Stoughton.

Bowles A, Gleeson D and Smith P, *Sociology A Modular Approach*, Oxford University Press.

Boyle S and Ardill J, *The Greenhouse Effect*, New English Library.

Bullock A and Stallybrass O, *The Fontana Dictionary of Modern Thought*, Fontana/Collins.

Button J, *How to be Green*, Century.

Central Office of Information (HMSO), *Britain, An Official Handbook*, (published annually).

Central Statistical Office (HMSO), *Social Trends*, (published annually).

Cherfas J, *Zoo 2000*, BBC Books.

Clarke J, *Population Geography*, Pergamon.

Crump A, *Dictionary of Environment and Development*, Earthscan.

Donnellon C, *Changing Roles in the Family*, Independence.

Farmer M, *The Family*, Longman.

Fernie J, *A Geography of Energy in the UK*, Longman.

Fletcher R, *The Family and Marriage in Britain*, Penguin.

Friday L and Laskey R (eds), *The Fragile Environment*, Cambridge University Press.

Hodder & Stoughton   © *1994 Paul Higginson. The publishers grant permission for multiple copies of this sheet to be made in the place of purchase for use solely in that institution.*

George S, *How the Other Half Dies: The Reasons for World Hunger*, Penguin.

Gibson C, *Population*, Basil Blackwell.

Goudie A, *The Human Impact on the Natural Environment*, Basil Blackwell.

Karas J and Kelly P, *The Heat Trap: The Threat Posed by Rising Levels of Greenhouse Gases*, Friends of the Earth.

Leeds C, *Peace and War A First Sourcebook*, Stanley Thornes.

Lowry JH, *World Population and Food Supply*, Hodder & Stoughton.

Morris D, *The Animal Contract*, Virgin.

New Scientist, IPC Magazines Ltd, Haywards Heath, West Sussex, RH16 3ZA.

New Internationalist, 42 Hythe Bridge Street, Oxford OX1 2EP.

Oxfam, Christian Aid and CAFOD publish a wide variety of excellent material on North-South and development issues.

Patterson WC, *The Energy Alternative*, Channel 4.

Pearce F, *Acid Rain*, Penguin.

Porritt J, *Where On Earth Are We Going?*, BBC Books.

Sawyer J, *Acid Rain and Air Pollution*, World Wide Fund for Nature.

Seager J (ed.), *The State of the Earth (An Atlas of Environmental Concern)*, Union Hyman.

Seymour J and Girardet H, *Blueprint for a Green Plant*, Dorling Kindersley.

Smyth A and Wheater C, *The Green Guide*, Argus Books.

Townsend P, *The Family Life of Old People*, Penguin.

Warnock JW, *The Politics of Hunger*, Methuen.

Warnock M, *A Question of Life, The Warnock Report on Human Fertilisation and Embryology*, Basil Blackwell.

FURTHER ACTIVITIES

1   Invite your local MP or councillor to take part in a question and answer session on an important issue such as the Coal Crisis or Defence Policy.

2   Most pressure groups (like Oxfam, Help the Aged, the Samaritans) will send speakers to schools and colleges to explain their work (usually through slide presentations and discussion). Ask such a group to talk to you.

3   Organise a debate with speakers from two conflicting organisations, for example, LIFE and the National Abortion Campaign; the League Against Cruel Sports and the British Field Sports Society; the Research Defence Society and Animal Aid.

4   Organise a Development Day or Environment Day in your college with workshops and displays on various topics. Most of the organisations and charities mentioned in this book will help by suggesting ideas, or sending speakers.

5   Hold a model UN meeting and invite representatives from other schools and colleges in the area to participate.

6   Organise an 'Underdeveloped Countries Week' in the college with various fundraising activities for development charities, such as a sponsored 24-hour fast, lunchtime concert, sponsored car wash, or fancy dress day. You can get details from Oxfam, Christian Aid or CAFOD.

7   Conduct college-wide surveys on contemporary issues such as vegetarianism, nuclear weapons or animal research.

8   Hold a college referendum on a contemporary issue like nuclear power or fox-hunting with campaigns, manifestos and video broadcasts.

9   Start a recycling group in your school or college. Start with newspapers and aluminium cans. You can get details from Friends of the Earth.

Hodder & Stoughton   © 1994 Paul Higginson. The publishers grant permission for multiple copies of this sheet to be made in the place of purchase for use solely in that institution.

Past Paper Essay Questions

The following essay questions have been selected from a typical range of past papers in A-level General Studies.

1 Outline the causes and effects of two of the following: a) holes in the ozone layer; b) acid rain; c) oil pollution at sea. How far should we try to minimise them? (Oxford 1991)

2 Currently much publicity is given to 'alternative' sources of power such as solar, wind, geothermal, tidal and wave. Evaluate two of these as practical possibilities for replacing the conventional provision in both a) an isolated farm and b) a major city. (JMB 1991)

3 Why is it sometimes claimed that overseas aid benefits the donor more than the recipient? To what extent do you believe this claim to be true? Outline the kinds of aid which you think are most likely to be effective. (JMB 1992)

4 What is the 'Greenhouse Effect', what causes are suggested for it and how would you attempt to measure if such an effect was occurring? Why is it important to study this effect? (Oxford 1990)

5 Discuss the feasibility of generating electricity from sources other than fossil fuels and nuclear energy. (Cambridge 1990)

6 Discuss the problems associated with the fact that men and women are living longer than was the case fifty years ago. (Cambridge 1990)

7 How effective do you consider charitable organisations are in coping with the problems they seek to overcome? You should illustrate your answer by referring to two different types of charities, one home-based and the other at work in the Third World. (Cambridge 1989)

8 Since world population is increasing rapidly, should nature be allowed to take its course? (Cambridge 1989)

9 The manufacturing industries are sometimes associated with undesirable effluents, some of which have lasting effects. Consider two or three examples of the problem and suggest solutions. (Cambridge 1989)

10 How far do you share the view that the motor car is a mixed blessing? (Northern Examinations and Assessment Board 1991)

11 What factors are suggested as causing the 'Greenhouse Effect', and what might be some of the long term consequences? (Northern Examinations and Assessment Board 1990)

12 'Let him who desires peace prepare for war.' (Vegetius, fourth century AD). State four ways in which the British Government observes this advice. (Northern Examinations and Assessment Board 1991)

13 Parliament sometimes considers matters which can be regarded as posing moral dilemmas. Choose one or two of these, summarise the arguments and consider whether Parliament is the right forum for such discussions and whether legislation is appropriate for these issues. (Cambridge 1991)

14 Since 1900 life expectancy in the United Kingdom has increased substantially. Consider the implications of this change. (Cambridge 1991)

15 What are the arguments both for and against the keeping of animals in zoos? (Cambridge 1993)

16 Discuss with reference to specific examples how those facing famine can best be helped. (Cambridge 1993)

17 In view of the lengthy waiting lists for many hospital operations, and the financial restraints that exist in the NHS, is it right to expect the NHS to devote resources and finance to spectacular, yet costly operations such as transplants? (AEB 1990)

18 Nuclear families are now a minority of all households. Does it matter? (Oxford 1993)

19 Comment briefly on the assertion that the production of electricity from nuclear power has a valuable future, indicating the problems which are associated with this particular form of generation. (AEB 1993)

20 How far can the invasion of one country by another ever be justified? Illustrate your answer by reference to conflicts that have occurred since 1945. (AEB 1993)

Hodder & Stoughton

© 1994 Paul Higginson. The publishers grant permission for multiple copies of this sheet to be made in the place of purchase for use solely in that institution.

G000037922

Guess What!

Teacher's Book 2
with DVD

American English

Lucy Frino

CAMBRIDGE
UNIVERSITY PRESS

University Printing House, Cambridge CB2 8BS, United Kingdom

One Liberty Plaza, 20th Floor, New York, NY 10006, USA

477 Williamstown Road, Port Melbourne, VIC 3207, Australia

314–321, 3rd Floor, Plot 3, Splendor Forum, Jasola District Centre, New Delhi – 110025, India

103 Penang Road, #05–06/07, Visioncrest Commercial, Singapore 238467

Cambridge University Press is part of the University of Cambridge.

It furthers the University's mission by disseminating knowledge in the pursuit of education, learning, and research at the highest international levels of excellence.

www.cambridge.org
Information on this title: www.cambridge.org/9781107556812

© Cambridge University Press 2016

This publication is in copyright. Subject to statutory exception and to the provisions of relevant collective licensing agreements, no reproduction of any part may take place without the written permission of Cambridge University Press.

First published 2016

Printed in Great Britain by CPI Group (UK) Ltd, Croydon CR0 4YY

A catalog record for this publication is available from the British Library

ISBN 978-1-107-55681-2 Teacher's Book with DVD Level 2
ISBN 978-1-107-55673-7 Student's Book Level 2
ISBN 978-1-107-55678-2 Workbook with Online Resources Level 2
ISBN 978-1-107-55682-9 Class Audio CDs Level 2
ISBN 978-1-107-55683-6 Flashcards Level 2
ISBN 978-1-107-55684-3 Presentation Plus DVD-ROM Level 2
ISBN 978-1-107-55672-0 Teacher's Resource and Tests CD-ROM Levels 1–2

Additional resources for this publication at www.cambridge.org/guesswhatamericanenglish

Cambridge University Press has no responsibility for the persistence or accuracy of URLs for external or third-party Internet websites referred to in this publication and does not guarantee that any content on such websites is or will remain accurate or appropriate. Information regarding prices, travel schedules, and other factual information given in this work is correct at the time of first printing but Cambridge University Press does not guarantee the accuracy of such information thereafter.

Contents

Language Summary

Introduction

About *Guess What!*

Guess What! is an innovative six-level course for primary-age students learning English who want to learn about the world around them as they do so. *Guess What!* aims to motivate students and excite young minds, to feed their natural curiosity about the world, and fuel their imaginations. It not only offers a well-paced syllabus with clearly marked goals for language learning, but also aims to develop students' learning and life skills in a broader sense, with opportunities for learning across the wider curriculum and for exploring social skills and values.

Guess What! has been written with the busy teacher in mind and offers clear lesson planning with flexibility for teachers with between two and four lessons per week.

The global classroom

With the use of stunning international photographs and an emphasis on real-life contexts, *Guess What!* brings the world into the English classroom. Students learn and are motivated to practice new language by following the examples of real children shown at home, at school, on vacation, on exciting trips, or in various recreational activities. The photographs from around the world motivate students to engage with each topic in a broad sense and make cross-cultural comparisons.

An imaginative journey

The realm of fantasy and imagination is as important to young learners as the discovery of the world around them. *Guess What!* uses engaging characters and fun and exciting stories to fuel students' imaginations. In *Guess What!* Level 2, students follow Olivia, David, Ben, and Tina through a magic portal in a tree house, where they have exciting adventures with their funny robot friend, iPal.

Social values

An understanding of social values gives young learners the skills they need to be successful in life. They need to learn about how to behave with other people, as well as taking responsibility for themselves and the world around them. Stories, fairy tales, and fables have traditionally been used to promote social values in a way that children relate to and find interesting. The stories in *Guess What!* build on this tradition. Each story episode illustrates a social value for students to discuss and apply to their own behavior. The social values covered in *Guess What!* Level 2 include sharing things, eating healthy food, and being neat.

Skilled learners

Students need to be skilled in reading, listening, speaking, and writing in order to use language effectively. As students will be learning to read and write in their own language, *Guess What!* Level 2 focuses on listening and speaking skills while providing a gradual introduction to the written word in English. Students will progress steadily from understanding and matching to tracing and then writing words to completing sentences by the end of Level 2.

Confident speakers

Speaking skills are further developed in functional language and pronunciation activities. In the Talk time feature, students learn and practice a simple and useful functional dialog, such as asking to take turns and offering to help. Then students will enjoy practicing their pronunciation with the amusing Animal sounds feature.

Keen thinkers

Guess What! aims to encourage students to become good thinkers as well as good language learners. The different kinds of activities develop a range of thinking skills, including: observation, concentration, prediction and guessing, using memory, sequencing, and classifying. Regular thinking skills activities are clearly signposted with the Think icon. The inclusion of Content and Language Integrated Learning activities also encourages wider thinking and knowledge across the primary curriculum.

The wider curriculum

The Content and Language Integrated Learning (CLIL) material in *Guess What!* has been selected from popular primary school subjects across the curriculum. Teachers can therefore integrate learners' understanding of age-related subject concepts while developing their English language skills. *Guess What!* offers CLIL learning with the combination of materials in the Student's Book and Workbook, and using short dynamic videos. This innovative and motivating approach provides a language-rich experience and develops learners' listening skills while they process subject content.

Digital competence

Successful young learners need to be competent in information technology (IT) and digital skills. These can be combined with language practice by using the Online Resources and Presentation Plus.

Cambridge English: Young Learners (YLE) tests

The language syllabus in *Guess What!* is well paced and achievable, with plenty of recycling built in throughout the course. *Guess What!* supports students aiming to take the Cambridge English: Young Learners (YLE) tests. *Guess What!* Level 2 is informed by the YLE Starters syllabus. The Starters syllabus is covered in full by the end of *Guess What!* Level 3.

Guess What! Level 2 components

Student's Book

The 104-page full-color and highly photographic Student's Book contains:

- A Hello again! unit, which reviews language from *Guess What!* Level 1 and presents ways of giving different kinds of information.
- Eight further teaching units, each presenting new language within a topic of interest to students of this age.
- Four Review spreads, designed to be used after every two main teaching units.

Each unit opens with an eye-catching photographic spread, followed by eight easy-to-use, single-lesson pages, which contain:

- Engaging topics and presentation contexts.
- Clear progression from presentation to practice in each lesson.
- A wide variety of activities, including humorous contextual dialogs, chants, songs, games and communication activities, functional dialogs, role-playing, and pronunciation activities.
- An exciting story adventure.
- Two pages of CLIL activities.
- Regular activities to develop a range of thinking skills.
- About Me activities for students to personalize their language learning.

Workbook with Online Resources

The 96-page full-color Workbook provides further consolidation of all the language and topics presented in the Student's Book. It can be used at home or in class and contains:

- Nine units and four reviews, following the same easy-to-use single-lesson format as the Student's Book.
- Puzzles and matching and task-based activities providing reading and writing practice at word level, with completion of sentences by the end of Level 2.
- An Evaluation providing a record of learning for each unit.
- A full-color Picture dictionary.
- A puzzle page feature.
- Regular Think and About Me activities.
- An access code to the Online Resources, which include games and extra grammar, vocabulary and writing activities for every unit. Student's online work can be tracked and reviewed by the teacher. Teachers can register for free at www.cambridgelms.org/primary.

Audio CDs

The three Audio CDs contain all the recorded material for the Student's Book and Workbook, including the songs (plus karaoke versions), chants, and stories. The audio script is included in each lesson in the teaching notes when it is not seen on the Student's Book page.

Teacher's Book with DVD

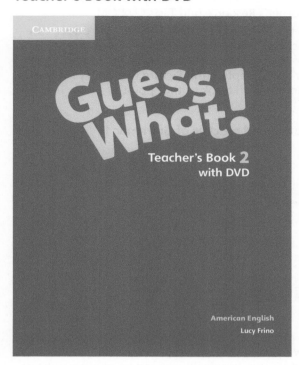

The 224-page Teacher's Book is interleaved with the Student's Book. It has been written with the busy teacher in mind and provides:

- Step-by-step guidance for each lesson in the teaching notes. This includes a summary of lesson aims and materials needed, a simple warmer and end-of-lesson activity, clear instructions for using the Student's Book and Workbook, audio scripts, answer keys, and suggested classroom instructions for you to use with your class.
- Photocopiable word cards for each unit to match the flashcards. Ideas for using the word cards are provided in the teaching notes.
- Extra games and activities for every lesson, as well as a Games bank that can be used as a dip-in resource.
- A DVD. This contains the videos for the CLIL lessons.

Teacher's Resource and Tests CD-ROM

The Teacher's Resource and Tests CD-ROM contains 106 pages of optional photocopiable material for you to use alongside *Guess What!* Levels 1 and 2. You can dip in and choose the material at different times, depending on the specific needs of your class. For *Guess What!* Level 2, the CD-ROM provides 53 pages of additional material as follows:

- Nine two-page Unit tests, which evaluate student's progress in each unit. These cover the core vocabulary and grammar structures of each unit, with listening and speaking activities on the first page and reading and writing activities on the second page.
- Four two-page Review tests, which evaluate student's progress. These can be used after each Review spread, and they also provide practice in listening, speaking, reading, and writing skills.
- 27 pages of extra worksheets (three pages per unit). These provide extra reinforcement activities for the core vocabulary and grammar structures of each unit.

Presentation Plus

Presentation Plus includes Interactive Whiteboard tools, a fully interactive Student's Book and Workbook, digital versions of the Teacher's Book, a multimedia library including video from the DVD, a Teacher's Resource and Tests CD-ROM, an Audio CD, and access to online teacher training support. Presentation Plus enables you to plan your lessons paper-free from a tablet or computer.

Flashcards

There are 91 flashcards to accompany *Guess What!* Level 2. They illustrate the key vocabulary from the main teaching units. Ideas for using the flashcards in class are included in the main teaching notes and in the Games bank.

Tour of a unit

Guess What! Level 2 has nine teaching units, each divided into eight lessons, along with an introduction to the topic. In addition, there are four Review spreads of two units each. As well as offering further practice, the Workbook provides a Picture dictionary and Evaluations. There are additional resources on the Teacher's Resource and Tests CD-ROM.

Unit introduction

The topic of the unit is introduced with a double-page, highly engaging photograph, chosen to stimulate children's imaginations and to encourage them to relate the topic to the wider world. The teaching notes for each unit suggest ways of exploiting the photographs. This introduction can be included as part of Lesson 1 or as a separate introductory lesson.

Lesson 1
Presentation of vocabulary

New vocabulary is presented in the context of a colorful illustration featuring the *Guess What!* characters. This is accompanied by a short and lively dialog on the Audio CD. Students will listen and repeat the vocabulary, and also read the vocabulary labels on the page. Students then listen and identify the new vocabulary in contextual sentences.

- The flashcards and word cards can also be used to present new words and review them in a variety of games.
- The Workbook provides further vocabulary recognition activities, including matching, tracing, and writing.

Lesson 2
Practice of vocabulary

Students practice the new vocabulary further with an engaging chant, followed by an activity that encourages them to use a particular thinking skill, such as spotting differences, working out sequences, and finding mistakes.

- Both activities practice vocabulary while also recycling language from previous units.
- The Workbook provides further practice, including a sticker feature. Students are also directed to the Picture dictionary at the end of this lesson.

- There is an additional vocabulary worksheet available in the Teacher's Resource and Tests CD-ROM.

Note: In the Hello again! Unit, Lesson 1 introduces the new character names rather than a vocabulary set. The letters of the alphabet are presented in Lesson 3, and students also complete the Picture dictionary numbers activity in the Workbook at that point.

Lesson 3
Presentation and practice of Grammar 1

The two grammar points of the unit are presented either with a lively song that also reuses the unit vocabulary or in a short dialog, usually illustrated by photographs of children using English in real and engaging contexts. The position of the song or contextual dialog varies between Lesson 3 and Lesson 4.

The activities on the page follow a clear and enjoyable path from presentation, through practice, to production. Students are supported through their learning with example speech bubbles on the page, and the new grammar point is summarized at the bottom of the page for the teacher.

- The Workbook provides a variety of activities and puzzles, designed to reinforce the target grammar, while providing support with early reading and writing.
- There is an additional grammar worksheet available in the Teacher's Resource and Tests CD-ROM.

Lesson 4
Presentation and practice of Grammar 2

The second new grammar point is presented either with a song or a short contextual dialog (depending on the format used in Lesson 3).

There is clear progression from this context to active production. Students are supported through their learning with example speech bubbles on the page, and the new grammar point is summarized at the bottom of the page for the teacher.

- The Workbook provides a variety of reinforcement activities and puzzles that support early reading and writing. There is also an About Me activity that encourages students to use the new grammar to talk about the unit topic.
- There is an additional grammar worksheet available in the Teacher's Resource and Tests CD-ROM.

Lesson 5
Story and value

Students reinforce and extend their learning further with a dynamic cartoon strip story featuring the *Guess What!* characters. Each story introduces a social value in a light-hearted way, as well as a functional dialog that students practice more fully in Lesson 6.

- The Workbook provides story sequencing and comprehension activities.

Lesson 6
Talk time and Animal sounds

Students practice a functional dialog, first introduced in the story and then applied in this lesson to real-world contexts. Students therefore learn how the function can be used within the different contexts of their own lives. Students will also focus on and practice a specific English sound in the engaging context of a humorous sentence about an animal.

- The Workbook provides a values activity and additional pronunciation practice.

Lesson 7
CLIL (Content and Language Integrated Learning)

Students explore a fascinating topic selected from primary school subjects across the curriculum. Students use the stimulating introductory photograph to engage with the topic and share any knowledge they already have. They then learn some new vocabulary and watch a short dynamic video, which is provided on the DVD with the Teacher's Book. Instructions for using the video and the video script are provided on pages TB124–128.

- The Workbook provides further activities exploring the CLIL topic.

Lesson 8
CLIL project and Evaluation

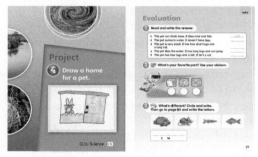

Students work together to do a simple project activity linked to the CLIL topic. The kind of project varies from unit to unit and include drawings, craft activities, a food poster, picture sums, and a research project about animals. Students then complete an Evaluation in the Workbook.

Review lessons (after every second unit)

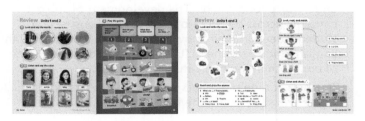

Language is reinforced through vocabulary puzzles and a task-based listening activity based on real children. There is also a full-page board game with clearly marked linguistic aims.

CLIL (Content and Language Integrated Learning)

Introduction

The two Content and Language Integrated Learning (CLIL) pages at the end of each unit in *Guess What!* are selected from primary school subjects across the curriculum. The subjects chosen for Levels 1 and 2 are the popular CLIL subjects of art, geography, math, physical education, and science. With the CLIL pages, teachers can develop students' understanding of age-related subject concepts while also developing their English language skills.

In order to integrate content and language meaningfully, each CLIL subject is supported with a short, dynamic video. Students can therefore watch and listen to highly contextualized, supportive CLIL input chosen from the real world outside the classroom. This innovative approach provides a language-rich experience and develops students' listening skills while they process subject content. The video and book activities also develop students' thinking processes by helping them to:

- understand, recognize, and produce new subject-specific vocabulary (Activity 1).
- develop lower-order processing skills, such as remembering, identifying, and comparing new subject-specific vocabulary presented in the Student's Book and then seen in the video (Activity 2).
- recognize new concepts and interpret what's shown in the pictures (Activity 3).
- develop higher-order processing skills such as critical and creative thinking (Activity 4).
- generate ideas through planning and produce subject-specific projects (Activity 5).

What is new and different about CLIL in *Guess What!* is that students build on their knowledge of subject concepts presented in the videos as they work through each level of the course. An example is the science topic of plants. In Level 1, students find out which foods come from plants, then in Level 2, they discover that materials for clothes are made from plants. In subsequent levels, students find out about parts of plants we can eat, and explore how we can use plants for shelter, food, fabric, and medicine and also how plants play a role in underwater food chains. The development of subject concepts across all levels of *Guess What!* ensures that students deepen their knowledge of both content and the English language. The CLIL topic is related to the theme of each unit in the main Student's Book.

Teachers can help learners enjoy the CLIL sections in *Guess What!* by doing the following:

Activating students' prior knowledge of the subject

Use the stimulating one-page photograph in the first CLIL page and the learner-friendly video to find out what students already know about each CLIL topic. Ask students closed questions and then an open question to help develop thinking skills. For example, in Level 2, Unit 3, What are clothes made of? ask:

1 *Can you see the T-shirts?* (recognizing and identifying words presented earlier in the book)
2 *What is it made of?* (establishing if students know this concept)

Finding out what students already know about subject-specific vocabulary at the start of a CLIL lesson is a stage when many students want to use their first language (L1). If students use L1 to say some words related to the CLIL topic, translate into English.

Word-level support

New vocabulary presented in the CLIL sections needs to be revisited because it is important that students can produce new language clearly and with confidence. You can achieve this by playing the videos more than once and by doing the following:

- Turning off the sound, pausing the video and asking students to repeat new vocabulary slowly/quickly/quietly/loudly.
- Pausing the video and eliciting new words through mime or questioning.
- Making flashcards to show the new CLIL vocabulary in a different order from that presented in the book or video.

You could compare some new CLIL vocabulary with words in the LI, e.g.,

- Level 1 Hello! Unit: *purple*, Unit 1: *plastic*, Unit 2: *electric*
- Level 2 Hello again! Unit: *sculpture*, Unit 1: *water*, Unit 2: *shelter*

Ask students *Do they sound the same? Do they look the same?* If there are students from other countries, find out the words in their languages, in order to focus on culture as well as language.

Sentence-level support

Encourage students to communicate new CLIL vocabulary in sentences, using grammar presented in the Student's Book. Provide sentence starters, fill-in-the-blank sentences (using *is/isn't*, *are/aren't*), and substitution tables so students feel confident when speaking, e.g.,

An apple is a _____ .	A pea _____ a vegetable.
Bananas are _____ .	Rice _____ a grain.
A carrot is a _____ .	Olives _____ fruit.
Beans are _____ .	Sausages _____ meat.

apples carrots oranges potatoes	are	fruits vegetables

You will need to provide students with plenty of support for CLIL. And remember, some learners need more support than others.

Schedule

There are 80 lesson plans provided in the teaching notes of *Guess What!* Level 2. These consist of eight lessons in each of the nine teaching units, and eight review lessons. Each teaching unit has two vocabulary lessons, two grammar lessons, one story lesson, one functional language and pronunciation lesson, one CLIL lesson, and one additional optional lesson for the CLIL project and Evaluation.

The course is aimed at teachers with classes of between two and four lessons per week (75 to 150 lessons per year). Extra materials provided on the Teacher's Resource and Tests CD-ROM can therefore be used to adapt the material to accommodate these different needs, along with the many ideas for Extra activities in each unit (pages TB114–TB127) and in the Games bank (pages xiv–xx).

Use these ideas to help you tailor the course to your own teaching situation. Each additional lesson type provides nine lessons (one per unit) unless otherwise stated.

Additional lesson type	Description	Three lessons per week (127 per year)	Four lessons per week (163 per year)
Introduction	Use the opening photographic spread for each unit, along with the flashcards, to preteach the new vocabulary. Use ideas from the Games bank (pages xiv–xx) for preparatory vocabulary work.		✓
Evaluation	Use the Evaluation at the end of the unit in the Workbook. Use ideas from the Extra activities (pages TB114–TB127), the Games bank, or the extra worksheets from the Teacher's Resource and Tests CD-ROM.		✓
Test and reinforcement	Use the End-of-unit test in the Teacher's Resource and Tests CD-ROM. Reward students with activities from the Games bank when they've completed the test. Extra vocabulary and grammar worksheets from the Teacher's Resource and Tests CD-ROM can also be used.	✓	✓
Portfolio	A portfolio is a large folder or box in which students store work they produce throughout the year. Use ideas from the Extra activities or the Games bank to review work and then encourage students to add any worksheets, posters, or other materials to their portfolio.	✓	✓
Progress to fun	Use ideas from the Extra activities and the Games bank, including the more time-consuming ideas, such as craft activities, research projects, and class trips. Students can also repeat their favorite activities.	✓	✓
Picture dictionary	Use the Picture dictionary in the Workbook, the flashcards and word cards, and ideas from the Extra activities or the Games bank. The extra vocabulary worksheet from the Teacher's Resource and Tests CD-ROM can also be used.		✓
Creativity	Base this around one of the craft activities suggestions in the Extra activities.		✓
IT	These lessons should be conducted in an area where you have access to computers. Use the Online Resources or base this on a research project from those suggested in the Extra activities.	✓	✓
End-of-term test (four lessons)	Use the test from the Teacher's Resource and Tests CD-ROM after each Review.	✓	✓
Class celebration (one lesson)	Prepare a course completion certificate for each student and have a ceremony where you hand these out.	✓	✓
End-of-year show (six lessons)	Rehearse and perform a class show. Students can present their work, perform songs or chants, or act out the story. They can also design invitations and programs.		✓

Games bank

The Games bank provides the instructions for games and communication activities that are referred to in the lesson notes. It can also be used as a dip-in resource whenever you need a simple and fun activity to use in class.

Act and guess
Use any set of flashcards or word cards. Students take turns choosing a flashcard without showing the rest of the class. They mime the item on the flashcard or word card for the rest of the class to guess.

Act it out
Students think of an activity or a word they know in English (e.g., *run*, *swim*, *eat*). They write this down on a slip of paper (in Unit 8, they write the present participle, e.g., *running*) and put the slips of paper into a box or bag. Students or pairs of students take turns drawing out a slip of paper, reading the activity, or the word (silently), and acting it out for the class to guess. They guess by saying the word or by asking a question, e.g., for Unit 8, students can guess the actions by asking: *Is it "running?" (Yes, it is.)*

Action treasure hunt
Write actions on slips of paper (one slip for each pair of students): *play field hockey, ride a horse, roller-skate, fly a kite*, etc. Hide these around the classroom. Students take turns finding a slip of paper and do or mime the action on it. Alternatively, students can find an action, and use it to make a question, e.g., *Can you (play field hockey)? (Yes, I can./No, I can't.)* Alternatively, they can use it to make a suggestion which they then both mime: *Let's (swim).* If time, when students have finished talking/miming, they can hide the slip of paper in a different place for another pair of students to find, and look for a new slip of paper.

Alphabetical order
Hand out slips of paper to each student (one slip for each word you want to practice spelling). Dictate the words. Students write one on each piece of paper. Tell students to turn the slips of paper over and mix them up. Say *Look at the words!* Students turn over their slips of paper and put them in alphabetical order, as quickly as they can. When they have finished, they raise their hands. Check the spelling and order of the words as each student puts up his/her hand. Fast finishers can mix up the words again and repeat the activity. To make the game competitive, the first student to finish with all the words correctly spelled and in the right order is the winner.

Anagrams
Write anagrams of target vocabulary on the board, e.g., for Unit 3 SB38, *tcajke (jacket)*. Students work in pairs to solve the anagrams. When they have solved each one, they raise their hands and say a word. Ask How do you spell (jacket)? The students spell it out correctly. This can also be played as a team game.

Bingo
Use this game to review any vocabulary set, letters or numbers. Use flashcards or write the letters/numbers on the board to review. Students then choose four of these words/letters/numbers and draw simple pictures or write them down. Say sentences defining each of the words e.g., for the farm animals/places in Unit 8 *This is a small bird. It is white or brown. It can swim.* (or just say the letters/numbers). Students who have drawn or written the word/letter cross it out. The first student to cross out all four of their words/letters calls out *Bingo!*

Blindfold game
Tie a piece of material around a student's eyes so that he or she is blindfolded. This student stands in the middle of the classroom. Other students walk around him or her until the blindfolded student reaches out and touches one of them. This student then stands still and asks *What's my name?* The blindfolded student guesses by their voice and replies *Your name's (Ana).* In SB41 the student then has to guess one item the student is wearing, by asking, e.g., *Are you wearing black shoes?* When (Ana) answers *Yes, I am*, she then has a turn at being blindfolded.

Bluff
Invite three or four students to the front of the class. Give each one a flashcard or picture and ask them to keep them secret from the class. These students decide (without telling the rest of the class) who is going to be the *bluffer* (the one who doesn't tell the truth). The students then each say a sentence that might or might not correspond with the flashcard or picture they are holding (e.g., in Unit 7 SB88, when the clothing store flashcard is on the board: *The toy store is next to the clothing store*). Students guess who is bluffing. Students say *Bluff* and the name of the student they think is the bluffer. Check by showing the pictures, and then repeat the activity with other groups of students. Students can also play this as a team game.

Can I have … ?

Students play this game in teams. Make a request, e.g., *Can I have (ten books / a red pen), please?* The team which finds the requested item the most quickly wins a point. When students are reading and writing more, you can also play this game with the requests written down on slips of paper for them to read.

Categories

Use flashcards or word cards from different vocabulary sets (or in Unit 5, from different food groups). Write the category headings for each vocabulary set on the board. Distribute the flashcards or word cards to different students in the class. Students with a card take turns saying or reading the word(s). The class decides which category the word is from. Students can then come to the front of the class and put their card into piles for each category. When the piles are completed, invite other students to come and take two cards from one pile and one from another. They read them out in a jumbled order. The rest of the class listen and say which word is the odd one out. Repeat until all students have been involved.

Circle it!

Write a selection of 10 to 12 numbers or stick pictures/flashcards on the board at a height your students can reach. Practice saying the numbers/items with the whole class. Divide the class into two teams, lined up facing the board. Give a different-colored board pen to the student at the front of each team. Say one of the numbers/items on the board. The two students race to circle the number. Whoever gets to the number first, circles it with their board pen. The two students then pass their board pen to the next student in their team and go to the back of the line. Repeat with the new students, saying a different number/item from the board. Repeat until all the numbers are circled. Count the circles in each color. The team with the most circles wins.

Class survey

Class surveys can be used to compare a range of students' experiences, e.g., finding out how many students like or don't like different foods. Stick a flashcard to the board, e.g., carrots, and use it to make a sentence or ask a question, e.g., *Do you like carrots?* Count the number of hands up and write this number next to the flashcard of the carrots. Repeat with other food and drink flashcards. At the end of the activity, you can compare the numbers for each food and drink item to find out the most and the least popular foods (*How many children like carrots?*)

Correct my mistakes

This game can be played with photographs, pictures, or texts or about your class/classroom. Make false sentences for students to correct, e.g., if there is a TV on a table, say *The TV is on the closet.* Nominate individual students to correct the sentences (*No (it isn't). It's on the table.* etc.).

Count and collect

Students play this game in teams. Say a number, e.g., *Eight.* One student from each team has to find and name eight of the same classroom objects, e.g., *eight books.* The first student to do so scores a point for their team.

Describe and draw

This is a picture dictation game. Students choose and draw four or five items, e.g., in Unit 4, a bedroom with three or four things on/in/under items of furniture. They don't show their drawing to their partner. Students then take turns describing what they've drawn to a partner or asking and answering questions, e.g., *The phone is on the table*, or *The supermarket is next to the café.* Their partner listens and draws the same items/picture onto another piece of paper. He/She can ask questions to help, e.g., *Is the supermarket between the café and the movie theater?* They then compare their drawings and check that they match. If there are any mistakes, they can comment on them: *No. The phone isn't under the table. It's on the table.*

Does it match?

Use flashcards and matching word cards. Stick four flashcards on the board face down so students can't see the pictures. Invite four students to the board and give each one a word card. Students stick the word cards face up below the flashcards so they can be read. Point to the first word card and students read out the word. Turn over the flashcard above it. Ask the rest of the class *Does it match?* (*Yes/No.*) When all word cards are turned over, students move them around so that they match the flashcards correctly. Repeat with other groups of students. See which group can guess the most number of flashcards correctly.

Drawing game

Choose a vocabulary item students know that is simple to draw. Draw a picture of the item on the board, line by line, pausing to ask each time What am I drawing? Can you guess? Students try to guess what the picture is before you have finished it. They can also play this in teams, with students taking turns doing the drawing. Alternatively, they can play the game in pairs.

Drawing in the air

Trace the outline of a number or an item in the air. Students have to watch and guess what you are "drawing."

Find a partner

Students draw or write down something that is their favorite/they like/they can do/they are wearing, e.g., for Unit 3 SB42, they draw an item of clothing they are wearing and color it in (e.g., a pink T-shirt). Then they have to find someone, who has drawn or written the same thing. They do this by asking different students a question about what they have on their paper, e.g., *Are you wearing a pink T-shirt?* (*Yes, I am./No, I'm not.*) When they find a partner they make a pair by standing or sitting together.

Find something (red/plastic)
Give students simple instructions to find objects of a color or a material: *Find something (red/cotton)*. Students have to look around the classroom to find all the items they can that are of that color or material. This can also be played as a team game with students seeing which team can find the most objects. If they know the words, students list the objects they have found: *a red pencil/a cotton shirt*, etc.

Follow my instructions
Give a student an instruction, e.g., *Put a pencil on the cabinet*. When the student has done so, ask the rest of the class *Where's the pencil? (It's on the cabinet.)* If the student has obeyed your instruction correctly congratulate him/her and say *Thank you. The pencil is on the cabinet*. If the student has made a mistake, e.g., the pencil is on your chair, say *Sorry (Clara)*, and repeat the instruction. Repeat, giving instructions about other items to other students. This can also be played as a team game with the team getting a point when a student carries out the instruction correctly.

Guess what?
This is a simple description game. You/Students describe a word or a picture for others to guess what it is, e.g., for Unit 2 SB26, *It's a pet. It's small. It's orange. (It's a fish.)*

Guess where?
Ask students to close their eyes while you hide a flashcard or a small item somewhere in the classroom. Students then open their eyes. Ask *Where's the (ball)?* Students look around and if they can see the item/flashcard, they answer *It's next to the window*.

Hangman
Write short lines on the board representing the letters in a word you want to practice (e.g., in Hello again! SB13 for *yellow* you write: _ _ _ _ _ _ .) Students take turns guessing letters. If they're correct, you write the letter in the word, on the appropriate line. If they're wrong, you note down the letter they guessed and draw one line of a picture made of nine lines, e.g., a simple house (with a triangular roof and rectangular door). If students guess the word before the picture is finished, they win. If you draw the whole house before they guess the word, you win.

I can see
Play this observation game with photographs or illustrations in the Student's Book. Ask students to look at the photographs/ illustrations and make sentences about them, e.g., *I can see a red bus*. Students find and point to the correct items in the photograph/illustration. Students can also take turns making more sentences for the class, or do the same activity in pairs.

Jigsaw matching
Find pictures of items from your target vocabulary set (e.g., from the Internet or magazines) and cut these up into two or three pieces to make a simple jigsaw. Distribute the pieces of the pictures to students so each student has one. Students have to guess what their item is. They then have to find other students in the class with the same item by asking questions. For example, they ask *Do you have a horse? (Yes, I do./No, I don't.)* They put their pieces together to make a complete picture.

Last one standing
Start the game with all students standing. Make a sentence, practicing a target structure, e.g., in Unit 3 SB38 with items of clothing and *I have: I have a skirt*. Students who agree with you (or, in Unit 3, those who are wearing the same item of clothing) stay standing. Those who don't agree sit down. Ask a standing student *Do you have (a skirt)? (Yes, I do.)* Then ask a sitting student, to elicit *No, I don't*. Repeat with different sentences using *I have* and *I don't have*. In Unit 3, include practice of colors, e.g., *I have blue socks*. The last student left standing wins.

Listen and do
Say a mixture of words that have two target sounds, e.g., for /g/ and /h/ in Unit 1: *go, get, help, green, how, head, great, hair, grandma, give, helicopter*. Students listen and do a specifi c action or mime for each target sound (e.g., in Unit 1 they look at you and wave as if saying "hello" for the /h/ words and they wave and then turn around as if saying "goodbye" for the /g/ words).

Match the pictures and words
Use any set of flashcards and matching word cards. Hold up the word cards and read them with the class. Then stick them to the board, or put them on your desk. Distribute the matching flashcards to pairs of students in the class. One student shows the flashcard and names the item or place on it. The other student finds the matching word card and brings it back. Check with the class that each word card collected matches with the flashcard correctly.

Me too!
Each student writes a list of sentences about themselves which are true, e.g., *I'm seven. I have a sister. I like art. I don't like soccer. I can swim. I can't dance*. They work in pairs. Student A reads his/her first sentence. Student B responds *Me too!* if the sentence is true for him/her, or *Not me*. if it isn't true. Student A checks the sentence if the response is *Me too!* Then Student B reads his/her first sentence and Student A responds. Students continue in this way until they have said all their sentences. See which pair have the most in common. If time, students can swap partners and repeat the activity (with the same sentences).

Meet and greet

Ask students to stand up. If you have some music, play it while students move around the classroom. Then stop the music. Students turn to the student on their left and introduce themselves, e.g., In the Hello again! unit SB6, saying *Hello/Hi! I'm (name). I'm (age). What's your name?* … They can wave to each other, or shake hands, and say *Pleased to meet you.* Repeat several times. (Note if you don't have music, just do this activity with students moving around until you say *Stop!* Alternatively students do the same activity from their seats, turning to ask the students next to them, behind, and in front of them in turn.)

Memory 1 through 10

Play this game with any set of ten flashcards. Show the cards to the students one by one and elicit the word, or a sentence about the card. Then stick the flashcard to the board face down and write a number underneath it from 1 through 10. Students have to try and remember where each flashcard is. Divide the students into two teams. Students from one team name a card and ask you a question about it, e.g., *Number 3. Is it a (baby)?* Turn the chosen flashcard over. If it is a baby, answer *Yes, it is,* and the guessing team keeps the card. If it isn't a baby, say *No, it isn't,* and turn it face down on the board again in the same position. Continue the game until all the cards have been guessed correctly. The team with the most flashcards wins the game.

Memory pairs

Play this game with any set of five matching flashcards and word cards. Distribute the flashcards and word cards to ten students and ask them to stand at the front of the class – the students with flashcards to the left and the students with word cards to the right. Students show their flashcards and word cards and say or read the word. They then hold the cards facing away from the class. Other students in the class take turns remembering who is holding the matching flashcards and word cards. They name a pair of students, e.g., Jacques and Laura. The named students show their cards. If they match, they give the cards to the student who guessed correctly. If they don't, they keep them and turn them to face away from the class. At the end of the game, the winners are students who have matching pairs of cards. Repeat with the other five pairs of matching flashcards and word cards.

Messages

Students write a message down on a slip of paper and put the slips of paper into a box or bag. The message can be an offer, an instruction, a request, or an invitation. For example, for Unit 5 SB65, students write messages offering food *Would you like an apple?* Students then take turns drawing out a message, and passing on the message to another student by reading it. The other student responds (e.g., *Yes, please./No, thank you.*), and the student who reads the message mimes carrying out the message, if appropriate (e.g., in Unit 5, handing over the food if the other student says "yes").

Mime and match

Use flashcards and the matching word cards for a target vocabulary set. Distribute the flashcards to half the class, and matching word cards to the other half of the class. Ask a student with a flashcard to mime doing something with the word shown on his/her card, e.g., flying a plane for plane, getting ready to serve for play tennis or swimming like a duck for duck. The student with the matching word card stands up, shows the word and reads it aloud, e.g., *I have "plane".* Check that the answer is correct, and then repeat with other students.

Mirror game

Students stand facing each other in pairs. They take turns touching an item of clothing/part of the body or face, e.g., touch their shoes. Their partner has to do the same action at exactly the same time, as if they are looking in the mirror. They can both then say the action: *Touch your shoes!* Students can make this activity more challenging by tricking their partner with their movements, i.e., seem to be about to touch their shoes and touch their socks instead.

Tic-tac-toe

Use any nine flashcards or word cards. Draw a tic-tac-toe grid on the board (a 3 X 3 grid). Stick one flashcard or word card face down into each of the nine squares. Divide the class into two teams – the Xs and the Os. The teams take turns selecting a card and turning it over. They have to say or read the word on the card, or make a sentence, or ask a question using it. If they do this correctly, they score an X or O in the square. If they make a mistake, the other team scores the X or O. The first team to get three Xs or Os in a row wins.

The one that doesn't belong

Choose and show four flashcards or word cards – three from the same category and one that is different (e.g., three places in town and one place on a farm). Students have to look at the word and say which one doesn't belong. When they can, encourage students to say why the item they chose doesn't belong, e.g., *It's on a farm.*

Pass the actions

Use any word cards for actions or action phrases. Distribute these to students in the class. Play some music while students pass the word cards around the class. Then stop the music or say *Stop!* Students with word cards take turns reading their action silently and acting it out for the rest of the class to guess.

Pass the ball

Students pass a soft ball or another object carefully around the class. Play some music or ask students to pass the ball around the class. Then stop the music or say *Stop!* The student holding the ball has to answer a question posed by you or another student in the class.

Pass the flashcards
Use any set of flashcards or objects. Distribute these to students in the class. Play some music or ask students to pass the flashcards around the class. Then stop the music or say *Stop!* Students with flashcards or objects take turns naming or making a sentence about the item on their flashcard.

Pass the present
Wrap a classroom object, a piece of food (e.g., a carrot or a banana) or a small toy (e.g., a helicopter) in layers of wrapping paper. Play some music and ask students to *Pass the present*. Students pass the present carefully round the class. Then stop the music and ask the student holding the parcel a question, e.g., *What are you wearing?* The student answers and can then unwrap one layer of the present. Continue until one student opens and names the final object inside the present.

Point to (red)
Give students simple color instructions: *Point to (red)*. Students have to look around the class and be the first one to find and point to something of that color. Repeat with other colors. This pointing game can also be played with any nouns – e.g., *Point to a cabinet*. Students try to be the first one to find and point to a cabinet in the classroom.

Questions tic-tac-toe
Draw a tic-tac-toe grid on the board (a 3 X 3 grid). Stick a flashcard into each of the nine squares. Divide the class into two teams – the Xs and the Os. The teams take turns asking and answering an appropriate question using the picture in the square. If the question and answer is grammatically correct, they score an X or O in the square. The first team to get three Xs or Os in a row is the winner.

Reading race
Use any set of flashcards or a mix of flashcards from different sets. Write sentences on pieces of paper, each describing one of the flashcards you have chosen, e.g., *It's a purple skirt* for the skirt flashcard or *I like cereal for breakfast* for the cereal flashcard. Stick the flashcards you have chosen to the board. Divide the class into two teams and give each team half the sentences (face down in a pile). Say *Ready, Steady, Go!* One student from each team stands up, picks up a sentence, reads it and sticks it below the correct flashcard on the board. They then walk quickly back to their team and sit down, naming the next student to read a sentence. The first team to stick up all its sentences is the winner.

Sentence chain game
This is a chain activity. Start with an initial sentence, e.g., for Unit 2 SB30 as if you have lost your pet: *I can't find my mouse.* Ask a student to continue, repeating your sentence and adding a pet of their own: *I can't find my mouse or my spider.* The game continues until someone forgets a

pet or can't think of one to add. Repeat the activity, seeing how long you can make the sentence chain.

Simon says
This is an instructions game. Students listen and follow instructions, but only if you say *Simon says*, e.g., if you say *Put on your jacket*, students should do nothing, but if you say *Simon says, "Put on your jacket,"* students must find their jacket and put it on (or mime doing so). Students can also give the instructions.

Sound bingo
Students think of four words with the target sound in them and write them on a piece of paper, e.g., with the /f/ sound in Unit 2: *frog, fish, five, fox*. Then call out a mixture of words that have /f/ (*four, fruit, feet*) or other sounds to contrast, e.g., /v/ and /θ/ for Unit 2: *vulture, think, van, three, violin*. Students listen carefully. When you say a word with the target sound (e.g. /f/), they say *Yes* and cross it off their list if they have written it down. When you say a word without this target sound in it, students say *No*. The first student to cross out all of his/her words calls out *Bingo!*

Sound pairs
Draw or write pairs of sound words on the board in a jumbled order, e.g., for words with /y/, /j/, /m/, and /n/, *yak* and *yellow*, *juice* and *giraffe*, *man* and *mom*, *nine* and *nice*. Make sure the words you choose only contain one of the target sounds in them (e.g., avoid *name*, as it contains both /n/ and /m/). Students then work in pairs to see who can match up the correct sound pairs the most quickly.

Stand in order
Use any set of flashcards or number cards. Distribute these to students in the class and ask these students to come to the front. Name the items on the flashcards in a random order (or say the numbers in ascending or descending order). Students with the flashcards have to arrange themselves in the correct order.

Stand up and sit down
This is an agreement game. Make sentences about something relating to students, e.g. for Unit 5, *I like toast for breakfast*. Students for whom this is true stand up, the others remain seated. Repeat with different sentences.

Test the teacher
Students test your knowledge by asking you questions. The questions can be about themselves or other students in the class, about flashcards, the coursebook or general knowledge questions they know the answer to. Students can just take turns thinking of and asking you questions, or you can arrange this as a team game, with teams taking turns thinking of and asking you a question. If you know the answer, you get a point. If you don't know the answer, their team or group gets a point. The team or group with the most points at the end of the game is the winner.

The last word
Say a sentence from the lesson/using target language, but stop before you say the last word each time. Students

say the word. For example, in Hello again! SB10 say lines from the story with the last word missing, e.g., *This is our … We have a surprise for … Stand … Hello, Ben. Let's …*

Traffic lights
Move students to a large open space or make a space in the classroom. Give classroom instructions or name target words (animals, actions) for students to mime. Say *Green light!* and show a circle of green card. Students follow your instruction. Say *Red light!* and show a circle of red card. Students stop what they are doing.

You can also use these cards for classroom management (e.g., to start and stop pair or group work). If you want to let students know they only have a few minutes left for a particular activity, you can say *Yellow light!* and show a circle of yellow card.

True or false?
Make true and false sentences about a picture, photograph, text, story, students in the class, or factual statements. Students listen and say *true* or *false*. Students can also take turns making the sentences. They can correct the false sentences to make them all true ones.

Two minutes
Write a category heading for words you want to brainstorm on the board (e.g., for Unit 8 Animals). Divide the class into teams of five or six students. Each team chooses someone to write for them. Tell them to write the names of as many things in the category as they can in English. Set a time limit of two minutes (use a timer if you have one or ring a bell after two minutes). Teams stop writing when the time is up. Ask students to count how many items are on their list. Elicit the words from the team with the most items and write them on the board (or invite the student with the list to write on the board). The other teams cross off the ones they have on their lists. Elicit any extra items from the other teams. Check comprehension and practice any new words.

What's in the bag?
Put an object or objects in a bag for a student to feel (e.g., classroom objects or small toys). Ask *What's this?* or *What are these?* Students must feel and guess the object(s) *(It's a (pencil)./They're (teddy bears))* without looking.

What's missing?
Stick flashcards or word cards to the board or lay them on the floor where all students can see them. Allow students a few minutes to look at them. Then ask students to close their eyes while you remove one or two of the cards. Students then open their eyes and answer the question *What's missing?*

Where's the (lamp)?
Show students the flashcards of pieces of furniture: closet, bookcase, cabinet, table and couch. Elicit the words, then stick them face down to the board in a row. Then show the following flashcards: phone, TV, mirror, lamp and clock, elicit the words, and stick one above each of the five furniture flashcards. Turn over the first furnishings flashcard in the top row. Using the item on the flashcard, ask *Where's the (phone)?* Tap the piece of furniture below. Students have to guess *It's on the table./Is the phone on the table?* Turn the furniture flashcard over. If it's the table, give both flashcards to the student who guessed correctly. If not, turn both cards over again and ask about another item, returning to the phone again later. At the end of the game, students who have the most pairs of cards are the winners of the game.

Whisper down the line
Make four teams. Teams line up facing the board. Give the student at the front of each team a board pen. Whisper a different number between 1 and 20 or a word to each of the students at the front of the teams. Students whisper it back along the line and the student at the back of their team comes and writes it on the board. Teams get a point for writing the number (in figures) correctly (or the word). The four students at the front go to the back of the line. Repeat with different numbers or words.

Who said it?
Books closed. Say a line from the story. Students say the name of the character who said it, e.g., in Unit 5 SB65 *Let's go for lunch (Ben). Oh, dear! (Tina) More cake, please. (iPal) That's enough! (Olivia).*

Who has it?
Hand out the unit flashcards at random. Students with flashcards stand up, show them to the class and make a sentence, e.g., in Unit 1 SB18 *I have a helicopter.* Give students two minutes to look at the flashcards and remember who has what. Then the students with flashcards put them face down on their desks. You can make a sentence, e.g., *She has a helicopter.* Students guess the name or say, e.g., *Umberto has a helicopter.* When someone guesses correctly, the student with the flashcard says *Yes. I have a (helicopter)* and gives the card back to you. Alternatively, ask a question, e.g., *Who has a helicopter?* Students guess the name in the same way. When students have the idea, repeat but this time volunteers can try to say where all the cards are by pointing to the students and making sentences

themselves, e.g., *She has a helicopter. He has a tractor.* etc. You can make the game competitive by giving students who guess correctly points.

Word race
Stick the word cards for the unit on the board (or write the words). Give students a time limit of five minutes to look at the words and practice spelling (e.g., by writing them out or testing each other). Divide the class into teams (there should be no more students on each team than there are words to remember, so that each student gets a turn – e.g., if there are nine words to remember you need teams of nine or fewer). Remove/Erase the words from the board. Divide the board into as many sections as you have teams, by drawing vertical lines (i.e., if you have four teams, there will be four sections). Students line up in their teams, facing the board. Give the first person on each team a board marker. Say *Write the words!* These four students come to the front and write one of the words they practiced earlier, in their team's section. Then they pass the board pen to the next person in the team, who writes a different word from the list, and so on. Students must not copy other teams but they can help the members of their team with words and spelling. Make sure a different student writes each word (and that there isn't a stronger student writing/spelling out all the words). The team which finishes first and has the most correctly spelled words wins.

Yes/No game
This game can be used for various vocabulary items. Think of an item students know the English word for. Students have to guess what you are thinking of by asking yes or no questions only, e.g., in Unit 6 *Is it a team sport?/ Do you need a racket?* Allow them a maximum number of questions to ask, e.g., five. This can also be played as a team game. If students guess correctly within this number of questions they score a point for their team.

Hello again!

Unit aims Students review language from Level 1 and learn to give different kinds of information. This includes:

- introducing themselves
- introducing their friends and family
- saying the letters of the alphabet and spelling their name
- reviewing numbers from 1 through 10 and saying how old they and others are
- learning about different kinds of art and reviewing colors and parts of the body

Background information The photograph shows students in school having a teleconference with students in a different country.

Introduction to the unit

- Greet the class. Introduce any new students. Say *Hello, I'm/My name's … What's your name?* When the student says his/her name reply *Nice to meet you, (Sam)!* Explain the meaning and encourage the rest of the class to repeat the phrase after you. Greet any students you already know by saying *Hello again, (Flavia).*
- Distribute or make sure each student has a Student's Book and a Workbook.
- Say *Open your books to pages 4 and 5, please.* Then say *Now listen and look.* Play the theme song on the recording.
- Students look at the photograph and read the title of the unit while listening to the recording. Confirm the meaning of *again*.
- Point to the three children in the foreground of the photograph and say *Look. Where are they? They're at …* *(school.)* Point to the teacher and ask *Is this their mom? (No.)* Say *No. It's the teacher.* Ask *Are they happy?* Use gesture to help show the meaning of *happy*. Point to the screen and ask *Who's this? (Boys and girls./Children.) Are they at school? (Yes, they are.) What are they doing?* Explain/Elicit that the children in the foreground are saying *Hello!* to some children in a school in a different country, via the Internet.
- Then ask further questions: *How many children can you see on the screen? (Seven.) Is their teacher in the classroom, too? (Yes, she is.) What colors can you see? (Pink, yellow, purple, white, green.) Are there any chairs in the photograph? (Yes, there are.) Are there any desks? (Yes, there are.) Are there any bags? (No, there aren't.) Do the children have pencils? (No, they don't.)*

`CD1:02`

(Theme song lyrics)

Guess What! Come and see.
Guess What! Come and play.
Guess What! What can we learn today?

Guess What! Come and see.
Guess What! Come and play.
Guess What! It's time to learn today!
Guess What!

1 [CD1 03] Listen. Who's speaking?

2 [CD1 04] Listen, point, and say.

1 Ben   2 Olivia   3 David   4 Tina

5 Leo

3 [CD1 05] Listen and find.

Find Leo

6 Vocabulary

→ Workbook page 4

Lesson aims Students review introducing themselves and saying how old they are. They review character names and are introduced to a new character.

New language *Ben, My name's … , Nice to meet you. This is (my sister/brother, Tina). His/Her name's … , He's/She's my (brother/sister/friend). pet, How old is he? He's two.*

Recycled language *Olivia, Tina, David, Leo* (character names), *Hello/Hi, What's your name? I'm … , Who's this? lizard, iPal,* numbers 1–5

Materials CD1 | Flashcards: 1–6 | CD of lively music (optional)

Warmer

● Point to a student and ask his/her neighbor *Who's this?* Encourage the second student to reply with a sentence, e.g., *It's Rosa.* Repeat for different students. Use *What's his/her name?* sometimes.

● Ask students if they remember the names of the characters from Level 1. Show the character flashcards and ask about each character *What's his/her name?*

Student's Book page 6

1 Listen. Who's speaking?

● Say *Open your books to page 6, please.* Ask *Who can you see? (Olivia, Tina, David, Leo) Are they at home? (No, at school.)*

● Ask *What are they saying?* Demonstrate waving your hand in greeting and elicit *Hello!* Point to the new character and ask *What are they saying to this boy? (What's your name? / Nice to meet you!)* Say *Let's listen to the children. Who's speaking?* Play the recording. Students listen and point to the characters as they speak.

● Play the recording again, pausing to elicit each character's name and that of the new boy, Ben. Ask *Is David Olivia's friend? (No, brother.) How old is Leo? (Two.)*

● Point to iPal (on Olivia's backpack) and ask *Who's this?* Remind students/Elicit that this is iPal and that he is a magic robot.

● If time, ask about the other items in the picture *What's this? / What can you see? / What color is it? (a yellow book, a blue bike, a ball).*

CD1:03

Ben: Hello. My name's Ben. What's your name?
Olivia: Hi, Ben. Nice to meet you. I'm Olivia. And this is David. He's my brother.
Ben: Hi, David.
David: Hi, Ben. This is Tina. She's my friend.
Tina: Hello.
Ben: And who's this?
David: He's my pet lizard. His name's Leo.
Ben: How old is he?
David: He's two.
Ben: Cool!
Leo: *Crick!*

2 Listen, point, and say.

● Show the character flashcards in the same order as they appear in the picture. Ask *Who's this? (Ben).* Repeat for the other characters.

● Say *Now listen, point, and say.* Play the recording. Students listen and point to the numbered characters in the picture as they hear them mentioned in the recording. Then play again. Students listen and say the characters' names.

CD1:04

1 Ben 3 David 5 Leo
2 Olivia 4 Tina

3 Listen and find.

● Say *Now listen and find.* Play the recording, pausing for students to find and point to the correct character, (the character who is named, not the speaker). Students can also say the correct number.

Key: Ben (1) Olivia (2) Tina (4) Leo (5) David (3)

CD1:05

Ben: Hello. My name's Ben.
David: This is my sister. Her name's Olivia.
Tina: I'm Tina.
David: This is Leo. He's two.
Tina: This is my friend. His name's David.

Find Leo.

● Point to the *Find Leo* icon at the bottom of the page. Ask *What's his name? (Leo.)* Say *Now find Leo.* Students find and point to Leo in the picture (David is holding him).

Workbook page 4

1 Order the letters. Look and draw lines.

● Students solve the anagrams to make names. They match the names to the picture by drawing lines.

Key: 2 David 3 Ben 4 Olivia 5 Tina

2 Look at Activity 1 and put a check ✓.

● Students read the sentences and look at the picture in activity 1. They check the *yes* or *no* box for each sentence.

Key: 2 yes 3 no 4 yes 5 yes

Ending the lesson

● Ask students to look at the picture in the Student's Book. Make true or false sentences about each character, e.g., point to David and say *This is Ben.* or point to Leo and say *He's two.* Students make a thumbs-up for true and a thumbs-down for false.

Extra activities: see page TB114 (if time)

Lesson aims Students learn to introduce family and friends and ask about someone's age.

New language *This is (my sister/brother, Tina).* | *friend*

Recycled language character names, numbers 1–10, *Who's this? What's his/her name? His/Her name's … , How old is he/she? He's/She's (eight). brother, sister*

Materials CD1 | Flashcards: 7–16 | Word cards: see page TB105 | Classroom objects – up to ten of each – placed around the classroom (erasers, books, pens, pencils, pencil cases) (optional)

Warmer

- Practice counting from 1 through 10 in chorus. Repeat several times. Then practice counting in reverse from 10 through 1.
- Write the numbers 1–10 on the board or show the number flashcards and point to them. Students say each number in chorus, then, when they are confident, individually.

Presentation

- Point to a student and ask *Who's this? / What's his/her name?* Encourage students to make a full sentence *This is Esteban.* Ask *How old is he/she?* Students guess, e.g., *Eight.* Repeat for different students.
- Stand next to a student and ask him/her to stand up. Introduce him/her to the class, e.g., *This is my friend. His name's Erik. He's seven.* Encourage the rest of the class to say *Hello, Erik. Nice to meet you.* Repeat for different students. Confirm the meaning of *friend* and practice pronunciation.

Student's Book page 7

4 Say the chant.

- Say *Open your books to page 7, please.* Point to each character and ask *What's his/her name? How old is he/she?* Make sure students realize the numbers in the orange circles are the characters' ages. Point to the labels *brother* and *sister* and elicit the meaning.
- Say *Listen to the chant.* Play the recording. Students listen and point to the pictures in turn.
- Then say *Now listen and say the chant.* Play the recording again. Students can clap along to the rhythm at first, joining in with as many words as they can. Then repeat as often as necessary until students are chanting confidently.

CD1:06

David: This is my sister. Her name's Olivia.
Ben: How old is she?
David: She's eight.
Olivia: This is my brother. His name's David.

Ben: How old is he?
Olivia: He's seven.
David: This is my friend. Her name's Tina.
Ben: How old is she?
David: She's seven.

Olivia: This is my friend. His name's Ben.
Tina: How old is he?
Olivia: He's eight.

5 Find the mistakes and say.

- Point to the first card and read the information. Ask *Is that correct? (No.)* Say *No. There are mistakes.* Read the example speech bubble, emphasizing the corrected information (*Ben, eight*).
- Say *Find the mistakes and say.* Students work in pairs. They read the cards and practice correcting the information, using activity 4 and the example speech bubble to help them.
- Elicit answers from different pairs. Write them on the board, if necessary. Make sure students are choosing *his/her* and *he/she* as appropriate.

Key: Number 2. Her name's Olivia. She's eight. **Number 3.** His name's David. He's seven. **Number 4.** Her name's Tina. She's seven.

Workbook page 5

3 Listen and stick.

- Students will need the Hello again! unit stickers from the back of the Workbook.
- Play the recording. Students listen and stick the stickers into the correct position.

CD1:07

1 **David:** Hello. My name's David.
2 **Ben:** Hi, I'm Ben.
3 **David:** This is my sister, Olivia.
4 **David:** This is my friend. Her name is Tina.
5 **David:** And this is Leo. He's two.

4 Look, read, and match.

- Students read and match the sentence halves.

Key: 1 Her name's Sue. She's nine. **2** This is my brother. He's eight. His name's Dan.

My picture dictionary → Go to page 84. Check the words you know and trace.

- Before students do the picture dictionary activity, introduce the number words using the word cards. Hold up each word card and read it aloud with the class.
- Students then turn to page 84 and look at the numbers. They check the number words they know. They then trace over the number words.

Ending the lesson

- Stand next to a confident student and ask about the person sitting next to him/her. Say, e.g., *Who's this? Is this your brother?* The student replies *This is my friend.* Encourage the student to continue, saying the friend's name and age, e.g., *His name's David. He's eight.* Repeat with different students. If time, students repeat the activity in groups of four.

Extra activities: see page TB114 (if time)

Say the chant.

This is my sister.
Her name's Olivia.
How old is she?
She's eight.

sister

brother

friend

friend

  Find the mistakes and say.

Number 1. His name's Ben. He's eight.

1

Name:
David

Age:
6

2

Name:
Tina

Age:
7

3

Name:
Ben

Age:
5

4

Name:
Olivia

Age:
9

6 (CD1 08) **Sing the song.**

Happy, happy, look and see,
We can sing our ABCs.

7 (CD1 09) **Listen and point.**

 Dan

 Jill

 Sam

 Sue

 Tom

8 (About Me) **Ask and answer.**

What's your name?   My name's Harry.

How do you spell "Harry"?   It's H-A-R-R-Y.

Lesson aims   Students learn to say the alphabet and to ask about spelling and to spell their name.

New language   letter names a–z | *How do you spell (Dan)? It's (D–A–N).* | *happy, look and see, We can sing our ABCs.*

Recycled language   *What's your name? My name's (Dan).*

Materials   CD1 | Pieces of thin cardboard with numbers on for the ages of your class (e.g., one card with number 7 and one card with number 8) | A photograph of your family (e.g., mom, dad, and siblings) (optional)

Warmer

- Ask a student to choose a number card to show his/her age. Introduce the student to the class, e.g., *This is my friend. Her name's Elena. She's seven.* Ask a second student to choose the correct number card for his/her age. The first student introduces the second student to the class just as you did (*This is my friend. His name's … *). Ask other students to continue.

Presentation

- Write letters *a*, *b*, *c* on the board. Say the letters. Students repeat. Write the other letters on the board and say *Let's learn our ABCs.* Explain that students are going to practice saying the letters in English so that they can spell their names.

Student's Book page 8

6 Sing the song.

- Say *Open your books to page 8, please. Let's say the alphabet.* Point to each letter and say it. Students repeat.
- Say *Now sing the song.* Play the recording a few times, until students are singing confidently. The first time students can hum to the tune and join in with any letters they know. You can also divide the class into four groups, with each group singing one line of the alphabet and the whole class joining in with the chorus.
- Students can sing along to the version of the song with the words or to the karaoke version.

CD1:08

A, B, C, D, E, F, G (x2)
Happy, happy, look and see
We can sing our ABCs.

H, I, J, K, L, M, N, O, P (x2)
Happy, happy, look and see
We can sing our ABCs.

Q, R, S, T, U, V (x2)
Happy, happy, look and see
We can sing our ABCs.

W, X, Y, and Z (x2)
Happy, happy, look and see
We can sing our ABCs.

7 Listen and point.

- Point to the first photograph and ask *What's his name?* (*Dan*). Repeat for the other photographs. Students ask and answer about the children in pairs in the same way.
- Say *Listen and point.* Play the recording. Students listen and point to the correct photograph. Ask *How do you spell "Dan"?* (*It's D–A–N.*) Practice saying the letters with the class. Repeat for the other photographs.

Key: Students point to Tom, Jill, Dan, Sue, and Sam.

CD1:09

Adult: Hello. What's your name?
Boy: My name's Tom.
Adult: How do you spell "Tom"?
Boy: T–O–M.
Adult: T–O–M. Tom! Thank you.

Adult: Hello. What's your name?
Girl: My name's Jill.
Adult: How do you spell "Jill"?
Girl: J–I–L–L.
Adult: J–I–L–L. Jill! Thank you.

Adult: Hello. What's your name?
Boy: My name's Dan.
Adult: How do you spell "Dan"?
Boy: D–A–N.
Adult: D–A–N. Dan! Thank you.

Adult: Hello. What's your name?
Girl: My name's Sue.
Adult: How do you spell "Sue"?
Girl: S–U–E.
Adult: S–U–E. Sue! Thank you.

Adult: Hello. What's your name?
Boy: My name's Sam.
Adult: How do you spell "Sam"?
Boy: S–A–M.
Adult: S–A–M. Sam! Thank you.

8 Ask and answer.

- Students work in pairs. They ask and answer about their own name, e.g., *What's your name? My name's Irina. How do you spell "Irina"? It's I–R–I–N–A.* They can make a name sign or badge before starting the activity.

Workbook page 6

5 Listen and circle the name.

- Students listen and circle the correct name each time. Elicit answers and ask, e.g., *How do you spell Tom?*

Key: 2 Pat **3** Nick **4** Katy

CD1:10

1 **Teacher:** What's your name?
Tom: My name's Tom.
Teacher: How do you spell "Tom"?
Tom: T–O–M.

2 **Teacher:** What's your name?
Girl: My name's Pat.
Teacher: How do you spell "Pat"?
Girl: P–A–T.

3 **Teacher:** What's your name?
Nick: My name's Nick.
Teacher: How do you spell "Nick"?
Nick N–I–C–K.

4 **Teacher:** What's your name?
Girl: My name's Katy.
Teacher: How do you spell "Katy"?
Girl: K–A–T–Y.

6 Draw and say. Then write and circle.

- Students draw a picture of a friend or sibling. They complete the sentences with the person's name and age and circle the correct option: *His/Her* and *He's/She's.*

Key: Students' own answers.

Ending the lesson

- Say *Listen. Who's this?* Spell out a student's name. The first student to guess the name correctly says *It's (Mauricio)* and spells the next name.

Extra activities: see page TB114 (if time)

Lesson aims Students learn to ask about objects using *What's this? It's a/an …* and *What are these? They're …*

New language *What are these? They're … rulers.*

Recycled language *What's this? It's a/an …* | classroom objects and furniture | *bike, computer, camera* | colors (e.g., *a pink computer*) | *How many (chairs) can you see?* | numbers 1–10

Materials CD1 | Classroom objects – pencil, pencil case, eraser, book, pen – or flashcards from Level 1 (17–26) | An orange, an apple | A blindfold, a bag, a collection of items students know in English (e.g., an apple, an orange, some bananas, an egg, a small bottle of water, two teddy bears, two or three balls, a doll) (optional)

Warmer

- Play the alphabet song from the previous lesson (CD1:08). Students join in and point to the letters on Student's Book page 8.

Presentation

- Hold up a pen and ask *What's this? (It's a pen.)* Repeat for other classroom objects (*pencil, book, pencil case, eraser*) and for furniture students can name in English (*desk, chair, door, window, board*). Show an apple or orange and ask *What's this?* to elicit *It's an …* Show a ruler and teach the new word.
- Hold up two items, e.g., two pens, and ask *What are these?* Help students reply *They're …* Repeat with more pairs and groups of items.

Student's Book page 9

9 Listen, look, and say.

- Say *Open your books to page 9, please. Listen and point.* Play the recording. Students point to the children in the photographs as they speak.
- Then say *Now listen and say.* Play the recording again, pausing for students to listen and repeat the questions and answers.

CD1:11

(See Student's Book page 9.)

10 Listen and point.

- Review colors using the flashcards or items in the classroom (point and ask *What color is this?*)
- Say *Listen and find. A2. What's this?* Students find the correct item (the computer) and say, e.g., *It's a computer.* Ask *What color is it? (Pink).* Say *Yes. It's a pink computer.* Repeat several times until students understand the way the grid works. Make sure you ask some plural questions (*What are these?*)

- Explain that students are going to listen to some children playing the same game. Say *Now listen and point.* Play the recording. Students point to the correct item. Play the recording again, pausing to ask *What's this? / What are these?* Students say, e.g., *They're brown chairs.*

CD1:12

Girl: A1. What are these?
Boy: They're brown chairs.
Girl: Yes. Your turn.

Boy: B2. What are these?
Girl: They're purple pencil cases.
Boy: Yes. Your turn.

Girl: A3. What are these?
Boy: They're blue doors.
Girl: Yes. Your turn.

Woman: B3. What's this?
Girl: It's a yellow camera.
Woman: Yes. Good job!

Boy: A2. What's this?
Girl: It's a pink computer.
Boy: Yes. Good job!

Girl: B1. What's this?
Boy: It's a red bike.
Girl: Yes. Good job!

11 Ask and answer.

- Students play the same game in pairs, using the speech bubbles to help them. Circulate and make sure they are forming singular or plural questions and answers as appropriate.

Workbook page 7

7 Look, read, and circle the answer.

- Students look at the photographs, read, and circle the correct sentence each time.

Key: 2 They're pencils. **3** It's an eraser. **4** They're pens.

8 Look and write.

- Students look at the pictures and complete the questions and answers.

Key: 2 this, a chair **3** are these, They're rulers. **4** 's this, It's a camera.

Ending the lesson

- Play *Drawing game* (see page xv) using classroom objects, toys, or food vocabulary. Draw both single things (e.g., an apple) and groups of things (e.g., an egg carton full of eggs) in order to practice *What's this?* and *What are these?* Encourage students to reply with full sentences (e.g., *It's an apple. / They're eggs.*) Color the pictures when possible, and ask students to describe the color, too, e.g., *It's a red apple.* You can also practice the alphabet by asking, e.g., *How do you spell "apple"?*

Extra activities: see page TB114 (if time)

9 CD1 11 Listen, look, and say.

1 What's this?

It's a ruler.

2 What are these?

They're books.

10 CD1 12 Listen and point.

11 Ask and answer.

b, 1. What's this?

It's a red bike.

Grammar: *What's this?*   9

Lesson aims Students reinforce language with a story. They also discuss the value of playing together.

New language *our, We have a surprise for you! You hold, Let's play. Help! Don't worry. What a big surprise! We're back again. Look and see. Come with us. Come and play. today*

Recycled language *colors | This is … , | tree house, Stand here, iPal, magic tree, Hello, Do you like … ? Yes, I do. / No, I don't. Oh, dear! Wow! Look, your, lion, crocodile, happy*

Materials CD1 | Cards/Materials for a game (e.g., dominoes, Happy Families, Ludo) (optional)

Warmer

- Draw a tree on the board and ask *What's this? (It's a tree)*. Draw a tree house in the tree. Point and ask *What's this in the tree? (It's a tree house)*. Ask students if they have ever been inside a tree house (they can explain where and when).

- Ask students what they remember about the tree house in the story in Level 1. Elicit *magic tree* and see if students remember the rhyme the characters say when they're at the tree house in Level 1 (*1, 2, 3, Magic tree, Clap your hands and come with me*). Tell students they are going to revisit the magic tree house in the stories in this book.

Student's Book page 10

12 Listen and read.

- Say *Open your books to page 10, please.* Ask *Can you see the tree house?* Point to the characters in frame 1 in turn and ask *Who's this? / What's his/her name?* (*Ben, Olivia, Tina, David.*) Remind students that David and Olivia are brother and sister and that the tree house is in their yard. Explain/Elicit that Ben is visiting the tree house for the first time. Point to iPal in frame 2 and ask *Who's this? (It's iPal)*. Encourage students to guess what happens in the story by looking at the other frames.

- Say *Now listen and read.* Play the recording while students listen and follow the story in their books. At the end of the story, point to the picture of the lion in frame 6 and ask *What's this? (It's Ben's lion)*.

- Then play the recording again, pausing at the end of each frame to ask more questions: Frame 1: *What do Olivia and Tina have? (Paint and brushes.)* Frame 2: *What color is the paint? (Red, green, and yellow.)* Frame 3: *Who has the yellow paint? (iPal.)* Frame 4: *What animals can you see? (A lion and a crocodile.)* Frame 5: *What does Ben say? (Oh, dear! Help!)* Elicit the meaning of *Help!* Frame 6: *Is Ben happy? (Yes.)*

- Make sure students realize that at first Ben is surprised/ scared when iPal comes to life, but at the end of the story, he's happy and says *What a big surprise!*

- Students can listen to the story again for pleasure, or pause after key lines for students to repeat. Encourage students to use gestures and intonation from the story as appropriate.

CD1:13

Olivia: This is our tree house.
David: We have a surprise for you!
Olivia: Stand here. You hold iPal.
All: 1, 2, 3, Magic tree.
We're back again. Look and see.
Come with us. Come and play
In our magic tree today.

Tina: This is iPal.
iPal: Hello, Ben! Let's play.

iPal: Do you like animals?
Ben: Yes, I do.

Lion: *Roar!*
Ben: Oh, dear! Help!
Olivia: Don't worry.

All: 3, 2, 1, that was fun.
Time to go. The magic's done!
Ben: Wow! What a big surprise!
David: And look, Ben! Your lion!

(Value) *Play together*

- Play the dialog for frame 3 of the story again, pausing and asking students to repeat iPal's line: *Hello, Ben. Let's play!* Show/Confirm with gesture the meaning of this expression. Then read the value with the class *Play together*. Make sure that students understand the meaning of *together*. Point to frame 2 and ask *Who's in the tree house? (Everyone)*. Ask *Who paints in the story? (Everyone)*. Talk about how important it is to include everyone in games and play together. Point out that Olivia and David share their tree house with their friends, and they want their new friend, Ben, to enjoy having adventures there, too.

- Divide the class into three groups and give each group a character name – Tina, Ben, and iPal. Then play the dialog from frames 3 and 4 again. Students listen and repeat the lines for their group's character.

- You can then rearrange the class into groups of three, each with one Tina, one Ben, and one iPal. Students practice the dialog, smiling and laughing to reinforce the idea of playing together.

Workbook page 8

9 Read and number. Then listen and check.

- Students number the pictures from the story to show the order of events. Play the recording for students to check.

Key: 2 c 3 b 4 f 5 d 6 a

CD1:14

(Repeat of story – see above for story script)

Ending the lesson

- Play *The last word* (see page xviii), with lines from the story.

Extra activities: see page TB114 (if time)

Lesson aims Students learn and practice *Let's play* and review asking about likes and dislikes. Students also practice saying the sounds /r/ and /l/.

New language *Me, too.* | *rabbit* | *The (rabbit) can (run).* | *lazy*

Recycled language *Let's play.* | *Do you like (computer games)? Yes, I do.* | *run, lion*

Materials CD1 | Music CD | Ball, toys (doll, teddy bear, art set, kite, robot, computer game, and board games popular with your students), or flashcards: 27–36 from Level 1 Unit 2, a picture of a robot

Warmer

- Ask a student *Do you like crocodiles?* Encourage the student to reply with a short answer *Yes, I do. / No, I don't.* Repeat with different students, asking about animals, colors, toys, and food and drink students know in English.
- Play *Pass the ball* (see page xvii). When the music stops, ask the student holding the ball *Do you like (teddy bears)?* He/She answers *Yes, I do.* or *No, I don't.* Alternatively, the student holding the ball asks his/her neighbor a question with *Do you like … ?*

Presentation

- Remind students of the story from the previous lesson. Say *iPal says to Ben "Hello! Let's … "* (play). He asks *"Do you like … ?"* (animals). Explain that students are going to practice talking about playing in this lesson.

Student's Book page 11

13 Listen and act.

- Say *Open your books to page 11, please.* Point to the controllers the children are holding in the photograph and ask *What toy is it? Is it an art set? Is it a camera? (It's a computer game).* Do not confirm answers. Say *Listen and find out. What does the boy say?* Play the recording. Elicit *Do you like computer games?*
- Ask students if they have ever played on a game like this and which computer games are their favorites.
- Ask different students *Do you like computer games?* When a student replies *Yes, I do.* say *So do I.* Explain/Confirm the meaning.
- Say *Now listen and repeat.* Play the CD again, pausing for students to repeat the lines.
- Hand one of the toys you've brought to class to each pair of students (or use the toy flashcards from Level 1). Students practice the exchange in pairs, using the toy they have. They swap roles so that each student gets a chance to ask. Go around the class, helping with the names of any new games/toys. Ring a bell or say *Stop!* Students swap their toy/flashcard with another pair and repeat the activity.

Alex: Let's play. Do you like computer games?
Abbi: Yes, I do.
Alex: Me, too.

14 Listen and say.

- In this activity, students practice saying the sounds /r/ and /l/.
- Say *Look at activity 14. What can you see?* Elicit *It's a lion.* and teach *rabbit.* Say *Look. The rabbit can …* Mime running to elicit *run.* Say *Look at the lion. It's lazy.* Mime being lazy and explain the meaning.
- Then say *rabbit – /r/ /r/ /r/ – rabbit.* Students repeat, emphasizing the /r/ sound in *rabbit.*
- Say *lion – /l/ /l/ /l/ – lion.* Students repeat, emphasizing the initial sound in the same way.
- Say *Listen and say.* Play the sound sentences on the recording. Students listen and repeat, emphasizing the initial /r/ and /l/ sounds.
- Students can then repeat the sound sentences without the recording, saying them faster and faster each time. See how fast they can say them.
- Ask students to think of any other words they know that begin with the sounds /r/ and /l/. For example, *robot, ride (a bike), look, living room, leg.*

CD1:16

/r/ /l/ The rabbit can run. The lion is lazy. (x2)

Workbook page 9

10 What's missing? Look and draw. Then stick.

- Remind students of the value from the previous lesson. Students look at the picture and think about what's missing. They then choose the correct toy from the three options shown and draw it into the picture.
- Students then select a smiley sticker from the back of the book and stick it next to the value.

Key: Students should draw the soccer ball (b).

11 Trace the letters.

- Students trace the letters *r* and *l* in the sound sentences.

12 Listen and circle l or r.

- Play the recording. Students listen and circle the letter *l* or *r* according to the initial sound of the word.

Key: 2 l 3 r 4 l

CD1:17

1 robot, robot 2 legs, legs 3 rabbit, rabbit 4 lion, lion

Ending the lesson

- Show students a picture of a robot or draw a robot on the board. Color the legs red if possible. Write the tongue twister *A lazy robot with red legs* on the board. Students practice saying it repeatedly, as fast as they can.

Extra activities: see page TB114 (if time)

13 **Talk Time Listen and act.**

Animal sounds

14 CD1 16 Listen and say.

The rabbit can run. The lion is lazy.

What kind of **art** is it?

1 CD1 18 Listen and say.

photography drawing sculpture painting

2 Watch the video.

3 Look and say the kind of art.

Number 1. Sculpture. Yes.

Guess What!

Project

4 Make a class sculpture.

Lesson aims   Students learn to identify and name different kinds of art.

New language   *Which kind of art is it?* | *photography, sculpture, drawing, painting*

Recycled language   *art* | *numbers 1–4* | *colors* | *photograph, picture, Which (colors) can you see? I can see …* | *Do you like … ? Yes, I do. / No, I don't.*

Materials   CD1 | DVD (optional) | Photographs of different kinds of art, if possible ones that are familiar to students (sculptures found in their hometown/ nearest city, famous paintings, or photographs by artists from their country) | Materials for making paintings and drawings, cameras, objects for a still life (e.g., toys, fruit in a bowl) (optional)

Warmer

- Show the pictures of art you've brought to class. Say *Look! Art.* Show each photograph and ask *Do you like it? Where is it?* (for a local sculpture) *What can you see? Which colors can you see?* Ask students *Where can you see art?* (Elicit names of local galleries, museums, or open spaces with sculptures.) Ask students if they have ever visited an art gallery and which pieces of art they liked best.

Student's Book page 12

What kind of art is it?

- Say *Open your books to page 12, please.* Ask questions about the photograph, e.g., *Where is it? What can you see? How many children are there?*
- Ask students what kind of art it is. Present *sculpture.* Ask students to think of different kinds of art and elicit ideas (in L1).

Student's Book page 13

1 Listen and say.

- Say *Now look at page 13, please.* Use the photographs to present the words for kinds of art.
- Say *Listen and say.* Play the recording. Students listen and repeat the words.
- Hold up the pictures you've brought to class and ask *What kind of art is it? Which kind of art do you like?* Find out which kind of art is most popular in the class (painting/photography/sculpture, or drawing).

CD1:18

1 photography **2** drawing **3** sculpture **4** painting

2 Watch the video.

- Play the video.
- If you don't have the video, provide students with reference materials – e.g., guides from art galleries/ museums, Internet access – so they can look for an example of each kind of art. Students work in pairs or small groups. They try to find and write the title and artist of one sculpture, one painting, one photograph, and one drawing. Circulate and ask questions about the art students find, e.g., *What's this? Do you like it? What color is it? What's it called? Who's the artist?*

Video 00 : see page TB128

3 Look and say the kind of art.

- Students look at the photographs and say the kind of art they can see. They use the speech bubbles to help them.
- Check the activity by saying the number of the photograph. Students say the kind of art.

Key: 2 photograph **3** painting **4** drawing

Guess What!

- Students look at the swirled image and guess which of the photographs on the page it's from. Check by asking *What's this? (It's a sculpture.)*

Key: It's a sculpture (photograph 1 in activity 3).

Workbook page 10

1 Look, read, and circle the word.

- Students look at the pictures and circle the correct word each time.

Key: 2 photograph **3** painting **4** sculpture

2 Look and copy the painting.

- Students copy the painting on the left into the frame on the right. Ask *Which colors can you see? Can you see a nose? Point to the eyes*, etc.

Ending the lesson

- Mime making one of the kinds of art in the lesson (e.g., taking a photograph). Students say the art form. Repeat for the other kinds of art. Students can also play this game in pairs.

Extra activities: see page TB115 (if time)

Lesson aims Students make a class sculpture. They can also complete the Evaluation in the Workbook.

Recycled language *What kind of art is it?* *photography, sculpture, drawing, painting* | parts of the body (*head, arms, legs, hands, feet*) | Students review all unit vocabulary and grammar in the Evaluation.

Materials CD1 | Examples of different kinds of art (made by students or pictures of works by professional artists) | Materials for the project: eight 30-cm pipe cleaners, plasticine/play clay, foil (a large square of foil and lots of strips) for each student | Optional: PVA glue and metallic or brown paint | Example of a person made from pipe cleaners, foil, etc. | Five slips of paper per student (optional)

Warmer

- Show different kinds of art from the previous lesson (either the ones students made in the Extension activity or pictures of works of art by professional artists. For each one, ask *What kind of art is it? Do you like it? What can you see? Which colors can you see?*

Student's Book page 13

4 Make a class sculpture.

- Say *Open your books to page 13, please.* Point to the photographs in activity 3. Ask *Which number's the sculpture? (Number 1.)* Ask students if there are any sculptures in their town/nearest city and if they've ever made a sculpture.
- Point to the photograph and explain that students are going to make their own class sculpture. Ask *What's this sculpture? What can you see? (People.)* Hold up an example you've made and elicit parts of the body. Ask, e.g., *What's this? (It's a head.) What are these? (They're legs.)* If you can, show some photographs of similar sculptures made of bronze by Alberto Giacometti (e.g., *Three Men Walking*).
- Give each student eight pipe cleaners, foil, and plasticine. Show students how to make their sculpture step by step. To make the head, scrunch a square of foil into a ball. Twist two pipe cleaners together and bend them in half. Wrap them around the ball of foil and twist below to make a neck. Attach the ends to the legs (formed by twisted pipe cleaners). Wrap two more pipe cleaners around the body to make arms. Students can fold the ends to make hands.
- Hand out strips of foil (about 3 cm wide). Show students how to wrap these around the sculpture, like a mummy. Form two pieces of Plasticine into foot shapes and wrap them around the bottom of each leg. Cover the feet with squares of foil, too.
- As students work, circulate and help. Ask questions, e.g., *What's this? / What are these? Do you like the sculpture? Is it a man or a woman? What's his/her name?*

- Students put their sculptures together in groups to make a class sculpture. They can arrange them so they seem to be walking, running, holding hands, playing soccer, etc.

Workbook page 11 – Evaluation

1 Look and write the name.

- Students look at the photographs and complete the names of the characters by writing letters on the lines. Review the alphabet first (e.g., by playing the alphabet song, CD1: 08).

Key: 2 Tina **3** Ben **4** Olivia **5** David

2 What's your favorite part? Use your stickers.

- Students choose their favorite part of the unit – the story, the song, or the video – and put a sticker under their chosen preference.

3 What's different? Circle and write. Then go to page 93 and write the letters.

- Students circle the picture that doesn't belong and write the name of the character. They then go to page 93 and write the letters in the puzzle.

Key: Tina, letters for the puzzle – n, a

Ending the lesson

- Students repeat their favorite activity from the unit.

Extra activities: see page TB115 (if time)

1 Transportation

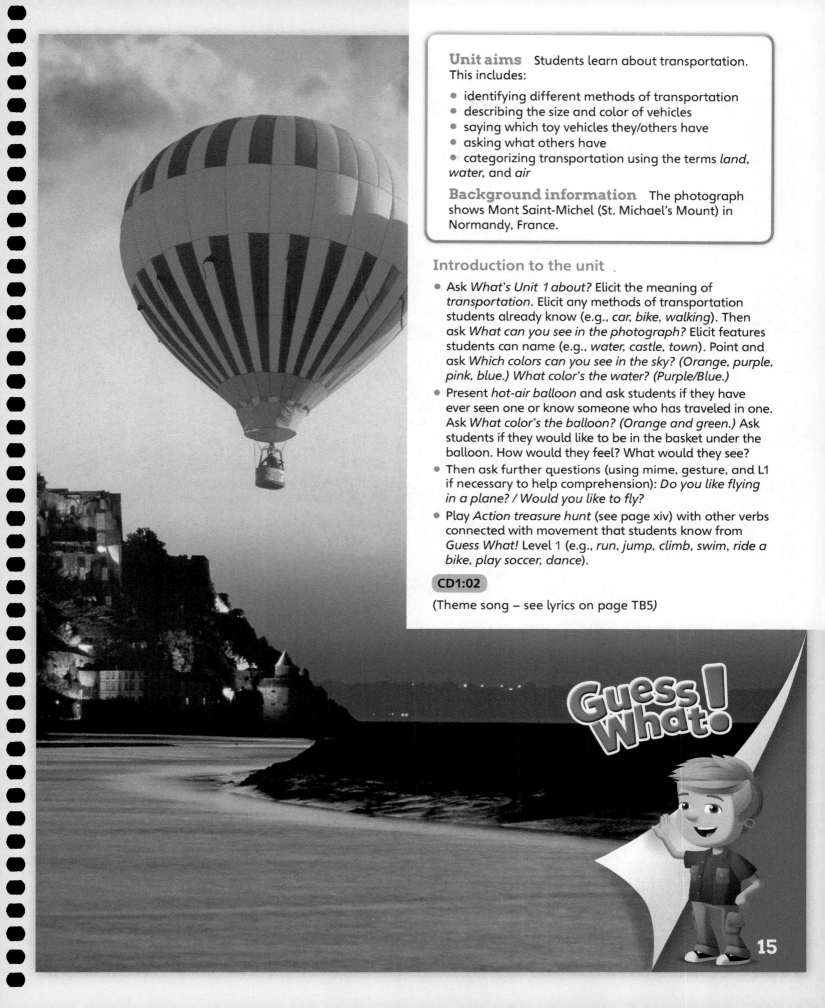

Unit aims Students learn about transportation. This includes:

- identifying different methods of transportation
- describing the size and color of vehicles
- saying which toy vehicles they/others have
- asking what others have
- categorizing transportation using the terms *land*, *water*, and *air*

Background information The photograph shows Mont Saint-Michel (St. Michael's Mount) in Normandy, France.

Introduction to the unit

- Ask *What's Unit 1 about?* Elicit the meaning of *transportation*. Elicit any methods of transportation students already know (e.g., *car, bike, walking*). Then ask *What can you see in the photograph?* Elicit features students can name (e.g., *water, castle, town*). Point and ask *Which colors can you see in the sky? (Orange, purple, pink, blue.) What color's the water? (Purple/Blue.)*
- Present *hot-air balloon* and ask students if they have ever seen one or know someone who has traveled in one. Ask *What color's the balloon? (Orange and green.)* Ask students if they would like to be in the basket under the balloon. How would they feel? What would they see?
- Then ask further questions (using mime, gesture, and L1 if necessary to help comprehension): *Do you like flying in a plane? / Would you like to fly?*
- Play *Action treasure hunt* (see page xiv) with other verbs connected with movement that students know from *Guess What!* Level 1 (e.g., *run, jump, climb, swim, ride a bike, play soccer, dance*).

CD1:02

(Theme song – see lyrics on page TB5*)*

15

1 [CD1 19] **Listen. Who's speaking?**

2 [CD1 20] **Listen, point, and say.**

1 plane

2 helicopter

3 bus

4 car

5 truck

6 motorcycle

7 train

8 boat

9 tractor

3 [CD1 21] **Listen and find.**

Find Leo

Lesson aims Students learn vocabulary for methods of transportation.

New language *plane, helicopter, bus, car, truck, motorcycle, train, boat, tractor, Here we are, transportation museum | Look around you. | It's so (small). | How about you? What do you like?*

Recycled language *character names | teacher | numbers 1–9 | colors | What's this/that? It's a plane. | big, small, long | What can you see? I can see a (red bus). | I like (trains). | He's in the (boat).*

Materials CD1 | Flashcards: 17–25 | Word cards: (see page TB106) (optional)

Warmer

- Say *Listen. Who's this?* Spell out the name of a student in the class. The first student to guess correctly says the whole name (e.g., *It's Joanna*) and can spell the next name.
- Say *Listen. What's this?* Spell out the word *transportation*, letter by letter. Write it on the board. Remind students this is the topic of Unit 1.

Presentation

- Hold up each transportation flashcard and say the new words. Students repeat in chorus and individually. Then hold up the flashcards in a random order. Students say the word.
- Hold up the car flashcard and ask *What color is it? (Blue.)* Repeat with the other flashcards, asking the same question.

Student's Book page 16

1 Listen. Who's speaking?

- Say *Open your books to page 16, please.* Ask *Who can you see? (Olivia, Tina, David, Ben).* Point to the new character and ask *Who's this?* Students guess. Tell them *This is their teacher.* Practice the word *teacher*, if necessary. Ask *Where are they? Are they at school? (No.)* Explain that the children are on a field trip to a museum. Ask *What kind of museum? What are they looking at? (Transportation / A transportation museum).*
- Say *Let's listen to the children. Who's speaking?* Play the recording. Students listen and point to the character they think is speaking each line (the teacher, Tina, David, Ben, or Olivia). Then play again, pausing for students to point to the methods of transportation in the picture as they hear the characters mention them.
- If time, ask about the color of the vehicles in the picture *What color's the plane? (It's blue.)*

CD1:19

Teacher: OK, children. Here we are at the transportation museum. Listen and look around you. … What's this, Tina?
Tina: It's a plane! A big blue plane. And listen to this … It's a big green helicopter!
Teacher: What can you see, David?

David: I can see a red bus and a yellow car. And I can see a truck. And listen … it's a motorcycle. It's so small!

Ben: Look at this long train. It's great. I like trains.
Teacher: How about you, Olivia? What do you like?
Olivia: I like this big white tractor.

Olivia: What's that?
Ben: It's Leo!

2 Listen, point, and say.

- Say *Now listen, point, and say.* Play the recording. Students listen and point to the numbered items in the picture. Then play again. Students listen and say the words.

CD1:20

1 plane 2 helicopter 3 bus 4 car 5 truck 6 motorcycle
7 train 8 boat 9 tractor

3 Listen and find.

- Say *Now listen and find.* Play the recording, pausing for students to find and point to the correct items in the picture. Students can also say the correct number.
- If you have time, students can then do a similar activity in pairs. One says a sentence, e.g., *It's a train*, and the other says the number: *Number 7* (or points to the item).

Key: Students point to the items in the following order: 3, 6, 1, 7, 4, 9, 2, 8, 5.

CD1:21

It's a red bus.	It's a yellow car.
It's a small orange motorcycle.	It's a big white tractor.
	It's a green helicopter.
It's a blue plane.	It's a boat.
It's a long train.	It's a blue truck.

Find Leo.

- Say *Now find Leo.* Students search for Leo in the picture (he's in the boat).

Workbook page 12

1 Look, read, and check ✓ or put an ✗.

- Students look at the pictures and read the words. They put a check if the word matches the picture and an ✗ if it doesn't match.

Key: plane ✗ tractor ✗ car ✓ train ✗ motorcycle ✓

2 Follow the transportation words.

- Students begin at the *Start* square and draw arrows connecting all the transportation words.

Key: Students draw lines between the following words: train, truck, bus, plane, helicopter, tractor, boat.

Ending the lesson

- Act out driving/sailing/flying or riding on one of the vehicles from the lesson. Students guess (*It's a boat*). Then they can repeat the activity in pairs.

Extra activities: see page TB115 (if time)

Lesson aims Students learn to describe the size and color of vehicles.

New language *It's a (big) (red) (car). And it goes like this.*

Recycled language transportation words | colors | *big, small, bike, This is my (car).*

Materials CD1 | Flashcards: 17–25 | Picture of a bike or flashcard from Level 1 Unit 2 (27) | Music CD (optional)

Warmer

- Review the transportation words with the flashcards. Show a picture of a bike or the flashcard from Level 1 Unit 2 (27) to review *bike*. Play *Act and guess* (see page xiv). Encourage students to make the noises of the different vehicles when they mime.

Student's Book page 17

4 Say the chant.

- Say *Open your books to page 17, please.* Point to each vehicle in activity 4 and ask *What's this? (It's a (car).) What color is it? (Red.) Is it big or small? (It's big.)* Make a longer sentence about each vehicle, e.g., *Yes. It's a big red car.* Encourage students to repeat the sentence with the two adjectives.
- Say *Listen to the chant.* Play the recording. Students listen and point to the pictures in turn.
- Then say *Now listen and say the chant.* Play the recording again. Students can clap along to the rhythm at first, joining in with as many words as they can. Then repeat as often as necessary until students are chanting confidently. Encourage them to join in with the vehicle sounds as loudly as they can.

CD1:22

This is my car,
It's a big red car.
This is my car,
And it goes like this.
Vroom! Vroom! (x3)

This is my bike,
It's a big pink bike.
This is my bike,
And it goes like this.
Ding! Ding! (x3)

This is my train,
It's a big green train.
This is my train,
And it goes like this.
Toot! Toot! (x3)

This is my boat,
It's a big blue boat.
This is my boat,
And it goes like this.
Honk! Honk! (x3)

5 Match and say.

- Point to the example and say *Look! Number 1 is a tractor, and c is a tractor. They match.* Students match the other close-up photographs to the vehicles in the second row. They make sentences in pairs, using the speech bubble to help them. Check answers by asking, e.g., *Number 2 ... ?* Students say the letter and *It's a ... .*

Key: 2 d It's a bus. **3** b It's a motorcycle. **4** a It's a helicopter.

6 Ask and answer.

- Ask different students about the methods of transportation, e.g., *Vitoria, do you like trains?* Students reply with short answers (*Yes, I do. / No, I don't.*) Students repeat the activity in pairs.

Workbook page 13

3 Listen and stick.

- Students will need the Unit 1 stickers from the back of the Workbook.
- Play the recording. Students listen and stick the stickers into the correct position.

CD1:23

1 It's a long green truck.
2 It's a yellow and white tractor.
3 It's a blue and white boat.
4 It's a yellow bus.
5 It's a small green car.

4 Look, read, and write the words.

- Make sure students understand what the two categories are (vehicles that travel on roads, vehicles that don't travel on roads). They copy the words from the word bank into the correct category.

Key: Road: car, motorcycle, bus; Not on the road: boat, helicopter, plane, train.

My picture dictionary → Go to page 85. Check the words you know and trace.

- Students turn to page 85 and check the transportation words they know. They then trace over the word labels for each picture.

Ending the lesson

- Play the chant again. Students join in and mime as follows: driving a car (holding the steering wheel, pressing the accelerator for "vroom, vroom"), riding a bike (holding the handle bars and ringing the bell), driving a train (holding and pulling down an old-fashioned whistle), and sailing a boat (e.g., pulling on ropes and then honking a horn).

Extra activities: see page TB115 (if time)

4 Say the chant.

This is my car.
It's a big red car.
This is my car,
And it goes like this.
Vroom! Vroom!

car

bike

train

boat

5 Match and say.

Number 1, c. It's a tractor!

 1

 2

 3

 4

 a

 b

 c

 d

6 About Me Ask and answer.

Do you like motorcycles?   Yes, I do.

7 (CD1 24) **Sing the song.**

I have a ,
You have a ___ .
He has a ___,
And she has a ___.

Let's play together.
Let's share our toys.
Let's play together.
All the girls and boys.

I have a ___,
You have a ___ .
He has a ___,
And she has a ___ .

Let's play together …

I have a ___,
You have a ___.
He has a ___,
And she has a ___ .

Let's play together …

8 (CD1 25) **Listen and say the name.**
(She has a train.) (May.)

Tim

May

Alex

Lucy

Lesson aims
Students talk about toys they and others have.

New language *You have a (train). He/She has a (motorcycle).* | *Let's share our toys, girls, boys*

Recycled language transportation words | toys (*teddy bear, doll, robot, ball, kite, bike*) | *I have a (truck).* | *play together*

Materials CD1 | Flashcards: 17–25 | Toy flashcards from Level 1, Unit 2 (if available) | A blank piece of paper for each student (optional)

Warmer
- Play a game of *Find something (red)* (see page xvi) with objects in the classroom or pictures in the Student's Book. Students make sentences about the items as they find them, e.g., *It's a red pencil. / It's a yellow car.* If you wish, include practice of size (*Find something big/small.*)

Presentation
- Review the transportation words with the flashcards. Ask *What's this?* (*It's a big red tractor*). Stick the cards on the board and make sentences with *I have*, e.g., *I have a big red tractor.*
- Call nine volunteers to the front. Give each one a flashcard. The students hold up their cards and say, e.g., *I have a blue car.*
- Say *You have a blue car.* The student with the car flashcard waves it. Point to the card and say to the class *Yes. Look. He/She has a blue car.* Repeat for the other cards (in random order).

Student's Book page 18
7 Sing the song.
- Say *Open your books to page 18, please.* Point to the picture of the children. Say *What can you see?* Elicit the transportation and toy words. Use the toy flashcards from Level 1 to review/present toys if necessary. Ask, e.g., *Where's the ball?* Students point.
- Say *Listen and point.* Play the recording. Students listen and point to the vehicles and toys as they are mentioned in the song. At the end, remind students of the meaning of *play together* and explain *share our toys, girls,* and *boys*.
- Then say *Now sing the song.* Play the recording a few times, until students are singing confidently. The first time students can hum to the tune and join in with any words they know. Then students can sing along, following the song text. Make sure they realize that the chorus is repeated at *Let's play together*. **Note:** Students can sing along to the version of the song with the words or to the karaoke version.

CD1:24

I have a truck,
You have a train.
He has a motorcycle,
And she has a plane.

Let's play together.
Let's share our toys.
Let's play together.
All the girls and boys.

I have a teddy bear,
You have a doll.
He has a robot,
And she has a ball.

Let's play together.
Let's share our toys.
Let's play together.
All the girls and boys.

I have a helicopter,
You have a kite.
He has a tractor,
And she has a bike.

Let's play together.
Let's share our toys.
Let's play together.
All the girls and boys.

8 Listen and say the name.
- Point to the first picture and ask *What's his name? (Tim).* Point out that this is the boy from the picture in activity 7. Repeat for the other pictures. Students ask and answer in pairs in the same way.
- Say *Listen and say the name.* Play the recording. Students listen and say the correct name, referring to the picture in activity 7.

Key: 2 Alex **3** Tim **4** Lucy

CD1:25

1 She has a train.
2 He has a tractor.
3 He has a helicopter.
4 She has a plane.

Workbook page 14
5 Listen and check ✓.
- Students listen and check the correct picture each time. Check answers by asking, e.g., *Number 1?* Students say, e.g., *b She has a car.*

Key: 2 b **3** b **4** b

CD1:26

1 She has a car.
2 He has a helicopter.
3 She has a bus.
4 He has a truck.

6 Look at the pictures and say.
- Students work individually or in pairs to find five more differences. They make sentences, using the example speech bubble to help them.

Key: In picture a, she has a motorcycle. In picture b, she has a boat. In picture a, he has a plane. In picture b, he has a helicopter. In picture a, he has a boat. In picture b, he has a motorcycle. In picture a, she has a tractor. In picture b, she has a bus. In picture a, she has a truck. In picture b, she has a tractor.

Ending the lesson
- Students work in pairs. Student A makes a sentence about one of the children in the picture in the Student's Book (e.g., *She has a red and black ball.*). Student B says the name (e.g., *Lucy*). Then they swap roles.

Extra activities: see page TB115 (if time)

Lesson aims   Students learn to ask about what others have.

New language   *Does he/she have a (plane)? Yes, he/she does. / No, he/she doesn't.*

Recycled language   transportation words | toys | classroom objects | food

Materials   CD1 | Six classroom objects/toys (e.g., a teddy bear, a doll, a kite) and/or items of known food (e.g., an orange, an apple, a banana) | Six bags that are not transparent | Music CD

Warmer

- Play the song from the previous lesson (CD1:24). Students join in with as many of the words as they can. If you wish, teach mimes for each of the vehicles and toys mentioned.

Presentation

- Call six volunteers to the front. Give each student an item to hold that students can name in English (e.g., a toy car, a pencil case, a doll, a teddy bear, an orange, and a banana). Ask each student to say what he/she has, e.g., *I have a car.* Then they each hide their item in a bag. Ask the class about what the volunteers have in random order with *Does … have*, e.g., *Does Lily have a banana?* Help students reply with short answers, e.g., *Yes, she does.* When a student answers *Yes, he/she does* correctly, the volunteer gives his/her item to that student and sits down.

Student's Book page 19

9 Listen, look, and say.

- Say *Open your books to page 19, please. What can you see?* Elicit the different toys on the table. Explain that the items are prizes for charity.
- Say *Listen and point.* Play the recording. Students point to the toys in the photograph as they are mentioned.
- Then say *Now listen and say.* Play the recording again, pausing for students to listen and repeat the questions and answers.

CD1:27

Man: Does he have a plane?
Woman: Yes, he does.

Man: Does she have a plane?
Woman: No, she doesn't. She has a car.

10 Look and match. Then listen and answer.

- Read the question in the speech bubble and show students how to follow the line from the photograph of the girl to find out the answer. Elicit the answer (*No, she doesn't.*) and the correct sentence (*She has a robot.*).

- Say *Look and match.* Give students time to follow the other lines to find out what each child has. They can check in pairs. Elicit the answers as numbers. Then say *Now listen and answer.* Play the questions, pausing after each one to elicit the answer. Ask students to make correct sentences for the *No* answers.

Key: 2 c Yes, he does. **3** b Yes, she does. **4** d No, he doesn't. (He has a ball.) **5** a No, she doesn't. (She has a plane.)

CD1:28

1 Does she have a ball?
2 Does he have a tractor?
3 Does she have a doll?
4 Does he have a plane?
5 Does she have a robot?

11 Ask and answer.

- Students play the same game in pairs, using the speech bubbles to help them. Circulate and make sure they are using *he* and *she* appropriately.

Workbook page 15

7 Look, read, and circle the answer.

- Students look at the pictures, read, and circle the correct answer each time.

Key: 2 Yes, he does. **3** No, he doesn't. **4** No, she doesn't.

8 Look at the picture and answer the questions.

- Students look at the picture and write the correct short answers.

Key: 2 Yes, she does. **3** Yes, she does. **4** No, he doesn't.

9 Draw and say. Then circle and write.

- Students draw a picture of their friend with a toy, vehicle, or other known item. Then they complete the sentence to describe the picture. They talk about their picture in pairs.

Key: Students' own answers.

Ending the lesson

- Hand out the objects from the beginning of the lesson. Play some music. Students pass the objects around. Stop the music. Point to one of the students holding an object and ask another student, e.g., *Does she have a banana?* The student replies *Yes, she does. / No, she doesn't.* Encourage students to respond as quickly as possible. Play the music again. Students pass the objects, as before.

Extra activities: see page TB115 (if time)

9 CD1 27 **Listen, look, and say.**

Does he have a plane?

Yes, he does.

Does she have a plane?

No, she doesn't. She has a car.

10 CD1 28 **Look and match. Then listen and answer.**

Number 1. Does she have a ball?   No, she doesn't.

11 **Ask and answer.**

Number 1. Does she have a ball?   No, she doesn't.

Lesson aims   Students reinforce language with a story. They also discuss the value of taking turns.

New language   *Let's go to the park.* | *Can I have a turn, please? Yes, of course. This is fun. Be careful. Take turns.*

Recycled language   methods of transportation, *(Ben) has a (helicopter). Does (Ben) have a (robot)? No, he doesn't. It's a (helicopter).* | *Thank you. Sorry. It's OK.* | *Let's play. Wow!*

Materials   CD1 | Flashcards: 17–25 | A toy and a dice for each group of four students OR a large game (e.g., floor-sized jigsaw puzzle, cars on a track, building blocks), slips of paper or small pieces of thin cardboard, half with "yes" written on them, half with "no" (enough for one for each student), a bag or a box (optional)

Warmer

- Call nine volunteers to the front. Give each one a flashcard that they show in turn and say *I have a (motorcycle).* Then they turn their flashcards around. Ask the rest of the class questions about the volunteers, e.g., *Does he/she/(name) have a (boat)?* If students answer incorrectly (e.g., they say *Yes, he does*, but the student doesn't have that flashcard), make a mark on the board. If you get to nine marks, the students at the front win.

Introduction

- Ask questions about the story so far: *What are the children's names? (Ben, David, Olivia, and Tina.) What's in the yard? (A tree house.) What's the surprise for Ben? (iPal is magic.) Which animal does Ben paint? (A lion.)*

Student's Book page 20

12 Listen and read.

- Say *Open your books to page 20, please.* Point to the characters in frame 1 and ask *Does Ben have a plane? (No, he has a helicopter).* Point to frame 4 and ask *Does Ben have the helicopter? (No, he doesn't. iPal has the helicopter.)* Ask students to guess what happens by looking at the other frames.
- Say *Now listen and read.* Play the recording while students listen and follow the story in their books. Then point to the helicopter in frame 6 and ask *What's this? (It's a helicopter, and it's iPal.)*
- Play the recording again, pausing to ask more questions: Frame 1: *Where are Olivia and David? (In the tree house.)* Frame 2: *Does Ben have a robot? (No, he doesn't. He has a helicopter.)* Frame 3: *Who plays with the helicopter? (iPal.)* Frame 4: *Are Ben, David, and Olivia happy? (No, they're worried.)* Elicit/Explain the meaning of *Be careful.* Frame 5: *Is the helicopter OK? (Yes, it is.)* Frame 6: *Are the children happy? (Yes.)*
- Students can listen to the story again for pleasure, or pause after key lines for students to repeat. They can join in with the rhymes before frame 2 and at the end of

the story using gestures and intonation from the story as appropriate.

CD1:29

Olivia: Ben has a helicopter!
David: Let's go to the park!

All: 1, 2, 3, Magic tree.
We're back again. Look and see.
Come with us. Come and play
In our magic tree today.

iPal: Does Ben have a robot?
Olivia: No, he doesn't. It's a helicopter.

iPal: Can I have a turn, please?
Ben: Yes, of course.

iPal: Thank you. This is fun!
David: Be careful, iPal!

Ben: It's OK.
iPal: Sorry. Now let's play with my helicopter!

Ben: Wow! The helicopter is iPal!

All: 3, 2, 1, that was fun.
Time to go. The magic's done!

(**Value**) *Take turns*

- Play the dialog for frame 3 of the story again, pausing after iPal's line: *Can I have a turn, please?* Explain/Elicit that iPal says this to ask to play with the helicopter. Play Ben's response, *Yes, of course*, and ask students to guess the meaning.
- Read the value *Take turns.* Explain the meaning and say how important it is to take turns when we play. Point out that iPal asks politely for his turn, without grabbing.
- Divide the class into two groups and give each group a character name – Ben or iPal. Then play the dialog from frame 3 again. Students listen and repeat the line for their group's character. You can then rearrange the class into pairs, each with one Ben and one iPal. Students practice the dialog in their pairs.

Workbook page 16

10 Read and write the letter. Then listen and check.

- Students match the text with the story frames. They write the correct letter in each speech bubble. Play the story again, which is repeated in full on the recording. Students listen and check their answers.

Key: 2 c 3 a 4 e 5 b 6 d

CD1:30

(Repeat of story – see above for story script)

Ending the lesson

- Make a sentence about the story. Students say the number of the frame, e.g., *Ben, David, and Olivia aren't happy. (4) The helicopter is iPal. (6) Ben says, "Yes, of course." (3) iPal plays with the helicopter. (4) Olivia and David are in the tree house. (1) The helicopter is OK. (5).*

Extra activities: see page TB116 (if time)

Lesson aims Students practice taking turns. Students also practice saying the sounds /g/ and /h/.

New language *gorilla, on the grass*

Recycled language *toys* | *methods of transportation* | *Let's play, Can I have a turn, please? Yes, of course.* | *take turns, computer game, hippo, house*

Materials CD1 | Small toy for each pair of students (if possible one they can name in English) | Large pictures of flowers and trees, windows, and a door (optional)

Warmer

- Say *Let's play soccer.* Students mime playing soccer. Repeat with different games and sports students know (e.g., *Let's play with a toy car. Let's play with a kite. Let's play with a camera. Let's run. Let's jump.*) Make the last instruction *Let's play with a computer game.*

Student's Book page 21

13 Listen and act.

- Say *Open your books to pages 20 and 21, please.* Remind students of the story from the previous lesson. Say *iPal asks Ben, "Can I have a … ?"* (turn, please). Elicit Ben's reply *(Yes, of course.)*
- Tell students they are going to listen to more people taking turns. Remind them of the expression *take turns.* Say *Now look at page 21. Who's speaking? Listen and point.* Play the recording. Students listen and point to the people in the photograph as they speak each line.
- Then say *Now listen and act.* Play the recording again, pausing for students to repeat each line with the correct pronunciation and intonation.
- Students act out similar dialogs in pairs. One student mimes playing with the controller for a computer game and handing it over when the other asks *Can I have a turn, please?*

CD1:31

Alex: Can I have a turn, please?
Carlos: Yes, of course.
Alex: Thanks. I like computer games.

14 Listen and say. /g/ /h/

- In this activity, students practice saying the sounds /g/ and /h/.
- Say *Look at activity 14. What can you see?* Elicit *hippo* and teach *gorilla* and *grass.* Ask *Where's the gorilla? (On the grass.)* and *Where's the hippo? (In the house.)*
- Then say *gorilla – /g/ /g/ /g/ – gorilla.* Students repeat, emphasizing the /g/ sound in *gorilla.*
- Say *hippo – /h/ /h/ /h/ – hippo.* Students repeat, emphasizing the initial sound in the same way.

- Say *Listen and say.* Play the sound sentences on the recording. Students listen and repeat, emphasizing the initial /g/ and /h/ sounds.
- Students can then repeat the sound sentences without the recording, saying them faster and faster each time. See how fast they can say them.
- Ask students to think of any other words they know that begin with the sounds /g/ and /h/. For example, *goodbye, grandpa, grandma, green, game, go, hello, hallway, head, hair, how, helicopter.*

CD1:32

/g/ /h/ A gorilla on the grass. A hippo in the house. (x2)

Workbook page 17

11 What's missing? Look and draw. Then stick.

- Remind students of the value from the previous lesson. Students look at the picture and think about what's missing. They then choose the correct toy from the three options shown and draw it into the picture.
- Students then select a smiley sticker from the back of the book and stick it next to the value.

Key: Students should draw the kite (b).

12 Trace the letters.

- Students trace the letters *g* and *h* in the sound sentences.

13 Listen and match the pictures with g or h.

- Play the recording. Students listen and match each picture with the letter *g* or *h* according to the initial sound of the word.

Key: 2 h **3** g **4** h

CD1:33

1 gorilla, gorilla **2** house, house **3** grass, grass **4** hippo, hippo

Ending the lesson

- Give a small toy to each pair of students. They practice taking turns. Student A plays with the toy. Student B asks *Can I have a turn, please?* Student A replies *Yes, of course.* and hands over the toy. Student B says *Thank you. I like …* They repeat, handing the toy over each time.

Extra activities: see page TB116 (if time)

13 CD1 31 Talk Time **Listen and act.**

Animal sounds

14 CD1 32 **Listen and say.**

A gorilla on the grass. A hippo in the house.

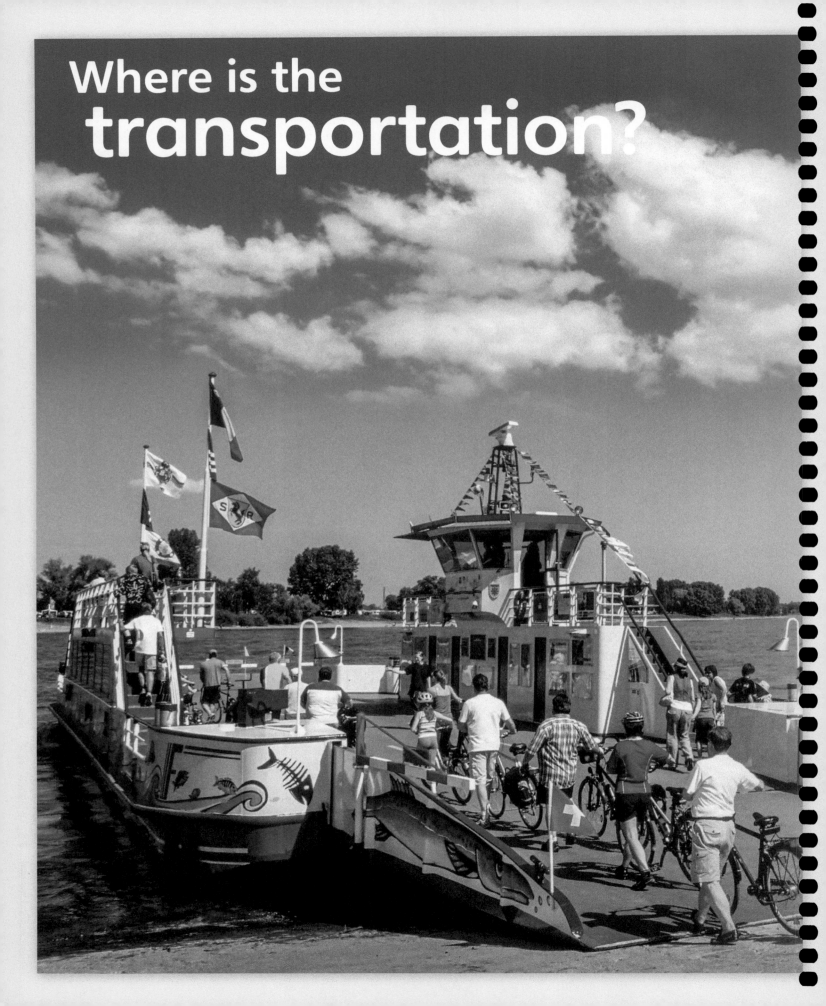

Where is the transportation?

1 CD1 34 **Listen and say.**

1

2

3

on land   on water   in the air

2 **Watch the video.**

3 **Look and say *on land*, *on water*, or *in the air*.**

Number 1. On land.   Yes.

Guess What!

1

2

3

4

Project

4 **Find transportation on land, on water, and in the air.**

Lesson aims Students learn to categorize methods of transportation according to where they go.

New language *on land, on water, in the air*

Recycled language *Where is the (transportation)?* | methods of transportation | numbers

Materials CD1 | DVD (optional) | If you don't have the DVD: pictures of ways of traveling on land, on water, or in the air (e.g., someone walking, four-wheel-drive vehicle, go-kart, hovercraft, paddle boat, surfboard, hot-air balloon, large commercial plane, hang glider) | Flashcards: 17–25 | Word cards: see page TB106 | Map of students' country (to show ferry routes, if appropriate) | 2 circles of thin cardboard, one red and one green, OR a water tray with objects that float or sink (e.g., a toy boat, a paper boat, a piece of wood, a cardboard tube, a toy car) (optional)

Warmer

- Review the methods of transportation using the flashcards. Stick all of the flashcards on the board and say *They are …* Elicit/Remind students of the category name *transportation*. Students can play *Drawing game* (see page xv) with the words in pairs.

Student's Book page 22

Where is the transportation?

- Say *Open your books to page 22, please.* Ask questions about the photograph, e.g., *What transportation can you see? (bikes, boat) Is there a plane? (No, there isn't.) How many people can you see? Can you see a family?*
- Ask students if they have ever traveled on a ferry like the one in the photograph (if yes, ask where they went, how long it took, and whether they liked it). If appropriate, show students a map of their country and point out ferry routes on rivers/lakes or across the ocean.
- Then point to the ferry and ask the opening question *Where is the transportation?* Point and say *The boat's on water.* Point to the last bike and say *The bike's on land.*

Student's Book page 23

1 Listen and say.

- Say *Now look at page 23, please.* Use the photographs to present the words for places where we can see methods of transportation.
- Say *Listen and say.* Play the recording. Students listen and repeat the words.
- Hold up the transportation flashcards and elicit the correct phrase (e.g., plane – *in the air*, boat – *on water*, truck – *on land*).

CD1:34

1 on land **2** on water **2** in the air

2 Watch the video.

- Play the video.
- If you don't have the video, show students the pictures of different methods of transportation you have found. For each one ask *Where's the transportation? (On land/ water. / In the air.)* and additional questions, e.g., *What color is it? Do you like it?* Ask students if they have traveled in any of the ways in the pictures.

Video 01 : see page TB129

3 Look and say on land, on water, *or* in the air.

- Students look at the photographs and say where the method of transportation is. They use the speech bubbles to help them.
- Check the activity by saying the number of the photograph. Students say the kind of transportation.

Key: **2** on water **3** in the air **4** on land

Guess What!

- Students look at the swirled image and guess what it is. Check by asking *What's this? (It's a boat.)*

Key: It's a boat (in photograph 2 of activity 3).

Workbook page 18

1 Look, read, and circle the words.

- Students look at the pictures and circle the correct words each time.

Key: **2** on land **3** in the air **4** on land **5** in the air **6** on water

2 Look and draw. Say.

- Students draw the four kinds of transportation in photographs 2, 4, 5, and 6 in the correct place (e.g., a bus on a road). They work in pairs and take turns making sentences about where the vehicles are in their picture (e.g., *The bus is on land.*)

Key: Students draw the car and truck on the road, the plane in the air, and the big boat on water.

Ending the lesson

- Draw three columns on the board, with the headings *on land, on water, in the air.* Stick the transportation word cards below the columns in random order (at a height your students can reach). Call volunteers to the front to choose a word card and put it into the correct column. The other students help decide if he/she is right.

Extra activities: see page TB116 (if time)

Lesson aims   Students make a transportation collage. They also complete the Evaluation in the Workbook.

Recycled language   *Where is the transportation? on land, on water, in the air* | methods of transportation | Students review all unit vocabulary and grammar in the Evaluation.

Materials   CD1 | Flashcards: 17–25 | Materials for the project: pictures of methods of transportation for students to cut out (e.g., car calendars/magazines, brochures for boat or train rides, airline ads), scissors, glue, a large sheet of paper for each student | Word cards: see page TB106 OR words to a traditional song about a method of transportation (e.g., "Row, Row, Row your Boat") and, if possible, music (optional)

Warmer

- Show a transportation flashcard and ask *What's this? (It's a tractor.) Is it on land, on water, or in the air? (On land).* Repeat for the rest of the flashcards.

Student's Book page 23

4 Find transportation on land, on water, and in the air.

- Say *Open your books to page 23, please.* Point to the photograph in activity 4 and ask *What's this?* Explain that it's a *chart.* Point to the columns in the chart (you may wish to copy it on the board first) and ask *How many? (Three).* Confirm the column headings (*on land, on water, in the air*).

- Give each student a large sheet of paper and tell them to draw the same three-column chart with headings. Hand out printed materials that have pictures of methods of transportation, such as magazines, calendars, catalogs, and ads. Students cut out photographs and stick them into the correct column of their chart. They can also draw more methods of transportation. Help them label the pictures, if they wish.

- As students work, circulate and help. Ask, e.g., *What's this? Where is it – on land or in the air? What color is it? Do you like it?*

- When students have finished their collages, they show them to the class or another group and name the different methods of transportation they've found, saying where they usually travel (e.g., *Motorcycle – on land*).

- You can see if anybody found a method of transportation that's different from everybody else's, e.g., a taxi, a hang glider, an all-terrain vehicle.

Workbook page 19 – Evaluation

1 Look, match, and write the word.

- Students match the people with the methods of transportation. They write transportation words to label the pictures on the right.

Key: 2 d tractor 3 b boat 4 a bus

2 What's your favorite part? Use your stickers.

- Students choose their favorite part of the unit – the story, the song, or the video – and put a sticker under their chosen preference.

3 What's different? Circle and write. Then go to page 93 and write the letters.

- Students circle the picture that doesn't belong and write the method of transportation. They then go to page 93 and write the letters in the puzzle.

Key: motorcycle, letters for the puzzle – r, y

Ending the lesson

- Students repeat their favorite activity from the unit.

Extra activities: see page TB116 (if time)

2 Pets

Unit aims Students learn about people and pets. This includes:

- identifying pet animals
- identifying people as baby, boy, girl, woman, or man
- describing people and animals
- asking and answering questions with *be* (*Is it … ? / Are they … ?*)
- learning about what animals need

Background information The photograph shows a pajama cardinalfish (scientific name: *Sphaeramia nematoptera*).

Introduction to the unit

- Say *Open your books to pages 24 and 25, please*. Play the theme song on the recording. Students look at the photograph and read the title of the unit while listening to the song.
- Ask *What's Unit 2 about?* Students guess the meaning of *pets*. Then ask *What can you see in the photograph?* See if anyone already knows the word *fish*. Ask *What can a fish do? Can it jump/run/walk?* (*It can swim.*)
- Ask *What color's the fish?* (*Yellow, brown/orange, black*, and *white*.) Review parts of the body: say *Look at the fish. Does it have legs/arms/feet/hands?* (*No, it doesn't.*) *Point to its eye.* (Students point.) Repeat for *head, tail*, and *mouth*. Students can repeat this game in pairs. One student names parts of the fish's body, and the other student points.
- Then ask further questions to personalize the topic: *Do you/your grandma and grandpa/your cousins have a pet? What is it? What's its name? Is it in the house or in the yard?*

CD1:02

(Theme song – see lyrics on page TB5)

Guess What!

1 CD1 35 **Listen. Who's speaking?**

2 CD1 36 **Listen, point, and say.**

1 woman

2 man

Pet Show

3 girl

4 cat

5 mouse

6 fish

7 boy

8 dog

9 baby

10 frog

3 CD1 37 **Listen and find.**

Find Leo

26

→ Workbook page 20

Lesson aims
Students learn vocabulary for people and pets.

New language *pet, pet show | woman, man, girl, boy, baby | cat, mouse, fish, dog, frog | What does he/she/that man have? It has (long ears).*

Recycled language *character names | numbers 1–10 | colors | big, small | He/She has a (white) (cat). It's (fat). I like the (dog). Can you see the (boy)? Be careful, Where's (my pet)?*

Materials **CD1** | Flashcards: 26–35 and animal flashcards from Level 1 Unit 8: 86–95, if available.

Warmer

- Review animals from Level 1 – say the animal, then students mime and make the appropriate noise. Stick the flashcards from Level **1** Unit 8 on the board, if available, or write the animal names. Point to each animal and ask *Is it a pet?* Students answer *Yes, it is.* for *snake, bird,* and *spider.*

Presentation

- Explain that students are going to learn words for more pets and also words for people.
- Hold up each flashcard and say the new word. Students repeat in chorus and individually. Then show the flashcards in random order. Students say the words.
- Show the pet flashcards and encourage students to say the word and then mime/make the appropriate noise for each animal.

Student's Book page 26

1 Listen. Who's speaking?

- Say *Open your books to page 26, please.* Ask *Can you see Olivia, Tina, David, and Ben?* Students point to the children's backs. Ask *Where are they? (At a pet show.)* Point to the sign in the picture and confirm the meaning. Ask students if they have ever been to a pet show.
- Say *Let's listen to the children. Who's speaking?* Play the recording. Students listen and point to the character they think is speaking each line (Tina, David, Ben, or Olivia). Then play again, pausing for students to point to the people and pets in the picture as they hear the characters mention them.
- If time, ask about the items in the background of the picture: *What transportation can you see? (A bus, a plane.) What color's the bus? (It's red.)*

CD1:35

Tina: It's a pet show! Look at that woman. She has a white cat. It's fat!
David: Ha, ha! What does that man have?
Olivia: A fish. An orange fish.
Ben: And look at that girl. She has a brown dog. I like the dog. It has long ears!
Olivia: Can you see the boy? He has a black mouse.
David: Be careful, mouse! The woman has a big cat.
Ben: What about the baby? What does he have?

Tina: It's small and green … He has a frog!
David: Where's *my* pet? … Leo?
Leo: *Crick!*

2 Listen, point, and say.

- Say *Now listen, point, and say.* Play the recording. Students listen and point to the numbered items in the picture as they hear them mentioned. Then play again. Students listen and say the words.

CD1:36

1 woman **2** man **3** girl **4** cat **5** mouse **6** fish **7** boy **8** dog **9** baby **10** frog

3 Listen and find.

- Say *Now listen and find.* Play the recording, pausing for students to find and point to the correct animals/people in the picture, as they hear them mentioned. Students can also say the correct number.
- If you have time, students can then do a similar activity in pairs. One says a sentence, e.g., *It's a cat,* and the other says the number or points to the animal/person in the picture.

Key: Students point to the items in the following order: 1, 4, 2, 6, 3, 8, 7, 5, 9, 10.

CD1:37

It's a woman.	It's a girl.	It's a baby.
It's a cat.	It's a dog.	It's a frog.
It's a man.	It's a boy.	
It's a fish.	It's a mouse.	

Find Leo.

- Say *Now find Leo.* Students search for Leo in the picture and raise their hands when they find him. (He's in Tina's bag.)

Workbook page 20

1 Order the letters and match.

- Students solve the anagrams and write the words. Then they match each person with their pet by drawing lines.

Key: 2 c girl, dog **3** b woman, fish **4** a boy, mouse

2 What's next? Look and circle the word.

- Students look at the pictures and circle the correct word in each pair.

Key: 2 frog **3** baby **4** dog

Ending the lesson

- Stick the flashcards *man, woman, girl, boy,* and *baby* on the board in a column. Stick a pet flashcard next to each person flashcard (e.g., frog next to man). Point to one pair of flashcards, name the person, and make a sentence, e.g., *Man. He has a frog.* Say the name of another person on the board and choose a volunteer to make a sentence about his/her pet. Repeat for the other people. Then swap the pets around and ask different students.

Extra activities: see page TB116 (if time)

Lesson aims Students practice the people and pet vocabulary and learn irregular plural words. Students practice counting.

New language *Come on now. Let's count them all. mice, fish* (plur.), *women, men, babies*

Recycled language people and pets | numbers 1–10 | colors | *big, small* | *I can see …*

Materials CD1 | Flashcards: 26–35 | Picture of a rabbit

Warmer

- Review the people and pet words with the flashcards. Students work in pairs and play *I can see* (see page xvi) with the picture on Student's Book page 26. Encourage students to include colors and to talk about the details in the background, e.g., *I can see a red bus.*, as well as the people and pets. Teach *white, brown,* and *black* if necessary.

Student's Book page 27

4 Say the chant.

- Say *Open your books to page 27, please.* Point to one of the pets in each group in activity 4 and ask *What's this? (It's a mouse.)* Ask *What color is it? (White.) Is it big or small? (It's big.)* Then point to the whole group of mice and say *Look and count. How many mice? (Seven.)* Say *Yes. There are seven mice. Seven mice.* Students repeat *mice.* Do the same for the other groups of animals, pointing out that we also say *Five fish,* not *Five fishes.*
- Say *Listen to the chant.* Play the recording. Students listen and point to the pictures in turn.
- Then say *Now listen and say the chant.* Play the recording again. Students can clap along to the rhythm at first, joining in with as many words as they can. Then repeat as often as necessary until students are chanting confidently. Encourage them to join in with the sound effects, when possible.

CD1:38

One frog, two frogs,
Big and small.
Come on now, let's count them all.
One, two, three.
Three green frogs.

One dog, two dogs,
Big and small.
Come on now, let's count them all.
One, two, three, four.
Four brown dogs.

One fish, two fish,
Big and small.
Come on now, let's count them all.
One, two, three, four, five.
Five orange fish.

One mouse, two mice,
Big and small.
Come on now, let's count them all.
One, two, three, four, five, six, seven!
Seven white mice!

5 Look, find, and count.

- Point to each photograph on the left and say, e.g., *Look! One woman, two women.* Students repeat after you.

Then say *Look at the picture. Let's count the women. … I can see two women.*

- Say *Look, find, and count.* Students work in pairs to count the number of men, babies, and children in the picture. They make sentences, using the speech bubble to help them. Check answers by asking, e.g., *How many men can you see?* Students say *I can see …* Ask more questions about the animals, pausing for students to look and count: *How many cats/rabbits/dogs/mice/fish can you see?* (not including the small pictures on the mouse and cat food).

Key: men – 3, babies – 4, children – 5, rabbits – 5, mice – 7, cats – 7, dogs – 3, fish – 2

6 Look at your classroom. Then say.

- Point to the example speech bubble. Say *Look at our class. How many boys?* Students count and say (remind them to include themselves!). Repeat for *girls, children, men,* and *women.* Write the numbers on the board and help students say them in English if they are bigger than ten and also, e.g., *I can't see any men.*

Workbook page 21

3 Listen and stick.

- Students will need the Unit 2 stickers from the back of the Workbook.
- Play the recording. Students listen and stick the stickers into the correct position.

CD1:39

1 The man has a small white dog. **2** The baby has a frog. **3** The girl has a big orange cat. **4** The woman has a small black cat. **5** The boy has a big black dog.

4 Write the words and find.

- Students label the pictures, then find the words in the word search puzzle.

Key: 2 women **3** babies **4** children

```
c h i l d r e n
n b j k l o p l
b c m e n s a o
c y m b c g h j
v t m w o m e n
m e e t y u k a
a w b a b i e s
q n e r t f n c
```

My picture dictionary → Go to page 86. Check the words you know and trace.

- Students turn to page 86 and check the words they know. They then trace over the word labels for each picture.

Ending the lesson

- Play the chant again for students to join in. Divide the class into groups to represent the animals in the chant: seven "mice," four "dogs," five "fish," and three "frogs." The groups mime being their animal when they are mentioned, and students point to them in turn for the counting in the last two lines of the verse.

Extra activities: see pages TB116 to TB117 (if time)

4 CD1 38 Say the chant.

mice

One frog, two frogs.
Big and small.
Come on now, let's count them all.
One, two, three.
Three green frogs.

fish

dogs

frogs

5 Look, find, and count. I can see two women.

women

men

babies

children

6 About Me Look at your classroom. Then say. I can see five boys.

→ Workbook page 21

7 CD1 40 Listen, look, and say.

1 beautiful

2 ugly

3 old

4 young

5 happy

6 sad

7 big

8 small

8 CD1 41 Listen, find, and say.

They're cats.

They're happy.

9 Make sentences. Say *yes* or *no*.

Number 1. It's a bird. It's ugly.

No. It's beautiful.

Lesson aims   Students describe animals.

New language   *beautiful, ugly, old, young, happy, sad | It's/He's/She's (beautiful). They're (happy).*

Recycled language   people and pets | numbers | *women, men, children, babies | big, small*

Materials   CD1 | Flashcards: 26–35 | Word cards: see page TB107, plus four homemade word cards with the words *women, men, children, babies* | Pictures of two or more women, two or more men, two or more children, two or more babies, two or more elephants | A piece of blank paper for each student (optional)

Warmer

- Review the people and pet words with flashcards and word cards (e.g., show the word cards, students do a mime for each, show the flashcards, students say the words). Show the boy and girl flashcards again to review/elicit *child* and *children*.
- Stick the flashcards for man, woman, baby, and boy on the board (at a height your students can reach). Add pictures of women, men, children, and babies (or draw simple pictures yourself). Show a word card for one of these eight items and invite a volunteer to stick it on the board below the correct picture. Students practice reading the words aloud. Remove the word cards and number the pictures 1 through 8. Students practice asking and answering in pairs, e.g., Student A: *Number 6?* Student B: *Women.*

Presentation

- Stick the flashcards of the dog and the mouse on the board. Point to the dog and ask *What's this? (It's a dog.) Is it small? (No).* Say *It's big.* Students repeat. Do the same for the mouse (*It's small*). Draw two elephants on the board or show a picture of some elephants. Ask *What are these? (They're elephants).* Ask *Are they small? (No.)* Say *They're big.* Students repeat.
- Practice *big* and *small* with mime. Students stand up. Say *Elephants! They're big.* Students stamp their feet and make themselves as big as possible. Say *Mice! They're small.* Students pretend to be mice and curl up as small as they can. Repeat with different animals and people (e.g., giraffes, crocodiles, lions, men, babies, frogs, fish). Students join in with the *They're small / They're big* as they get the idea.

Student's Book page 28

7 Listen, look, and say.

- Say *Open your books to page 28, please. What can you see?* Elicit the different animals (*birds, elephants, cats, dogs, frogs*).
- Say *Listen and point.* Play the recording. Students point to the pairs of animals as they are mentioned. Confirm the meaning of each adjective. Then say *Now listen and say.* Play the recording again, pausing for students to listen and repeat.

CD1:40

1 It's beautiful.	5 They're happy.
2 It's ugly.	6 They're sad.
3 She's old.	7 They're big.
4 He's young.	8 They're small.

8 Listen, find, and say.

- Point to the speech bubble and read it aloud. Point to the picture of the cats in activity 7 and elicit/say *They're happy.*
- Say *Listen, find, and say.* Play the recording, pausing after each sentence. Students listen, find the animal(s) in activity 7, and say a sentence with *It's/He's/She's/They're* … and the appropriate adjective each time.

Key: It's a pink and blue bird. It's beautiful. They're brown frogs. They're big. They're dogs. They're sad. She's an elephant. She's old. He's an elephant. He's young. It's a gray bird. It's ugly. They're green frogs. They're small.

CD1:41

They're cats.	She's an elephant.
It's a pink and blue bird.	He's an elephant.
They're brown frogs.	It's a gray bird.
They're dogs.	They're green frogs.

9 Make sentences. Say yes or no.

- Students work in pairs. Student A chooses one of the pictures in activity 7 and says two sentences to describe it, as in the example. These can be either true or false. Student B says *yes* if the description is correct and *no* if it isn't. Encourage students to correct the false sentences, as in the example. Circulate and check that students are using the correct pronouns and singular/plural verb forms.

Workbook page 22

5 Look, write the words, and match.

- Students label the pictures using the words in the box, then draw lines to match the adjectives with their opposites in the right-hand column.

Key: 2 young **3** sad **a** happy **b** beautiful **c** old (2–c, 3–a)

6 Look, read, and check ✓.

- Students look at the pictures, read, and check the correct sentence in each pair.

Key: 2 It's big. **3** She's old. **4** He's ugly.

7 Draw and say. Then write.

- Students draw a picture of a real or imaginary pet. They complete the sentences with the kind of pet and two adjectives, as in the example.

Key: Students' own answers.

Ending the lesson

- Books closed. Play a memory game with the pictures on Student's Book page 28. Say, e.g., *They're sad.* Students say *(They're) dogs.* Repeat several times. Students can play the same game in pairs.

Extra activities: see page TB117 (if time)

Lesson aims Students learn to ask questions with adjectives and *be*.

New language *at | pet store | Can you guess which (pet/pets) is/are (my favorite/favorites) | Is it (happy)? Are they (beautiful)? Are they (spiders)? | Yes, they are. / No, they aren't.*

Recycled language *animals | adjectives | I'm (at the pet store). | Is it a (dog)? Yes, it is. / No, it isn't. | my favorite*

Materials CD1 | Flashcards: 26–35 | Pictures of spiders, snakes, and other known animals, e.g., giraffes, elephants, lions | Pictures of an ugly spider/snake, two or more beautiful animals (e.g., fish), some elephants / other big animals, two or more small animals (e.g., mice/frogs), a happy child / some happy children, a sad person, an old person / group of old people, a baby / some babies (optional) | Eight word cards: *ugly, beautiful, big, small, happy, sad, old, young*

Warmer

● Stick the flashcards on the board, putting the boy and girl close to each other. Say *Listen. Can you guess?* Describe one of the pictures, e.g., *It's small. It's green. It can jump. (Frog).* Students guess the person/animal. For the flashcards of the boy and the girl say, e.g., *They're happy. They're a boy and a girl. (Children).* Take the people flashcards off the board, leaving the pets.

Presentation

● Add pictures of other animals to the board, making sure some of them show more than one animal.

● Point to one of the flashcards with just one animal and ask, e.g., *Is it a mouse?* Help students with the answers *Yes, it is. / No, it isn't.* Repeat with different single animals and with items around the classroom, e.g., *Is it a pen?* Add questions with adjectives, e.g., *Is it small?*

● Point to one of the pictures of two or more animals and ask, e.g., *Are they elephants?* Teach the answers *Yes, they are. / No, they aren't.* Repeat with different animals and objects around the classroom. Add questions with adjectives, e.g., *Are they beautiful?*

Student's Book page 29

10 Sing the song.

● Say *Open your books to page 29, please.* Say *Look. It's a pet store.* Confirm the meaning and ask students if they've ever been to a pet store. Ask *What can you see?* Elicit the animals and encourage students to describe them, e.g., *It's a dog. It's brown. It's sad.* Make sure they realize the green animal on the branch is a lizard.

● Say, e.g., *They're snakes. They're happy.* Students point.

● Say *Listen and point.* Play the recording. Students listen and point to the pets. Remind students of the meaning of *Can you guess?* and *favorite.* Ask *Which pet is your favorite?*

● Then say *Now sing the song.* Play the recording a few times, until students are singing confidently. The first time students can hum to the tune and join in with any words they know. Then students can sing along, following the song text.

● Students can sing along to the version of the song with the words or to the karaoke version.

CD1:42

I'm at the pet store. I'm at the pet store.
Can you guess which pet is my favorite?
Is it small? No, it isn't. Is it big? Yes, it is.
Is it beautiful? No, it isn't. Is it ugly? Yes, it is.
It's big and ugly.
Let me guess, let me guess. Oh, yes!
It's a fish! It's a fish!

I'm at the pet store. I'm at the pet store.
Can you guess which pets are my favorites?
Are they old? No, they aren't. Are they young? Yes, they are.
Are they sad? No, they aren't. Are they happy? Yes, they are.
They're young and happy.
Let me guess, let me guess. Oh, yes!
They're dogs! They're dogs!

11 Play the game.

● Read the speech bubbles with the class and ask them to point to the correct pet(s).

● Tell students you are thinking of one of the animals in the picture. Students ask you questions, as in the speech bubbles, until they guess. Repeat until students get the idea. Students can then play the game in pairs.

Workbook page 23

8 Listen and circle the answer.

● Students listen to the question, look at the picture, and circle the correct answer. Pause the recording as necessary.

Key: 2 No, they aren't. **3** Yes, it is. **4** Yes, he is.

CD1:43

1 Is she old?   **3** Is it happy?
2 Are they ugly?   **4** Is he sad?

9 Look at the picture and answer the questions.

● Students look at the picture and write the correct short answers.

Key: 2 No, they aren't. **3** No, it isn't. **4** Yes, they are. **5** Yes, they are. **6** No, they aren't.

Ending the lesson

● Stick the pet flashcards on the board, together with a picture of a spider and a snake. Say *Can you guess which pet is my favorite?* Students ask you Yes/No questions with adjectives and colors, e.g., *Is it small? Is it black?* until they guess the pet. Students repeat the game in pairs.

Extra activities: see page TB117 (if time)

10 CD1 42 Sing the song.

I'm at the pet store.
I'm at the pet store.
Can you guess which
pet is my favorite?

Is it small? No, it isn't.
Is it big? Yes, it is.
Is it beautiful? No, it isn't.
Is it ugly? Yes, it is.
It's big and ugly.
Let me guess, let me
guess. Oh, yes!
It's a fish! It's a fish!

I'm at the pet store.
I'm at the pet store.
Can you guess which
pets are my favorites?

Are they old? No, they aren't.
Are they young? Yes, they are.
Are they sad? No, they aren't.
Are they happy? Yes, they are.
They're young and happy.
Let me guess, let me guess. Oh, yes!
They're dogs! They're dogs!

11 Think Play the game.

Is it happy?   No it isn't.

Is it a dog?   Yes, it is!

Are they beautiful?   No, they aren't.

Are they spiders?   Yes, they are!

→ Workbook page 23

Grammar: *Is it small?* **29**

Lesson aims
Students reinforce language with a story. They also discuss the value of being helpful.

New language Can I/we help? | I can't find (my cat). | What's his name? | Mr. | You're welcome. | be helpful

Recycled language frog, cat | sad, big, beautiful | What's that? It's a (frog). | Aunt | Hello | Oh, dear | He's/She's (sad). | Thank you.

Materials CD1 | Materials for making a poster (display paper, blank sheet of paper, pens, scissors, glue) for each group of students (optional)

Warmer
- Play the song from the previous lesson (CD1:42). Divide the class into two groups. One group sings the *I'm at the pet store …* sections and all the short answers (*No, it isn't.* etc.). The other group sings all the questions, as if they were the person guessing (*Is it small?* etc.), *Let me guess …* and the last line *It's a fish! / They're dogs!* Repeat, with the groups swapping roles.

Introduction
- Ask questions about the story so far: *What are the children's names? (Ben, David, Olivia, and Tina.) Is Ben a girl? (No, he's a boy.) Which toy does Ben have? (A helicopter.) What's the magic robot's name? (iPal.)*

Student's Book page 30
12 Listen and read.

- Say *Open your books to page 30, please.* Point to the characters in frame 1 and ask *Where are the children? (In the tree house).* Say *Point to iPal.* (Students point – he's next to Tina). Point to the new character in frame 2 and ask *Who's that?* Explain that the woman is Tina's aunt and her name is Sue. Ask *What animals can you see in the story? (A frog, a cat.)* Encourage students to guess what happens by looking at the other frames.

- Say *Now listen and read.* Play the recording while students listen and follow the story in their books. At the end of the story, point to the cat in frame 6 and ask *What's this? (It's Aunt Sue's cat.)* Make sure students realize that the cat is lost and iPal and the children find it.

- Then play the recording again, pausing to ask more questions: Frame 1: *Which animal is in the tree house? (A frog.)* Frame 2: *Is Aunt Sue happy? (No, she isn't. She's sad.)* Frame 3: *What's in the picture? (Aunt Sue's cat.)* Explain the meaning of *I can't find …* Pretend you have lost something yourself and mime looking for it, saying, e.g., *Oh, dear! I can't find my pen.* Frame 4: *What's the cat's name? (Mr. Tom.) Is he small? (No, he isn't. He's big.) Is he ugly? (No, he isn't. He's beautiful.)* Frame 5: *What's under the tree? (The frog.)* Explain that it's helping the children find the cat. Frame 6: *Is Aunt Sue happy? (Yes, she is.) What does she say? (Thank you.)* Point out Tina's reply (*You're welcome.*) and explain the meaning.

- Students can listen to the story again for pleasure, or pause after key lines for students to repeat. They can join in with the rhymes after frame 1 and at the end of the story. Encourage students to use gestures and intonation from the story as appropriate.

CD1:44

Olivia: Look! What's that?
David: It's a frog!
All: 1, 2, 3, Magic tree.
We're back again. Look and see.
Come with us. Come and play
In our magic tree today.

Tina: It's Aunt Sue! Hello.
David: Oh, dear! She's sad.

Tina: Can we help?
Aunt Sue: Yes, please. I can't find my cat.
David: What's his name?
Aunt Sue: Mr. Tom. He's big … and he's beautiful!

David: What's that?

Aunt Sue: Thank you.
Tina: You're welcome!
All: 3, 2, 1, that was fun.
Time to go. The magic's done!

Value Be helpful
- Play the dialog for frame 3 of the story again, pausing after Tina's line *Can we help?* Explain/Elicit that Tina says this because Aunt Sue looks sad. Play Aunt Sue's response, *Yes, please.*
- Read the value *Be helpful.* Explain the meaning and talk about how important it is to offer help when we can. Ask students for examples of when they helped someone at school or at home.
- Divide the class into two groups and give each group a character name – Tina or Aunt Sue. Then play the dialog from frame 3 again. Students listen and repeat the line for their group's character.
- Rearrange the class into pairs, each with one Tina and one Aunt Sue. Students practice the dialog in their pairs.

Workbook page 24
10 Look and write the words. Then listen and check.

- Students complete the speech bubbles with words from the box. Play the story again, which is repeated in full on the recording. Students listen and check their answers.

Key: 2 sad 3 cat 4 beautiful 5 What's 6 you

CD1:45

(Repeat of story – see above for story script)

Ending the lesson
- Play *Sentence chain game* (see page xviii), using the starting sentence *I can't find my (mouse).*

Extra activities: see page TB117 (if time)

Lesson aims   Students practice offering help. Students also practice saying the sounds /f/ and /v/.

New language   *fox, vulture, vegetables, with*

Recycled language   *pets | I can't find my (dog). | Can I help? | Here you are. Thank you. | Hello, five, soccer*

Materials   CD1 | A picture of a firefly (optional)

Warmer

- Before class, hide your Student's Book (or your board marker) somewhere in the room. Look very worried, say *Oh, dear! Where is it?* and search in your bag. Encourage students to ask you *Can we help?* Say *Yes, please. I can't find my (book).* Students help look for it. When a student finds it, help him/her say *Here you are* and hand it over. Look very relieved and say *Thank you. You're very helpful.*

Student's Book page 31

13 Listen and act.

- Say *Open your books to pages 30 and 31, please.* Remind students of the story from the previous lesson. Say *Aunt Sue is sad. Tina asks, "Can we … ?" (help).* Elicit Aunt Sue's reply. *(Yes, please. I can't find my cat.)*
- Tell students they're going to listen to someone else offering help. Remind them of the expression *be helpful.* Say *Now look at page 31. Who's speaking? Listen and point.* Play the recording. Students listen and point to the people in the photograph as they speak each line.
- Then say *Now listen and act.* Play the recording again, pausing for students to repeat each line with the correct pronunciation and intonation.
- Students act out similar dialogs in pairs. One student mimes looking for a pet (e.g., in the air if it is a bird, under the desk if it is a mouse), saying *I can't find my …* The other student asks *Can I help?*, mimes finding the pet and handing it over (*Here you are*). Remind the first student to say *Thank you.*

CD1:46

Abbi: I can't find my dog.
Ed: Can I help?

Ed: Here you are.
Abbi: Thank you! Hello, Rover!

14 Listen and say.   /f/ /v/

- In this activity, students practice saying the sounds /f/ and /v/.
- Say *Look at activity 14. What can you see?* Elicit *fish* and teach *fox, vulture,* and *vegetables.*
- Then say *fox – /f/ /f/ /f/ – fox.* Students repeat, emphasizing the /f/ sound in *fox.*
- Say *vulture – /v/ /v/ /v/ – vulture.* Students repeat, emphasizing the initial sound in the same way.
- Students can also practice the sounds one after the other

(/f/, /v/), with their hands on their throats, so that they can feel the difference between the unvoiced /f/ and voiced /v/.

- Say *Listen and say.* Play the sound sentences on the recording. Students listen and repeat, emphasizing the initial /f/ and /v/ sounds.
- Students can then repeat the sound sentences without the recording, saying them faster and faster each time. See how fast they can say them.
- Ask students to think of any other words they know that begin with the sound /f/ or contain the sound /v/. For example, *four, five, fine, find, feet, frog, living room, five, have, seven.*

CD1:47

/f/ /v/ A fox with a fish. A vulture with vegetables. (x2)

Workbook page 25

11 What's missing? Look and draw. Then stick.

- Remind students of the value from the previous lesson. Students look at the picture and think about what's missing. They then choose the correct pet from the three options shown and draw it into the picture.
- Students then select a smiley sticker from the back of the book and stick it next to the value.

Key: Students should draw the cat (a).

12 Trace the letters.

- Students trace the letters *f* and *v* in the sound sentences.

13 Listen and check ✓ v or f.

- Play the recording. Students check the box next to *v* or *f* according to the initial sound of the word.

Key: 2 v **3** f **4** f

CD1:48

1 four, four **2** vegetables, vegetables **3** fox, fox **4** fish, fish

Ending the lesson

- Show a picture of a firefly and teach the word. Write the tongue twister *Five fireflies* on the board. Students practice saying it repeatedly, as fast as they can.

Extra activities: see page TB117 (if time)

Listen and act.

Animal sounds

14 CD1 47 **Listen and say.**

A **f**ox with a **f**ish. A **v**ulture with **v**egetables.

What do animals need?

1  **Listen and say.**

water

food

shelter

2 **Watch the video.**

3 **Look and say** *water*, *food*, or *shelter*.

Number 1. Water.

Yes!

Guess What!

Project

4 **Draw a home for a pet.**

→ Workbook page 26

Lesson aims Students learn about what animals need.

New language *What do (animals) need? shelter, wild animals*

Recycled language animals | colors | numbers | *water, food*

Materials **CD1** | DVD (optional) | Flashcards of pets: 28–31 and 34 | Pictures of elephants, zebras, giraffes, crocodiles, hippos, monkeys, snakes, spiders, lions (or flashcards from Level 1 Unit 8: 86–95) | Pictures of different animal food (e.g., meat, fish, leaves, insects), shelter (e.g., cave, tree, kennel, nest), and water (river, stream, water hole) OR a blank piece of paper for each student (optional)

Warmer

- Mix up the flashcards of pets and pictures of wild animals and stick them on the board. Elicit the names by asking *What's this? (It's a fish.)* or *What are these? (They're giraffes.)* Move three of the pet flashcards into a group (e.g., cat, dog, and mouse) and ask *What's the same?* Move more pet cards into the group if students don't guess *(They're all pets)*. When students get the idea, ask which of the other animals are pets. Explain that the others are *wild animals*.

Student's Book page 32

What do animals need?

- Say *Open your books to page 32, please.* Ask questions about the photograph, e.g., *What animals can you see? (Elephants.) Where are the elephants? (In the water.) Are they small? (No, they aren't. They're big.)*
- Ask students if they like elephants and if they have ever seen a real elephant.
- Then point to the photograph and ask the opening question *What do animals need?* Point to the water and say *Animals need water.* Point to the trees and say *They need food.* Confirm/Explain the meaning of *need*.

Student's Book page 33

1 Listen and say.

- Say *Now look at page 33, please.* Use the photographs to review/present the words for things animals need.
- Say *Listen and say.* Play the recording. Students listen and repeat the words.
- Draw a picture of a banana on the board and ask *Is it water? (No.) Is it shelter? (No.) What is it? (Food.)* Draw more pictures of food animals eat (e.g., a worm, some grass, a spider), forms of water animals might drink from (e.g., river, waterfall, dog's bowl with water), and kinds of shelter for animals (e.g., a rabbit hutch, a dog's kennel, a tree with a hole in it). Students say *food, water,* or *shelter* each time.

CD1:49

1 water **2** food **3** shelter

2 Watch the video.

- Play the video.
- If you don't have the video, write the word *cat* in the center of the board. Draw a mind map around the word, with three branches: food, water, shelter. Next to each word draw a picture of food for a cat (e.g., a tin of food with a fish on it), water for a cat (a bowl with water in it), and shelter for a cat (a house). Give each student in the class a different pet animal from the list *(dog, mouse, fish, frog)*. Tell them to draw a similar mind map for their animal. Circulate and provide new language if students wish to label their pictures (e.g., *cheese, tank, aquarium*).

Video 02 : see page TB129

3 Look and say water, food, or shelter.

- Students work in pairs. They look at the photographs and say what each one is. They use the speech bubbles to help them.
- Check the activity by saying the number of the photograph. Students say *water, food,* or *shelter*.

Key: 2 water **3** food **4** shelter

Guess What!

- Students look at the swirled image and guess what it is. Check by asking *What's this? (Shelter.)*

Key: It's the nest in photograph 4 of activity 3.

Workbook page 26

1 Look, read, and match.

- Students look at the pictures and match them with the sentences by drawing lines.

Key: b 2 **c** 3 **d** 1

2 Look at the picture and check ✓ the box.

- Students look at the picture and read the sentences. They check the correct sentence.

Key: 2 A mouse needs food.

Ending the lesson

- With their books closed, ask students *What do animals need?* Draw pictures on the board as prompts, if necessary. Elicit the words *(water, food, shelter)* and ask students to help you spell them as you write them on the board.

Extra activities: see page TB118 (if time)

Lesson aims Students draw a home for a pet. They also complete the Evaluation in the Workbook.

New language *for a (pet)*

Recycled language *What do animals need? shelter, water, food, home | pets and people | numbers | Students review all unit vocabulary and grammar in the Evaluation.*

Materials CD1 | Flashcards: 26–35 | Materials for the project (a blank sheet of paper, colored markers or pencils for each student)

Warmer

● Play *Memory 1 through 10* (see page xvii) with the pet and people flashcards.

Student's Book page 33

4 Draw a home for a pet.

● Write the question from the previous lesson (*What do animals need?*) on the board and see if students can remember the three things you talked about (*shelter, water, food*).

● Say *Open your books to page 33, please.* Point to the picture in activity 4 and ask *Which pet is this? (A rabbit.)* Ask *Where's the rabbit? (In its house/shelter.)* Say *Yes. The rabbit needs shelter. It needs a home.* Confirm the meaning of *home.*

● Say *Draw a home for a pet.* Give each student a sheet of paper and tell them to draw a picture showing a pet in its home, with food and water. Help students label the pictures, if they wish.

● As students work, circulate and help. Ask, e.g., *What's this? Is it food, water, or shelter?*

● When students have finished their pictures, they show them to the class or a partner and say which animal the home is for (e.g., *This is a home for a frog*).

Workbook page 27 – Evaluation

1 Read and write the answer.

● Students read the definitions and write the animals on the right.

Key: 2 fish 3 mouse 4 frog 5 dog

2 What's your favorite part? Use your stickers.

● Students choose their favorite part of the unit – the story, the song, or the video – and put a sticker under their chosen preference.

3 What's different? Circle and write. Then go to page 93 and write the letters.

● Students circle the picture that doesn't belong and write the pet. They then go to page 93 and write the letters in the puzzle.

Key: mouse, letters for the puzzle – o, u

Ending the lesson

● Students repeat their favorite activity from the unit.

Extra activities: see page TB118 (if time)

Review   Units 1 and 2

1 **Look and say the words.**   *Number 1. Bus.*

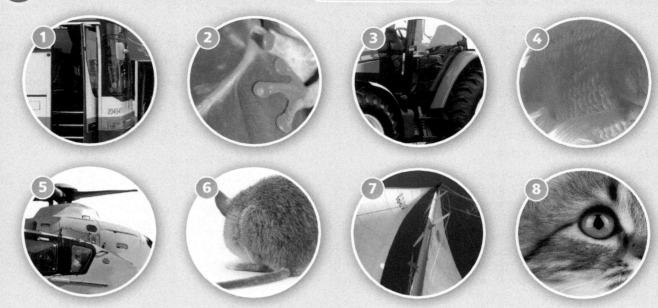

2 CD1 50 **Listen and say the color.**

   Tony

   Anna

   May

   Bill

→ Workbook pages 28–29

Lesson aims Students reinforce the language of the Hello again! unit through Unit 2.

New language on the weekend | snow center, lake

Recycled language numbers 1–10 | the alphabet | transportation | people and pets | colors | big, small, old, young, beautiful, ugly, happy, sad | What's this? Is it a (bus)? Is it (big)? Yes, it is. / No, it isn't. | Hello. I'm (Tony). I'm (eight). | Do you have a (pet)? I have (two). It's /He's / She's (small). It/He/She isn't (beautiful). They're (white). Are they (mice)? Yes, they are. / No, they aren't. His/Her name's (Domino). How do you spell (Anna)?

Materials CD1 | Flashcards: 17–35 (optional) | Word cards: see pages TB105, TB106, and TB107

Warmer

- Ask *What can you remember from the Hello again! unit, Unit 1, and Unit 2? Let's find out.* Allow students time to look through the units and at any work displayed in class. Encourage them to say what is easy or difficult. Ask *What is your favorite activity?*

Student's Book page 34

1 Look and say the words.

- Say *Open your books to page 34.* Students look at the close-up photographs and guess the words. Check the activity by saying the picture number, e.g., *Number 1.* Students say the word: *Bus.* Alternatively, check the activity by asking *What's number (1)? / What's this?* Elicit *It's a (bus).*
- If you have time, provide further review by asking questions about the photographs, e.g., *Number 8. Is it a bus? (No, it isn't.) Is it big/small? Is it a pet?*

Key: 2 frog **3** tractor **4** fish **5** helicopter **6** mouse **7** boat **8** cat

2 Listen and say the color.

- Say *Look at the children.* Point to the children in the top row of the activity in turn and ask *Is this a boy or a girl? What's his/her name? (His/Her name's ...)*
- Point to each photograph in the bottom row and ask *What color is it?* Students answer with the color of the picture frame, e.g., *Red.* Then say *Look at the (red) photograph. What pet(s) can you see?* Students look at each photograph and name the pet (*a fish, a dog, mice, a cat*).
- Say *Now listen. Say the name and the color.* Play the recording. Students listen and find which pet each child has. They then say the name, color, and pet. Play the recording again, if necessary, pausing to ask *What color? Which pet? How old is (Tony)? What color are Anna's fish? Is May's cat old? What's the name of Bill's dog?*

Key: Tony – green (mice), Anna – red (fish), May – blue (cat), Bill – yellow (dog)

CD1:50

Tony: Hello. I'm Tony. I'm eight.
Adult: Do you have a pet?
Tony: I have two! They're small, and they're white.
Adult: Are they mice?
Tony: Yes, they are! Good job!
Anna: Hi. I'm Anna.
Adult: How do you spell "Anna"?
Anna: A–N–N–A.
Adult: Do you have a pet?
Anna: I have two pets! I have two fish. They're yellow and black, and they're beautiful.
May: Hello. My name's May. I'm nine. I have a cat. She isn't beautiful. She's ugly!
Adult: Is she old?
May: No, she's young.
Bill: Hello! My name's Bill. I'm seven. I have an old pet. He's happy. He's a dog! His name's Domino.
Adult: How do you spell "Domino"?
Bill: D–O–M–I–N–O.

Workbook page 28

1 Look and write the word.

- Students look at the pictures and complete the words in the puzzle grid.

Key: 1 Olivia **2** Leo **3** mouse **4** tractor **5** frog **6** Ben **7** motorcycle **8** helicopter **9** Tina

2 Read and circle the answer.

- Students read the questions and answers and circle the correct option each time.

Key: 2 has **3** They're **4** spell **5** Does, have **6** it, it

Ending the lesson

- Play *Stand up and sit down* (see page xviii) with a variety of sentences from the first three units, e.g., *I have a pet. My pet is young. My mom has a bike. I'm seven. I have a baby sister.*

Extra activities: see page TB118 (if time)

Lesson aims Students play a board game and continue reinforcing the language of the Hello again! unit through Unit 2.

Recycled language the alphabet | transportation | people and pets | colors | *What's this? It's a (fish). What are these? They're (cars). How do you spell ("helicopter")? What does he/she have? He/She has a (frog). Is he / Are they (beautiful/old/ young/sad)? What's the matter? I can't find my (car). Can I help? Yes, please. Here you are. Thanks. Do you like cars? Yes, I do. Can I have a turn? Of course. Let's play.*

Materials CD1 | Flashcards: 17–35 | Small squares of colored paper or colored game pieces for covering the game board squares (four of one color for each student)

Warmer

- Use the flashcards to play *The one that doesn't belong* (see page xvi). The one that doesn't belong can be from a different category (e.g., *bus, dog, boat, motorcycle* – dog doesn't belong because it isn't a method of transportation), or it can be different because of spelling or sound (e.g., *baby, bus, boat, fish* – fish doesn't belong because it doesn't start with the sound /b/).

Student's Book page 35

3 Play the game.

- This is a tic-tac-toe-style game. The aim is to be the first to get a row of four (vertically, horizontally, or diagonally).
- Students play in pairs. Each student has four pieces of colored paper or four game pieces (all the same color). The student who's starting the game chooses where to place his/her game piece by saying the color of the row and the column number, e.g., *Blue 2*. The other student then makes a question according to the color of the square on the board. For example, for square 2 on the blue row, he/she asks *How do you spell "motorcycle"?* If the first student answers the question correctly, he/she puts a game piece on the square. It is then the second student's turn. The first student with four game pieces in a row wins.
- Students use the prompts at the top of the page to help them when they are playing the game.

Key: Red 1 What's this? It's a fish. Red 2 What are these? They're cars. Red 3 What's this? It's a tractor. Red 4 What are these? They're mice. Blue 1 How do you spell "helicopter"? (Student spells the word aloud.) Blue 2 How do you spell "motorcycle"? (Student spells the word aloud.) Blue 3 How do you spell "plane"? (Student spells the word aloud.) Blue 4 How do you spell "train"? (Student spells the word aloud.) Yellow 1 What does he have? He has a frog. Yellow 2 What does she have? She has a truck. Yellow 3 What does he have? He has a boat.

Yellow 4 What does she have? She has a cat. Green 1 Are they beautiful? No, they aren't. They're ugly. Green 2 Is he old? Yes, he is. Green 3 Are they young? Yes, they are. Green 4 Is he/she sad? No, he/she isn't. He's/She's happy.

Workbook page 29

3 Look, read, and match.

- Students look at the pictures, read the questions, and match them with the answers by drawing lines.

Key: 2 d **3** c **4** a

4 Listen and check ✓.

- Students listen and check the correct picture in each pair.

Key: 1 picture 1 **2** picture 2

CD1:51

1 Girl: Oh! I can't find my car.
  Boy: Can I help?
  Girl: Yes, please.
  Boy: Here you are.
  Girl: Thanks. Do you like cars?
  Boy: Yes, I do. Can I have a turn?
  Girl: Of course!

2 Boy: Let's play.
  Girl: OK. Do you like soccer?
  Boy: Yes, I do.
  Girl: Me, too.
  Boy: What's the matter?
  Girl: I can't find my soccer ball.
  Boy: Here you are.
  Girl: Thank you!

Ending the lesson

- Play a game of *Correct my mistakes* (see page xv) using the pictures in the game squares on Student's Book page 35. While students are looking at the game, make false sentences for them to correct, e.g., *Yellow 4. She has a dog. (No, she doesn't. She has a cat.)*

Extra activities: see page TB118 (if time)

3 Play the game.

What's this? / What are these?	How do you spell ... ?	What does he/she have?	Is he / Are they ... ?
1	**2**	**3**	**4**

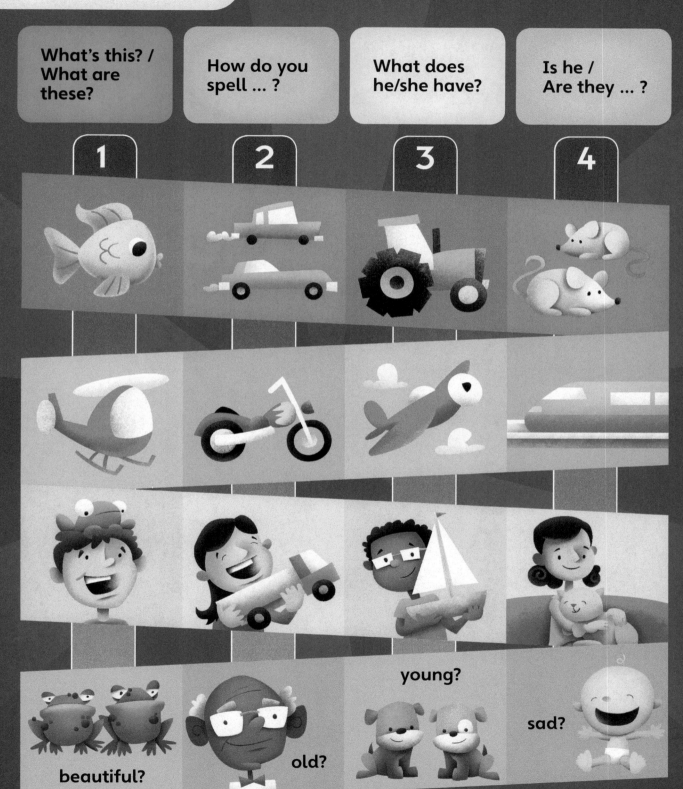

beautiful?

old?

young?

sad?

3 Clothes

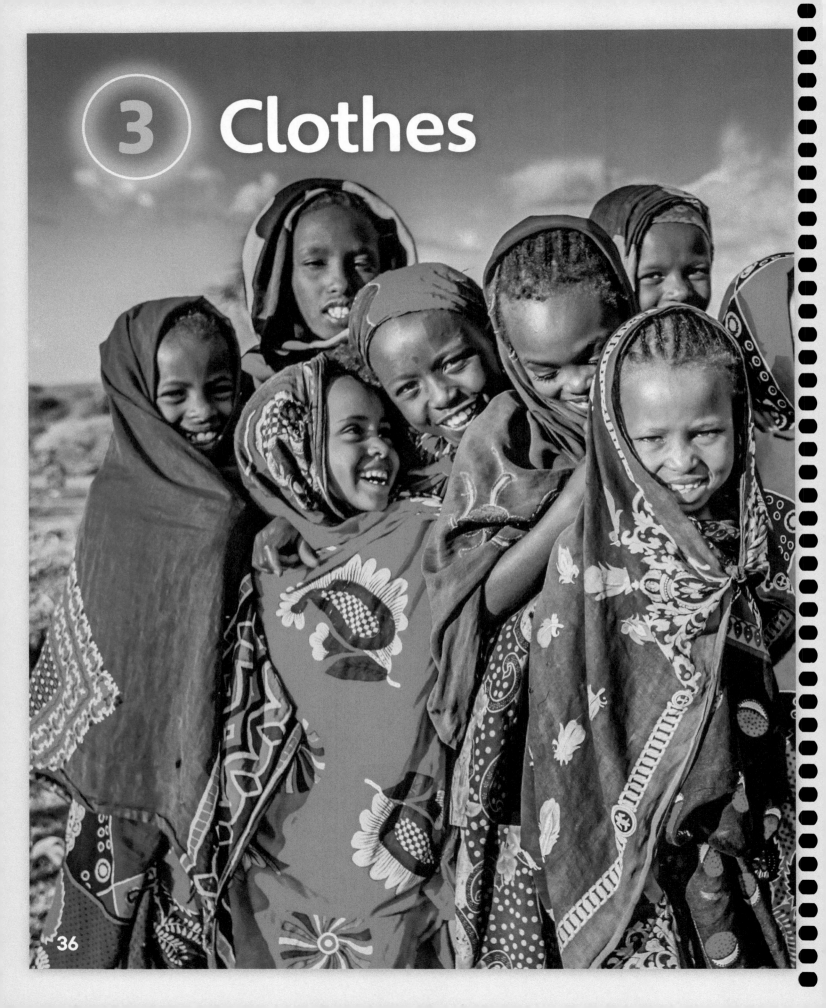

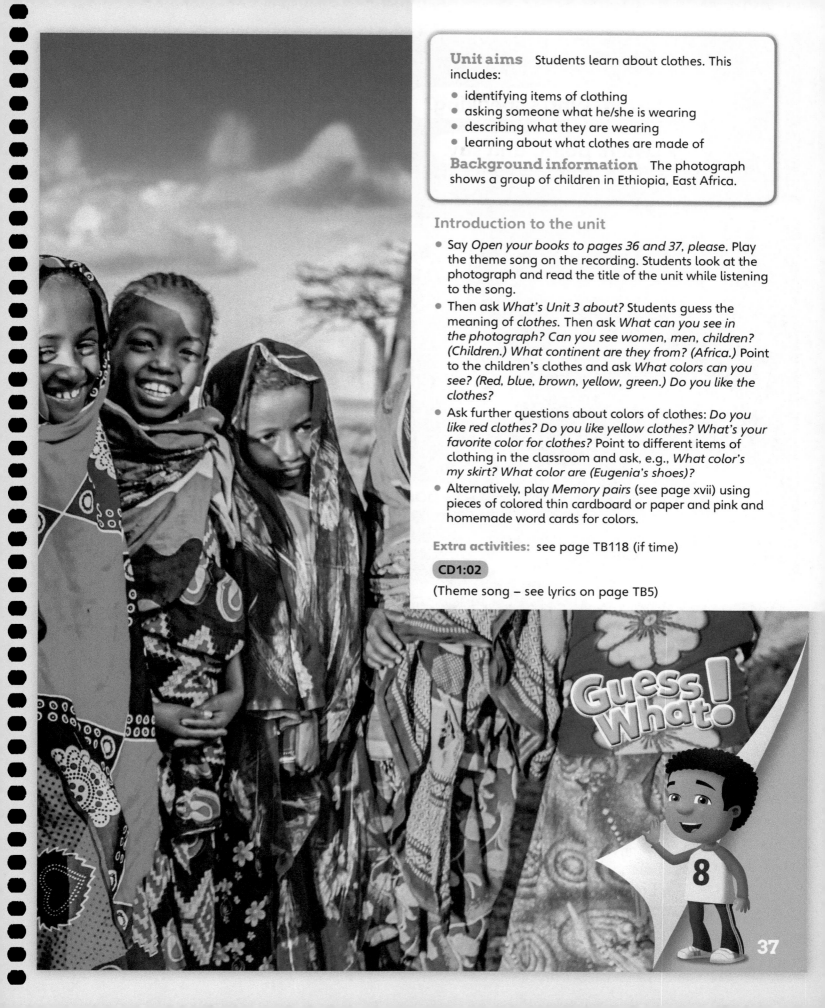

Unit aims Students learn about clothes. This includes:

- identifying items of clothing
- asking someone what he/she is wearing
- describing what they are wearing
- learning about what clothes are made of

Background information The photograph shows a group of children in Ethiopia, East Africa.

Introduction to the unit

- Say *Open your books to pages 36 and 37, please*. Play the theme song on the recording. Students look at the photograph and read the title of the unit while listening to the song.
- Then ask *What's Unit 3 about?* Students guess the meaning of *clothes*. Then ask *What can you see in the photograph? Can you see women, men, children? (Children.) What continent are they from? (Africa.)* Point to the children's clothes and ask *What colors can you see? (Red, blue, brown, yellow, green.) Do you like the clothes?*
- Ask further questions about colors of clothes: *Do you like red clothes? Do you like yellow clothes? What's your favorite color for clothes?* Point to different items of clothing in the classroom and ask, e.g., *What color's my skirt? What color are (Eugenia's shoes)?*
- Alternatively, play *Memory pairs* (see page xvii) using pieces of colored thin cardboard or paper and pink and homemade word cards for colors.

Extra activities: see page TB118 (if time)

CD1:02

(Theme song – see lyrics on page TB5)

Guess What!

8

1 (CD1 52) **Listen. Who's speaking?**

2 (CD1 53) **Listen, point, and say.**

THE THEATER
presents
WOOF!

1 jacket

2 pants

3 socks

5 shoes

4 skirt

6 dress

7 T-shirt

8 jeans

9 shirt

3 (CD1 54) **Listen and find.**

Find Leo

Lesson aims   Students learn vocabulary for clothes.

New language *jacket, pants, socks, skirt, shoes, dress, T-shirt, jeans, shirt, Do you like … or … ?, the (yellow) one*

Recycled language *character names | numbers 1–9 | colors | old, favorite | Do you have … ? What do you have? this/these, I have (these black shoes). This is my … Oh, dear. Where's … ? I don't like it.*

Materials CD1 | Flashcards: 36–44

Warmer

- Point to something you are wearing or your purse and say the color(s). Point to more items of clothing. Students say the colors. Play *Point to (red)* (see page xviii). Encourage students to point to items of clothing (theirs or someone else's) first.

Presentation

- Explain that students are going to learn words for clothes in today's lesson.
- Hold up each flashcard and say the new word. Students repeat in chorus and individually. Then show the flashcards in random order. Students say the words.
- Show the flashcards and elicit a phrase for each with the correct color, e.g., *a purple skirt / blue jeans*.

Student's Book page 38

1 Listen. Who's speaking?

- Say *Open your books to page 36, please*. Elicit the characters' names and ask *Where are the children? (At school)*. Point to the teacher and ask *Who's this? (The teacher.)* Say *Look! They're in the school auditorium.* Point to the stage and the rack of clothes and elicit/explain that the children are preparing a school play. Use the picture to teach *costume*. Ask students if they have taken part in a performance at school / worn a costume.
- Say *Let's listen. Who's speaking?* Play the recording. Students listen and point to the character they think is speaking each line (Tina, David, Ben, Olivia, or the teacher). Then play again, pausing for students to point to the items of clothing as they hear the characters mention them in the recording.
- If time, ask about the colors of the clothes *(What color's the skirt?/What color are the shoes?)* and the items in the background: *Can you see any pets? (A dog, some fish, a lizard.) What color's the dog? (It's brown.) How many fish can you see? (Four.)*

CD1:52

Teacher: Hello, everyone. Do you all have your costumes?
Children: Yes, Teacher.
Teacher: David, what do you have?
David: This black jacket and these red pants. And I have these black shoes.
Teacher: Good! What about you, Ben?
Ben: This is my costume! My pants, my jacket, and these red socks.

Teacher: Hmm. Do you have any shoes?
Ben: No, I don't.
Teacher: Oh, dear.
Tina: Look, Olivia! I have this green skirt. And do you like this pink shirt or the yellow shirt?
Olivia: I like the yellow one.
Tina: What about you, Olivia? Where's your costume?
Olivia: It's this purple dress! But I don't like it. I just like my old jeans and my favorite T-shirt.
Teacher: Oh, Olivia!

2 Listen, point, and say.

- Say *Now listen, point, and say.* Play the recording. Students listen and point to the numbered items in the picture as they hear them mentioned in the recording. Then play again. Students listen and say the words.

CD1:53

1 jacket **2** pants **3** socks **4** skirt **5** shoes **6** dress
7 T-shirt **8** jeans **9** shirt

3 Listen and find.

- Say *Now listen and find.* Play the recording, pausing for students to find and point to the correct clothes in the picture, as they hear them mentioned. Students can also say the correct number.
- If you have time, students can then do a similar activity in pairs. One says a sentence, e.g., *She has a white T-shirt*, and the other says the name (e.g., *Olivia*) or points to the person in the picture.

Key: Students point to the items in the following order: 6, 8, 5, 1, 7, 2, 4, 3, 9.

CD1:54

I like this dress.	I like these pants.
I like these jeans.	I like this skirt.
I like these shoes.	I like these socks.
I like this jacket.	I like this shirt.
I like this T-shirt.	

Find Leo.

- Say *Now find Leo.* Students search for Leo in the picture (he's behind the fish tank).

Workbook page 30

1 Look and match. Then read and color.

- Students match the labels with the clothes by drawing lines. Then they read the instructions and color the clothes accordingly.

Key: Students color according to the instructions on page 30 of the Workbook.

Ending the lesson

- Play *Last one standing* (see page xvi) with items of clothing and colors.

Extra activities: see pages TB118 to TB119 (if time)

Lesson aims   Students practice the clothes vocabulary.

New language   *Here's your (jacket). Here are your (shoes). Put on your (jacket).* | *go out*

Recycled language   clothes | colors | *favorite* | *Let's … (play)!* | *His/Her (T-shirt) isn't (red). It's (yellow). His/Her (shoes) aren't (orange). They're (red).*

Materials   CD1 | Flashcards: 36–44 | Real items of clothing in different colors on hangers, pairs of shoes in different colors | Pictures of people wearing different clothes (e.g., from clothes catalogs or magazines), scissors, glue, blank paper (optional)

Warmer

● Review the clothes words with the flashcards or real items of clothing. Display these in the classroom (e.g., clothes on hangers, shoes on top of shoe boxes). Then play *Can I have … ?* (see page xv). Call students to find the correct item of clothing, e.g., *Paul, can I have a blue T-shirt, please?*

Presentation

● Ask a student *What's your favorite lesson?* (*Math.*) Then ask *Do we have math today?* (*Yes, we do. / No, we don't.*) Confirm by saying *We have math today. We have math on Monday.* or *We don't have math today. We have math on Tuesday.* Students repeat the sentences in chorus and individually. Repeat with other students' favorite lessons, eliciting and practicing as a class and individually.

Student's Book page 39

4 Say the chant.

● Say *Open your books to page 39, please.* Point to each jacket in the first photograph in activity 4 and ask *What's this?* (*It's a jacket.*) Ask *What color is it?* (*Black/Red.*) Make a phrase for each item, e.g., *Yes. It's a black jacket.* Repeat for the other photographs, e.g., *What are these?* (*They're shoes.*) *What color are they?* (*They're purple.*) *Yes. They're purple shoes.*

● Say *Listen to the chant.* Play the recording. Students listen and point to the photographs in turn. Use gesture and mime to show the meaning of *Here's/Here are* and *Put on your …* Check that students understand *Let's go out and play.*

● Then say *Now listen and say the chant.* Play the recording again. Students can clap along to the rhythm at first, joining in with as many words as they can. Then repeat as often as necessary until students are chanting confidently. Encourage them to mime putting on the different items of clothing as they chant.

CD1:55

Here's your jacket,
Your favorite red jacket.
Put on your jacket,
Let's go out and play.

Here are your shoes,
Your favorite purple shoes.
Put on your shoes,
Let's go out and play.

Here's your T-shirt,
Your favorite green T-shirt.
Put on your T-shirt,
Let's go out and play.

Here are your pants,
Your favorite blue pants.
Put on your pants,
Let's go out and play.

5 Find the mistakes and say.

● Point to the picture and say *They're in a clothing store.* Explain that they're trying on clothes before they buy. Then say *Look at the picture. Is it OK?* Make sure students realize that the mirror is strange, and the clothes in the reflection are not the right colors. Read the speech bubbles and encourage students to point to the items of clothing.

● Say *Find the mistakes and say.* Students work in pairs to find more differences between the clothes and their reflections. They take turns making sentences using *his/her* and the singular or plural form of *be* (*isn't/aren't/It's/They're*) as appropriate and using the speech bubbles to help them. Check answers by asking, e.g., *What about the girl's jacket?* Students say *Her jacket isn't purple. It's blue.*

Key: *His pants aren't green. They're blue. His socks aren't purple. They're green. His T-shirt isn't red. It's yellow. Her dress isn't pink. It's purple. Her jacket isn't purple. It's blue.*

Workbook page 31

2 Listen and stick.

● Students will need the Unit 3 stickers from the back of the Workbook.

● Play the recording. Students listen and stick the stickers into the correct position.

CD1:56

1 Oh, look! I like this pink T-shirt and purple skirt!
2 This white T-shirt is great! And look at these orange socks!   3 A short green jacket! I like short jackets. And I like these blue jeans, too.   4 I like these black jeans. And this long green jacket is my favorite.   5 This yellow dress is beautiful. I like these black shoes, too.

3 Look and write the words.

● Students label the picture using the words in the box.

Key: 1 T-shirt 2 shirt 3 jacket 4 jeans 5 skirt 6 pants 8 shoes

My picture dictionary → Go to page 87. Check the words you know and trace.

● Students turn to page 87 and check the words they know. They then trace over the word labels for each picture.

Ending the lesson

● Ask a student to stand up. Say a verse from the chant, using any item of clothing/color. Mime handing over the item of clothing, e.g., *Here's your dress. Your favorite blue dress. Put on your dress. Let's go out and play.* The student mimes putting on the item. Repeat with other students. Students can repeat the activity in pairs, using the words of the chant or their own ideas.

Extra activities: see page TB119 (if time)

4 CD1 55 **Say the chant.**

red jacket

green T-shirt

purple shoes

blue pants

Here's your jacket,
Your favorite red jacket.
Put on your jacket,
Let's go out and play.

Here are your shoes,
Your favorite purple shoes.
Put on your shoes,
Let's go out and play.

5 Think **Find the mistakes and say.**

His T-shirt isn't red. It's yellow.

Her shoes aren't orange. They're red.

6 (CD1 57) **Sing the song.**

What are you wearing?
What are you wearing?
What are you wearing today?

I'm wearing red
And a green .
I'm wearing a blue
And a yellow .
Oh! I look great today!

I'm wearing blue
And an orange .
I'm wearing a green
And a purple .
Oh! I look great today!

7 (CD1 58) (Think) **Listen and say the name.**

Sammy

Sally

8 (About Me) **Ask and answer.**

What are you wearing today?

I'm wearing a blue skirt.

Lesson aims Students ask someone what he/she is wearing and describe what they themselves are wearing.

New language *What are you wearing (today)? I'm wearing (a) (red jacket/pants) and a (green skirt). I look great.*

Recycled language clothes | colors | parts of the body | *man, woman, boy, girl*

Materials CD1 | Pictures of people from clothes catalogs | A ball, a music CD OR flashcards: 36–44, and handmade clothes cards, e.g., red shoes, pink pants, an orange jacket, yellow socks (if possible, make a set of 15 cards for each group of students – see Extra activities for details) (optional)

Warmer

● Point to a picture of a person in the Student's Book or show a picture from a catalog. Ask, e.g., *Is this a man? (No, it's a woman.)* Describe the clothes, making mistakes with colors (as in Student's Book page 39, activity 5). Students say, e.g., *Her jacket isn't brown. It's orange.* They can repeat the activity in pairs, using pictures in their books.

Presentation

● Say *Today I'm wearing (black pants and a red T-shirt). I'm wearing (black socks and black shoes).* Help a volunteer describe his/her clothes. Repeat with different students. Ask each student *What are you wearing today?*

Student's Book page 40

6 Sing the song.

● Say *Open your books to page 40, please.* Point to the large picture and say *Look. Two monsters. A boy and a girl.* Ask *Which clothes can you see?* Elicit the clothes and colors, e.g., *a yellow T-shirt.* Review parts of the body by asking, e.g., *Where's the yellow T-shirt? (On his head.)*

● Say *Listen and point.* Play the recording. Students listen and point to the clothes that are mentioned in the song. At the end, explain the meaning of *I look great today.*

● Then say *Now sing the song.* Play the recording a few times, until students are singing confidently. The first time students can hum to the tune and join in with any words they know. Then students can sing along, following the song text. You can also divide the class into two groups, with one group singing the part of Sammy and the other Sally. They all join in with the questions *What are you wearing (today)?* **Note:** Students can sing along to the version of the song with the words or to the karaoke version.

CD1:57

What are you wearing?
What are you wearing?
What are you wearing today? (x2)

I'm wearing red pants
And a green skirt.
I'm wearing a blue jacket
And a yellow T-shirt.

Oh! I look great today!
What are you wearing?
What are you wearing?
What are you wearing today?

I'm wearing blue shoes
And an orange skirt.

I'm wearing a green dress
And a purple sock.
Oh! I look great today!
What are you wearing?
What are you wearing?
What are you wearing today? (x2)

7 Listen and say the name.

● Point to the picture on the left and say *Look. It's the boy monster from the song. What's his name? (Sammy.)* Practice pronunciation of the name. Repeat for Sally.

● Say *Listen and say the name. Sammy or Sally?* Play the first item on the recording. Pause and elicit the name *(Sammy).* Ask *What's he wearing? (A blue jacket.)* Then play the rest of the recording, pausing after each sentence. Students listen, look at the picture in activity 6, and say *Sammy* or *Sally.*

● If time, students can repeat this activity in pairs. Student A makes a sentence with *I'm wearing …* as if he/she were one of the monsters. Student B says *Sammy* or *Sally.*

Key: 1 Sammy 2 Sally 3 Sally 4 Sammy

CD1:58

1 **Voice:** What are you wearing?
  Sammy: I'm wearing a blue jacket.
2 **Voice:** What are you wearing?
  Sally: I'm wearing blue shoes.
3 **Voice:** What are you wearing?
  Sally: I'm wearing an orange skirt.
4 **Voice:** What are you wearing?
  Sammy: I'm wearing a yellow T-shirt.

8 Ask and answer.

● Read the speech bubbles aloud. Practice pronunciation if necessary. Students work in pairs to ask and answer about their clothes. **Note:** If your students wear a uniform, ask them to draw a picture of themselves wearing their favorite clothes. They ask and answer about the picture (*What are you wearing in the picture?*).

Workbook page 32

4 Look, read, and check ✓.

● Students read the questions and answers and check the correct picture in each pair.

Key: 2 b 3 b 4 b

5 Look at the pictures and write.

● Students look at the pictures and complete the sentences.

Key: 2 a dress, a jacket, shoes 3 jeans, a T-shirt, socks 4 pants, a shirt, shoes

Ending the lesson

● Play *Sentence chain game* (see page xviii), using the starting sentence: *I'm wearing purple pants.*

Extra activities: see page TB119 (if time)

Lesson aims Students ask and answer about what they are wearing.

New language *Are you wearing a (blue T-shirt)? Are you wearing (brown shoes)? Yes, I am. / No, I'm not.* | *My turn.*

Recycled language clothes | colors | *What are you wearing (today)? I'm wearing (a) (red jacket/ pants) and a (green skirt). I look great.* | *take turns*

Materials CD1 | Flashcards: 36–44 | A scarf / piece of thick fabric to use as a blindfold (optional)

Warmer

- Play the song from the previous lesson. Students sing along. Stick the clothes flashcards on the board in the order they appear in the song (pants, skirt, jacket, T-shirt, shoes, skirt, dress, sock). Play the karaoke version of the song. Students sing the song, changing the colors to match the items on the flashcards.

Presentation

- Tell a confident volunteer to stand up. Ask *What are you wearing today?* Suggest something the student isn't wearing, e.g., *Are you wearing a green skirt?* Help the student reply *No, I'm not.* Repeat with different items he/ she isn't wearing (make them funny, if possible), e.g., *Are you wearing red shoes? Are you wearing a purple jacket?* Then ask about something he/she is wearing, e.g., *Are you wearing blue jeans?* Help the student reply *Yes, I am.*

Student's Book page 41

9 Listen, look, and say.

- Say *Open your books to page 41, please. What can you see?* Elicit clothes and colors in the photograph (e.g., *black pants, a blue T-shirt, a yellow T-shirt, a gray skirt*).
- Say *Listen and point.* Play the recording. Students point to the children in the photograph as they speak. Then say *Now listen and say.* Play the recording again, pausing for students to listen and repeat the questions and answers.
- If time, students can ask and answer about their clothes in pairs, using the speech bubbles to help them.

CD1:59

1 **Katie:** Are you wearing a blue T-shirt?
 Alex: Yes, I am.

2 **Alex:** Are you wearing brown shoes?
 Katie: No, I'm not.

10 Listen and point. Then play the game.

- Point to the colors and elicit the name of each. Do the same with the clothes.
- Say *Listen and point.* Play the first line of the recording, pausing after *pants.* Students listen and point to the correct color and item of clothing. Play the question.

Students repeat. Explain that the boy has chosen a color and an item of clothing and then made a question for his partner. Play the girl's answer. Students repeat. Do the same with the second part of the recording.

- Say *Play the game. Take turns.* Students take turns choosing a color and an item of clothing and making a question. They answer according to what they're actually wearing.

CD1:60

Boy: Pink. Pants. Are you wearing pink pants?
Girl: No, I'm not. My turn!

Girl: Purple. Socks. Are you wearing purple socks?
Boy: Yes, I am!

Workbook page 33

6 Listen and number the pictures.

- Students listen and number the pictures.

Key: a 2 **b** 1 **c** 3

CD1:61

1 **Woman:** Are you wearing a skirt and a T-shirt?
 Girl: No, I'm not. I'm wearing jeans and a T-shirt.

2 **Man:** Are you wearing pants and a jacket?
 Boy: No, I'm not. I'm wearing jeans and a jacket.

3 **Man:** Are you wearing a dress and shoes?
 Woman: No, I'm not. I'm wearing a skirt, a shirt, and shoes.

7 Look, read, and circle the word.

- Students look at the picture, read the question, and circle the correct word each time.

Key: 2 shirt **3** shoes **4** jeans

8 Draw. Ask and answer with a friend.

- Students draw a picture of themselves, either in the clothes they're wearing or in a different outfit. They ask and answer in pairs, using the speech bubbles to help them.

Key: Students' own answers.

Ending the lesson

- Turn your back to the class or close your eyes. Ask individual students about what they're wearing, using Yes/No questions, e.g., *Irene, are you wearing a pink T-shirt?* Try to get as many *Yes* answers as possible. You can make this game competitive by scoring a point each time a student answers *Yes, I am*, but giving the class a point for a *No* answer. See who can get to ten points first, you or the class.

Extra activities: see page TB119 (if time)

9 CD1 59 **Listen, look, and say.**

1 Are you wearing a blue T-shirt?

2 Are you wearing brown shoes?

Yes, I am.

No, I'm not.

10 CD1 60 **Listen and point. Then play the game.**

Pink. Pants.
Are you wearing pink pants?

No, I'm not. My turn!

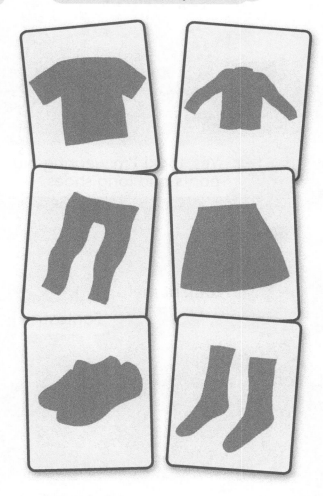

→ Workbook page 33   Grammar: *Are you wearing a blue T-shirt?* **41**

Lesson aims   Students reinforce language with a story. They also discuss the value of sharing.

New language   hat, party | *You can use my (hat).* | *Fantastic! first prize, share things*

Recycled language   clothes | *costume* | *Look at … , clothes, Here's a … for you, What are you wearing? They're … , I'm wearing … , big, long, Here you are. Thanks. robot*

Materials   CD1 | A piece of blank paper for each student | A hat (optional)

Warmer

- Ask different students about their clothes (e.g., *Serena, are you wearing white socks? (Yes, I am. / No, I'm not.)*
- Give a piece of paper to each student and ask them to draw an item of clothing they are wearing. Play *Find a partner* (see page xv), with students asking about their drawing, e.g., *Are you wearing a white shirt?* When students find a partner, they describe what they're wearing to one another. **Note:** If your students wear a uniform, they draw a favorite item of clothing instead.

Introduction

- Remind students of the story so far, asking who the children helped in the last episode (*Tina's Aunt Sue*), which pet Aunt Sue has (*a cat*), and which animal helped the children (*a frog*). Ask students to guess what the children will do with iPal today.

Student's Book page 42

11 Listen and read.

- Say *Open your books to page 42, please.* Point to frame 1 and ask *What do the children have? (Clothes).* Teach *hat* with a real hat or the picture. Ask *Are these clothes for school?* Encourage students to guess what the clothes are for by looking at the other frames.
- Say *Now listen and read.* Play the recording while students listen and follow the story. At the end, ask *What are the children wearing? (Costumes).* Explain/Elicit that there is a costume contest. Point to frame 6 and ask *Who's the winner? Who's number 1? (iPal.)* Explain the meaning of *first prize.* Ask students if any of them have been to a parade/street party like the one in the story.
- Then play the recording again, pausing to ask more questions: Frame 1: *What color's the hat for David? (Red.)* Frame 2: *What's Tina wearing? (A pink and purple dress.) Who's wearing yellow pants? (David.) What are the clothes for? (A party).* Explain the meaning of *party.* Frame 3: *Are David's shoes small? (No. They're big.)* Frame 4: *Is iPal happy? (No, he's sad.)* Make sure students realize he wants to wear a costume. Explain the meaning of *You can use my …* Frame 5: *Is iPal happy? (Yes, he is.) What's on iPal's head? (A bird.) Where are they? (At the party).* Frame 6: *Is iPal a robot? (No, not at this party!)* Explain/Elicit that the man thinks iPal is dressed as a robot, but his costume is a pirate costume.

- Students can listen to the story again for pleasure, or pause after key lines for students to repeat. They can join in with the rhymes, using gestures and intonation from the story as appropriate.

CD1:62

Tina: Look at these clothes.
Olivia: Here's a hat for you!
All: 1, 2, 3, Magic tree. We're back again. Look and see. Come with us. Come and play In our magic tree today.

iPal: What are you wearing?
Ben: They're clothes for a party!
iPal: A party?
David: Yes, look! I'm wearing big pants and long shoes.
Olivia: Here you are, iPal. You can use my hat.
Ben: And my jacket.
iPal: Thank you.

iPal: Look at me!
David: Fantastic!

Judge: First prize … The robot!
iPal: Thanks! But I'm not a robot!
All: 3, 2, 1, that was fun. Time to go. The magic's done!

(Value)   *Share things*

- Point to frame 4 and remind students that iPal is sad because he doesn't have a costume. Ask students what happens next. Play the dialog for frame 4 of the story again, pausing after Olivia's lines: *Here you are, iPal. You can use my hat.* and after Ben's line *And my jacket.* Explain/Elicit that Olivia and Ben are sharing their things with iPal. Ask what iPal says next (*Thank you*).
- Read the value *Share things.* Explain the meaning and ask students for examples of things they can share at school or at home (classroom items, food, toys).
- Divide the class into three groups, one each for Olivia, iPal, and Ben. Then play the dialog from frame 4. Students repeat the lines for Olivia and Ben, and if they are iPal, they act being sad, then happy. They then say *Thank you.* Rearrange the class into groups of three, with one of each character per group. Students practice the dialog in their groups.

Workbook page 34

9 Read and number. Then listen and check.

- Students number the pictures to show the order of events. Play the recording for students to check.

Key: a 4 b 1 c 5 d 2 e 6 f 3

CD1:63

(*Repeat of story – see above for story script*)

Ending the lesson

- Imagine you are a character in the story and describe your clothes, e.g., *I'm wearing a pink and purple dress.* Students say the name of the character (e.g., *Tina*). They can play the same game in pairs.

Extra activities: see page TB119 (if time)

Lesson aims Students practice sharing. Students also practice saying the sounds /dʒ/ and /j/.

New language *You can use this one, jackal, jello, yak, yogurt*

Recycled language clothes | classroom objects | *I don't have a (pen). Here you are. Thank you. don't like*

Materials CD1 | Six or seven hats | Music CD | A selection of clothes (jackets, hats, skirts, boots) for costumes (e.g., a pirate hat that goes with some pirate pants or a toy parrot, a fairy skirt with a matching top and hat, cowboy pants and a matching jacket) (optional)

Warmer

● Put on a hat and ask *What am I wearing? / What's this? (A hat).* Students stand up, if possible. Give the hat to one student and say *Here you are. You can use my hat.* He/She puts the hat on. Encourage the student to say *Thank you.* Hand out another five or six hats in the same way. Play some music. Students walk around. Stop the music. Students who are wearing hats pass them to the student closest to them, saying *Here you are. You can use my hat.* These new students put them on and say *Thank you.* Play the music. The game continues in this way. **Note:** If you have limited space in your classroom, students can remain seated and pass the hats around the class when the music plays.

Student's Book page 43

12 Listen and act.

● Say *Open your books to pages 42 and 43, please.* Remind students of the story from the previous lesson. Say *The children have costumes for a party. iPal is sad.* Ask why *(iPal doesn't have clothes for the party).* Ask what happens *(Olivia and Ben share the clothes).* Remind students of the meaning of *share.* Write *You ___ use my hat.* on the board and elicit the missing word *(can).*

● Tell students they are going to listen to someone else sharing their things. Say *Now look at page 43. Who's speaking? Listen and point.* Play the recording. Students listen and point to the boys in the photograph as they speak each line.

● Then say *Now listen and act.* Play the recording again, pausing for students to repeat each line with the correct pronunciation and intonation. Explain the meaning of *this one.*

● Students act out similar dialogs in pairs, using real classroom objects. One student looks sad as he/she says *I don't have a …* The other student offers to share his/ her things *(Here you are. You can use this one).* Remind the first student to say *Thank you.*

CD1:64

Alex: Oh, no! I don't have a pen.
Carlos: Here you are. You can use this one.
Alex: Thank you.

13 Listen and say.

● In this activity, students practice saying the sounds /dʒ/ and /j/.

● Say *Look at activity 13. What can you see?* Teach *jackal, yak, Jell-O,* and *yogurt.*

● Then say *jackal – /dʒ/ /dʒ/ /dʒ/ – jackal.* Students repeat, emphasizing the /dʒ/ sound in *jackal.*

● Say *yak – /j/ /j/ /j/ – yak.* Students repeat, emphasizing the initial sound in the same way.

● Students can also practice the sounds one after the other (/dʒ/, /j/), with their hands on their throats, so that they can feel the difference between the unvoiced /j/ and voiced /dʒ/.

● Say *Listen and say.* Play the sound sentences on the recording. Students listen and repeat, emphasizing the initial /dʒ/ and /j/ sounds.

● Students can then repeat the sound sentences without the recording, saying them faster and faster each time. See how fast they can say them.

● Ask students to think of any other words they know that begin with the sounds /dʒ/ and /j/. For example, *juice, giraffe, jacket, jeans, jump, yellow, you, yes, young, use.*

CD1:65

/dʒ/ /j/ Jackals don't like jello. Yaks don't like yogurt. (x2)

Workbook page 35

10 Look, read, and stick.

● Remind students of the value from the previous lesson. Students look at the pictures and think about which one shows the value. They stick the smiley face sticker in the circle next to the correct picture.

● Students then select a smiley sticker from the back of the book and stick it next to the value.

Key: Students put the sticker next to the second picture.

11 Trace the letters.

● Students trace the letters *j* and *y* in the sound sentences.

12 Listen and circle j or y.

● Play the recording. Students circle *j* or *y* according to the initial sound of the word.

Key: 2 y 3 j 4 y

CD1:66

1 jello, jello 2 yak, yak 3 jacket, jacket 4 yogurt, yogurt

Ending the lesson

● Write the tongue twister *Do you like jeans or do you like jackets?* on the board. Students practice saying it repeatedly, as fast as they can.

Extra activities: see page TB119 (if time)

TB43

12   **Listen and act.**

Animal sounds

13 CD1 65 Listen and say.

Jackals don't like jello. Yaks don't like yogurt.

What are **clothes** made of?

1 CD1 67 Listen and say.

cotton   silk   leather   wool

2 Watch the video.

3 Look and say the material.

Number 1. Wool.   Yes!

Guess What!

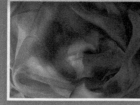

Project

4 Make a collage of clothes from different countries.

Clothes

Lesson aims Students learn about what clothes are made of.

New language *What are clothes made of? cotton, silk, leather, wool*

Recycled language clothes | colors

Materials CD1 | DVD (optional) | Real items of clothing made of cotton, silk, leather, and wool (if possible, at least two items made from each material) (optional)

Warmer

- Show two or more items of clothing made from the same material (e.g., a shirt, a T-shirt, and some socks, all made of cotton). For each item ask *What's this? (A shirt)* and *Are you wearing a (shirt)? (Yes, I am. / No, I'm not.)* Give the items of clothing to the students to pass around the class. Ask them to feel the clothes and ask *What's the same?* Students guess. If they guess that the material is the same, tell them they are going to learn about the different materials clothes are made of in today's lesson.

Student's Book page 44

What are clothes made of?

- Say *Open your books to page 44, please.* Ask questions about the photograph, e.g., *What clothes can you see? (…) What colors can you see? Can you see a/some … ?*
- Ask students where they usually get their clothes.
- Then point to the photograph and ask the opening question *What are clothes made of?* Explain the meaning of the question. Show the different clothes you've brought to class and elicit the materials in L1.

Student's Book page 45

1 Listen and say.

- Say *Now look at page 45, please.* Use the photographs to present the words for materials.
- Say *Listen and say.* Play the recording. Students listen and repeat the words.
- Hold up each item of clothing you've brought to class and ask *What's it made of? (Cotton/Wool/Silk/Leather.)*

CD1:67

1 cotton **2** silk **3** leather **4** wool

2 Watch the video.

- Play the video.
- If you don't have the video, draw a simple four-column chart on the board, with the four materials at the top of each column. Students copy the chart, then write the names of items of clothing that can be made of each material in the correct column. They compare their charts in pairs or small groups. Elicit ideas and complete the chart on the board (note that some items of clothing can be made of more than one material).

Key: Possible items of clothing for the chart: cotton: shirt, T-shirt, jacket, socks, skirt, pants, dress, jeans; silk: shirt, skirt, dress, pants, jacket; leather: jacket, shoes, pants, skirt, dress; wool: socks, jacket, pants, skirt, dress, socks

Video 03 : see page TB130

3 Look and say the material.

- Students work in pairs. They look at the photographs and say the material each item is made of. They use the speech bubbles to help them.
- Check the activity by saying the number of the photograph. Students say *cotton/silk/leather/wool.*

Key: **2** cotton **3** silk **4** wool **5** leather

Guess What!

- Students look at the swirled image and guess what it is. Check by asking *What's this? (It's wool.)*

Key: It's wool (last photograph, activity 1).

Workbook page 36

1 Look and write the number.

- Students look at the picture and number the materials to match the items of clothing.

Key: wool 4 silk 3 leather 2

2 Look, read, and circle the word.

- Students look at the photograph and circle the correct material each time.

Key: cotton wool leather

Ending the lesson

- Point to different items you're wearing / that you've brought to class and ask, e.g., *What are my pants made of? (Cotton.) What's this scarf made of? (Wool.)*

Lesson aims Students make a clothes collage. They also complete the Evaluation in the Workbook.

New language collage

Recycled language What are clothes made of? cotton, silk, leather, wool, clothes | Students review all unit vocabulary and grammar in the Evaluation.

Materials CD1 | Flashcards: 36–44 | Word cards: see page TB108 | Pictures of clothes from around the world (e.g., thobe from the Middle East, Japanese kimono, Scottish kilt) | Materials for the project: blank paper, scraps of material (cotton, wool, silk, and others), scissors, glue, colored markers/pencils for each student (optional)

Warmer

- Play Word race (see page xx) with the word cards for Unit 3.

Student's Book page 45

4 Make a collage of clothes from different countries.

- Write the question from the previous lesson (What are clothes made of?) on the board and see if students can remember the materials (cotton, silk, wool, leather).
- Show pictures of clothes from around the world and ask What's this made of? Ask students to guess the materials and which country/region each outfit comes from.
- Say Open your books to page 45, please. Point to the picture in activity 4 and ask How many people can you see? (Four.) What are they wearing? What colors can you see? Check that they understand the meaning of collage.
- Say Make a collage of children's clothes. Give each student a piece of paper and each group some pieces of material, a scissors, and glue. Students make a collage picture of two to four different outfits. Help students label the pictures, if they wish.
- As students work, circulate and help. Ask, e.g., What's the skirt made of? Is it from Poland?
- When students have finished their collages, they show them to a partner / small group, say what each person is wearing, and name the materials.

Workbook page 37 – Evaluation

1 Write the words and find.

- Students label the pictures and find the words in the word search puzzle.

Key: 2 pants **3** skirt **4** jeans **5** dress **6** shoes

```
g  s  k  i  r  t  f  s  h  o  e  s  d
f  s  d  r  e  s  s  d  v  b  c  m  q
j  e  a  n  s  n  a  j  k  o  a  l  o
a  w  t  q  o  p  a  n  t  s  p  l  l
s  o  c  k  s  m  c  n  v  b  w  i  k
```

2 What's your favorite part? Use your stickers.

- Students choose their favorite part of the unit – the story, the song, or the video – and put a sticker under their chosen preference.

3 What's different? Circle and write. Then go to page 93 and write the letters.

- Students circle the picture that doesn't belong and write the item of clothing. They then go to page 93 and write the letters in the puzzle.

Key: pants, letters for the puzzle – t, s

Ending the lesson

- Students repeat their favorite activity from the unit.

④ Rooms

Unit aims Students learn about houses and rooms. This includes:

- identifying rooms and furnishings inside the home
- asking about and describing where things are in a room
- learning numbers 11 through 20
- learning about things on a street
- interpreting and drawing a bar chart

Background information The photograph shows a building in Little India, Singapore.

Introduction to the unit

- Say *Open your books to pages 46 and 47, please.* Play the theme song on the recording. Students look at the photograph and read the title of the unit while listening to the song.
- Ask *What's Unit 4 about?* Explain the meaning of *rooms*. Then point to the photograph and ask *What can you see? (A house/a door/windows.) What colors can you see on the door? (Green, yellow, orange, red.)*
- Ask *Which rooms can you see in a house? (Bedroom, living room, bathroom, kitchen, dining room, hallway.)* Elicit other parts of the home that students already know in English, e.g., from *Guess What!* Level 1: *hallway, yard, balcony.*
- Ask further questions about homes: *Do you like houses or apartments? What color's your bedroom? What's your favorite room at home?*
- Then play *True or false?* (see page xix), making statements about the students' classroom and/or school, to review rooms, furniture, and the prepositions *in, on,* and *under,* e.g., *My desk's under the window. We have two doors in our classroom. The computer's on a black chair.*

CD1:02

(Theme song – see lyrics on page TB5)

47

→ Workbook page 38

Lesson aims   Students learn vocabulary for furnishings.

New language   closet, phone, TV, bookcase, mirror, cabinet, lamp, table, clock, couch, Welcome to … , video diary, We're playing hide and seek. Who's in/on/under the (closet)? It's me. Who can you see in/on/under the (couch)?

Recycled language   character names | numbers 1–10 | rooms | colors | bed, Come and see. This is the (bookcase). My (books) are in/on/under the (bed). The (phone) is in/on/under the (couch). books, clothes, toys, I have a (TV). Here's a (table). It's in/on/under the (mirror).

Materials   CD2 | Flashcards: 45–54 | Word cards: see page TB109 | Poster putty

Warmer

- Draw a house with two floors and five rooms (three downstairs, two upstairs) on the board, at a height your students can reach. Ask *What's this? (A house). How many rooms can you see? (Five.)* Point to the upstairs part. Ask *Which rooms are here? (Bedroom and bathroom.)* Draw a bed in the bedroom and a bathtub and toilet in the bathroom. Repeat for downstairs (*living room, dining room, kitchen*), adding simple details. Point and ask *What's this room?* or ask *Where's the (living room)?* Students point. Say *Draw a yard/balcony, please.*

Presentation

- Ask *What's in a room? Let's look.* Hold up each flashcard and say the new word. Students repeat in chorus and individually. Then show the flashcards in random order. Students say the words.

Student's Book page 48

1 Listen. Who's speaking?

- Say *Open your books to page 48, please.* Ask *Is this Tina's bedroom?* Students guess (*No*). Explain that it's Ben's room. Say *They're playing a game. Which game?* Teach *hide and seek.* Ask students if they play hide and seek. Point to the camera and explain that Ben is making a video diary.

- Say *Let's listen. Who's speaking?* Play the recording. Students listen and point to the characters. Play again, pausing for students to point to the furnishings. Review/Teach *bed.* If time, ask *Who's in the closet? (Olivia.) Who can you see under the bed? (Tina.) Where's David? (In the cabinet.)* Ask about the clothes and other items, e.g., *Where are Ben's shoes? (Under the couch.) Can you see a chair? (Yes. It's blue.)*

CD2:02

Ben: Hello. Welcome to my video diary! We're playing hide and seek in my bedroom. Come and see. This is the bookcase, and this is the closet. My books are in the bookcase, and my clothes are in the closet. The phone is on the bookcase. And who is in the closet?

Olivia: It's me, Olivia!
Ben: This is my cabinet for my toys. And I have a TV on the cabinet. And who can you see in the cabinet?
David: It's me, David!
Ben: This is my bed, and here's a table. I have a lamp on the table and a red clock. And who is under the bed?
Tina: It's me, Tina!
Ben: This is the couch. It's under the mirror. And who is under the couch?
Leo: *Crick!*
Ben: It's Leo!

2 Listen, point, and say.

- Say *Now listen, point, and say.* Play the recording. Students listen and point to the numbered items in the picture. Then play again. Students listen and say the words.

CD2:03

1 closet **2** phone **3** TV **4** bookcase **5** mirror
6 cabinet **7** lamp **8** table **9** clock **10** couch

3 Listen and find.

- Say *Now listen and find.* Play the recording, pausing for students to find and point to the correct items. Students can also say the correct number. If time, students can repeat in pairs. One says a sentence, e.g., *It's a lamp*, and the other says the number (e.g., *Seven*) or points to the item.

Key: Students point to the items in the following order: 1, 9, 3, 7, 4, 10, 6, 8, 5, 2.

CD2:04

It's a closet.   It's a bookcase.   It's a mirror.
It's a clock.   It's a couch.   It's a phone.
It's a TV.   It's a cabinet.
It's a lamp.   It's a table.

Find Leo.

- Say *Now find Leo.* Students search for Leo in the picture (he's under the couch).

Workbook page 38

1 Look, read, and circle the word.

- Students look at the picture and circle the correct word.

Key: 2 lamp **3** phone **4** couch **5** TV **6** table

2 Look, read, and write.

- Students look at the pictures, read the sentences, and write the missing words.

Key: 2 clock **3** couch **4** phone

Ending the lesson

- Put poster putty on the back of the word cards. Hand out the cards. Students take turns finding the object written in the classroom and sticking the card onto it (e.g., the word *bookcase* onto the bookcase). Remove the cards, mix them up, and repeat with different students.

Extra activities: see pages TB119 to TB120 (if time)

Lesson aims Students practice the furnishings vocabulary. They practice asking about and describing where things are in a room.

New language *Is the (lamp) on/in the (table)? The (lamp)'s/It's on/in the (table). Are the (books) in/ on the (bookcase)? The (books) are / They're in/on the (bookcase).*

Recycled language furnishings | *Yes, it is. / No, it isn't. Yes, they are. / No, they aren't.*

Materials CD2 | Flashcards: 45–54 | Two pieces of blank paper for each student (optional)

Warmer

- Review the furnishings words with the flashcards or using items around the classroom.
- Play *Correct my mistakes* (see page xv), making sentences about the color and position of items in the classroom, e.g., *The clock is white. (No. It's red.) The lamp is on the closet. (No. It's on the cabinet.)* You can also point to items and say the wrong word, e.g., point to a table and say *This is a couch. (No. It's a table.)*

Student's Book page 49

4 Say the chant.

- Say *Open your books to page 49, please.* Point to each of the photographs and ask *What's this? (It's a table.)* Review *in* and *on* by asking *Where's the lamp? (On the table.) Where are the books? (In the bookcase.)* Repeat for *clock* and *clothes*.
- Say *Listen to the chant.* Play the recording. Students listen and point to the photographs in turn.
- Then say *Now listen and say the chant.* Play the recording again. Students can clap along to the rhythm at first, joining in with as many words as they can. Then repeat as often as necessary until students are chanting confidently. Encourage them to mime putting something on a table and putting books in a bookcase / clothes in a closet as they chant.

CD2:05

Is the lamp on the table?
Yes, it is. Yes, it is.
The lamp's on the table.

Are the books in the
  bookcase?
Yes, they are. Yes, they are.
The books are in the
  bookcase.

Is the clock on the table?
Yes, it is. Yes, it is.
The clock's on the table.

Are the clothes in the
  closet?
Yes, they are. Yes, they are.
The clothes are in the
  closet.

5 Look, ask, and answer.

- Point to the main picture and ask *What can you see? (A living room, a couch, a cabinet, a bookcase, a table).* Explain that there are some pieces missing from the picture – point to the jigsaw pieces on the right. Read the question in the speech bubble. Point to the picture, then read the example answer.
- Say *Look, ask, and answer.* Students work in pairs to ask

and answer about the picture, using the speech bubbles to help them. Circulate and make sure students are using *Is* and *Are* correctly.
- Check answers by asking, e.g., *Are the lamps on the table? (No, they aren't. They're on the bookcase.)*

Key: Students' own answers.

6 What's in your bedroom? Think and say.

- Tell students to close their eyes and think about their bedroom at home. *What's in the bedroom? Where's the bed? Where's the chair? What's in the cabinet?* Students work in pairs. They take turns describing where things are in their bedroom, using the speech bubble to help them. Circulate and help with new language.

Key: Students' own answers.

Workbook page 39

3 Listen and stick.

- Students will need the Unit 4 stickers from the back of the Workbook.
- Play the recording. Students listen and stick the stickers into the correct position.

CD2:06

1 The computer isn't in the closet. It's in the cabinet.
2 The clock isn't on the bookcase. It's on the table.
3 The phone isn't on the table. It's on the couch.
4 The mirror isn't under the TV. The TV is under the mirror.
5 The lamp isn't on the table. It's on the bookcase.

Key: computer in the cabinet, clock on the table, phone on the couch, mirror above the TV, lamp on the bookcase

4 Look, match, and write the words.

- Students match the missing items with the rooms by drawing lines. Elicit a sentence about each picture, e.g., 1 *The TV is in the living room.* 2 *The clothes are in the closet.* 3 *The books are in the bookcase.* 4 *The phone is on the table.*

Key: 2 c closet 3 a bookcase 4 b phone

My picture dictionary → Go to page 88. Check the words you know and trace.

- Students turn to page 88 and check the words they know. They then trace over the word labels for each picture.

Ending the lesson

- Ask students to look at the picture on Student's Book page 48. Ask questions with *Is/Are*, e.g., *Is the lamp on the table? (Yes, it is.) Are the shoes under the bed? (No, they aren't. They're under the couch.)* Students can repeat the activity in pairs, taking turns asking the questions.

Extra activities: see page TB120 (if time)

4 **Say the chant.**

Is the lamp on the table?
Yes, it is. Yes, it is.
The lamp's on the table.

Are the books in the bookcase?
Yes, they are. Yes, they are.
The books are in the bookcase.

lamp

bookcase

clock

closet

5 **Look, ask, and answer.**

Is the phone on the bookcase?

No, it isn't. It's on the table.

1

2   **3**

4

6   **What's in your bedroom? Think and say.**

My computer is on my desk.

→ Workbook page 39

Vocabulary **49**

7  **Sing the song.**

It's moving day, it's moving day,
And everything's wrong
on moving day.

There's a  in the bathroom.
There's a 🛋 in the hallway.
There's a 🗄 in the kitchen.
And I can't find my ball today!

It's moving day …

There are four 🛋s in the yard.
There are two 📺s on my bed.
There are three ⏰s on the couch.
And where is baby Fred?

It's moving day …

8 **Listen and say *yes* or *no*.**

Lesson aims   Students describe where things are in a room/house.

New language   *moving day, everything's wrong, There's a (couch) in/on the (bathroom). There are (four lamps) in/on the (yard).*

Recycled language   *furnishings, furniture, rooms, in/on, I can't find my (ball). Where is … ? baby*

Materials   CD2 | *Five or six known toys, toy animals, items of clothing or food (some singular, some plural)* | *A scarf / piece of thick fabric to use as a blindfold OR a large bag and six to eight objects or flashcards (toys, animals, items of clothing, or classroom objects) (optional)*

Warmer

- Before the class, put some furnishings in unusual places (e.g., the clock in a cabinet (with the door open), a lamp under a table, your purse on a cabinet).
- Ask *What's wrong in the classroom today?* Explain the meaning of *wrong*. Students make sentences, e.g., *The clock is in the cabinet (today).* If possible, students also tell you where the clock should be, e.g., *It isn't in the cabinet. It's on the wall.* Move each item back to its usual position.

Presentation

- Place some singular and plural items around the room, e.g., a teddy bear on your chair, a toy animal under a chair, a pair of socks on someone's desk, some bananas on the cabinet. Ask *What toy can you see? (A teddy bear).* Say *Yes! There's a teddy bear.* Encourage students to repeat *There's a teddy bear.* Ask *Where is it? (It's on your chair.)* Repeat for the other items, making sure you introduce *There are …* (e.g., *There are three bananas.*)

Student's Book page 50

7 Sing the song.

- Say *Open your books to page 50, please.* Point to the picture and ask *What's this? (A house.)* Ask *What can you see?* Elicit rooms, furniture, and other items. Point to the family and ask *Who's this? (Mom/Dad/A baby/A boy.)* Point to the men who are wearing blue. Say *Look at these men. Are they in the family? (No, they aren't.)* Elicit/Explain that they are helping the family move. Say *It's moving day.* Explain the meaning. Ask students if they have ever moved.
- Point to one thing that's in the wrong place (e.g., the bookcase). Say *Oh, dear! Look! There's a bookcase in the bathroom. That's wrong!* Explain/Review the meaning of *wrong*. Elicit more examples of things that are in the wrong place (e.g., *There are lamps in the yard.*).
- Say *Listen and point.* Play the recording. Students listen and point to the items. At the end, explain the meaning of *everything* and *I can't find (my ball).*
- Then say *Now sing the song.* Play the recording a few times, until students are singing confidently. The first time students can hum to the tune and join in with any words they know. Then students can sing along, following the song text. You can also divide the class into two groups,

one singing the first verse, the other the second verse. They all join in with the chorus (*It's moving day …*).
Note: Students can sing along to the version of the song with the words or to the karaoke version.

CD2:07

It's moving day, it's moving day,
And everything's wrong on moving day. (x2)

There's a couch in the bathroom.
There's a table in the hallway.
There's a closet in the kitchen.
And I can't find my ball today!

It's moving day, it's moving day
And everything's wrong on moving day. (x2)

There are four lamps in the yard.
There are two mirrors on my bed.
There are three clocks on the couch.
And where is baby Fred?

It's moving day, it's moving day,
And everything's wrong on moving day. (x2)

8 Listen and say yes or no.

- Say *Listen and say yes or no.* Play the recording, pausing after each sentence. Students listen, look at the picture in activity 7 and say *yes* or *no*. Ask students to make true sentences for the "no" answers.

Key: 1 yes **2** no (There are four lamps in the yard.) **3** no (There's a closet in the kitchen.) **4** yes **5** no (There's a mirror / There are two mirrors in the bedroom.) **6** yes

CD2:08

1 There's a couch in the bathroom.

2 There are four lamps in the living room.

3 There's a bed in the kitchen.

4 There are two TVs on the chair.

5 There's a bookcase in the bedroom.

6 There's a baby in the cabinet.

Workbook page 40

5 Look, read, and write yes or no.

- Students look at the picture, read the sentences, and write *yes* or *no*. Elicit correct sentences for the "no" answers.

Key: 2 yes **3** no (There's one clock in the bedroom.) **4** no (There's a closet in the bedroom.) **5** yes **6** yes

6 Draw your room and say. Then write.

- Students draw a picture of their bedroom. They take turns talking about their rooms, then completing the sentences.

Key: Students' own answers.

Ending the lesson

- Make true or false sentences using *There's / There are* about the classroom (make the false sentences funny, if possible), e.g., *There's a robot in the cabinet.* Students say *Yes* or *No.* They can repeat the game in pairs.

Extra activities: see page TB120 (if time)

Lesson aims Students ask and answer questions about quantity. Students practice counting and learn numbers 11–20.

New language numbers 11–20 | *How many (books) are there?*

Recycled language furnishings and furniture | pets | clothes | numbers 1–10

Materials CD2 | Two different-colored board markers, one for each team of students (optional)

Warmer

- Play the song from the previous lesson. Students sing along. Teach mimes for the furniture and the other key items in the song (couch, table, closet, ball, lamp, mirror, clock, baby). Play the song again for students to sing and mime.

Presentation

- Practice counting from 1 through 10 with the class forward and in reverse. See if any students know numbers larger than ten already. Ask questions about items in the classroom (with answers of ten or less), e.g., *How many windows are there in our classroom? How many girls are there?*

Student's Book page 51

9 Listen, look, and say.

- Say *Open your books to page 51, please. What's this?* (*A bookcase.*) *What's in the bookcase?* (*Books.*) Say *How many books are there?* Give students time to look at the picture.
- Say *Listen and point.* Play the recording. Students point to the books one by one as they hear the numbers. Then say *Now listen and say.* Play the recording again, pausing for students to listen and repeat. Practice counting from 1 through 20 in chorus several times.

CD2:09

Boy: How many books are there?
Girl: 1, 2, 3, 4, 5, 6, 7, 8, 9, 10, 11, 12, 13, 14, 15, 16, 17, 18, 19, 20. Twenty! There are twenty books.

10 Listen, count, and answer the questions.

- Point to the picture and ask *What can you see?* (*A bedroom*). Elicit as many items students know in the room as possible (e.g., planes, clocks, fish, socks, pencils, chair, jackets, lamps, spiders).
- Say *Listen, count, and answer.* Play the first question on the recording, pause and count the fish with the students, then play the answer. Point to the speech bubbles above the picture.
- Then play the rest of the recording, pausing after each question for students to count and answer. They can compare answers in pairs, if necessary, before telling you.

Key: 2 three **3** six **4** nine **5** sixteen

CD2:10

1 How many fish are there?
2 How many lamps are there?
3 How many clocks are there?
4 How many pencils are there?
5 How many socks are there?

11 Play the game.

- Read the speech bubbles with the class. Ask *How many spiders are there?* (*Four.*) Make a true sentence about the picture, e.g., *There are seven planes.* Ask *Yes or no?* (*Yes.*) Say *Play the game.* Students play in pairs, taking turns making a true or false sentence each time.

Workbook page 41

7 What's next? Read and write.

- Students complete the number sequences with words from the box.

Key: 2 twelve **3** fifteen **4** twenty

8 Count and write. Then answer the questions.

- Students look at the large picture and count the number of each of the items in the small pictures. They write the numbers in the boxes. Then they read and answer the questions.

Key: 2 There are thirteen fish. **3** There are sixteen cars. **4** There are fifteen shoes. **5** There are ten balls. **6** There are twenty books.

Ending the lesson

- Play *Drawing in the air* (see page xv) with numbers between **1** and **20**. Students can also play in pairs.

Extra activities: see page TB120 (if time)

9 (CD2 09) **Listen, look, and say.**

10 (CD2 10) **Listen, count, and answer the questions.**

How many fish are there?

Seventeen!

11 (Think) **Play the game.**

There are three spiders.   No!

12 CD2 11 **Listen and read.**

1. Oh, no! Where's my ring?
   Is it in the art set?

2. Look at this big bookcase!
   There's my doll. We're in my bedroom!

3. Let's go in. Walk on me!
   Thanks, iPal.

4. What a mess! Let's clean up.

5. Let's put the toys in the cabinet.
   Now it's neat.

6. What does iPal have?
   It's your ring, Tina!

52 Value: Be neat

→ Workbook page 42

Lesson aims   Students reinforce language with a story. They also discuss the value of being neat.

New language   *ring (n), We're in (my bedroom). Let's go in. Walk on me! What a mess! clean up, put, now, neat (adj)*

Recycled language   *furniture, Where's my … ? Is it in the … ? Look at this, big, There's my … , Thanks, What does … have?*

Materials   CD2 | Ten slips of paper for each student OR flashcards: bookcase, cabinet, and closet (45, 47, and 54) and flashcards of clothes: 36–44, pictures or flashcards of toys and books/magazines/comic books (optional)

Warmer

● Practice counting from 1 through 20 in chorus. Start counting and point to students at random to say the next number. Practice counting in different patterns, e.g., saying only odd or only even numbers or only multiples of three (students clap instead of saying the other numbers).

Introduction

● Remind students of the story so far, asking why iPal is sad in the last episode (he doesn't have a costume), where the children go (to a party), how iPal gets his costume (the children share their clothes), and what iPal dresses up as (a pirate). Ask students to guess what the children will do with iPal today.

Student's Book page 52

12 Listen and read.

● Say *Open your books to page 52, please.* Point to frame 1 and ask *Where are the children? (In the tree house).* Say *Look. Tina is sad. She can't find her ring.* Teach *ring* by drawing a picture on the board. Point to frame 2 and ask *Are the children big? (No, they're small.)* Encourage students to guess how they find the ring by looking at the other frames.

● Say *Now listen and read.* Play the recording while students listen and follow the story. At the end, ask *Where's Tina's ring? (On iPal's head).* Explain/Elicit that the children become small and they go inside Tina's dollhouse in her bedroom.

● Then play the recording again, pausing to ask more questions: Frame 1: *Is the ring in the art set? (No.)* Frame 2: *What's big in the picture? (The bookcase.)* Frame 3: *What do the children walk on? (iPal's arms.)* Frame 4: *Is the room OK? (No, it's messy.)* Explain the meaning of *What a mess!* and *Let's clean up.* Frame 5: *Where are the toys? (In the cabinet.) Where are the books? (In the bookcase).* Frame 6: *Is Tina sad? (No, she's happy. / She has her ring.)*

● Students can listen to the story again for pleasure, or pause after key lines for students to repeat. They can join in with the rhymes. Encourage students to use gestures and intonation from the story as appropriate.

CD2:11

Tina: Oh, no! Where's my ring?
Olivia: Is it in the art set?
All: 1, 2, 3, Magic tree. We're back again. Look and see. Come with us. Come and play In our magic tree today.
David: Look at this big bookcase.
Tina: There's my doll. We're in my bedroom!

iPal: Let's go in. Walk on me!
Children: Thanks, iPal.
Olivia: What a mess!
David: Let's clean up.
Tina: Let's put the toys in the cabinet.
David: Now it's neat.
Olivia: What does iPal have?
iPal: It's your ring, Tina!
All: 3, 2, 1, that was fun. Time to go. The magic's done!

(Value)   *Be neat*

● Point to frame 4 and play the first line of the dialog. Remind students of the meaning of *What a mess!* Say *Look! There are books on the couch.* Elicit more sentences about the room (e.g., *There's a ball on the couch. There's a book and a duck on the table.*) Play the next line of the story (*Let's clean up.*).

● Read the value *Be neat.* Confirm the meaning of *neat* and ask *Is your bedroom/house/desk neat?* Talk about how we can lose things if we aren't neat.

● Divide the class into two groups (Olivia and David). Then play the dialog from frame 4 again. Students repeat the lines for Olivia and David. Encourage them to use the same intonation as on the recording. Rearrange the class into pairs, with one of each character per pair. Students practice the dialog.

Workbook page 42

9 Read and write the letter. Then listen and check.

● Students match the text with the story frames. They write the correct letter in each speech bubble. Play the story again, which is repeated in full on the recording. Students listen and check their answers.

Key: 2 d **3** b **4** a **5** f **6** c

CD2:12

(Repeat of story – see above for story script)

Ending the lesson

● Ask questions about the position, color, and number of the things in the story, e.g., Frame 1: *Where's the art set? (On the table.)* Frame 2: *How many books are there in the bookcase? (Eight.)* Frame 3: *How many windows are there in the dollhouse? (Five.)* Frame 4: *What color's the mirror? (It's yellow.)* Frame 5: *Where's the ball? (It's in the cabinet.)* Frame 6: *What's Tina wearing? (Pink pants and a green and blue T-shirt.)* See which student/pair of students can get the most correct answers.

Extra activities: see page TB120 (if time)

Lesson aims Students practice *Let's clean up.* Students also practice saying the sounds /m/ and /n/.

New language *meerkat, newt*

Recycled language *furnishings | What a mess! Let's clean up! have, mouth, nose*

Materials CD2 | Books, toys, stuffed animals, items of clothing, magazines/comic books, classroom objects, a picture of an anemone

Warmer

- Before class, make the room messy by putting books, stuffed animals, items of clothing, bags and classroom items, etc. on the tables/under chairs/on the floor, etc. When students arrive say *What a mess!* Students repeat. Encourage them to join in with *Let's clean up!* Point to one of the items that's in the wrong place and say, e.g., *Look. There's a book under the chair. Let's put the book in the bookcase.* Repeat with two or three more items. Then call on volunteers to say where items are, suggest where to put them, and clean them up. At the end say *Great! Now it's neat.*

Student's Book page 53

13 Listen and act.

- Say *Open your books to pages 52 and 53, please.* Remind students of the story from the previous lesson. Say *Tina is sad. She can't find her ___ . (ring)* Ask where the children go *(To Tina's bedroom).* Ask *Are they big or small? (They're small.)* Remind students of the meaning of *What a mess!* Write *Let's ___ up!* on the board and elicit the missing word *(clean).*
- Tell students they're going to listen to someone else who is looking at a messy room. Say *Now look at page 53. What can you see? (…)* Then say *Who's speaking? Listen and point.* Play the recording. Students listen and point to the person in the photograph they think is speaking *(Mom).*
- Then say *Now listen and act.* Play the recording again, pausing for students to repeat with the correct pronunciation and intonation.
- Students practice the language in pairs, making a mess with books and other classroom objects on their desk first. One student points to the things and says *What a mess! Let's clean up!* The other student says *OK* and puts the things away. Then they swap roles and repeat.

CD2:13

Woman: What a mess! Let's clean up!

14 Listen and say.

- In this activity, students practice saying the sounds /m/ and /n/.
- Say *Look at activity 14. What can you see?* Teach *meerkat* and *newt.* Review mouth and nose by saying *Point to your nose/mouth.*
- Then say *meerkat – /m/ /m/ /m/ – meerkat.* Students repeat, emphasizing the /m/ sound.
- Say *newt – /n/ /n/ /n/ – newt.* Students repeat, emphasizing the initial sound in the same way.
- Say *Listen and say.* Play the sound sentences on the recording. Students listen and repeat, emphasizing the initial /m/ and /n/ sounds.
- Students can then repeat the sound sentences without the recording, saying them faster and faster each time. See how fast they can say them.
- Ask students to think of any other words they know that begin with the sounds /m/ and /n/. For example, *mom, my, milk, monkey, motorcycle, man, mouse, mice, mirror, name, number, nine, nineteen, now, not, nice.*

CD2:14

/m/ /n/ Meerkats have mouths. Newts have noses. (x2)

Workbook page 43

10 Look, read, and stick.

- Remind students of the value from the previous lesson. Students look at the pictures and think about which one shows the value. They stick the smiley face sticker in the circle next to the correct picture.
- Students then select a smiley sticker from the back of the book and stick it next to the value.

Key: Students put the sticker next to the first picture.

11 Trace the letters.

- Students trace the letters *M, m, N* and *n* in the sound sentences.

12 Listen and circle the pictures.

- Play the recording. Students circle the pictures that match the sound shown on the left of each row.

Key: 1 mouse, man **2** newt, nose

CD2:15

1 mouse, mouse **2** name, name **3** man, man
1 newt, newt **2** nose, nose **3** motorcycle, motorcycle

Ending the lesson

- Write the tongue twister *Many anemones see enemy anemones* on the board. Show a picture of an anemone, if possible. Students practice saying it repeatedly, as fast as they can.

Extra activities: see pages TB120 to TB121 (if time)

13   **Listen and act.**

Animal sounds

14 **Listen and say.**

Meerkats have mouths. Newts have noses.

How many are there?

54

1 (CD2 16) **Listen and say.**

1

2

3

4

streetlight   bus stop   mailbox   traffic light

2 **Watch the video.**

3 **Look and say the number.**

How many streetlights are there?   There are fourteen.

Guess What!

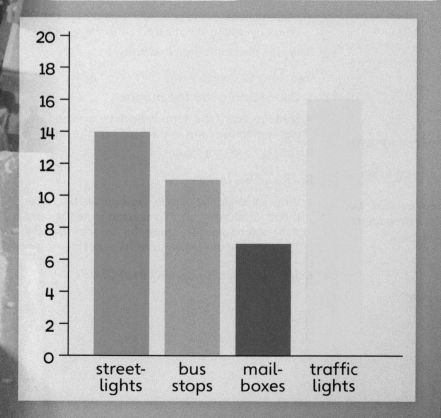

Project

4 Make a bar chart.

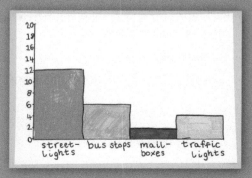

→ Workbook page 44

CLIL: Math **55**

Lesson aims Students learn about things on a street. They learn to interpret a bar chart.

New language *streetlight*, *bus stop*, *mailbox*, *traffic light*

Recycled language numbers 1–20 | *How many (streetlights) are there?*

Materials CD2 | DVD (optional) | Four board markers (one for each team of students in the Warmer) | Ten large number cards, each with a number between 11 and 20 on it OR a blank piece of paper and a clipboard for each student (optional)

Warmer

- Review numbers 1 through 20 by counting around the class, forward and in reverse.
- Play *Whisper down the line* (see page xix) with numbers 1–20.

Student's Book page 54

How many are there?

- Say *Open your books to page 54, please.* Ask questions about the photograph, e.g., *What transportation can you see? (…) How many people can you see? (…) Can you see a … ?*
- Ask students how the street looks different from a street in their hometown/city.
- Then point to the photograph and ask the opening question *How many are there?* Review the meaning of the question. Ask about objects, furnishings, and people in the class (there have to be 20 or fewer), e.g., *How many girls are there in our class? How many boys? How many desks are there? How many windows? How many bookcases?*

Student's Book page 55

1 Listen and say.

- Say *Now look at page 55, please.* Use the photographs to present the words for things on the street.
- Say *Listen and say.* Play the recording. Students listen and repeat the words.
- Students look at the photograph on page 54 again. Ask *Can you see some traffic lights? How many streetlights can you see? Is there a mailbox? What color is it? Where's the bus stop?*

CD2:16

1 streetlight 2 bus stop 3 mailbox 4 traffic light

2 Watch the video.

- Play the video.
- If you don't have the video, talk about how the things on the street in the photographs in activity 1 are different from the ones in your students' hometown (color, size, shape). Ask students for examples of other things we usually see on a street (e.g., crosswalks, trash cans, benches, road signs, railings, bike racks, parking meters) and talk briefly about what each one is for.

Video 04 : see page TB130

3 Look and say the number.

- Point to the picture of the bar chart and ask if students have seen a chart like this before. Read the labels on the x axis. Tell them that someone has done a survey, counting the number of each of these things on a street close to their house/school. Read the numbers on the y axis aloud with the students. Read the example speech bubbles and make sure students know how to read the answer on the bar chart.
- Students work in pairs to ask and answer about the rest of the items on the x axis of the chart (bus stops, mailboxes, and traffic lights). They use the speech bubbles to help them.
- Check the activity by choosing pairs to ask and answer about each thing.

Key: bus stops – eleven, mailboxes – seven, traffic lights – sixteen

Guess What!

- Students look at the swirled image and guess what it is. Check by asking *What's this? (A traffic light.)*

Key: It's the traffic light in activity 1.

Workbook page 44

1 Count and write the number.

- Students count the items in each picture and write the answers to the sums in the boxes on the right.

Key: 1 5   2 5   3 8   4 6

Ending the lesson

- Write six to eight addition sums on the board (or dictate them). Students work in pairs and write the answers in their notebooks. Make sure the answers are all 20 or less. Students can also write sums for a partner to work out.

Extra activities: see page TB121 (if time)

Lesson aims Students do a survey and make a bar chart. They also complete the Evaluation in the Workbook.

New language *bar chart*

Recycled language *How many (streetlights) are there? streetlight, bus stop, mailbox, traffic light* | numbers 1–20 | Students review all unit vocabulary and grammar in the Evaluation.

Materials CD2 | Materials for the project: blank paper for each student (if possible, graph paper), colored markers or pencils, rulers | Flashcards: 45–54 and word cards: see page TB109

Warmer

- Draw a long line across the board representing a street. Draw some houses along the street. Say *What is there on the street? Let's draw.* Students suggest things on the street, e.g., *Streetlight.* Ask *How many streetlights are there? (Five.)* Add the correct number of streetlights to your picture. Make sure you review *bus stop, mailbox,* and *traffic light.* You can also ask *How many men/women/children are there?* and/or *How many cars/bikes/motorcycles/buses are there?* and add these things to your picture.

- If you do not wish to draw, ask questions about the photograph on Student's Book page 54.

Student's Book page 55

4 Make a bar chart.

- Draw the axes of a simple bar chart on the board and remind students that they looked at a bar chart in the previous lesson. Teach *bar chart.* Point to the y axis and ask *What do I write here? (Numbers).* Explain that we can use bar charts to show the results of any kind of survey where we count groups of items/people/answers.

- Say *Open your books to page 55, please.* Point to the picture in activity 4 and ask questions about the chart, e.g., *How many streetlights are there? (Twelve.)*

- Say *Make a bar chart.* If you didn't take students for a walk outside school for the Extension activity in the previous lesson, take them before they make their bar chart (see page TB119 for instructions). Alternatively, walk to the road just outside the school and count each street item together with your class (streetlights, bus stops, traffic lights, mailboxes), recording the answers in a chart on a large piece of paper. If there are a number of additional pieces of things on the street outside your school, add those to the categories in your chart (e.g., benches, trash cans, parking spots).

- If you can't take your students outside, count the items yourself before the class.

- Write the results of the survey on the board as total numbers for each item, e.g., *streetlights – 8, bus stops – 2, traffic lights – 1, parking spots – 14.*

- Give each student a piece of paper (graph paper, if possible), a ruler, and colored markers/pencils. Show them how to draw the x axis, with equal space for each bar, and the y axis, with equal spacing for each number (either marked in single numbers or in twos). Students draw their bar chart and color each bar a different color. Circulate and help. Students compare their bar charts in pairs and ask and answer questions, using the speech bubbles in Student's Book activity 3 to help them.

Workbook page 45 – Evaluation

1 Order the letters and write the word.

- Students solve the anagrams and label the pictures.

Key: 2 table 3 clock 4 phone 5 mirror 6 couch

2 What's your favorite part? Use your stickers.

- Students choose their favorite part of the unit – the story, the song, or the video – and put a sticker under their chosen preference.

3 What's different? Circle and write. Then go to page 93 and write the letters.

- Students circle the picture that doesn't belong and write the item of clothing. They then go to page 93 and write the letters in the puzzle.

Key: closet, letter for the puzzle – t

Ending the lesson

- Students repeat their favorite activity from the unit.

Extra activities: see page TB121 (if time)

Review **Units 3 and 4**

1 **Look and say the words.** Number 1. Jeans.

2 **CD2 17** **Listen and say the color.**

→ Workbook pages 46–47

Lesson aims Students reinforce the language of Units 3 and 4.

New language *best friend*

Recycled language clothes | furniture and furnishings | numbers | colors | *bedroom* | *How old is he/she? He's/She's (eight).* | *What's he/she wearing? He's/She's wearing (jeans). What are you wearing? I'm wearing (a green T-shirt).* | *My favorite color is (green).* | *There's a (closet). There are (two beds). I have (a computer).* | *How many (cars) are there?* | *Who's this? Her name's (Sue). How old is she? She's (eight).*

Materials CD2 | Flashcards: 36–54, word cards: see pages TB108–TB109 (optional)

Warmer

- Ask *What can you remember from Units 3 and 4? Let's find out.* Allow students time to look through the units and at any work displayed in class. Encourage them to say what is easy or difficult. Ask *What's your favorite activity?*

Student's Book page 56

1 Look and say the words.

- Say *Open your books to page 56, please.* Students look at the close-up photographs and guess the words. Check the activity by saying the picture number, e.g., *Number 1.* Students say the word: *Jeans.* Alternatively, check the activity by asking *What's number (1)? / What's this? / What are these?* Elicit *It's a (clock). / They're (jeans).*
- If you have time, provide further review by asking questions about the photographs, e.g., *Number 1. Are they socks? (No, they aren't.) What color are they? (They're blue.) Are you wearing (jeans)? (Yes, I am. / No, I'm not.)*

Key: 2 clock 3 jacket 4 lamp 5 socks 6 table 7 shoes 8 closet

2 Listen and say the color.

- Say *Let's find out about the people and things in the photographs.* Explain that students will hear two people talking about the photographs. They have to decide which photograph matches each conversation.
- Ask *Can you see a boy? (Students point to the correct photograph.)* Ask *How old is he? (Students guess.) What's he wearing? (Jeans, a green T-shirt, green shoes.)* Repeat for the photograph of the girl. Point to the photograph of the toy cars and ask *What are these? (They're cars.) What colors can you see? (Red, black, blue, yellow, white, etc.)* Then point to the photograph of the bedroom and ask *Is this a living room? (No, a bedroom.)* Ask *What can you see? (A bed, toys, a computer, a bookcase with books, a closet.)* Say *Listen and say the color.*

- Play the recording, pausing after each mini-dialog. Students listen and guess which photograph is being talked about each time. They say the color of the correct photograph frame.
- Depending on time available, ask students further questions about the photographs: *What's the boy's name? (His name's Alex.) How old is he? (He's eight.) What's his favorite color? (Green.) Is it Alex's computer? (Yes, it is.) What's Alex's favorite toy? (Cars.) What's the girl's name? (Sue.) How old is she? (She's eight.) Is she Alex's sister? (No. She's his best friend.)* Explain the meaning of *best friend.*

Key: Yellow, Red, Blue, Green

CD2:17

Adult: Hello. What's your name?
Alex: Hello. I'm Alex. I'm eight years old. This is my picture!
Adult: What are you wearing in this picture?
Alex: Jeans … and my green T-shirt. And I'm wearing green shoes. My favorite color is green.
Adult: Is this your bedroom?
Alex: Yes, it is. There are two beds, and there's a closet, and I have a computer.
Adult: Wow! How many cars are there?
Alex: There are lots of cars! They're my favorite toy.
Adult: And who's this?
Alex: She's my best friend. Her name's Sue.
Adult: How old is she?
Alex: She's eight – the same age as me!

Workbook page 46

1 Look and write the word. Then draw Number 8.

- Students look at the pictures and complete the words in the puzzle grid. They work out the answer for number 8 by reading the word spelled in the outlined boxes in the grid. Then they draw the missing item and write the word.

Key: 2 lamp 3 table 4 mirror 5 phone 6 dress 7 pants 8 cabinet

2 Read and circle.

- Students read and circle the correct word each time.

Key: 2 are 3 are 4 dress

Ending the lesson

- Play *Point to (red)* (see page xviii) with clothes, furniture, and furnishings in the classroom (e.g., *Point to a blue jacket. / Point to a bookcase. / Point to some black shoes.*)

Extra activities: see page TB121 (if time)

Lesson aims Students play a board game and continue reinforcing the language of Units 3 and 4.

New language *Miss a turn. Go forward one. Go back one.*

Recycled language clothes | furniture and furnishings | *classroom, bedroom, living room, kitchen* | *Are you wearing (shoes)/(a skirt)? Yes, I am. / No, I'm not.* | *How many (tables) are there in your (classroom)? There are (ten).* | *Look at your bedroom. What a mess! Let's clean up. Let's put the T-shirts and jeans in the closet.* | *Thank you! You're welcome.* | *Oh, no! I don't have a pen. Here you are. You can use this one.*

Materials CD2 | Flashcards: 36–54 | Coin for each pair of students and buttons or game pieces for playing the game | Word cards: see pages TB108–TB109 (optional)

Warmer

- Play *What's missing?* (see page xix) with the flashcards. You can play using the sets for Units 3 and 4 separately or mix five cards from each set together each time to make a mixed selection of items to remember (more challenging).

Student's Book page 57

3 Play the game.

- The aim of this game is to be the first one to reach the *Finish* square (top right of the board). Students play in pairs with a coin and buttons or game pieces.
- Students place their game piece on the square marked *Start* (the green traffic light). They then take turns flipping the coin and moving their game piece along the board. If they flip the heads side of the coin, they move two spaces. If they flip the tails side of the coin, they move one space.
- When students land on a square with a picture on it, they ask and answer a question with those pictures and the words given, e.g., *Are you wearing shoes? Yes, I am.* or *How many tables are there in your classroom? (There are ten.)* If students make the question and answer correctly, they stay on the square they've landed on. If they make a mistake, they move back one square.
- When they land on a square with the words *Miss a turn*, their partner has two turns. When they land on a square with the words *Move forward one* or *Move back one*, they move their game piece accordingly. Make sure students understand what these phrases mean before they begin to play.
- Play continues until one student moves to the square marked *Finish* (by flipping the heads side of the coin, when on square 19).

Key: 1 Are you wearing shoes? (Yes, I am. / No, I'm not.) **2** How many tables are there in your classroom? (Students' own answers.) **3** Are you wearing a skirt? (Yes, I am. / No, I'm not.) **5** How many closets are there in your bedroom?

(Students' own answers.) **6** Are you wearing socks? (Yes, I am. / No, I'm not.) **7** How many couches are there in your living room? (Students' own answers.) **9** Are you wearing a T-shirt? (Yes, I am. / No, I'm not.) **10** How many chairs are there in your kitchen? (Students' own answers.) **11** Are you wearing pants? (Yes, I am. / No, I'm not.) **13** How many bookcases are there in your classroom? (Students' own answers.) **14** Are you wearing a jacket? (Yes, I am. / No, I'm not.) **15** How many mirrors are there in your bathroom? (Students' own answers.) **17** Are you wearing a dress? (Yes, I am. / No, I'm not.) **18** How many TVs are there in your house? (Students' own answers.) **19** Are you wearing a shirt? (Yes, I am. / No, I'm not.)

Workbook page 47

3 Look, read, and write the answers.

- Students read the questions and write the answers, referring to the pictures.

Key: 2 No, I'm not. **3** I'm wearing a dress and a jacket. **4** There are 11.

4 Listen and check ✓.

- Students listen and check the correct picture in each pair.

Key: 1 picture 1 **2** picture 2

CD2:18

1 Big Sister: What's the matter?
Little Sister: I can't find my favorite purple T-shirt!
Big Sister: Oh! Look at your bedroom. What a mess!
Little Sister: Let's clean up.
Big Sister: OK. Let's put the T-shirts and jeans in the closet.
Little Sister: Thank you!
Big Sister: You're welcome.

2 Boy: Can I have a turn, please?
Girl: Of course.
Boy: Oh, no!
Girl: What's the matter?
Boy: I don't have a pen.
Girl: Here you are. You can use this one.
Boy: Thank you!

Ending the lesson

- A volunteer stands at the front of the classroom, with his/her back to the class. The rest of the class takes turns asking about items in the classroom / what their classmates are wearing, e.g., *How many bookcases are there in the classroom? / What's Elena wearing?* This can also be played as a team game, with a representative from one team as the volunteer and only members of the other team asking the questions. Keep score on the board. The volunteer at the front swaps with a different student after answering a certain number of questions (e.g., three).

Extra activities: see page TB121 (if time)

TB57

③ Play the game.

Finish

Are you wearing a  ? **17**

How many  are there in your house? **18**

Are you wearing a ? **19**

GO BACK ONE! **20**

MISS A TURN! **16**

How many are there in your bathroom? **15**

Are you wearing a ? **14**

How many  are there in your classroom? **13**

Are you wearing a ? **9**

How many are there in your kitchen? **10**

Are you wearing ? **11**

GO BACK ONE! **12**

GO FORWARD ONE! **8**

How many are there in your living room? **7**

Are you wearing ? **6**

How many are there in your bedroom? **5**

 Are you wearing ? **1**

How many are there in your classroom? **2**

Are you wearing a ? **3**

MISS A TURN! **4**

Start

57

⑤ Meals

58

Unit aims   Students learn about meals and food.
This includes:

- learning vocabulary for meals and food
- asking about what others like to eat
- talking about what others like / don't like to eat
- offering food
- categorizing food into food groups

Introduction to the unit

- Say *Open your books to pages 58 and 59, please.* Play the theme song on the recording. Students look at the photograph and read the title of the unit while listening to the song.

- Ask *What's Unit 5 about?* Encourage students to work out the meaning of *meals*. Then point to the photograph and ask *What can you see? (Boys/Brothers) How many boys are there? (Two.) What do the boys have?* Explain that each boy has a *lunch box.* Ask students *Do you have a lunch box?* If necessary, explain that school children in different countries often take sandwiches to school to eat for lunch. Ask students what they eat at lunchtime / if they eat at home or at school. Ask what kind of food the boys in the photograph have *(sushi/rice).*

- Elicit food items that students already know in English or play *Two minutes* (see page xix) with the heading *Food.* (From *Guess What!* Level 1 students should know: *juice, apple, banana, orange, bread, chicken, egg, water, milk, cheese*). Write any words students come up with on the board. Ask individual students about the foods, e.g., *Do you like (chicken)? (Yes, I do. / No, I don't.)*

CD1:02

(Theme song – see lyrics on page TB5)

59

1 CD2 19 Listen. Who's speaking?

2 CD2 20 Listen, point, and say.

The Café
Breakfast 8–12
Lunch 12–3
Dinner 4–7

1 potatoes
2 carrots
3 rice
4 peas
5 sausages
6 fish
7 meat
8 beans
9 toast
10 cereal

3 CD2 21 Listen and find.

Find Leo

Lesson aims
Students learn vocabulary for food and meals.

New language *potatoes, carrots, rice, peas, sausages, fish, meat, beans, toast, cereal, I'm hungry, lots of, lunch, breakfast, What a funny lunch!*

Recycled language character names | numbers 1–10 | food and drink from *Guess What!* Level 1 | *What do you have? I have (carrots). I like / don't like (fish). What about you? What's that? There's / There are*

Materials CD2 | Flashcards: 55–64 | Level 1 food and drink flashcards: 66–75, if available | Music CD (optional)

Warmer

- Use the Level 1 food flashcards: 66–75, if available, to review food and drink vocabulary.
- Play the *Drawing game* (see page xv) with food from Level 1 (e.g., banana, orange, apple, egg, bread, chicken, cheese). Students can also play the game in pairs. If you don't wish to draw, mime eating one of the items, e.g., peeling and eating a banana and ask *What's this? (It's a banana.)* The student who guesses first does the next mime.

Presentation

- Say *Let's learn more food words.* Hold up each flashcard and say the new word. Students repeat in chorus and individually. Then show the flashcards in random order. Students say the words.
- Stick the flashcards on the board. Point and ask individual students *Do you like (rice)? (Yes, I do. / No, I don't.)* Point to the cereal flashcard. Mime waking up and eating a bowl of cereal and say *I like cereal for breakfast.* Confirm the meaning. Ask students *What do you like for breakfast?* Present *lunch* and *dinner* in the same way.

Student's Book page 60

1 Listen. Who's speaking?

- Say *Open your books to page 60, please.* Ask *Who can you see?* Students say the names of the characters. Ask *Where are the children? (At a café.)* Point to the trays and the clock and say *Look at the food and the clock. Is it time for breakfast, lunch, or dinner? (Lunch.)*
- Say *Let's listen. Who's speaking?* Play the recording. Students listen and point to the characters. Then play again, pausing for students to point to the foods.
- If time, ask about other items in the picture, e.g., *How many tables are there? (Three.) What drinks can you see? (Water, orange juice.) Who has a phone? (The woman.)*

CD2:19

David: Mmm, I'm hungry! What do you have for lunch, Tina?

Tina: I have fish, white rice, and peas. I like fish and rice. What about you?

David: I have meat and potatoes. I don't like rice. And I have lots of orange carrots. I like carrots.

Tina: What about you Olivia? What do you have?

Olivia: I have sausages and beans. And I have potatoes. Mmm! I'm hungry.

David: What's that, Ben?

Ben: It's toast and cereal.

Olivia: Toast and cereal? For lunch? What a funny lunch! I like toast and cereal for breakfast!

2 Listen, point, and say.

- Say *Now listen, point, and say.* Play the recording. Students listen and point to the numbered items in the picture. Then play again. Students listen and say the words.

CD2:20

1 potatoes **2** carrots **3** rice **4** peas **5** sausages **6** fish **7** meat **8** beans **9** toast **10** cereal

3 Listen and find.

- Say *Now listen and find.* Play the recording, pausing for students to find and point to the correct items in the picture. Students can also say the correct number.
- If you have time, students can repeat in pairs. One says a sentence, e.g., *I don't like meat,* and the other says the number (e.g., *Seven*) or points to the item.

Key: Students point to the items in the following order: 5, 6, 7, 1, 3, 9, 10, 4, 8, 2.

CD2:21

I like sausages.	I like rice.	I like beans.
I like fish.	I like toast.	I like carrots.
I like meat.	I like cereal.	
I like potatoes.	I like peas.	

Find Leo.

- Say *Now find Leo.* Students search for Leo in the picture (he's next to the counter, looking at the carrots).

Workbook page 48

1 Find and circle. Look and write the word.

- Students circle the words in the word snake and then use them to label the pictures.

Key: 2 peas **3** fish **4** cereal **5** carrots **6** toast

2 Look, read, and write yes or no.

- Students look at the picture, read the sentences, and write *yes* or *no*.

Key: 2 no **3** yes **4** yes **5** no

Ending the lesson

- Students work in pairs. Student A closes his/her book. Student B looks at the picture on Student's Book page 60 and makes a sentence about one of the characters' food, e.g., *She has fish.* Student A says the name (e.g., *Tina*). Then they swap roles.

Extra activities: see page TB121 (if time)

Lesson aims Students practice the food and meals vocabulary. They practice asking what others like to eat.

New language for (breakfast/lunch/dinner), Yum! shopping list

Recycled language food, breakfast, lunch, dinner, Do you like (toast) for (breakfast)? Yes, I do. plants

Materials CD2 | Flashcards: 55–64 | A shopping list | Ten sentences on slips of paper, each about one of the key food words in the unit (optional)

Warmer

- Review the food words with the flashcards. Write *dinner, breakfast, lunch* on the board and ask students to put the meals in order (*breakfast, lunch, dinner*). Play *Anagrams* (see page xiv), using some of the food words and the three meal words.

Student's Book page 61

4 Say the chant.

- Say *Open your books to page 61, please.* Point to the first photograph and ask *What's for breakfast? (Toast and cereal.)* Repeat for the other two photographs.
- Say *Listen to the chant.* Play the recording. Students listen and point to the photographs in turn.
- Then say *Now listen and say the chant.* Play the recording again. Students can clap along to the rhythm at first, joining in with as many words as they can. Then repeat as often as necessary until students are chanting confidently. You can also divide the class into two groups. One group chants the first two lines of each verse and one chants the second two lines. Then they swap.

CD2:22

Do you like toast for breakfast?
Do you like cereal, too?
Toast and cereal for breakfast?
Yum! Yes, I do.

Do you like sausages for lunch?
Do you like carrots, too?
Sausages and carrots for lunch?
Yum! Yes, I do.

Do you like fish for dinner?
Do you like potatoes, too?
Fish and potatoes for dinner?
Yum! Yes, I do.

5 Read, look, and say. What's missing?

- Ask students *Do you like grocery shopping? Who goes shopping for food in your family? Do you go shopping for food?* Hold up a shopping list and say *Look. This is my shopping list. It has lots of food on it.* Read some of the items, then mime using the list while walking down an aisle in a supermarket. Elicit the meaning.
- Say *Look at the shopping list.* Students read the shopping list in activity 5. Give them time to work out the meaning of each item. Point to the first item on the list. Then say *Let's look in the shopping bag. Where's the cereal?* Students find it and point. Mime checking the item on the list. Say *What's missing?* Explain that students need to check the rest of the items on the list and find the things that aren't in the bag.
- Check answers by asking, e.g., *Are there any (sausages) in the bag? / Is there any (meat) in the bag? (Yes/No.)*

Key: The missing items are peas, rice, and fish.

Workbook page 49

3 Listen and stick.

- Students will need the Unit 5 stickers from the back of the Workbook.
- Play the CD. Students listen and stick the stickers into the correct position.

CD2:23

1 I have sausages and peas for lunch.
2 I have fish and rice for dinner.
3 I have cereal and toast for breakfast.
4 I have meat and potatoes for lunch.
5 I have sausages and carrots for dinner.

4 Look and write the words.

- Review the meaning of *plants* and check that students understand the column headings. Students write each word in the box in the correct column.

Key: These foods are plants: cereal, peas, rice, potatoes, carrots
These foods aren't plants: meat, fish, sausages

My picture dictionary → Go to page 89. Check the words you know and trace.

- Students turn to page 89 and check the words they know. They then trace over the word labels for each picture.

Ending the lesson

- Play *Stand up and sit down* (see page xviii), using sentences about foods for different meals (e.g., *I like toast for breakfast. I don't like milk for breakfast. I like rice for lunch. I like meat for dinner.*)

Extra activities: see page TB120 (if time)

Say the chant.

breakfast

Do you like toast for breakfast?
Do you like cereal, too?
Toast and cereal for breakfast?
Yum! Yes, I do.

lunch

dinner

5 Think **Read, look, and say. What's missing?**

Shopping list

cereal

sausages

meat

peas

potatoes

beans

rice

fish

6 (CD2 24) **Sing the song.**

My friend Sammy likes
🍗 for lunch.
He doesn't like 🥔,
And he doesn't like 🫛.
He likes 🫘 and 🥕,
And he likes 🧀.

Munch, Sammy.
Munch your lunch!

My friend Sally likes
🐟 for lunch.
She doesn't like 🧀,
And she doesn't like 🍗.
She likes 🫘 and 🥕,
And 🥔 and 🫛.

Munch, Sally.
Munch your lunch!

7 (CD2 25) **Listen and say *Sammy* or *Sally*.**

8 (About Me) **Ask and answer. Then say.**

Do you like fish?

Yes, I do.

Alex likes fish.

Lesson aims Students talk about what others like / don't like to eat.

New language *My friend/He/She/Alex likes (meat) for (lunch). My friend/He/She/Alex doesn't like (beans). munch*

Recycled language food, *friend, Do you like (fish)? Yes, I do. / No, I don't. shopping bag, There is/are …*

Materials CD2 | A shopping bag | Flashcards: 55–64 | A photograph of a friend of yours (optional)

Warmer

- Review the food words using the flashcards and stick them on the board. Show a shopping bag and say *I have my bag. Let's go shopping.* Play *Sentence chain game* (see page xviii). Take a flashcard and say *There are (peas) in my shopping bag.* Put the flashcard in your bag. Ask a student to choose another flashcard, add the new item he/she has chosen to the sentence, e.g., *There are peas and sausages in my shopping bag.*, and put the flashcard in the bag. Repeat until there are no flashcards left. You can show the flashcards in the bag as prompts, if necessary.

Presentation

- Draw two large circles on the board (at a height your students can reach). Draw a smiley face at the top of one circle and a sad face at the top of the other. Give a volunteer a flashcard and ask *Do you like (potatoes)?* If the student replies *Yes, I do*, help him/her to put the flashcard in the circle with the smiley face. Ask about different foods, each time encouraging the student to put the flashcard in the correct circle. When there are four flashcards in each circle, ask the student to sit down. Make a sentence about one of the foods in the "like" circle, e.g., *Look! Leo likes sausages.* Make another positive sentence. Invite students to make similar sentences. Then make a negative sentence, e.g., *Look! Leo doesn't like cereal.* Give more example sentences, inviting students to help.

Student's Book page 62

6 Sing the song.

- Say *Open your books to page 62, please.* Point to the monsters and ask *Who's this? (Sammy and Sally.)* (These are the monsters from Student's Book page 40.) Say *Sammy and Sally are friends.* Elicit the meaning of *friend*. Point to the foods at the bottom and ask *What can you see?* Make sentences about what each monster likes (e.g., *Sammy likes meat. Sally likes fish.*).
- Say *Listen and point.* Play the recording. Students listen and point to the food. Point to the foods where the circles overlap and say *What foods do Sammy and Sally like? (Carrots and beans.)* Explain the meaning of *Yum!* and *munch*.
- Then say *Now sing the song.* Play the recording a few times, until students are singing confidently. The first time students can hum and join in with any words they know. Then students can sing along, following the song

text. You can divide the class into boys and girls. **Note:** Students can sing along to the version of the song with the words or to the karaoke version.

CD2:24

My friend Sammy likes
   meat for lunch.
He doesn't like potatoes,
And he doesn't like peas.
He likes beans and carrots,
And he likes cheese.
Munch, Sammy.
Munch your lunch! (x4)

My friend Sally likes fish
   for lunch.
She doesn't like cheese,
And she doesn't like meat.
She likes beans and carrots,
And potatoes and peas.
Munch, Sally.
Munch your lunch! (x4)

7 Listen and say Sammy or Sally.

- Say *Listen and say Sammy or Sally.* Play the recording, pausing after each sentence. Students listen, look at the picture in activity 6, and say *Sammy* or *Sally*.

Key: 1 Sammy **2** Sally **3** Sally **4** Sammy **5** Sammy **6** Sally

CD2:25

1 He doesn't like peas. **2** She likes peas. **3** She doesn't like meat. **4** He doesn't like potatoes. **5** He likes carrots. **6** She likes carrots.

8 Ask and answer. Then say.

- Ask students to draw four pictures of foods. Students work in pairs. Student A shows each of his/her pictures to Student B and asks, e.g., *Do you like beans?* Student B answers *Yes, I do* or *No, I don't.* Then they swap. Make groups of four. Students take turns talking about the person they asked in the pairwork, e.g., *Lucia likes toast. She doesn't like peas.*

Workbook page 50

5 Listen and match. Draw a happy face or a sad face.

- Students listen and draw lines to match each child with the food. They draw a happy or a sad face on each child, depending on whether he/she likes or dislikes the food.

Key: 2 rice, sad **3** beans, sad **4** fish, happy

CD2:26

1 She likes potatoes.
2 He doesn't like rice.
3 She doesn't like beans.
4 He likes fish.

6 Look, read, and circle the words.

- Students read each sentence, look at the picture, and circle *likes* or *doesn't like*.

Key: 2 doesn't like **3** doesn't like **4** likes

Ending the lesson

- Students cover the song words, leaving the picture of Sammy and Sally and the circles visible. Play a game of *True or false?* (see page xix), making sentences with *Sally/ Sammy likes / doesn't like …* Students can also play in pairs.

Extra activities: see page TB122 (if time)

Lesson aims Students ask and answer about what others like to eat.

New language *Is it a boy or a girl? Does he/she like (meat)? Yes, he/she does. No, he/she doesn't.*

Recycled language food, *boy, girl, It's (Tony).*

Materials CD2 | Flashcards: 55–64

Warmer

- Play the song from the previous lesson. Students sing along. They can act looking happy/hungry for lines with the word *likes* and mime being disgusted for the lines with *doesn't like.*

Presentation

- Hand out five of the flashcards to volunteers. Ask a student with a flashcard to stand up. Tell the class they need to guess whether the student likes or dislikes this food. Ask individuals to guess, e.g., *Does Adriana like (beans)?* Help them reply *Yes, he/she does.* or *No, he/she doesn't.* Keep a tally of guesses on the board. Then ask the student *Do you like (beans)?* He/She answers *Yes, I do.* or *No, I don't.* See if the students guessed correctly. Repeat with different students.

Student's Book page 63

9 Listen, look, and say.

- Say *Open your books to page 63, please. What can you see? (Orange juice, cereal, toast.)* Give students time to look at the picture and think about whether the children like or dislike the foods.
- Say *Listen and point.* Play the recording. Students point to the children. Then say *Now listen and say.* Play the recording again, pausing for students to listen and repeat.

CD2:27

1 Does he like cereal?
  No, he doesn't.
  Does she like toast?
  No, she doesn't.

2 Does he like toast?
  Yes, he does.
  Does she like cereal?
  Yes, she does.

10 Ask and answer.

- Tell students they are going to play a guessing game using the photographs in activity **10**. Point to Tony and ask, e.g., *Does he like potatoes? (Yes, he does.) Does he like sausages? (No, he doesn't.)* Ask two questions about each child in the photographs, one with a positive answer, one negative, in the same way.
- Ask two volunteers to read the example speech bubbles and make sure students understand that the person asking questions can only ask questions that can be answered *Yes* or *No* (after question 1, *Is it a boy or a girl?*). Play an example round of the game, with you choosing one of the children in the photographs and the class asking you questions, if necessary.

- Say *Play the game.* Students play in pairs, taking turns choosing a child in the photographs and asking questions. Circulate and help with language.

Workbook page 51

7 Look, read, and circle the words. Then answer the questions.

- For the first two items, students look at the pictures, read the questions and answers, and circle the correct words. For the second two items they look, read, and write the correct answer.

Key: Kim **2** peas **4** No, she doesn't. Jim **1** carrots **2** fish **3** Yes, he does. **4** No, he doesn't.

8 Draw and say. Then write and circle.

- Students choose a member of their family to write about. They draw two plates – one with things he/she likes eating for dinner and one with things he/she doesn't like. Then they complete the sentences about the person. They use the model on the left to help them.

Key: Students' own answers.

Ending the lesson

- Students work in pairs. Student A points to one of the children in Student's Book activity 10 and asks *Does he/she like (rice)?* Student B answers *Yes, he/she does.* or *No, he/she doesn't.* as quickly as possible. Then they swap. They can also play this as a memory game, with Student A looking at the book (asking, e.g., *Does Pat like bread?*) and Student B answering from memory.

Extra activities: see page TB122 (if time)

9 CD2 27 **Listen, look, and say.**

1

2

10 Think **Ask and answer.**

Tony

Kim

Is it a boy or a girl?

It's a boy.

Does he like meat?

Yes, he does.

Does he like carrots?

No, he doesn't.

It's Tony!

Tom

Pat

Grammar: *Does he like cereal?* **63**

Lesson aims Students reinforce language with a story. They also discuss the value of eating healthy food.

New language Hawaii, café, Let's go, chocolate cake, more, That's enough! a lot, eat, healthy food

Recycled language food, look, lunch, Yes, please. No, thank you. Oh, dear! I like ... , What's the matter? He likes ...

Materials CD2 | Toy mouse (or mouse flashcard from Unit 2:34) | Bag | Selection of six food flashcards or toy food (e.g., bananas, cheese, toast, fish, rice, carrots) | Picture of a "food wheel" | Pictures of healthy and unhealthy foods (bananas, juice, oranges, peas, fish, cookies, cake, chips, etc.) (optional)

Warmer

- Show the mouse flashcard/toy mouse and say *This is my pet mouse, Minnie.* Hold up the bag with flashcards/toy food inside and say *This is Minnie's food. Guess what she likes.* Students take turns asking, e.g., *Does Minnie/ she like (potatoes)?* If a student guesses correctly, say *Yes, she does!* and give the flashcard/toy food to that student. If a student guesses incorrectly, you score a point. If students guess all the items before you get six points, they win. If you get six points, you win.

Introduction

- Remind students of the previous episode of the story. Say *Tina can't find her ... (ring). The children go to (Tina's bedroom). They say, "What a mess! Let's ... " (clean up).* Ask if they find Tina's ring (*Yes, iPal does.*). Ask students to guess where the children will go with iPal today.

Student's Book page 64

11 Listen and read.

- Say *Open your books to page 64, please.* Point to frame 1 and ask *What can the children see? (A plane.)* Point to the banner and explain the meaning of *café.* Ask students what they know about Hawaii and show where it is. Point to frame 2 and ask *Where are the children? (At Café Hawaii.)* Elicit the food they can see. Ask *What food does iPal like?* Ask students to look at the story and guess.

- Say *Now listen and read.* Play the recording while students listen and follow the story. Ask *What does iPal like? (Chocolate cake.)* Check that students know what chocolate cake is. Then play the recording again, pausing to ask questions: Frame 1: *Do the children want breakfast? (No, lunch.)* Frame 2: *Does iPal like fish and potatoes? (No, he doesn't.)* Frame 3: *Does iPal like carrots or peas? (No, he doesn't.)* Frame 4: *Is the chocolate cake small? (No, it's big.)* Frame 5: *Why are the children sad? (iPal is eating a lot of / too much cake.)* Explain the meaning of *more* and *That's enough.* Frame 6: *Is iPal OK? (No.) What's the matter?* Confirm that iPal's feeling sick because he's eaten too much cake. Explain the meaning of *a lot.*

- Students can listen to the story again for pleasure, or pause after key lines for students to repeat. They can join in with the rhymes. Encourage students to use gestures and intonation from the story.

CD2:28

David: Look! Café Hawaii!
Ben: Let's go for lunch!
All: 1, 2, 3, Magic tree. We're back again. Look and see. Come with us. Come and play In our magic tree today.
Café attendant: Would you like fish and potatoes?
Olivia: Yes, please!
iPal: No, thank you!
David: What about carrots or peas, iPal?
iPal: No, thank you.
Tina: Oh, dear! What would you like, iPal?
iPal: Cake! I like chocolate cake.
iPal: More cake, please!
Olivia: No, iPal. That's enough!
Ben: What's the matter?
David: He likes chocolate cake – a lot!
All: 3, 2, 1, that was fun. Time to go. The magic's done!

(**Value**) *Eat healthy food*

- Point to frame 5 and play the first line. Remind students of the meaning of *more.* Ask *Is it a good idea? (No.)* Play the next line. Ask students *How many arms does iPal have? (Four.) What does iPal have in his hands? (A lot of cake.)* Ask students what happens next *(iPal feels sick)* and play the dialog for frame 6.

- Read the value *Eat healthy food.* Explain the meaning and ask *Is chocolate cake healthy food? (No, it isn't.)* Talk about how important it is to eat all kinds of food, but only a small amount of unhealthy foods. Ask *What healthy food is there in the story? (Fish, potatoes, carrots, peas, bananas, oranges, apples, beans.)* Elicit examples of unhealthy food *(cake, cookies, ice cream, chips, fries).* If possible, show a picture of a "food wheel" to explain how much of each different kind of food we should eat. Divide the class into two groups (iPal and Olivia). Play the dialog from frame 5 again. Students repeat the lines, then practice the dialog in pairs (iPal and Olivia).

Workbook page 52

9 Look and write the words. Then listen and check.

- Students complete the speech bubbles with words from the box. Play the story again, which is repeated in full on the recording. Students listen and check their answers.

Key: 2 fish **3** peas **4** Cake **5** please **6** likes

CD2:29

(Repeat of story – see above for story script)

Ending the lesson

- Play *Who said it?* (see page xix).

Extra activities: see page TB122 (if time)

> **Lesson aims** Students practice offering, refusing, and accepting food. Students also practice saying the sounds /s/ and /z/.
>
> **New language** *seal, sun, zoo* | *Would you like (beans)? What about (carrots)? What would you like?*
>
> **Recycled language** food | *Yes, please. / No, thank you.* | *zebra*
>
> **Materials** CD2 | Flashcards: 55–64 | Selection of healthy and unhealthy breakfast foods / pictures of foods (e.g., oat cereal, sugary cereal, cupcakes, bread, cola, empty milk or juice bottle/carton) | A slip of paper for each student, a box or bag (optional)

Warmer

- Put the unhealthy breakfast foods / pictures on a table at the front of the class (or draw a picture of a glass of cola and a plate with cupcakes on it). Say *Look. This is my breakfast. What do I have for breakfast?* Students say the foods they know. Ask *Is my breakfast healthy? (No, it isn't.)* Ask *What healthy food can I eat for breakfast?* Students make suggestions (e.g., *cereal, milk, juice*). Show the healthy foods as prompts.

Presentation

- Offer one of the foods you've brought to class (or a food flashcard) to a confident student. Ask *Would you like (cereal)?* Encourage the student to reply politely (*Yes, please. / No, thank you.*). If the student says "yes," hand him/her the food. If the student says "no," offer something else, e.g., ask *What about (cupcakes)?* Repeat with different students until you have handed out all the food.

Student's Book page 65

12 Listen and act.

- Say *Open your books to pages 64 and 65, please.* Remind students of the story from the previous lesson. Say *The children are hungry. They go to … (Café Hawaii).* Ask *Which foods does the café have? (fish, potatoes, carrots, peas).* Ask *What does iPal like? (Chocolate cake). Is it healthy? (No.)* Remind students that the children try to get iPal to eat other kinds of food. Ask *What does iPal say? (No, thank you. / More cake.)*

- Tell students they are going to listen to more people offering food. Say *Now look at page 65. What can you see? (A woman, a boy, a school cafeteria, sausages, potatoes, beans).* Then say *Who's speaking? Listen and point.* Play the recording. Students listen and point to the person in the photograph they think is speaking.

- Then say *Now listen and act.* Play the recording again, pausing for students to repeat with the correct pronunciation and intonation.

- Students practice the language in pairs. Student A mimes offering different foods and says *Would you like … ? / What about … ?* Student B accepts or refuses politely. Then they swap roles and repeat.

CD2:30

Woman: Would you like potatoes?
Boy: Yes, please.

Woman: What about beans?
Boy: No, thank you.

13 Listen and say.

- In this activity, students practice saying the sounds /s/ and /z/.

- Say *Look at activity 13. What can you see?* Teach *seal, sun,* and *zoo.*

- Then say *seal – /s/ /s/ /s/ – seal.* Students repeat, emphasizing the /s/ sound.

- Say *zebra – /z/ /z/ /z/ – zebra.* Students repeat, emphasizing the initial sound in the same way.

- Say *Listen and say.* Play the sound sentences on the recording. Students listen and repeat, emphasizing the initial /s/ and /z/ sounds.

- Students can then repeat the sound sentences without the recording, saying them faster and faster each time. See how fast they can say them.

- Ask students to think of any other words they know that begin with the sound /s/ or contain the sound /z/. For example, *see, sit, six, seven, sister, sing, swim, snake, spider, skirt, socks, lazy, lizard.*

CD2:31

/s/ /z/ A seal in the sun. A zebra in the zoo. (x2)

Workbook page 53

10 Look, read, and stick.

- Remind students of the value from the previous lesson. Students look at the pictures and think about which one shows the value. They stick the smiley face sticker in the circle next to the correct picture.

- Students then select a smiley sticker from the back of the book and stick it next to the value.

Key: Students put the sticker next to the second picture.

11 Trace the letters.

- Students trace the letters *s* and *z* in the sound sentences.

12 Listen and circle s or z.

- Play the recording. Students look at the picture, listen, and circle the correct sound each time.

Key: 2 z **3** z **4** s

CD2:32

1 sock, sock **2** zebra, zebra **3** zoo, zoo **4** sing, sing

Ending the lesson

- Write the tongue twister *Six lazy lizards* on the board. Students practice saying it repeatedly, as fast as they can.

Extra activities: see page TB122 (if time)

12   **Listen and act.**

Animal sounds

13 CD2 31 **Listen and say.**

A seal in the sun. A zebra in the zoo.

→ Workbook page 53   Functional language: *Would you like potatoes?*   Pronunciation: *s, z* **65**

What kind of **food** is it?

1 (CD2 33) **Listen and say.**

 **1**

 **2**

 **3**

 **4**

 **5**

fruit   vegetables   meat   grains   dairy

2 **Watch the video.**

3 **Look and say what kind of food it is.**

Number 1. Fish.   Yes.

 **1**

 **2**

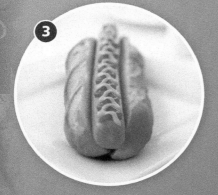 **3**

 **4**

Guess What!

Project

4 **Make a food poster.**

Lesson aims Students learn about food groups and categorize foods.

New language *fruit, vegetables, grains, dairy, ice cream*

Recycled language food, *What kind of (food) is it? meat, fish, Would you like (an apple)? Yes, please. / No, thank you.*

Materials CD2 | DVD (optional) | Flashcards: 55–64 | Food flashcards from Level 1 Unit 6: 66–75 or pictures of known foods | Music CD

Warmer

- Review language for offering, accepting, and refusing by offering students food flashcards (or real/toy food), e.g., *Would you like (an apple)?* Remind students to reply politely. (*Yes, please. / No, thank you.*)
- Play *Pass the flashcards* (see page xviii). When the music stops, students with flashcards turn to the person on their right and offer the food on the card, e.g., *Would you like (toast)?* The person says *Yes, please.* and takes the card or *No, thank you.* and doesn't take it.

Student's Book page 66

What kind of food is it?

- Say *Open your books to page 66, please.* Ask questions about the photograph, e.g., *Where is it? What food can you see? (Oranges.) Can you see a (banana)? Can you see any meat? (No.)*
- Ask students if there is a market like this in their hometown/city.
- Then point to the whole stall in the photograph and ask the opening question *What kind of food is it?* Review the meaning of *What kind … ?* See if students know the food group name already (*fruit*) or the names of any other food groups (e.g., *vegetables*). Ask *How many kinds of fruit can you see?*

Student's Book page 67

1 Listen and say.

- Say *Now look at page 67, please.* Use the photographs to present the words for food groups.
- Say *Listen and say.* Play the recording. Students listen and repeat the words.
- Students look at the photograph on page 66 again. Ask about the new food groups: *Are there any dairy foods in the photograph? Are there any grains?*

CD2:33

1 fruit **2** vegetables **3** meat **4** grains **5** dairy

2 Watch the video.

- Play the video.
- If you don't have the video, write the food groups as headings on the board. Show flashcards (from this unit and Level 1 Unit 6, if available) or pictures of foods from each group (mixed up). Ask volunteers to come to the front, choose a card/picture, say which food group it belongs in, and stick it in the correct place on the board. Possible groups: *fruit: apple, banana, orange; vegetables: peas, carrots, beans, potatoes; grains: rice, bread, toast, cereal; meat: chicken, sausages; dairy: milk, cheese, egg.*

Video 05 : see page TB131

3 Look and say what kind of food it is.

- Students work in pairs. They look at the photographs and say which food group(s) each food belongs in. They use the speech bubbles to help them.
- Check the activity by saying the number of the photograph. Students say, e.g., *fruit and dairy.* Teach *ice cream.*

Key: 2 fruit and dairy **3** meat and grains **4** fruit

Guess What!

- Students look at the swirled image and guess what it is. Check by asking *What's this? (Ice cream.)*

Key: It's ice cream (photograph 2, activity 3).

Workbook page 54

1 Look and write the words in the chart.

- Students look at the pictures and write each food in the correct column of the chart.

Key: fruits and vegetables: peas, carrots; meat and fish: sausages, fish; grains and cereals: rice, bread; dairy: cheese, milk

Ending the lesson

- Play *House* (see page xv) with the names of the food groups.

Extra activities: see pages TB122 to TB123 (if time)

Lesson aims Students make a food poster, categorizing kinds of food. They also complete the Evaluation in the Workbook.

Recycled language food, *What kind of food is it? fruit, vegetables, grains, dairy, meat, fish* | Students review all unit vocabulary and grammar in the Evaluation.

Materials CD2 | Flashcards: 55–64 | Food flashcards from Level 1 Unit 6: 66–75 or pictures of known foods | Materials for the project: large piece of blank paper for each group of students, colored markers or pencils, pictures of food (e.g., from supermarket advertising leaflets or fridge catalogs), scissors, glue

Warmer

- Hand out a selection of food flashcards/pictures of food, making sure there are at least two from each food group. Name a food group, e.g., *Vegetables*. Ask *Where are the vegetables?* Students with a flashcard/picture of a food from that group hold it up or stand up and say, e.g., *Potatoes are vegetables*. Repeat for the other food groups (*fruit, dairy, meat and fish, grains*).

Student's Book page 67

4 Make a food poster.

- Say *Open your books to page 67, please*. Point to the picture in activity 4 and ask questions about the poster, e.g., *What fruit can you see? (Orange, bananas, apples.) What foods are grains and cereals? (Rice, bread.) What kind of food is cheese? (Dairy.)*
- Say *Make a food poster*. Students work in small groups. Give each group a large piece of blank paper, pictures of food to cut out (e.g., leaflets from supermarkets, pictures of fridges from catalogs), scissors, and glue. Each group divides their paper into four sections, writes the food groups, and makes a poster like the one in the Student's Book. They don't need to use pictures of food they can name in English – as long as they can identify the food group it belongs to. If you don't have leaflets/catalogs, students can draw and color the pictures themselves.
- Circulate and help, asking the names of the different foods, providing new vocabulary and asking, e.g., *What kind of food is this? Do you like (broccoli)?*
- Display the posters in the classroom and give students time to look at their classmates' work.

Workbook page 55 – Evaluation

1 Read and write the word.

- Students complete the food words.

Key: 2 (C)arrots 3 (F)ish 4 (P)eas 5 (m)eat 6 (R)ice

2 What's your favorite part? Use your stickers.

- Students choose their favorite part of the unit – the story, the song, or the video – and put a sticker under their chosen preference.

3 What's different? Circle and write. Then go to page 93 and write the letters.

- Students circle the picture that doesn't belong and write the name of the food. They then go to page 93 and write the letters in the puzzle.

Key: rice, letters for the puzzle – r, e

Ending the lesson

- Students repeat their favorite activity from the unit.

Extra activities: see page TB123 (if time)

Activities

> **Unit aims**   Students learn about free-time activities. This includes:
>
> - learning vocabulary for activities
> - talking about what they can/can't do
> - talking about what they and others like doing
> - asking what others like doing
> - talking about playing nicely
> - learning vocabulary for sports equipment

Introduction to the unit

- Say *Open your books to pages 68 and 69, please.* Play the theme song on the recording. Students look at the photograph and read the title of the unit while listening to the song.

- Ask *What's Unit 6 about?* Encourage students to work out the meaning of *activities*. Then point to the photograph and ask *What can you see? How many boys are there? (Two.) How many girls? (Two.) What's the activity?* Teach or elicit *roller-skate.* Ask different students *Can you roller-skate?* Encourage them to reply with short answers *Yes, I can. / No, I can't.* If time, ask more questions about the photograph, e.g., *What are the children wearing? / Which colors can you see?*

- Elicit actions and activities that students already know in English (from *Guess What!* Level 1: *paint, draw, run, jump, sing, climb, swim, ride a bike, play soccer, dance*). Write these words on the board. Ask individual students *Can you (dance)? (Yes, I can. / No, I can't.)* Students ask and answer about the activities in pairs.

- If time, play *Pass the ball* (see page xvii). When the music stops (or you say *Stop!*), ask the student with the ball a question with *Can you … ?*, e.g., *Can you draw? (Yes, I can. / No, I can't.)* Students can also practice asking and answering about activities using *Can you … ?* in pairs.

CD1:02

(Theme song – see lyrics on page TB5)

Guess What!

69

Activity Day *What can you do?*

1. play tennis
2. play field hockey
3. play basketball
4. roller-skate
5. play baseball
6. ride a horse
7. fly a kite
8. take photographs

TODAY!

3 (CD2 36) **Listen and find.**

Find Leo

Lesson aims   Students learn vocabulary for activities.

New language   *play tennis, play field hockey, play basketball, roller-skate, play baseball, ride a horse, fly a kite, take photographs, Activity Day, Cool! enter, What can you do? I love (baseball). today*

Recycled language   character names | numbers 1–8 | Activities from Level 1: *paint, draw, run, jump, sing, climb, swim, ride a bike, play soccer, dance, I can/can't (paint). Can you (paint)? Yes, I can. No, I can't. Look at this. school, Let's (go). Me, too. What's your favorite sport? What about you/me? I have … , Great! Come on.*

Materials   CD2 | Flashcards: 65–72 | Word cards: see page TB111 | Level 1 action flashcards: 76–85, if available | Slips of paper, each with an activity from the lesson or an action from Level 1 written on it (optional)

Warmer

- Use the Level 1 action flashcards: 76–85, if available, to review vocabulary for activities.
- Play *Simon says* (see page xviii) with actions and activities from Level 1 (e.g., *Simon says "Ride a bike."*) (Students mime riding a bike.) Volunteers can also give the instructions.

Presentation

- Say *Let's learn more words for activities*. Hold up each flashcard and say the new word. Students repeat in chorus and individually. Then show the flashcards in random order. Students say the words.
- Stick the flashcards on the board. Make a positive and a negative sentence about two of the activities with *can* (e.g., *I can play basketball. I can't play field hockey.*) Write the sentences on the board.
- Ask *What can you do?* Elicit sentences from different students (e.g., *I can ride a bike.*) Students tell each other which things they can and can't do in pairs.

Student's Book page 70

1 Listen. Who's speaking?

- Say *Open your books to page 70, please.* Ask *Who can you see?* Students say the names of the characters. Ask *Where are the children? (At school.)* Point to the poster and say *Look! A poster. What's it for?* Explain/Elicit that the poster is for an Activity Day. Check that students understand *day* and *today*.
- Say *Let's listen. Who's speaking?* Play the recording. Students listen and point to the characters. Then play again, pausing for students to point to the activities on the poster as they hear the characters mention them.

CD2:34

Olivia: Look at this! A school Activity Day! Cool!
Ben: Let's enter. I can play tennis, and I can play field hockey.

Olivia: Me, too. And I can play basketball. Basketball is my favorite sport.
Ben: What about you, Tina? What can you do?
Tina: Roller-skate! I can roller-skate. And I can play baseball. I love baseball.
David: What about me? I can ride a horse. And, um – I can fly a kite! I have a fantastic kite.
Olivia: Yes! Great! And I can take photographs.
Ben: Look – it's today! Come on. Let's go!

2 Listen, point, and say.

- Say *Now listen, point, and say.* Play the recording. Students listen and point to the numbered activities on the poster as they hear them mentioned. Then play again. Students listen and say the words.

CD2:35

1 play tennis **2** play field hockey **3** play basketball **4** roller-skate **5** play baseball **6** ride a horse **7** fly a kite **8** take photographs

3 Listen and find.

- Say *Now listen and find.* Play the recording, pausing for students to find and point to the correct activity. Students can also say the correct number.
- If you have time, students can repeat in pairs. One says a sentence, e.g., *I can take photographs*, and the other says the number (e.g., *Eight*) or points to the picture of the activity.

Key: Students point to the activities in the following order: 6, 8, 5, 3, 1, 7, 2, 4.

CD2:36

I can ride a horse.   I can play tennis.
I can take photographs.   I can fly a kite.
I can play baseball.   I can play field hockey.
I can play basketball.   I can roller-skate.

Find Leo.

- Say *Now find Leo.* Students search for Leo in the picture (he's in Ben's bag).

Workbook page 56

1 Look, match, and write.

- Students match the activities with the equipment by drawing lines. Then they complete the phrases on the right.

Key: 2 a horse **3** c kite **4** b baseball

2 Look and write the words.

- Students look at the pictures and complete the dialogs with the words in the box.

Key: 1 play **2** ride, fly **3** roller-skate, take

Ending the lesson

- Play *Does it match* (see page xv) with the Unit 6 flashcards and word cards.

Extra activities: see page TB123 (if time)

Lesson aims Students practice the activities vocabulary. They practice talking about what they can/can't do.

New language *Good idea!*

Recycled language actions and activities | *I can/can't (play tennis). Let's (play tennis).* | letters a–e | numbers 1–5

Materials CD2 | Flashcards: 65–72 | Word cards: see page TB111 | A piece of blank paper for each student (optional)

Warmer

- Review the activities with the flashcards.
- Play *Mime and match* (see page xvii), using the flashcards and word cards. When the student with the matching word card stands up, encourage him/her to make a sentence with *can* or *can't* about the activity (e.g., *I can't roller-skate*).

Student's Book page 71

4 Say the chant.

- Say *Open your books to page 71, please.* Point to the larger photograph and say *I can play … (tennis).* Repeat for the other photographs. Make sure students understand the meaning of the checks and *X*s next to the photographs.
- Say *Listen to the chant.* Play the recording. Students listen and point to the photographs in turn. Explain the meaning of *Good idea!* and practice saying it with the whole class.
- Then say *Now listen and say the chant.* Play the recording again. Students can clap along to the rhythm at first, joining in with as many words as they can. Then repeat as often as necessary until students are chanting confidently. Students can also mime the different activities as they chant.

CD2:37

I can play tennis.	I can fly a kite.
I can't play field hockey.	I can't ride a horse.
Let's play tennis!	Let's fly a kite!
Good idea!	Good idea!
I can play basketball.	I can take photographs.
I can't play baseball.	I can't roller-skate.
Let's play basketball!	Let's take photographs!
Good idea!	Good idea!

5 Match and say.

- Write letters *a* through *e* on the board and practice pronunciation of the letter names.
- Point to the first sentence in the list in activity 5 and ask a volunteer to read it aloud. Ask *Which picture? (e).* Say *Match and say.* Students read and match the rest of the sentences in pairs.

- Check answers by saying the number of the sentence, e.g., *Two.* Students say, e.g, *c I can take photographs.*

Key: 2 c I can take photographs. 3 a I can ride a horse. 4 b I can play tennis. 5 d I can play field hockey.

6 Point and tell your friend.

- Students work in pairs. They take turns pointing to one of the pictures in activity 5 (a–e) and saying whether they can or can't do it. Circulate and check pronunciation of *can/can't*.

Key: Students' own answers.

Workbook page 57

3 Listen and stick.

- Students will need the Unit 6 stickers from the back of the Workbook.
- Play the recording. Students listen and stick the stickers into the correct position (the things the boy can do on the left and the things he can't do on the right).

CD2:38

1 I can roller-skate.	4 I can't ride a horse.
2 I can't play field hockey.	5 I can fly a kite.
3 I can take photographs.	6 I can't play basketball.

4 Look and write the words.

- Check that students understand the meaning of the pictures in the two columns (the left-hand column is for activities that require a ball, the right-hand column is for activities that don't require a ball). Students write the activities from the box in the correct columns.

Key: ball: play tennis, play baseball; no ball: ride a horse, roller-skate, take photographs

My picture dictionary → Go to page 90. Check the words you know and trace.

- Students turn to page 90 and check the words they know. They then trace over the word labels for each picture.

Ending the lesson

- Suggest activities with *Let's …* (e.g., *Let's roller-skate!*). Students all say *Good idea!* and mime doing the activity. When they get the idea, volunteers can come to the front to make the suggestions. Use the flashcards as prompts, if necessary.

Extra activities: see page TB123 (if time)

4 CD2 37 **Say the chant.**

I can play tennis.
I can't play field hockey.
Let's play tennis.
Good idea!

basketball
baseball

fly a kite
ride a horse

take photographs
roller-skate

5 About Me **Match and say.**

1, e. I can roller-skate.

1 I can roller-skate.
2 I can take photographs.
3 I can ride a horse.
4 I can play tennis.
5 I can play field hockey.

6 About Me **Point and tell your friend.**

Picture b. I can play tennis.

Picture e. I can't roller-skate.

→ Workbook page 57

Vocabulary **71**

7 CD2 39 **Listen, look, and say.**

1 I like playing basketball, I don't like swimming.

2 I like swimming. I don't like playing basketball.

8 CD2 40 **Listen and say the name.**

Ann

Pam

Jack

Bill

Alex

Grace

9 **Things you like. Think and say.**

I like painting.　　He likes painting.

Lesson aims
Students talk about what they and others like / don't like doing.

New language
I like / don't like (playing basketball). He/She likes / doesn't like (painting).

Recycled language
activities | family | *This is (me/my family). That's (my cousin). Who's this? Is it your (mom)? dog*

Materials
CD2 | Flashcards: 65–72 | Level 1 action flashcards: 76–85, if available

Warmer

- Review the activities using the flashcards. Review actions from *Guess What!* Level 1 with flashcards, if available, or using mime prompts.
- Students play a version of *Mirror game* (see page xvii) in pairs. They stand facing each other. Student A says, e.g., *Let's roller-skate.* Student B says *Good idea!* Then they both mime the activity, trying to do exactly the same actions at the same time, as if they were looking in a mirror. The game continues, with Student B suggesting an activity to mime.

Presentation

- Stick the activity flashcards on the board in a row. Point to one of the flashcards and say, e.g., *I like playing tennis.* Make a check next to the flashcard. Point to the next flashcard and say, e.g., *I don't like flying a kite.* Put an ✗ next to the flashcard. Repeat the sentences. Check that students understand the meaning. Make sentences about the rest of the flashcards.
- Invite students to make similar positive and negative sentences about different activities by asking, e.g., *What about dancing, Elena? (I like dancing.)*

Student's Book page 72

7 Listen, look, and say.

- Say *Open your books to page 72, please.* Point to activity 7 and ask *Which activities can you see? (Basketball, swimming.)*
- Say *Listen and point.* Play the recording. Students point to the children. Then say *Now listen and say.* Play the recording again, pausing for students to listen and repeat.

CD2:39

Boy: I like playing basketball. I don't like swimming.
Girl: I like swimming. I don't like playing basketball.

8 Listen and say the name.

- Say *Look at activity 8. This is a family. Let's read the names.* Point to each photograph and ask *What's his/her name?* Help students practice pronunciation of the names. Explain that they are going to listen to the boy (Alex) talking about the photographs. Review family words (*mom, dad, sister, brother, cousin, grandma, grandpa*).

- Say *Listen and say the name.* Play the recording, pausing after each sentence. Students listen, look at the photographs, and say the correct name each time.

Key: Alex, Grace, Pam, Ann, Bill, Jack

CD2:40

Alex: Look at my photographs. This is my family.
Girl: OK.
Alex: This is me. I like painting pictures. What's my name?
Girl: And who's this?
Alex: That's my cousin. She likes riding a horse. What's her name?
Girl: And who's this? Is it your mom?
Alex: Yes! She likes playing tennis.
Girl: Oh, yes. What's her name?
Girl: And who's this? Is it your grandma?
Alex: Yes, it is. She likes taking photographs. What's her name?
Alex: And this is my uncle. He likes singing.
Girl: What's his name?
Girl: And this is your dog!
Alex: Yes! He likes playing soccer. What's his name?

9 Things you like. Think and say.

- Students work in pairs. They take turns talking about things they like/dislike doing (e.g., *I like singing. I don't like playing soccer.*).
- Make groups of four. Students take turns talking about the person they worked with in the pairwork, e.g., *Gabriel likes singing. He doesn't like playing soccer.* They use the speech bubbles to help them.

Workbook page 58

5 Look at the chart. Circle the words and write.

- Students read, refer to the chart, and circle *like* or *don't like* in each speech bubble. Then they use the chart to complete the sentences below in the third person.

Key: 2 don't like 3 don't like 4 don't like 6 likes 7 likes 8 likes

Ending the lesson

- Make a sentence with *likes/doesn't like* about one of the photographs in Student's Book activity 8 (e.g., *She likes taking photographs.*). Students say the name (e.g., *Ann*). If time, they can play the same game in pairs.

Extra activities: see pages TB123 to TB124 (if time)

Lesson aims
Students ask and answer about what others like doing.

New language *Do you like (flying a kite)? Does he/she like (flying a kite)?*

Recycled language activities | *Yes, I do. No, I don't. Yes, he/she does. No, he/she doesn't. I like (flying a kite). He/She likes (flying a kite).*

Materials CD2 | Flashcards: 65–72

Warmer

- Play *True or false?* (see page xix), making sentences with *he/she likes +ing* about students in the class. Volunteers can lead the game by making sentences about their friends.

Presentation

- Hand out five of the flashcards to volunteers. Ask a student with a flashcard to stand up. Tell the class they need to guess whether the student likes or dislikes this activity. Ask individuals to guess, e.g., *Does Dominika like (playing basketball)?* Help them reply *Yes, he/she does.* or *No, he/she doesn't.* Keep a tally of guesses on the board. Then ask the student *Do you like (playing basketball)?* He/She answers *Yes, I do.* or *No, I don't.* See if the students guessed correctly. Repeat with different students.

Student's Book page 73

10 Sing the song.

- Say *Open your books to page 73, please.* Point to the large picture in activity 10 and ask *What activities can you see?* (playing tennis, riding a horse, riding a bike, flying a kite, roller-skating, playing soccer). Say *Listen and point.* Point to each of the people in the large picture (e.g., the boy riding a horse) and ask *Does he like (riding a horse)? (No, he doesn't.)*
- Say *Listen and point.* Play the recording. Students listen and point to the small pictures.
- Then say *Now sing the song.* Play the recording a few times, until students are singing confidently. The first time students can hum to the tune and join in with any words they know. Then students can sing along, following the song text and the small pictures. You can also divide the class into two groups, with one group singing all the questions and one singing the answers. **Note:** Students can sing along to the version of the song with the words or to the karaoke version.

CD2:41

Do you like flying a kite?	Does he like flying a kite?
No, I don't. No, I don't.	No, he doesn't. No, he
Do you like riding a bike?	doesn't.
Yes, I do. Yes, I do.	Does he like riding a bike?
I like riding a bike.	Yes, he does. Yes, he does.
	He likes riding a bike.

Do you like playing tennis?	Does she like playing tennis?
No, I don't. No, I don't.	No, she doesn't. No, she
Do you like playing soccer?	doesn't.
Yes, I do. Yes, I do.	Does she like playing
I like playing soccer.	soccer?
	Yes, she does. Yes, she does.
	She likes playing soccer.

11 Listen and say the number.

- Say *Look at the pictures. Find the children in the big picture.* Give students time to match the small pictures (1 to 6) with children in the picture in activity 11. Elicit a sentence for each picture, to make sure students understand which activity each person is doing and whether he/she likes it or not (e.g., *Number 4. She doesn't like playing tennis.*)
- Say *Listen and say the number.* Play the recording, pausing for students to find the picture and answer after each short dialog.

Key: 6, 5, 3, 2, 4, 1

CD2:42

Boy: Do you like roller-skating?	**Girl:** Do you like riding a bike?
Girl: Yes, I do.	**Boy:** Yes, I do.
Girl: Do you like riding a horse?	**Boy:** Do you like playing tennis?
Boy: No, I don't.	**Girl:** No, I don't.
Boy: Do you like playing soccer?	**Girl:** Do you like flying a kite?
Girl: Yes, I do.	**Boy:** No, I don't.

Workbook page 59

6 Look, read, and circle the answers.

- Students look at the pictures, read the speech bubbles, and circle the correct answer each time.

Key: **2** No, I don't. **3** Yes, he does. **4** No, she doesn't.

7 Complete the chart. Ask and answer.

- Students work in groups of three. They complete the chart by writing two more activities at the top of columns 3 and 4 and the names of the two other students in their group on the numbered lines in rows 3 and 4. They complete the Me row by circling "yes" for activities they like and "no" for activities they don't like. Then they ask the other two students in their group questions with *Do you like … ?* to find out their answers.

Key: Students' own answers.

Ending the lesson

- Students work in pairs. They look at the picture in Student's Book activity 10 and ask and answer about the different activities shown (e.g., *Do you like riding a bike? Yes, I do. / No, I don't.)*

Extra activities: see page TB124 (if time)

10 CD2 41 Sing the song.

Do you like ?
No, I don't. No, I don't.
Do you like ?
Yes, I do. Yes, I do.
I like !

Does he like ?
No, he doesn't. No, he doesn't.
Does he like ?
Yes, he does. Yes, he does.
He likes !

Do you like ?
No, I don't. No, I don't.
Do you like ?
Yes, I do. Yes, I do.
I like !

Does she like ?
No, she doesn't. No, she doesn't.
Does she like ?
Yes, she does. Yes, she does.
She likes !

11 CD2 42 Think Listen and say the number.

1

4

2

5

3

6

Grammar: *Do you like flying a kite?* **73**

Lesson aims Students reinforce language with a story. They also discuss the value of playing nicely.

New language *Are you OK? team, That's not fair! play nicely, Watch me, throw, like this, Good job.*

Recycled language activities, *It's a ... , favorite, Let's play, Put on (these shirts). I'm sorry. That's OK. ball, Thanks*

Materials CD2 | A selection of balls used to play different sports (e.g., basketball, soccer, tennis, baseball, rugby, Ping-Pong, field hockey, volleyball) OR four board markers – one for each team of students (optional)

Warmer

- Play the song from the previous lesson. Students join in and mime doing the different activities.

Introduction

- Remind students of the previous episode of the story. Ask *Do the children go out for breakfast? (No, lunch.) What's the name of the café? (Café Hawaii.) What's iPal's favorite food? (Chocolate cake.) Does iPal eat a little bit of cake? (No, a lot.) Is that healthy? (No.) Is he OK? (No. He's sick.)* Ask students to guess which sport the children will play with iPal today.

Student's Book page 74

12 Listen and read.

- Say *Open your books to page 74, please.* Point to frame 1 and ask *Who can you see? What does Olivia have on her neck? (A camera.) Does Olivia have a soccer ball? (No, she has a basketball.)* Point to the basketball players in frame 2 and say *Look. There's a red team and a blue team.* Check that students know the meaning of *team.* Ask *Do you like basketball? What's your favorite team?*

- Point to frame 3 and ask *What's iPal wearing? (A red shirt).* Say *Look at Olivia. Is she happy? Why not? What happens?* Encourage students to guess by looking at the other frames.

- Say *Now listen and read.* Play the recording while students listen and follow the story. At the end, ask *Who's the winner? (The red team.) Is Olivia happy? (Yes, she is.)*

- Then play the recording again, pausing to ask questions: Frame 1: *Who does the ball hit?* (use gesture to convey the meaning) *(David.)* Frame 2: *What's the name of the basketball team? (The All Stars.)* Frame 3: *Are iPal's arms and legs short? (No, they're long.) Is it OK? (No, it isn't.)* Frame 4: *What does iPal say? (I'm sorry.)* Frame 5: *Can Olivia play basketball? (Yes, she can.)* Explain the meaning of *Watch me* and *throw.* Frame 6: *What does iPal say? (Good job!)* Explain the meaning of *Good job!*

- Students can listen to the story again for pleasure, or pause after key lines for students to repeat. They can join in with the rhymes. Encourage students to use gestures and intonation from the story.

CD2:43

Olivia: It's a basketball!
Tina: Are you OK, David?
All: 1, 2, 3, Magic tree.
    We're back again. Look and see.
    Come with us. Come and play
    In our magic tree today.
David: The *All Stars* are my favorite team!
iPal: Let's play! Put on these shirts!
Players: That's not fair!
Olivia: Play nicely, iPal.
iPal: I'm sorry.
Player: That's OK.
Olivia: Watch me! Throw the ball like this.
Player: Yes!
iPal: Good job, Olivia!
Olivia: Thanks, iPal.
All: 3, 2, 1, that was fun.
    Time to go. The magic's done!

Value *Play nicely*

- Point to frame 3 and play the first line. Explain the meaning of *That's not fair.* Ask why it isn't fair (iPal is using magic to help him reach the basket). *Is it a good idea? (No.)* Play the next line. Explain the meaning of *Play nicely.* Ask students what happens next (iPal says, "I'm sorry.") and play the dialog for frame 4.

- Read the value *Play nicely.* Talk about how important it is to play by the rules when we play sports or games with other people. Ask for another example of playing nicely in the story (iPal says "Good job!" to Olivia). Elicit examples of when students have played nicely at school or at home.

- Divide the class into two groups (basketball player and Olivia). Then play the dialog from frame 3 again. Students repeat the lines. Rearrange the class into pairs (basketball player and Olivia). Students practice the dialog.

Workbook page 60

8 Read and number. Then listen and check.

- Students number the pictures to show the order of events. Play the recording for students to check.

Key: a 6 b 4 c 2 d 5 e 3 f 1

CD2:44

(Repeat of story – see above for story script)

Ending the lesson

- Play *The last word* (see page xviii) with the following lines from the story: *Are you ... ? (OK) The All Stars are my favorite ... (team). Put on these ... (shirts). That's not ... (fair). I'm ... (sorry). Watch ... ! (me) Good ... ! (job).*

Extra activities: see page TB124 (if time)

Lesson aims Students practice playing nicely. Students also practice saying the sound /k/ and learn that the sound can be represented by two different letters.

New language *camel*, *kangaroo*

Recycled language activities, *camera*, *kite*, *That's not fair! Play nicely.*

Materials CD2 | Flashcards of words spelled with the letter *c* or *k*: *car*, *bike*, *helicopter*, *tractor*, *cat*, *skirt*, *socks*, *bookcase*, *cabinet*, *clock*, *carrots*, *basketball*, *field hockey*, *roller-skate* | A board marker for each team of ten students (optional)

Warmer

- Ask different students *What's your favorite sport?* and *What's your favorite team?* If students completed the Home–school link task for the previous lesson, ask them to show the pictures/photographs they brought to class. Ask about the teams' uniforms, e.g., *What color are your team's shirts? Do you have a team shirt?*

Student's Book page 75

13 Listen and act.

- Say *Open your books to pages 74 and 75, please.* Remind students of the story from the previous lesson. Ask *What sport do the children play? (Basketball.) Can iPal play basketball? (No, he can't. His arms and legs are long. / It's not fair.)* Ask *What does Olivia say to iPal? (Play nicely.)*
- Tell students they're going to listen to some other people asking their friends to play nicely. Say *Now look at page 75. What sport is it? (Soccer.)* Ask *How many boys are there? (Four.)* Then say *Who's speaking? Listen and point.* Play the recording. Students listen and point to the person in the photograph they think is speaking.
- Then say *Now listen and act.* Play the recording again, pausing for students to repeat with the correct pronunciation and intonation.
- Students practice the language in groups of three. They decide what sport/game they're playing. One student mimes playing the wrong way / not following the rules. The other two say *That's not fair!* and *Play nicely.* Encourage the first student to then say *I'm sorry.* Then they swap roles and repeat.

CD2:45

Ed: That's not fair! **Charlie:** I'm sorry.
Alex: Play nicely.

14 Listen and say.   /k/

- In this activity, students practice saying the sound /k/ and learn to recognize the two spellings ("c" and "k").
- Say *Look at activity 14. What can you see? (a camera, a kite).* Teach *camel* and *kangaroo*. Point out that the sound /k/ can be represented with the letters *c* and *k*.
- Then say *camel – /k/ /k/ /k/ – camel.* Students repeat, emphasizing the /k/ sound.

- Say *kangaroo – /k/ /k/ /k/ – kangaroo.* Students repeat, emphasizing the sound /k/ in the same way.
- Say *Listen and say.* Play the sound sentences on the recording. Students listen and repeat, emphasizing the initial /k/ sounds.
- Students can then repeat the sound sentences without the recording, saying them faster and faster each time. See how fast they can say them.
- Ask students to think of any other words they know that begin with the sound /k/ (spelled with either *c* or *k*). For example, *computer*, *cousin*, *climb*, *car*, *carrots*, *kitchen*. You may wish to point out that when the sound /k/ is in the middle or at the end of the word, it is usually represented with the letter *k* (e.g., *snake*, *like*, *bike*, *milk*, *book*, *look*, *take*) and that the letter *c* does not always make the sound /k/ (e.g., *cheese*, *cereal*).

CD2:46

/k/ /k/ A camel with a camera. A kangaroo with a kite. (x2)

Workbook page 61

9 Look, unscramble, and stick.

- Remind students of the value. They read the caption, solve the anagram, and write the word in the blank. Then students look at the pictures and think about which one shows the value. They stick the smiley face sticker in the circle next to the correct picture.
- Students then select a smiley sticker from the back of the book and stick it next to the value.

Key: Missing word: play; Students put the sticker next to the second picture.

10 Trace the letters.

- Students trace the letters *c* and *k* in the sound sentences.

11 Listen and number the pictures.

- Students listen to the words on the recording and number the pictures in the order they are mentioned.

Key: a 2 **b** 3 **c** 5 **d** 4 **e** 1 **f** 6

CD2:47

1 car, car **2** kite, kite **3** cat, cat **4** kangaroo, kangaroo **5** kitchen, kitchen **6** camera, camera

Ending the lesson

- Prepare a selection of flashcards of words from Level 2 that are spelled with *c*, *k*, or both. Show one of the flashcards (e.g., *tractor*). Students think about the spelling and say *C*, *K*, or *Both* (e.g., for *tractor*, they say *C*). Ask a volunteer to spell the word aloud and write it on the board to check.

Extra activities: see page TB124 (if time)

13   Listen and act.

Animal sounds

14 Listen and say.

A **c**amel with
a **c**amera.
A **k**angaroo
with a **k**ite.

What equipment do we need?

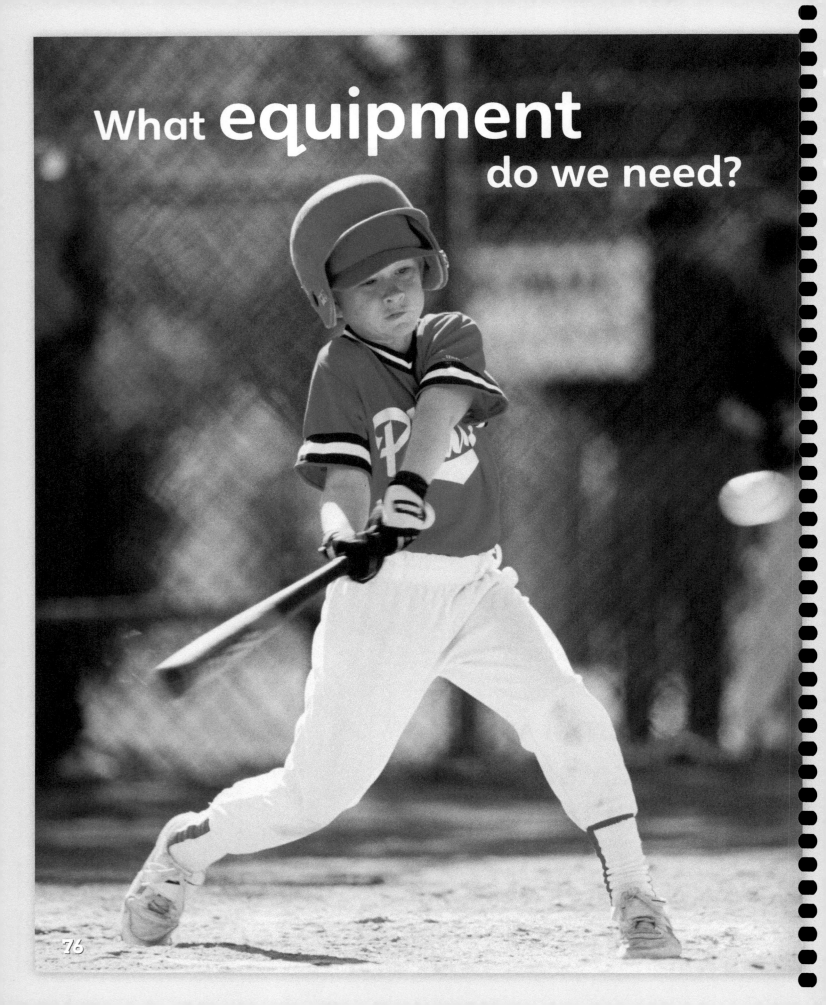

1 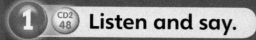 CD2 48 **Listen and say.**

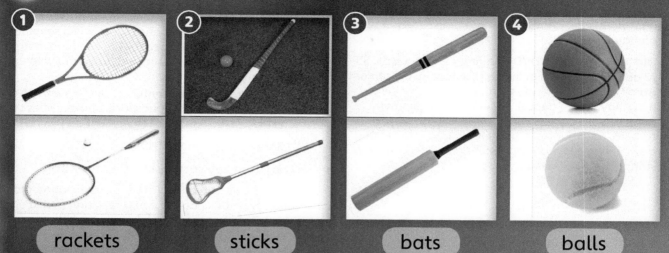

rackets   sticks   bats   balls

2 **Watch the video.**

3 **Look and say** *racket*, *stick*, *bat*, or *ball*.

 Number 1. Ball.   Yes!

Guess What!

Project

4 **Make a Carroll diagram.**

	We need a ball	We don't need a ball
We need a bat		
We don't need a bat		

→ Workbook page 62

Lesson aims   Students learn vocabulary for sports equipment.

New language   *What equipment do we need?* *racket, stick, bat*

Recycled language   activities, *ball, camera, hat, shoes, kite, I have a (camera). I like (taking photographs).*

Materials   CD2 | DVD (optional) | Flashcards: 65–72 and flashcards of activities that require equipment from Level 1 Unit 7 (e.g., paint, climb, swim, ride a bike, play soccer, dance) | Music CD | Equipment for activities students can name in English (e.g., a camera, roller skates, a basketball, a bicycle helmet, a swimming cap, dancing shoes / a music CD, a kite/string)

Warmer

- Show an item used in one of the activities students have learned about in the unit so far, e.g., a camera. Say *Look. I have a … (camera.) I like … (taking photographs.)* Repeat with other items. Tell students that all these items are *equipment* – things we need to do different activities. Write the words on the board.
- Then hand the items to students around the class. Play some music. Students pass the items around. When the music stops, students with the items stand up and say *I have a (cap). I like (swimming).*

Student's Book page 76

What equipment do we need?

- Say *Open your books to page 76, please.* Ask questions about the photograph, e.g., *Where are they? What sport is it? (…) How many children can you see? (…) Can you see a (ball)? Is it big or small?*
- Ask students if they can play baseball.
- Then point to the baseball bat in the photograph and ask the opening question *What equipment do we need?* Review the meaning of *need.* See if students know any words for sports equipment already.

Student's Book page 77

1 Listen and say.

- Say *Now look at page 77, please.* Use the photographs to present the words for *equipment* (and review *ball*).
- Say *Listen and say.* Play the recording. Students listen and repeat the words.
- Students look at the photograph on page 76 again. Ask about the new equipment: *Can you see a bat? Are there any sticks in the photograph? How many sticks are there?*

CD2:48

1 rackets 2 sticks 3 bats 4 balls

2 Watch the video.

- Play the video.
- If you don't have the video, ask students to think about their gym classes at school. Ask *What sports do you play? What equipment do you use?* Students think about what they wear and use for different sports in pairs. They write the name of each sport and a sentence about what they need, e.g., *soccer – We need soccer boots, shirts, and a ball.* Circulate and provide new language as necessary.
- Ask pairs to read their sentences and write them on the board. Ask students about sports and activities they do outside school. Ask *What equipment do you need?*

Video 06 : see page TB131

3 Look and say racket, stick, bat, or ball.

- Students work in pairs. They look at the photographs and say what kind(s) of equipment are used in each sport. They use the speech bubbles to help them.
- Check the activity by saying the number of the photograph. Students say *racket/stick/bat,* and/or *ball.*

Key: 2 stick, ball 3 racket, ball 4 ball

Guess What!

- Students look at the swirled image and guess what it is. Check by asking *What's this? (A bat.)*

Key: It's a bat (photograph 3, activity 1).

Workbook page 62

1 Look and match the pictures.

- Students draw lines to match each sport with the kinds of equipment needed.

Key: 2 tennis – racket – ball, 3 baseball – bat – ball, 4 field hockey – stick – ball

2 Look at Activity 1 and write the words.

- Students look at the pictures in activity 1 and complete the sentences.

Key: 2 racket, ball 3 bat, ball 4 stick, ball

Ending the lesson

- Show an activity flashcard (from this unit or from Level 1 Unit 7). Ask *What equipment do we need?* Students say the words. Stick the flashcard on the board and write the equipment words around it (or invite students to write the words). Repeat for different flashcards to review as much of the vocabulary from the lesson as possible.

Extra activities: see page TB124 (if time)

Lesson aims Students make a Carroll diagram, categorizing sports/activities. They also complete the Evaluation in the Workbook.

New language *Carroll diagram, We use a (bat). We don't use a (bat).*

Recycled language activities, *equipment, racket, stick, bat, ball* | Students review all unit vocabulary and grammar in the Evaluation.

Materials CD2 | Flashcards: 65–72 and flashcards of activities that require equipment from Level 1 Unit 7 (e.g., paint, climb, swim, ride a bike, play soccer, dance) | Materials for the project (large piece of blank paper for each group of students, colored markers or pencils, pictures of activities, scissors, glue) | Word cards: see page TB111 | Music CD (optional)

Warmer

- Play *True or false?* (see page xix) with the activity flashcards, e.g., show the tennis flashcard and say *We use a racket to play this sport. (True.)* Show the basketball flashcard and say *There are ten people on a basketball team. (False.)* Present *use* during the game.

Student's Book page 77

4 Make a Carroll diagram.

- Say *Open your books to page 77, please.* Point to the picture in activity 4 and say *Listen and point. We use a bat and a ball.* Help students point to the correct part of the diagram (the top left section). Repeat for *We don't use a bat, but we use a ball.* (the bottom left section) and *We don't use a bat, and we don't use a ball* (the bottom right section). Ask, e.g., *Which sports use a bat and a ball? (Baseball, cricket.) Which sports use a ball, but don't use a bat? (Soccer, tennis).* Explain that this kind of diagram is called a *Carroll diagram*.

- Say *Make a Carroll diagram.* Students work in small groups. Give each group a large piece of blank paper, pictures of activities/sports to cut out, scissors, and glue. Each group copies the three-column chart from the diagram in the Student's Book onto their paper and writes along the top and at the sides. They don't need to use pictures of sports they can name in English, they just need to categorize them according to which equipment is used/not used. Note that students can draw and color the pictures themselves or just write the names of the sports.

- Circulate and help, providing new vocabulary and asking, e.g., *Do we use a bat? Do we use a ball?*

- Display the diagrams in the classroom and give students time to look at their classmates' work.

Workbook page 63 – Evaluation

1 Look and write the activity.

- Students look at the pictures and complete the words.

Key: **2** (p)lay (b)asketball **3** (r)ide a (h)orse **4** (p)lay (t)ennis **5** (p)lay (f)ield (h)ockey **6** (p)lay (b)aseball

2 What's your favorite part? Use your stickers.

- Students choose their favorite part of the unit – the story, the song, or the video – and put a sticker under their chosen preference.

3 What's different? Circle and write. Then go to page 93 and write the letters.

- Students circle the picture that doesn't belong and write the name of the activity. They then go to page 93 and write the letters in the puzzle.

Key: ride a horse, letters for the puzzle – d, a, e

Ending the lesson

- Students repeat their favorite activity from the unit.

Extra activities: see page TB124 (if time)

Review Units 5 and 6

1 Look and say the words.

Number 1. Fly a kite.

2 CD2 49 Listen and say the color.

Sue

Dan

Lesson aims
Students reinforce the language of Units 5 and 6.

Recycled language meals and food | activities | *He/She likes (cereal). He/She doesn't like (sausages). Does (Sam) like (fish)? Yes, he/she does. / No, he/she doesn't. I like (playing tennis). I don't like (playing field hockey). He/She likes (riding a horse). Do you like (playing baseball)? Do you like (meat and potatoes) for (dinner)? Yes, I do. / No, I don't. What do you like doing?*

Materials CD2 | Flashcards: 55–72 | Music CD

Warmer

● Ask *What can you remember from Units 5 and 6? Let's find out.* Allow students time to look through the units and at any work displayed in class. Encourage them to say what is easy or difficult. Ask *What's your favorite activity?*

Student's Book page 78

1 Look and say the words.

● Say *Open your books to page 78, please.* Students look at the close-up photographs and guess the words/phrases. Check the activity by saying the picture number, e.g., *Number* 1. Students say *Kite/Fly a kite.* Alternatively, check the activity by asking *What's number (1)? / What's this? / What are these?* Elicit *It's (a kite).*

● If you have time, provide further review by asking questions related to the photographs, e.g., *Number* 1. *Do you like flying a kite? (Yes, I do. / No, I don't.) What color are carrots? (They're orange.)*

Key: 2 peas **3** carrots **4** ride a horse **5** rice **6** take photographs/camera **7** sausages **8** play tennis/racket

2 Listen and say the color.

● Say *Let's find out about the people in the photographs. What does the girl like? What does the boy like?* Explain that students will hear the children talking about the things in the photographs. They have to decide which photograph matches each conversation.

● Ask *What's the boy's name? (Dan.) What's the girl's name? (Sue.)* Point to the photographs in the bottom row and ask *What food/activity can you see?* Then say *Listen and say the color.*

● Play the recording, pausing after each mini-dialog. Students listen and guess which photograph is being talked about each time. They say the color of the correct photograph frame.

● Depending on time available, ask students further questions about the children: *Does Sue like playing tennis? (No, she doesn't. She likes roller-skating.) Does she like fish, rice, and carrots? (Yes, she does.) Does Dan like meat and potatoes? (No, he doesn't. He likes sausages and beans.) Does Dan like playing field hockey? (Yes, he does.)*

Key: Blue, Yellow, Red, Green

CD2:49

Adult: Hi! What's your name?
Sue: Hi! I'm Sue.
Adult: Do you like playing tennis?
Sue: No, I don't. I like roller-skating.

Adult: Hi! What's your name?
Dan: Hi! My name's Dan.
Adult: What do you like doing?
Dan: I like playing field hockey.

Adult: Do you like meat and potatoes for dinner, Sue?
Sue: No, I don't. I like fish, rice, and carrots.

Adult: Hello, Dan. What do you like for dinner, Dan?
Dan: I like sausages and beans.

Workbook page 64

1 Write and draw.

● Students use the alphabet code at the top of the activity to work out the letters. They write the words and draw pictures.

Key: 2 fly a kite **3** sausages **4** play basketball **5** cereal **6** roller-skate

2 Read and match.

● Students match the sentence/question halves by drawing lines.

Key: 2 f **3** e **4** a **5** b **6** c

Ending the lesson

● Play *Pass the flashcards* (see page xviii) with a selection of flashcards from Units 5 and 6. When the music stops, students have to ask a classmate a question using the food/activity on the card (e.g., *Do you like roller-skating? / Do you like cereal for breakfast?*). You can check that the rest of the class is listening by asking *Does (Thomas) like roller-skating? (Yes, he does. / No, he doesn't.)*

Extra activities: see pages TB124 to TB125 (if time)

Lesson aims Students play a board game and continue reinforcing the language of Units 5 and 6.

Recycled language meals and food | activities | *Do you like (playing basketball)? Yes, I do. No, I don't. Does he/she like (sausages)? Yes, he/she does. No, he/she doesn't. Would you like some (cereal)? Yes, please. / No, thanks. Me, too. That's not fair! Play nicely. I'm sorry. That's OK.*

Materials CD2 | Flashcards: 55–72 | A coin for each pair of students and buttons or game pieces for playing the game (optional)

Warmer

- Play *The one that doesn't belong* (see page xvi) with flashcards from Units 5 and 6, e.g., potatoes, fish, carrots, peas (fish – the rest are vegetables); play tennis, play baseball, play basketball, take photographs (take photographs – the rest are ball sports); cereal, rice, roller-skate, ride a horse (cereal – the rest start with the sound /r/); play basketball, play field hockey, ride a horse, play tennis (ride a horse – you need more than one person to do the other activities).

Student's Book page 79

3 Play the game.

- The aim of this game is to be the first one to get to the star at the *Finish*. Students play in pairs with a coin and buttons or game pieces. Elicit the food or activity on each of the picture squares before students begin the game.
- Students place their button or game piece on the green arrow marked *Start*. They then take turns flipping the coin and moving their game piece along the board. If they flip the heads side of the coin, they move two spaces. If they flip the tails side of the coin, they move one space.
- On each square of the game board, students make a question with the words given and the food or activity pictured. For example, square 1: *Does he like sausages?* and square 2 *Do you like playing basketball?* They use the happy and sad faces as prompts to answer the questions about other people (i.e., for a happy face they answer *Yes, he/she does.* and for a sad face they answer *No, he/she doesn't.*).
- If students make a question and answer correctly, they stay on the square they have landed on. If they make a mistake, they move back one square.
- Play continues until one student moves to the star marked *Finish*.

Key: 1 Does he like sausages? (No, he doesn't.) **2** Do you like playing basketball? (Students' own answers.) **3** Does she like rice? (Yes, she does.) **4** Do you like taking photographs? (Students' own answers.) **5** Does he like carrots? (No, he doesn't.) **6** Do you like flying a kite? (Students' own answers.) **7** Does she like meat? (Yes, she does.) **8** Do you like playing tennis? (Students' own answers.) **9** Does he like potatoes? (No, he doesn't.) **10** Do you like playing field hockey? (Students' own answers.) **11** Does she like peas? (No, she doesn't.) **12** Do you like roller-skating? (Students' own answers.) **13** Does he like cereal? (Yes, he does.) **14** Do you like playing baseball? (Students' own answers.) **15** Does she like fish? (No, she doesn't.) **16** Do you like riding a horse? (Students' own answers.) **17** Does he like toast? (Yes, he does.) **18** Do you like beans? (Students' own answers.)

Workbook page 65

3 Look, read, and write the words.

- Students look at the pictures and complete the questions and answers with words from the box.

Key: 2 fish, does **3** rice, doesn't **4** roller-skating, don't

4 Listen and check ✓.

- Students listen and check the correct picture in each pair.

Key: 1 picture 2 **2** picture 2

CD2:50

1 Girl: Do you like cereal?
Boy: Yes, I do.
Girl: Me, too. Would you like some?
Boy: No, thank you. Let's clean up.
Girl: OK. Put the cereal in the cabinet.
Boy: OK.
Girl: Thank you.

2 Boy: I like flying a kite.
Girl: Me, too. Can I have a turn?
Boy: No, May.
Girl: That's not fair!
Mom: Play nicely!
Boy: I'm sorry.
Girl: That's OK.

Ending the lesson

- Write the following phrases in a column on the left of the board: 1 *Would you like some toast? 2 I like roller-skating. 3 I'm sorry. 4 Can I have a turn?* Write the following responses in a column on the right: *a That's OK. b Yes, of course. c No, thanks. d Me, too.* Students match the phrases (they can work in pairs). Check answers (1 c, 2 d, 3 a, 4 b). Then give students time to practice the exchanges in pairs (Student A: *Would you like some toast?* Student B: *No, thanks.* etc.).
- Finish the class by saying phrases to students at random, encouraging them to reply as quickly as possible (erase the board to make it more challenging).

Extra activities: see page TB125 (if time)

3 Play the game.

7 In town

Unit aims Students learn about places in town. This includes:

- learning vocabulary for places in town
- describing where a place is
- asking where a place is
- talking about road safety
- learning vocabulary for public buildings
- drawing a map of their town

Background information The photograph shows the town square (Place du Chapitre) in Nimes, France.

Introduction to the unit

- Say *Open your books to pages 80 and 81, please.* Play the theme song on the recording. Students look at the photograph and read the title of the unit while listening to the song.
- Ask *What's Unit 7 about?* Encourage students to work out the meaning of *town*. Then point to the photograph and ask *What can you see?* Elicit, e.g., *building, house, apartment, window, balcony,* and the colors of the decorations.
  Ask *Where is this place?* Students guess which country the photograph was taken in. Tell students it's a picture of Nimes, in France, and show them where it is on a map.
- Write the word *town* on the board and ask students *What is there in our town?* Students say places in town that they already know in English (e.g., *café, park, school*). Write these on the board and add places that are similar in L1 (e.g., *hospital, movie theater, supermarket*). Ask *What's the name of this school/the hospital? What's the name of a café/movie theater/supermarket in town?*

CD1:02

(Theme song – see lyrics on page TB5)

Guess What!

1 (CD3 02) **Listen. Who's speaking?**

2 (CD3 03) **Listen, point, and say.**

1 park

2 movie theater

3 clothing store

4 café

5 toy store

6 bookstore

7 supermarket

8 street

9 school

10 playground

3 (CD3 04) **Listen and find.**

Find Leo

→ Workbook page 65

Lesson aims Students learn vocabulary for places in town.

New language *park, movie theater, clothing store, café, toy store, bookstore, supermarket, street, school, playground, store, Action! Welcome, down the street, lots of, outside, them all, There's a movie on about (robots). place, everyone*

Recycled language character names | numbers 1–10 | *This is … , I'm on … , There's/There are … , Can you see … ? small, I love … , robot, my favorite, I like (playing tennis). We like (our town). great, Good job!*

Materials CD3 | Flashcards: 73–82 | Map or photographs of students' hometown | Ten slips of paper for each student or pair of students (optional)

Warmer

- Show a map/photographs of the students' hometown and ask *What's the name of this place?* Teach *place.* If students don't recognize the town, point to the map and say, e.g., *This is (name) Street.* Ask *Where's our school?* Students say the name of the street/area.

Presentation

- Say *Let's learn more words for places in a town.* Hold up each flashcard and say the new word. Students repeat in chorus and individually. Then show the flashcards in random order. Students say the words.

Student's Book page 82

1 Listen. Who's speaking?

- Say *Open your books to page 82, please.* Ask *What's this? (A town.) Where's Ben? Is he at the supermarket? (No, the café.)* Point to David. (Students point.) Ask *Can you see Tina and Olivia? Where are they? (At school. / On the playground.)* Ask *What does Olivia have? (A camera. / A phone.)* Say *She's making a video.*

- If time, ask about other details, e.g., *How many cars are there? (Seven.) What's in the toy store window? (A teddy bear, a ball, a tractor.) Can you see someone flying a kite?* (Students point.)

- Say *Let's listen. Who's speaking?* Play the recording. Students listen and point to the characters. Then play again, pausing for students to point to the places.

CD3:02

Olivia: OK, Tina. Action!
Tina: Welcome to our town. This is our school. I'm on our playground.
David: Look down the street. There are lots of places along the street.
Ben: Yes. I'm outside the café. Can you see it? I like going to the café for lunch. And over there, there's a big supermarket. There are lots of cars outside the supermarket.
David: And there are three small stores. Can you see them all? There's a toy store, a bookstore, and a clothing store.

Tina: And there's a big movie theater. I love movies. There's a movie on about robots.
Ben: And there's a park. The park is my favorite place. I like playing tennis at the park.
All: We like our town.
Olivia: OK, great! Good job, everyone!

2 Listen, point, and say.

- Say *Now listen, point, and say.* Play the recording. Students listen and point to the numbered places in the picture. Then play again. Students listen and say the words.

CD3:03

1 park **2** movie theater **3** clothing store **4** café **5** toy store **6** bookstore **7** supermarket **8** street **9** school **10** playground

3 Listen and find.

- Say *Now listen and find.* Play the recording, pausing for students to find and point to the correct place. Students can also say the correct number. If you have time, students can repeat in pairs. One says a place and the other says the number or points to the picture.

Key: Students point to the places in the following order: 8, 1, 5, 7, 2, 4, 9, 6, 10, 3.

CD3:04

There's a street.	There's a café.
There's a park.	There's a school.
There's a toy store.	There's a bookstore.
There's a supermarket.	There's a playground.
There's a movie theater.	There's a clothing store.

Find Leo.

- Say *Now find Leo.* Students search for Leo in the picture (he's above the school gate).

Workbook page 66

1 Look at the picture and write the letter.

- Students look at the picture and write the letters next to the correct words.

Key: 2 d **3** a **4** f **5** b **6** c

2 Look at Activity 1 and write yes or no.

- Students look at the picture in activity 1 and write *yes* or *no.*

Key: 2 yes **3** no **4** yes **5** no **6** yes

Ending the lesson

- Ask *What's your favorite place/store/street in (name of town)?* Volunteers answer. If appropriate, ask further questions, e.g., *Can you ride your bike in (name) Park? What do you eat in (name) Café? What stores are there on (name) street?*

- Students can also ask and answer *What's your favorite place?* in pairs.

Extra activities: see page TB125 (if time)

Lesson aims   Students practice the town vocabulary. They practice talking about where people are.

New language   *Come with me, look around, My (cousin)'s on the (playground).*

Recycled language   places in town, *girl, boy, man, woman, sister, brother, mom, dad, cousin, aunt, uncle, grandma, grandpa, It's my (sister). Where's your (dad)? He's/She's in the (café). There's/There are …*

Materials   CD3 | Flashcards: 73–82 | Word cards (see page TB112) | Flashcards of family from Level 1: 37–45, if available

Warmer

- Review places in town with the flashcards. Stick the flashcards on the board. Ask students for an example of some/all of the places in their town, e.g., *What's the name of a (park) in (name of students' hometown)?*
- Play *Memory pairs* (see page xvii), using the flashcards and word cards.

Student's Book page 83

4 Say the chant.

- Say *Open your books to page 83, please.* Point to the photograph of the girl and ask *Where's the girl? (In a café).* Repeat for the other photographs. Review the family words in the captions or use flashcards from *Guess What!* Level 1.
- Say *Listen to the chant.* Play the recording. Students listen and point to the photographs in turn. Explain the meaning of *Come with me and look around* and practice saying it with the whole class.
- Then say *Now listen and say the chant.* Play the recording again. Students can clap along to the rhythm at first, joining in with as many words as they can. Then repeat as often as necessary until students are chanting confidently.

CD3:05

Come with me and look around.
Who's in the café in the town?
It's my sister! She's in the café.
She's in the café in the town!

Come with me and look around.
Who's in the toy store in the town?
It's my brother! He's in the toy store.
He's in the toy store in the town!

Come with me and look around.
Who's in the bookstore in the town?
It's my mom! She's in the bookstore.
She's in the bookstore in the town!

Come with me and look around.
Who's in the movie theater in the town?
It's my dad! He's in the movie theater.
He's in the movie theater in the town!

5 Match and say.

- If necessary, write letters *a* through *e* on the board and practice pronunciation of the letter names. Practice the family words (*aunt, uncle,* etc.) using flashcards from *Guess What!* Level 1 or by saying, e.g., *Point to the grandma.*
- Point to the first sentence in activity 5 and ask a volunteer to read it aloud. Ask *Which picture? (c).* Say *Match and say.* Students read and match the rest of the sentences in pairs.
- Check answers by saying the number of the sentence, e.g., *Two.* Students say, e.g., *d My aunt's in the clothing store.*

Key: 2 d 3 e 4 b 5 a

6 Think of a place. Say and guess.

- Students work in pairs. They take turns making a sentence about a place in town. Give some more examples, if necessary, e.g., *I can drink tea here. (Café) I can get a jacket here. (Clothing store)* Circulate and help with language.

Key: Students' own answers.

Workbook page 67

3 Listen and stick.

- Students will need the Unit 7 stickers from the back of the Workbook.
- Play the recording. Students listen and stick the stickers into the correct position.

CD3:06

1 **Man:** Where's your mom?
  Boy: She's in the clothing store.
2 **Man:** Where's your brother?
  Boy: He's in the movie theater.
3 **Man:** Where's your dad?
  Boy: He's in the supermarket.
4 **Man:** Where's your cousin?
  Boy: She's at the park.
5 **Man:** Where's your sister?
  Boy: She's in the toy store.

4 Look and write.

- Students look at the items and write the name of the place where they would usually see them.

Key: 2 café 3 street 4 school

My picture dictionary → Go to page 91. Check the words you know and trace.

- Students turn to page 91 and check the words they know. They then trace over the word labels for each picture.

Ending the lesson

- Students look at the photographs and pictures on Student's Book page 83. Say the name of a family member (e.g., *Grandma*). Students make a sentence (e.g., *She's in the supermarket.*) They can repeat the activity in pairs.

Extra activities: see page TB125 (if time)

4 CD3 05 Say the chant.

Come with me and look around.
Who's in the café in the town?
It's my sister! She's in the café.
She's in the café in the town.

sister

brother   mom   dad

5 Match and say.

1, c. My cousin's on the playground.

1 My cousin's on the playground.
2 My aunt's in the clothing store.
3 My uncle's in the school.
4 My grandma's in the supermarket.
5 My grandpa's at the park.

6 Think Think of a place. Say and guess.

There's a desk and green chairs.

It's a school.

→ Workbook page 67   Vocabulary **83**

7 CD3 07 **Sing the song.**

Come and visit my town,
My friendly little town.
It's nice to be in my town,
My little town.

There's a toy store and
a clothing store.
There's a bookstore
and a movie theater.
There's a café, and
there's a supermarket.
In my little town.

And the toy store is behind the
clothing store.
And the bookstore is in front of
the clothing store.
And the clothing store is between
the bookstore and the toy store!
In my little town.

And the movie theater is next to the café.
And the café is next to the supermarket.
And the café is between the supermarket
and the movie theater.

Come and visit my town …

8 CD3 08 **Look, listen, and find the mistakes.**

The movie theater is next to the supermarket.

No, it isn't. The movie theater is next to the café.

Lesson aims Students describe where places are in a town.

New language *Come and visit (my town). friendly, little, It's nice to be in (my town). The (movie theater) is next to/in front of/behind the (café). The (café) is between the (movie theater) and the (supermarket).*

Recycled language places in town, *In my town, There's a … , No, it isn't.*

Materials CD3 | Flashcards: 73–82 | Three soft toys (e.g., a mouse, a dog, and a frog) or toy vehicles (e.g., a car, a tractor, and a bus)

Warmer

● Play the chant from the previous lesson. Students join in. Write the names of two girls and two boys from your class on the board. Students say the chant, using these names instead of the family words.

Presentation

● Hold up each soft toy and ask *What's this? (It's a (mouse).)* Put one toy on a table where everyone can see it. Say *The (mouse) is on the table.* Put a second toy next to it and say, e.g., *The frog is next to the mouse.* Explain *next to*, using gesture and L1. Students repeat the sentence. Present *in front of* and *behind* by changing the position of the toys and making sentences (e.g., *The frog is behind the mouse. / The mouse is in front of the frog.*) Students repeat. Add the third toy and present *between* (e.g., *The frog is between the mouse and the dog.*). Move the toys and practice the sentences until students are familiar with the prepositions.

Student's Book page 84

7 Sing the song.

● Say *Open your books to page 84, please.* Point to the picture of the town and say *It's a town. Is it big? (No, it's small.)* Say *It's a little town.* Present *little*. Then ask *What places can you see? (A movie theater, a café, etc.).* Say *Look. The movie theater is next to the café.* (Point to the buildings.) Do the same with the rest of the places in the song.

● Say *Listen and point.* Play the recording. Students listen and point to the places in the picture. Explain the meaning of *Come and visit, It's nice to be in my town,* and *friendly*.

● Then say *Now sing the song.* Play the recording a few times, until students are singing confidently. The first time students can hum to the tune and join in with any words they know. Then students can sing along, following the song text and using the picture to help. **Note:** Students can sing along to the version of the song with the words or to the karaoke version.

CD3:07

Come and visit my town, my friendly little town.
It's nice to be in my town, my little town.

There's a toy store and a clothing store.
There's a bookstore and a movie theater.
There's a café, and there's a supermarket,
In my little town.
And the toy store is behind the clothing store.
And the bookstore is in front of the clothing store.
And the clothing store is between the bookstore and the toy store,
In my little town.
And the movie theater is next to the café.
And the café is next to the supermarket.
And the café is between the supermarket and the movie theater.
Come and visit my town.
Come and visit my town, my friendly little town.
It's nice to be in my town, my little town, my little town.

8 Look, listen, and find the mistakes.

● Say *Look at the town. Listen and correct.* Play the recording, pausing after each sentence. Students listen, look at the picture in activity 7 and correct the sentences. They use the speech bubbles to help.

Key: 2 No, it isn't. The clothing store is in front of the toy store. **3** No, it isn't. The café is between the movie theater and the supermarket. **4** No, it isn't. The toy store is behind the clothing store.

CD3:08

1 The movie theater is next to the supermarket.
2 The clothing store is in front of the bookstore.
3 The café is between the movie theater and the toy store.
4 The toy store is behind the movie theater.

Workbook page 68

5 Look, read, and match.

● Students match the prepositions with the pictures by drawing lines.

Key: 2 c **3** b **4** a

6 Look, read, and circle the words.

● Students look at the pictures and circle the correct preposition each time.

Key: 2 between **3** in front of **4** behind

7 Draw and say. Then write.

● Students draw a picture of their school and a nearby building/place. They compare their pictures in pairs and talk about where the school is, using the speech bubble to help. Circulate and check. Students then write a sentence describing where the school is.

Key: Students' own answers.

Ending the lesson

● Play *Guess where?* (see page xvi) with a flashcard or toy.

Extra activities: see page TB125 (if time)

Lesson aims   Students learn to ask where a place is.

New language   *Is there a (playground) next to/behind/in front of the (school)? Is there a (café) between the (movie theater) and the (supermarket)? Yes, there is. / No, there isn't.*

Recycled language   places in town, *No, it isn't. The (movie theater) is next to/in front of/behind the (café). The (café) is between the (movie theater) and the (supermarket).*

Materials   CD3 | Flashcards: 73–82 | Two pieces of blank paper per student (optional)

Warmer

- Review prepositions from the previous lesson by asking about where students are sitting in class, e.g., *Is Rafael next to Paulo? (Yes, he is. / No, he isn't.) Is Larissa in front of Igor? (Yes, she is. / No, she isn't.)* Then play *Correct my mistakes* (see page xv), making false sentences about where students and items are, e.g., *Julia is between Thais and Leonardo. (No, she isn't. She's between Thais and Olira.)* or *The TV is next to the window. (No, it isn't. It's next to the door.)*

Presentation

- Draw a horizontal line on the board and say *This is a street.* Stick four or five flashcards of places along the line (e.g., clothing store, bookstore, café, supermarket). Stick three or four more flashcards behind the places, (e.g., park, school, movie theater), making sure the positions of the second group of flashcards show *behind/ in front of*. Point to the flashcards and ask questions about where things are, e.g., *Is there a park behind the bookstore?* Help students to answer *Yes, there is. / No, there isn't.*

Student's Book page 85

9 Listen, look, and say.

- Say *Open your books to page 85, please.* Point to the map of the town and ask *Where's the (bookstore)?* Students point and say, e.g., *It's between the café and the toy store.* Students practice talking about where things are in pairs in the same way.

- Say *Listen and look.* Play the recording. Students point to the map as they listen. Then say *Now listen and say.* Play the recording again, pausing for students to listen and repeat.

CD3:09

Boy: Is there a playground behind the school?
Girl: Yes, there is.
Boy: Is there a café next to the movie theater?
Girl: No, there isn't.

10 Listen and say yes or no.

- Say *Look at the map. Listen and say "yes" or "no."* Play the recording, pausing for students to look at the picture and answer after each question.

Key: 1 Yes, there is. **2** Yes, there is. **3** No, there isn't. **4** No, there isn't. **5** Yes, there is. **6** No, there isn't.

CD3:10

1 Is there a park behind the movie theater?
2 Is there a bookstore between the café and the toy store?
3 Is there a café in front of the park?
4 Is there a toy store next to the clothing store?
5 Is there a clothing store in front of the school?
6 Is there a bookstore next to the school?

11 Play the game.

- Students work in pairs. Student A looks at the Student's Book page and Student B has his/her book closed. Student A asks a question or makes a sentence about the map, using the speech bubbles to help. Student B tries to remember the map and answers. Then they swap roles. They can make the game competitive by scoring a point for each correct answer.

Workbook page 69

8 Look, read, and check ✓.

- Students look at the picture, read the questions, and check the correct answer each time.

Key: 2 Yes, there is. **3** No, there isn't. **4** Yes, there is.

9 Complete the questions and the answers.

- Students complete the questions and answers.

Key: 2 Is there, there isn't **3** Is there, there is **4** Is there, there is

Ending the lesson

- Ask questions about the position of places in students' hometown, e.g., *Is there a playground behind our school? (Yes, there is. / No, there isn't.)* or items in the classroom (e.g., *Is there a chair next to my table?*). If time, students can repeat the activity in pairs.

Extra activities: see page TB125 (if time)

Listen, look, and say.

Is there a playground behind the school?

Yes, there is.

Is there a café next to the movie theater?

No, there isn't.

10 ^{CD3 10} **Listen and say *yes* or *no*.**

11 Think **Play the game.**

Is there a café in front of the supermarket?

Yes, there is.

The movie theater is next to the school.

No, it isn't. The movie theater is next to the supermarket.

→ Workbook page 69

Grammar: *Is there a playground behind the school?* **85**

Lesson aims
Students reinforce language with a story. They also discuss the value of road safety.

New language
tickets, They're from … , Be careful! Look left and right. It's safe now. Let's cross. It's closed today. Come with me. It's a movie about (robots). Be safe.

Recycled language
places in town, cousin, Where's the (movie theater)? It's (next to) the (supermarket). Let's go. I like (going to the movies.)

Materials
CD3 | Strips of thin black and white cardboard (to make a crosswalk) (optional)

Warmer

- Play the Unit 7 song (CD3:07). Students join in. They can act/mime showing people around while they sing.

Introduction

- Remind students of the previous episode of the story. Ask *What sport do the children play? (Basketball.) Does iPal play nicely? (No. / He has long arms and legs.) What does he say? (I'm sorry.) Who has the trophy? (Olivia.)* Ask students to guess where in town the children will visit today.

Student's Book page 86

12 Listen and read.

- Say *Open your books to page 86, please.* Point to frames 1 and 2 and ask *Which place do the children visit? (The movie theater.)* Point to frame 1 and say *I need tickets for the movie theater.* Students repeat *tickets.* Ask *What do we see at the movie theater?* Say the titles of some movies. Present *movie.* Point to frame 2 and ask *Are the children in the bus? (No. They're walking / on the street.)* Point to frame 5 and ask *Are the children in the movie theater? (No, they aren't.)* Say *Look. The movie theater is closed.* Explain the meaning of *closed.* Ask *Do the children see a movie?* Encourage students to guess by looking at the end of the story.

- Say *Now listen and read.* Play the recording while students listen and follow. At the end, point to frame 6 and ask *Where are the children? (At a movie theater, but in a car. The car is iPal.)* Explain/Elicit that this is a drive-in theater.

- Play the recording again, pausing to ask questions: Frame 1: *Who are the tickets from? (Tina's cousin.) What's her name? (Anna.)* Frame 2: *Where's Anna? (Students point.) Where's the movie theater? (Next to the supermarket.)* Frame 3: *Is the man in the car happy? (No, he isn't.) Where's iPal? (On the street. / In front of the car.)* Frame 4: *Are the children OK now? (Yes, they are.)* Frame 5: *Why are the children sad? (The movie theater is closed.)* Frame 6: *What's the movie about? (Robots.)*

- Students can listen to the story again for pleasure, or pause after key lines for students to repeat. They can join in with the rhymes. Encourage students to use gestures and intonation from the story.

CD3:11

David: Movie tickets!

Tina: They're from my cousin, Anna!

All: 1, 2, 3, Magic tree. We're back again. Look and see. Come with us. Come and play In our magic tree today.

iPal: Where's the movie theater?

Anna: It's next to the supermarket.

iPal: Let's go!

Anna: No, iPal! Be careful!

Olivia: Look left and right.

David: It's safe now. Let's cross.

Anna: Oh, no! It's closed today!

iPal: Come with me!

David: It's a movie about robots!

Tina: I like going to the movies.

All: 3, 2, 1, that was fun. Time to go. The magic's done!

Value — Be safe

- Point to frame 3 and ask *Where are the children?* Explain that they're at a crosswalk. Ask *What color's the man (in the traffic light)? (Red). Is it OK to cross? (No, it isn't.)* Play the recording for frame 3. Explain the meaning of *Be careful.* Point to frame 4 and ask *What color is the man? (Green.) Is it OK to cross? (Yes, it is.)* Play the first line of the recording for frame 4. Explain the meaning of *left* and *right.* Play the next line. Explain *It's safe now* and *Let's cross.*

- Read the value *Be safe.* Say how important it is to cross the road at the right place (e.g., at a crosswalk) and to wait for lights to change and/or cars to stop. Ask students which way they need to look before they cross (left, then right, if they live in a country where people drive on the right). Explain that in the U.K., people look right, then left, because the cars travel on the left.

- Divide the class into two groups (Olivia and David). Play the dialog from frame 4 again. Students repeat the lines. Rearrange the class into pairs (Olivia and David) to practice the dialog.

Workbook page 70

10 Read and write the letter. Then listen and check.

- Students match the text with the story frames. They write the correct letter in each speech bubble. Play the story again, which is repeated in full on the recording. Students listen and check their answers.

Key: 2 f 3 a 4 e 5 d 6 b

CD3:12

(Repeat of story – see above for story script)

Ending the lesson

- Describe one of the frames from Student's Book page 86 and ask students to say the number, e.g., *The movie theater is closed. (5) It's safe to cross the street. (4) The children are in the tree house. (1) iPal isn't safe. (3)*

Extra activities: see pages TB125 to TB126 (if time)

Lesson aims
Students practice crossing the road safely. Students will also practice saying words with the letters *qu* and *x*.

New language
quick, queen bee, ox, X-ray

Recycled language
places in town, *Look left and right / right and left. It's safe now. Let's cross.*

Materials
CD3 | Picture of the queen of England | Flashcards: 73–82, word cards: see page TB112 (optional)

Warmer

- Students stand up. Tell them to imagine they're on a street (*We're on the street.*). Say *Let's go to school. Let's walk.* Students walk on the spot. Say *Stop! Let's cross the street. We're at the crosswalk. Push the button.* Mime pushing the button on a traffic light. Students copy. Say *Look right and left / left and right.* Mime looking for cars. Students copy. Say *It's safe now. Let's cross.* Students walk on the spot as if crossing the street. Repeat the same instructions, encouraging students to join in with the actions and the language.

Student's Book page 87

13 Listen and act.

- Say *Open your books to pages 86 and 87, please.* Remind students of the story from the previous lesson. Ask *Where do the children go? (To the movie theater.) Can iPal cross the street? (No, he can't. He isn't safe.).* Say *Anna says, "Be careful" and Olivia says, "Look … " (left and right). David says, "It's safe now. Let's … " (cross).*
- Tell students they're going to listen to someone else being safe. Say *Now look at page 87. Who can you see? (Some children, a man with a stop sign.)* Ask *Is it safe? Can they cross the street? (Yes, they can.)* If you wish, explain that a person who helps children cross the road when they are on their way to/from school is called a *crossing guard* (because they take care of people wanting to use the crosswalk). Then say *Listen and point.* Play the recording. Students listen and point.
- Then say *Now listen and act.* Play the recording again, pausing for students to repeat with the correct pronunciation and intonation.
- Students practice the language in pairs. They mime waiting at a crosswalk and looking right and left / left and right. Then they say *It's safe now. Let's cross.* and mime walking across the road.

CD3:13

Boy: It's safe now. Let's cross.

14 Listen and say.

- In this activity, students practice saying words with the letters *qu* and *x*.
- Say *Look at activity 14. What can you see?* Teach *queen bee, ox,* and *X-ray.* Use a picture of the queen of England to present *queen,* if possible. Explain that the bee is

quick. Point out that the letter *q* is always followed by the letter *u* in English, and together they make the sound /kw/. Explain that the letter *x* usually represents the sound /ks/ (e.g., *ox, fox, box*) but that it represents the letter name "x" /eks/ in *X-ray.*

- Then say *quick – /kw/ /kw/ /kw/ – quick.* Students repeat.
- Say *ox – /ks/ /ks/ /ks/ – ox.* Students repeat, emphasizing the sound /ks/ at the end of the word.
- Say *X-ray – /eks/ /eks/ /eks/ – X-ray.* Students repeat, using the letter name this time.
- Say *Listen and say.* Play the sound sentences on the recording. Students listen and repeat.
- Students can then repeat the sound sentences without the recording, saying them faster and faster each time. See how fast they can say them.
- Ask students to think of any other words they know that have the letter *x.* For example, *Excuse me, fox, next to.*

CD3:14

/kw/ /ks/ A quick queen bee. An ox with an X-ray. (x2)

Workbook page 71

11 Look, unscramble, and stick.

- Remind students of the value. They read the caption, solve the anagram, and write the word in the blank. Then students look at the pictures and think about which one shows the value. They stick the smiley face sticker in the circle next to the correct picture.
- Students then select a smiley sticker from the back of the book and stick it next to the value.

Key: Missing word: safe; Students put the sticker next to the first picture.

12 Trace the letters.

- Students trace the letters *qu, x,* and *X* in the sound sentences.

13 Listen and write qu or x.

- Point to the picture of the man running and teach *quick.*
- Play the recording. Students complete the words with the letters *qu* or the letter *x.*

Key: 2 si(x) **3** o(x) **4** qu(ick)

CD3:15

1 queen bee, queen bee **2** six, six **3** ox, ox **4** quick, quick

Ending the lesson

- Play *Tic-tac-toe* (see page xvii) with nine words containing the letters *qu* and *x* (e.g., *queen, six, fox, excuse me, ox, question, quick, X-ray, quiet*). Write the words on the board, let students memorize them, and then cover each word with a piece of thin cardboard with a number between 1 and 9 on it or make nine word cards that can be turned over in the squares of the tic-tac-toe grid.

Extra activities: see page TB126 (if time)

13   **Listen and act.**

Animal sounds

14 CD3 14 **Listen and say.**

A **quick queen** bee. An o**x** with an **X**-ray.

Where are the
places?

1 CD3 16 **Listen and say.**

1

police station

2

fire station

3

hospital

4

sports center

2 **Watch the video.**

3 **Look and say the letter and number.**

A, 3.   Fire station.   Yes!

Guess What!

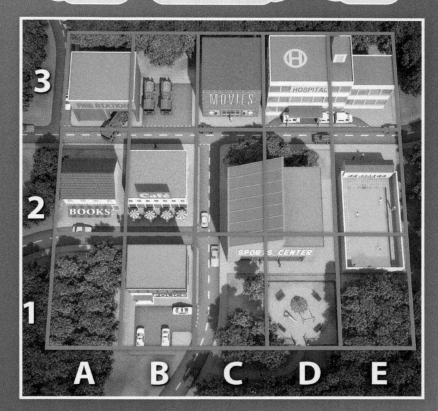

Project

4 **Draw a map of your town.**

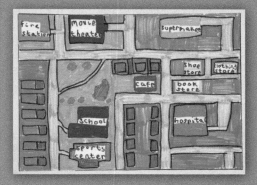

Lesson aims Students learn vocabulary for public buildings in town.

New language *police station, fire station, hospital, sports center*

Recycled language places in town, *town, Where are … ?*

Materials CD3 | DVD (optional) | Flashcards: 73–82 | A board marker for each team of students (if possible, each a different color) OR a piece of paper for each student with two blank grids of 15 squares, with letters A through E along the bottom and 1 through 3 on the left side (similar to the one on Student's Book page 89) (optional)

Warmer

- Review places in town using the flashcards. Play *Bluff* (see page xiv) with the flashcards. First stick a flashcard on the board, e.g., the clothing store flashcard. Say *There's a clothing store in my town.* Draw a square next to the clothing store with a question mark in it (as if it was a mystery building). Say *What's next to the clothing store?* Each of the students with a flashcard makes a sentence, either using the place on their flashcard if they are telling the truth or using a different place if they are the "bluffer" (e.g., *The toy store is next to the clothing store.*). The rest of the class guesses who is bluffing.

Student's Book page 88

Where are the places?

- Say *Open your books to page 88, please.* Ask questions about the photograph, e.g., *What's this? (A town.) What can you see? (Houses, a hospital, trees, a car park, etc.) Can you see some cars? Can you see a factory? Is there a park?*
- Then ask the opening question *Where are the places?* Review the meaning of *places.*

Student's Book page 89

1 Listen and say.

- Say *Now look at page 89, please.* Use the photographs to present the places.
- Say *Listen and say.* Play the recording. Students listen and repeat the words.
- Students look at the photograph on page 88 again. Ask about the new places: *Can you see the fire station? Is there a sports center in the photograph? Where's the police station? Is the hospital next to a school?*

CD3:16

1 police station **2** fire station **3** hospital **4** sports center

2 Watch the video.

- Play the video.
- If you don't have the video, ask students to think about their town. Ask, e.g., *Is there a (hospital)? What's the name of the hospital? Where's the sports center? What sports can you play there?* Ask students if they have ever visited any of these places or if anyone in their family works there.

Video 07 : see page TB132

3 Look and say the letter and number.

- Say the coordinates of one of the places on the grid (e.g., *2, A*). Students say the place (e.g., *Bookstore*). Repeat with different places until students get the idea. Then say a place (e.g., *Fire station*). Students say the coordinates (e.g., *A, 3*).
- Students then play the same game in pairs. Student A says the coordinates of one of the pictures, and Student B says the place. Then they swap over.

Guess What!

- Students look at the swirled image and guess what it is. Check by asking *What's this? (A fire station.)*

Key: It's a fire station (photograph 2, activity 1).

Workbook page 72

1 Look, read, and circle the word.

- Students read the sentences and circle the correct option.

Key: 2 movie theater **3** café **4** movie theater

2 Look at Activity 1 and answer the questions.

- Students read the questions and find the items on the grid in activity 1.

Key: 2 A2 **3** D/E3 **4** C/D1, C/D2

Ending the lesson

- Mime an action from one of the places in the lesson (e.g., putting out a fire with a fire hose). Ask *What place is it?* Students say, e.g., *Fire station.* Students can also play in pairs or small groups.

Extra activities: see page TB126 (if time)

Lesson aims Students draw a map of their town. They also complete the Evaluation in the Workbook.

New language *map*

Recycled language places in town | Students review all unit vocabulary and grammar in the Evaluation.

Materials CD3 | Flashcards: 73–82 | A map/plan of the center of the students' hometown / or nearby city | Equipment for making a video presentation, photographs / pictures of places students know well in their hometown (e.g., the park, the hospital, the sports center, your school, the movie theater) (optional)

Warmer

- Play *Memory 1 through 10* (see page xvii) with the flashcards.

Student's Book page 89

4 Draw a map of your town.

- Say *Open your books to page 89, please.* Point to the picture in activity 4 and ask *What's this?* Teach *map.* Ask *Do you have a map of* (the students' hometown) *at home? Do/Does your (mom and dad) use a map?* Hold up a plan of the center of the students' hometown or a nearby city and talk about where things are, e.g., *Look. This is the hospital. It's next to the park. Can you see the sports center? It's on* (name) *Street.*

- Say *Draw a map of your town.* Students work in pairs or small groups. Give each group a large piece of blank paper. Each pair/group decides which part of the town/city to show on their map. Tell them to choose just a few streets, as on the example map in the Student's Book. They draw a grid of streets in pencil. Check the layout and help each group decide where to put the places they want to show.

- Circulate and help, providing new vocabulary and asking, e.g., *What place is this? Where's the (fire station)? What's next to the (bookstore)?*

- Display the maps in the classroom and give students time to look at their classmates' work.

Workbook page 73 – Evaluation

1 Look and write the word.

- Students label the pictures.

Key: 2 school **3** movie theater **4** park **5** toy store **6** café

2 What's your favorite part? Use your stickers.

- Students choose their favorite part of the unit – the story, the song, or the video – and put a sticker under their chosen preference.

3 What's different? Circle and write. Then go to page 93 and write the letters.

- Students circle the picture that doesn't belong and write the name of the place. They then go to page 93 and write the letters in the puzzle.

Key: supermarket, letters for the puzzle – u, e

Ending the lesson

- Students repeat their favorite activity from the unit.

Extra activities: see page TB126 (if time)

8 On the farm

Unit aims   Students learn about animals and places on a farm. This includes:

- learning vocabulary for farm animals and places on a farm
- describing what an animal is doing
- asking what an animal is doing
- inviting someone to a party
- learning about what farmers do

Background information   The photograph shows a young golden alpaca on a farm.

Introduction to the unit

- Say *Open your books to pages 90 and 91, please.* Play the theme song on the recording. Students look at the photograph and read the title of the unit while listening to the song.

- Ask *What's Unit 8 about?* Encourage students to work out the meaning of *On the farm.* Then point to the photograph and ask *What can you see?* Elicit *an animal* and present *alpaca.* Ask *Is the alpaca a pet? Is it in a yard? (No.)* Confirm the meaning of *farm.*

- Write the word *farm* on the board and ask students if they have ever visited a farm or if they know anyone who lives on a farm. Ask what kind of products we get from farms (e.g., *wheat, rice, meat, eggs, milk, apples*).

- Ask *What is there on a farm?* Students suggest names of animals and places on the farm. Tell students they are going to learn the names in English in this unit.

- Alternatively, hand out paper and ask students to draw a picture of a farm. They can then compare their pictures in pairs or small groups (e.g., *I have a farmer in my picture. There's a red tractor.*) and ask you for any additional new vocabulary for the buildings, animals, or equipment they drew.

CD1:02

(Theme song – see lyrics on page TB5)

Guess What!

1 (CD3 17) **Listen. Who's speaking?**

2 (CD3 18) **Listen, point, and say.**

Café and Gift Store

1 field

2 barn

3 horse

4 donkey

5 sheep

6 goat

7 cow

3 (CD3 19) **Listen and find.**

8 duck

9 pond

Find Leo

Lesson aims Students learn vocabulary for animals and places on the farm.

New language *field, barn, horse, donkey, sheep, goat, cow, duck, pond, over there*

Recycled language character names, numbers 1–9, colors, *Welcome, Can you see it / the (gray donkey)? It's/She's in the (field). next to, I have (three sheep). There's a (black goat). There are (two ducks in the pond). What's your favorite (animal)? big, old, look, They have (babies). baby*

Materials CD3 | Flashcards: 83–91

Warmer

- Play *Two minutes* (see page xix) with the category heading *Animals*. Students may write *zebra, elephant, giraffe, crocodile, hippo, monkey, snake, bird, spider, lion, fish, mouse, dog, cat, frog, horse*, and some of the animals from the sound sentences (e.g., *rabbit, fox, camel*). Review the alphabet by asking students to spell some/all of the animal words aloud when you write them on the board.

Presentation

- Say *Let's learn more words for animals and places on a farm.* Hold up each flashcard and say the new word. Students repeat in chorus and individually. Then show the flashcards in random order. Students say the words.

Student's Book page 92

1 Listen. Who's speaking?

- Say *Open your books to page 92, please.* Ask *What's this? (A farm.) Where's the farmer? (Next to the pond.) Can you see the sheep? Where are they? (In the field.) How many chickens are there? (Five.) What color's the horse? (Brown.) Can you see the children? Who's next to the barn? (Ben.) Who's next to the field? (Olivia.)* Say *The children are visiting the farm. They're looking at the animals.* Present *gray*, using the picture of the donkey.
- If time, ask about other details, e.g., *Can you see a café?* (Students point.) *What's in the store window? (A sheep, a tractor.) Can you see a woman?* (Students point.) *Is she wearing a skirt? (No, pants/jeans.)*
- Say *Let's listen. Who's speaking?* Play the recording. Students listen and point to the characters. Then play again, pausing for students to point to the places as they hear the characters mention them.

CD3:17

Farmer: Hello! Welcome to my farm! Look! Can you see the gray donkey?
Olivia: Um – oh, yes. Over there. It's in the field. Next to the sheep.
Farmer: Yes. I have three sheep. And there's a black goat, too. Can you see it?
Olivia: Oh, yes.
David: What's your favorite animal?
Farmer: My big old horse, Bess. She's in the barn.

David: Oh, yes. She *is* big! And there's a black and white cow in the barn, too.
Tina: And look! There are two ducks in the pond. They have babies!
Olivia: Ahhh!
Tina: One baby *really* likes Leo!

2 Listen, point, and say.

- Say *Now listen, point, and say.* Play the recording. Students listen and point to the numbered animals and places in the picture as they hear them mentioned. Then play again. Students listen and say the words.

CD3:18

1 field **2** barn **3** horse **4** donkey **5** sheep **6** goat **7** cow **8** duck **9** pond

3 Listen and find.

- Say *Now listen and find.* Play the recording, pausing for students to find and point to the correct place. Students can also say the correct number.
- If you have time, students can repeat in pairs. One says an animal or place on the farm, and the other says the number or points to the picture.

Key: Students point to the animals and places in the following order: 2, 7, 3, 8, 1, 4, 6, 5, 9.

CD3:19

Can you see the barn?
Can you see the cow?
Can you see the horse?
Can you see the ducks?
Can you see the field?
Can you see the donkey?
Can you see the goat?
Can you see the sheep?
Can you see the pond?

Find Leo.

- Say *Now find Leo.* Students search for Leo in the picture (he's on the grass close to the pond, on the right).

Workbook page 74

1 Look, read, and circle the word.

- Students look at the pictures and circle the correct word each time.

Key: **2** goat **3** barn **4** donkey **5** pond **6** duck

2 Follow the animal words.

- Students begin at *Start* and draw arrows connecting all the animal words.

Key: Students draw lines between the following words: cow, goat, duck, sheep, donkey, cat, horse.

Ending the lesson

- Play *Guess what?* (see page xvi), describing animals and places in the picture on Student's Book page 92, e.g., *It's big and gray. (Donkey.) There's a cow and a horse in this place. (Barn.)*

Extra activities: see page TB126 (if time)

Lesson aims Students practice the farm vocabulary. They practice talking about where animals are on the farm.

New language *Where are the (goats)? They're (in the field).*

Recycled language farm animals and places, *Where's the (donkey)? It's in the (barn). What's your favorite animal? It's a (sheep).* swim, fly, water, ride, wool, house, fish

Materials CD3 | Flashcards: 83–91 | Word cards: see page TB113, a board marker for each team of students (each team has nine or fewer students) (optional)

Warmer

- Review the farm vocabulary with the flashcards. Then play *Act and guess* (see page xiv) with the farm animal flashcards (students can mime and make animal noises).

Student's Book page 93

4 Say the chant.

- Say *Open your books to page 93, please.* Point to the photographs of the animals and ask in turn *What's this? / What are these? (It's a donkey/cow. / They're goats/ ducks.)* Ask *Where's the donkey? (In the barn.) Where are the goats? (In the field.)*
- Say *Listen to the chant.* Play the recording. Students listen and point to the photographs in turn. Remind them of the meaning of *on the farm*.
- Then say *Now listen and say the chant.* Play the recording again. Students can clap along to the rhythm at first, joining in with as many words as they can. Then repeat as often as necessary until students are chanting confidently.

CD3:20

Where's the donkey?
It's in the barn.
It's in the barn on the farm!

Where are the goats?
They're in the field.
They're in the field on the farm!

Where's the cow?
It's in the barn.
It's in the barn on the farm!

Where are the ducks?
They're in the pond.
They're in the pond on the farm!

5 Read and follow. Then ask and answer.

- Choose two volunteers to read the example speech bubbles. Show students how to follow the tracks from the question to the photograph of the field. They work individually to follow the rest of the tracks and work out where each animal is. Then they work in pairs to ask and answer. Circulate and make sure students are using *It's/ They're* as appropriate in their answers.

- Check answers by asking a volunteer to read the next question and choose someone to answer. That person answers, then reads the next question and chooses a different classmate to answer.

Key: 2 They're in the pond. **3** They're in the field. **4** It's in the barn.

6 Ask and answer.

- Students work in pairs. They take turns asking the question *What's your favorite animal?* Remind students that they can choose from the animals they talked about at the beginning of the first lesson of the unit or a different animal. Circulate and provide new vocabulary, as necessary.

Key: Students' own answers.

Workbook page 75

3 Listen and stick.

- Students will need the Unit 8 stickers from the back of the Workbook.
- Play the recording. Students listen and stick the stickers into the correct position.

CD3:21

1 Where's the donkey?
It's in front of the barn.

2 Where are the ducks?
They're in the pond.

3 Where are the donkeys?
They're behind the barn.

4 Where are the sheep?
They're next to the barn.

5 Where's the horse?
It's in the field.

4 Read and write the word.

- Students read the definitions and write the animal or place.

Key: 2 duck **3** horse **4** sheep **5** barn **6** pond

My picture dictionary → Go to page 92. Check the words you know and trace.

- Students turn to page 92 and check the words they know. They then trace over the word labels for each picture.

Ending the lesson

- Students look at the picture on Student's Book page 92. Ask, e.g., *Where's the donkey? (It's in the field.) Where are the ducks? (They're in the pond.)* Students can repeat the activity in pairs.

Extra activities: see page TB126 (if time)

4 CD3 20 Say the chant.

donkey

goats

Where's the donkey?
It's in the barn.
It's in the barn.
On the farm.

Where are the goats?
They're in the field.
They're in the field.
On the farm.

cow

ducks

5 Read and follow. Then ask and answer.

Where's the cow?   It's in the field.

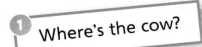
1 Where's the cow?

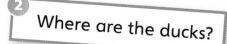
2 Where are the ducks?

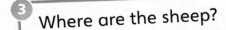
3 Where are the sheep?

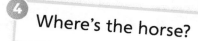
4 Where's the horse?

a

b

c

6 About Me Ask and answer.

What's your favorite animal?   It's a sheep.

7 CD3 22 Sing the song.

Field and pond, house and barn,
Look at the animals on the farm …

What's the  doing?
It's swimming. It's swimming.
It's swimming.
What's the duck doing?
It's swimming in the pond .

Field and pond …

What's the horse doing?
It's running. It's running. It's running.
What's the horse doing?
It's running in the field .

Field and pond …

What's the cat doing?
It's sleeping. It's sleeping.
It's sleeping.
What's the cat doing?
It's sleeping in the house .

Field and pond …

What's the cow doing?
It's eating. It's eating. It's eating.
What's the cow doing?
It's eating in the barn .

Field and pond …

8 CD3 23 Listen and answer the questions.

> What's the duck doing?

> It's swimming.

94 Grammar: *What's the duck doing?*

→ Workbook page 76

Lesson aims Students talk about what animals are doing.

New language *What's the (horse) doing? It's (running), swimming, sleeping, eating, sleep, eat*

Recycled language farm animals and places, *Look at … on the farm, run, swim, jump, dance*

Materials CD3 | A slip of paper for each student, a box or bag | Slips of paper with verbs/activities written on them (from this lesson and from Unit 6) (optional)

Warmer

- Play the chant (CD3:20). Students join in. Divide the class into two groups, boys and girls. One group chants the questions, the other the answers. They all join in with the phrase *On the farm*. Swap the groups and repeat.

Presentation

- Mime swimming and ask *What am I doing?* Explain the question if necessary. Students reply *Swim*. Make a present progressive sentence, e.g., *I'm swimming. Swimming.* Repeat with running, jumping, and dancing.
- Present *eating* and *sleeping* using mime.

Student's Book page 94

7 Sing the song.

- Say *Open your books to page 94, please.* Point to the small pictures of the animals and places in the song and ask *What's this?* Students say *It's a (horse/field).*
- Say *Listen and point.* Play the recording. Students listen and point to the photographs of the animals and places. Mime each of the actions (running, swimming, sleeping, eating) as students listen, to confirm the meaning of the verbs.
- Then say *Now sing the song.* Play the recording a few times, until students are singing confidently. The first time students can hum to the tune and join in with any words they know. Then students can sing along, following the song text and singing the words for the animals and places shown in the photographs. They can also mime the different actions as they sing.
- Students can sing along to the version of the song with the words or to the karaoke version.

CD3:22

Field and pond, house and barn,
Look at the animals on the farm.
Field and pond, house and barn,
Look at the animals.

What's the duck doing?
It's swimming. It's swimming. It's swimming.
What's the duck doing? It's swimming in the pond.

Field and pond …

What's the horse doing?
It's running. It's running. It's running.
What's the horse doing? It's running in the field.

Field and pond …
What's the cat doing?
It's sleeping. It's sleeping. It's sleeping
What's the cat doing? It's sleeping in the house.

Field and pond …

What's the cow doing?
It's eating. It's eating. It's eating.
What's the cow doing? It's eating in the barn.

Field and pond, house and barn,
Look at the animals on the farm.
Field and pond, house and barn,
Look at the animals. Look at the animals on the farm.

8 Listen and answer the questions.

- Say *Listen and answer the questions.* Play the first item on the recording and point to the example speech bubbles. Give students time to look at the rest of the photographs and discuss what each animal is doing in pairs.
- Play the recording, pausing after each question. Students listen, look at the photographs, and answer. They use the speech bubbles to help.

Key: 2 It's sleeping. **3** It's eating. **4** It's jumping. **5** It's running. **6** It's eating. **7** It's sleeping. **8** It's running.

CD3:23

1 What's the duck doing?	**5** What's the horse doing?
2 What's the sheep doing?	**6** What's the hen doing?
3 What's the cow doing?	**7** What's the cat doing?
4 What's the frog doing?	**8** What's the goat doing?

Workbook page 76

5 Look, read, and check ✓.

- Students look at the pictures and check the correct sentences.

Key: 2 The horse is running. **3** The duck is flying.

6 Look, read, and answer the questions.

- Students look at the pictures, then read and answer the questions.

Key: 2 It's swimming. **3** It's sleeping. **4** It's running/jumping.

7 Draw your favorite farm animal. Then write.

- Students draw a picture of their favorite farm animal doing one of the actions from the lesson. They complete the sentences.

Key: Students' own answers.

Ending the lesson

- Play *Act it out* (see page xiv).

Extra activities: see page TB126 (if time)

Lesson aims
Students practice asking what animals are doing.

New language *Is the (cat) (sleeping)?*

Recycled language farm animals, actions, *Yes, it is. / No, it isn't.*

Materials CD3 | Slips of paper with actions on them from this unit, Unit 6, and Level 1 (e.g., *run, jump, swim, eat, sleep, paint, draw, climb, ride a bike/ horse, play soccer/tennis/basketball/ field hockey, dance, take photographs, fly a kite, roller-skate*) OR farm animal flashcards (sheep, donkey, horse, cow, goat, duck) (optional)

Warmer

- Play *Simon says* (see page xviii) with the actions from the previous lesson (e.g., *Simon says "Swim"*). Review the present progressive by describing what students are doing, e.g., *Good job! You're swimming. / Oh, no! You're jumping.*

Presentation

- Say *Open your books to page 94, please.* Point to the first photograph in activity 8 and ask *Is the duck flying?* Explain the meaning of the question if necessary. Encourage students to reply *No, it isn't.* Repeat with more questions to practice positive and negative answers.

Student's Book page 95

9 Listen, look, and say.

- Say *Open your books to page 95, please.* Point to picture 1 and ask about what the different animals are doing, e.g., *Look at picture 1. What's the cat doing?* Students point and say, e.g., *It's sleeping.* Students can practice in pairs in the same way if time.
- Say *Listen, look, and say.* Play the recording. Students point to the animals in the pictures as they listen. Then say *Now listen and say.* Play the recording again, pausing for students to listen and repeat.

CD3:24

1 Is the cat sleeping?
  Yes, it is.
  Is the mouse sleeping?
  No, it isn't. It's eating.
  Is the duck swimming?
  No, it isn't. It's flying.
  Is the dog running?
  Yes, it is.
  Is the cow sleeping?
  No, it isn't. It's running.
  Is the horse jumping?
  Yes, it is.

10 Play the game.

- Read the example speech bubbles with the class. Check that they understand what they need to do. They work in pairs. Student A chooses a picture. Student B asks questions about what the different animals are doing and guesses which picture Student A has chosen. Then they swap.

Key: Students' own answers.

Workbook page 77

8 Listen and check ✓ or put an X.

- Students look at the pictures and name the animals they can see. Students then listen and put a check if the answer is correct or an X if the answer is incorrect.

Key: 2 X 3 X 4 ✓

CD3:25

1 Is the horse eating?
  Yes, it is.
2 Is the cow sleeping?
  No, it isn't.
3 Is the goat eating?
  No, it isn't.
4 Is the sheep sleeping?
  Yes, it is.

9 Look, read, and circle the word.

- Students read the questions and answers, and circle the correct word each time.

Key: 2 running 3 jumping 4 flying 5 eating 6 swimming

Ending the lesson

- Ask questions about the pictures on Student's Book page 95, activity 9, choosing students at random. For example, *Maxim, Picture 2, Is the frog jumping? (Yes, it is.)* Alternatively you could play a team game, asking each team in turn a question about one of the pictures. Students on each team can confer before they give you their answer. Keep score on the board.

Extra activities: see pages TB126 to TB127 (if time)

9 CD3 24 **Listen, look, and say.**

1 Is the cat sleeping? Yes, it is.

2 Is the duck swimming? No, it isn't. It's flying.

10 Think **Play the game.**

Is the dog running? Yes, it is.

Picture 1!

1. It's a message for iPal.
   Let's find him!

2. Would you like to come to a party?
   Yes, please!

3. Hold on!
   We're flying!

4. Welcome to the party!
   It's so nice to see you!
   WELCOME HOME iPAL

5. What's Ben doing?
   He's ... dancing!

6. Goodbye, iPal!
   Goodbye! Thanks for taking care of me!

96 Value: Love your home

→ Workbook page 78

Lesson aims Students reinforce language with a story. They also discuss the value of loving their home.

New language message, *Would you like to come to a party? Hold on, We're flying, It's so nice to see you. What's Ben doing? He's dancing.* take care of

Recycled language farm animals and places, *Let's find (him). Yes, please. Welcome to … , Goodbye!*

Materials CD3 | Flashcards: 83–91 | Word cards: see page TB113 (optional)

Warmer

- Play *Mime and match* (see page xvii) with the farm animal flashcards and word cards. Tell the students who are miming that they can also make the animal sounds, if necessary. When students guess correctly, check by asking, e.g., *What's the duck doing? (It's swimming.)*

Introduction

- Remind students of the previous episode of the story. Ask *Which place in town do the children visit? Is it a toy store? (No, a movie theater.) Do they go by bus? (No, they walk.) Is iPal safe on the street? (No, he isn't.)* Remind them that the children have to teach iPal to use the crosswalk and to look left and right before he crosses the road. Ask students to guess where the children will go with iPal today.

Student's Book page 96

11 Listen and read.

- Say *Open your books to page 96, please.* Point to frame 3 and ask *What are they doing? (Flying.)* Point to frame 4 and ask *What's this place? (iPal's home.) Who are the people? (iPal's family.)* Point to frame 5 and say *Look. They're having a party.* Check that students know the word *party*.

- Point to frame 6 and say *This is the end of the party.* Explain that the children are getting party favors (bags with little presents, usually given out at the end of parties in the United States). Ask *Is iPal going home with the children?* Encourage students to guess by looking at the picture and the words in the speech bubbles.

- Say *Now listen and read.* Play the recording, while students listen and follow. At the end, point to frame 6 and ask *Does iPal go home with the children? (No, he doesn't. He stays with his family.)*

- Then play the recording again, pausing to ask questions: Frame 1: *What does Olivia have? (A message for iPal.)* Explain the meaning of *message*. Frame 2: *Are the children happy? (Yes, they are.) Why?* Students explain that iPal has invited them to a party. Frame 3: *Are they walking to the party? (No, they're flying (in iPal).)* Frame 4: Point to the banner in the picture and ask students what *Welcome home, iPal* means. Explain the meaning of *It's so nice to see you.* Frame 5: *Who's dancing? (Ben, iPal, and his family.)* Frame 6: *What does iPal say? (Goodbye. Thanks.)* Explain the meaning of *Thanks for taking care of me.*

- Students can listen to the story again for pleasure, or pause after key lines for students to repeat. They can join in with the rhymes. Encourage students to use gestures and intonation from the story.

CD3:26

Olivia: It's a message for iPal.
Tina: Let's find him!

All: 1, 2, 3, Magic tree.
We're back again. Look and see.
Come with us. Come and play
In our magic tree today.

iPal: Would you like to come to a party?
Ben: Yes, please!

iPal: Hold on!
All: We're flying!

iPal's dad: Welcome to the party!
iPal's mom: It's so nice to see you!

Olivia: What's Ben doing?
David: He's … dancing!

Children: Goodbye, iPal!
iPal: Goodbye! Thanks for taking care of me!

All: 3, 2, 1, that was fun.
Time to go. The magic's done!

(**Value**) *Love your home*

- Point to frame 4 and ask *Is iPal happy? (Yes, he is.)* Point out that his dad is waving, and his mom has her arms out to welcome him and the children. Play the line *It's so nice to see you.* Remind students of the meaning. Students repeat the line.

- Read the value *Love your home.* Talk about how good it is to come home when you have been away somewhere. Ask students if they have ever been away on vacation or staying with relatives and how they felt when they came home. What did their parents/caregivers say or do? Did they have a special meal or a party? Ask students what they like best about their home.

Workbook page 78

10 Look and write the words. Then listen and check.

- Students complete the speech bubbles with words from the box. Play the story again, which is repeated in full on the recording. Students listen and check their answers.

Key: 2 party 3 flying 4 Welcome 5 dancing 6 Goodbye

CD3:27

(Repeat of story – see above for story script)

Ending the lesson

- Play *Who said it?* (see page xix) with lines from the story, e.g., *Let's find him. (Tina) Would you like to come to a party? (iPal) Yes, please. (Ben) Hold on! (iPal) It's so nice to see you. (iPal's mom) What's Ben doing? (Olivia) Thanks for taking care of me. (iPal)*

Extra activities: see page TB127 (if time)

> **Lesson aims** Students practice making, accepting, and refusing invitations. Students also practice saying words with the sound /w/.
>
> **New language** *wolf, whale, wheel, I'd love to.*
>
> **Recycled language** farm animals and places, *Would you like to come to my party? Yes, please. No, thank you. white, water*
>
> **Materials** CD3 | Flashcards: 83–91 | Music CD, a ball (optional)

Warmer

- Play *Stand in order* (see page xviii) with the farm flashcards.

Student's Book page 97

12 Listen and act.

- Say *Open your books to pages 96 and 97, please.* Remind students of the story from the previous lesson. Ask *Do the children go to the stores? (No, to a party.) Do they fly in a plane? (No, in iPal.) Where do they visit? (iPal's home.) Do they meet iPal's friends? (No, his family.) Does iPal go home with the children? (No, he doesn't. / He's with his family.)* Say *iPal asks the children to the party. He says, "Would you … to come to a party?"* (like). Remind students that Ben replies *Yes, please.*
- Tell students they are going to listen to someone else making an invitation. Say *Now look at page 97. Who can you see? (Two girls.)* Point to the girl with the invitation and ask *What does she have?* Explain/Elicit that it's a party invitation. Ask students if/when they've received an invitation to a party. Then say *Listen and point.* Play the recording. Students listen and point. Explain the meaning of *I'd love to.*
- Then say *Now listen and act.* Play the recording again, pausing for students to repeat with the correct pronunciation and intonation. Ask students what to say if they can't accept an invitation (*No, thanks.*).
- Students practice the language in pairs. They mime handing over an invitation and accepting it.

CD3:28

Girl 1: Would you like to come to my party?
Girl 2: Yes, please! I'd love to. Thanks.

13 Listen and say.   /w/ /wh/

- In this activity, students practice saying words with the sound /w/.
- Say *Look at activity 13. What can you see?* Review *water* and teach *wolf, whale,* and *wheel.* Point out that the letter *w* is often followed by the letter *h* in English, but it still makes the sound /w/.
- Say *wolf – /w/ /w/ /w/ – wolf.* Students repeat, emphasizing the sound /w/.
- Say *whale – /wh/ /wh/ /wh/ – whale.* Students repeat, emphasizing the sound in the same way.

- Say *Listen and say.* Play the sound sentences on the recording. Students listen and repeat.
- Students can then repeat the sound sentences without the recording, saying them faster and faster each time. See how fast they can say them.
- Ask students to think of any other words they know that have the sound /w/. For example, *what, window, wood, where, wash, woman, wearing, wool.* If necessary, explain that although the word *who* is written with the letter *w* the first sound is /h/, not /w/.

CD3:29

/w/ /w/ A wolf in the water. A white whale with a wheel. (x2)

Workbook page 79

11 Look, unscramble, and stick.

- Remind students of the value. They read the caption, solve the anagram, and write the word in the blank. Then students look at the pictures and think about which one shows the value. They stick the smiley face sticker in the circle next to the correct picture.
- Students then select a smiley sticker from the back of the book and stick it next to the value.

Key: Missing word: home; Students put the sticker next to the second picture.

12 Trace the letters.

- Students trace the letters *w* and *wh* in the sound sentences.

13 Listen and check ✓ w or wh.

- Play the recording. Students listen to the words and check the ones with the letter(s) *w* or *wh*.

Key: 2 wh **3** wh **4** w

CD3:30

1 water, water **2** where, where **3** wheel, wheel
4 wolf, wolf

Ending the lesson

- Play *Sound pairs* (see page xviii) with the sounds /w/ and /v/ (e.g., *vulture, wolf, white, very, window, vegetables, wool, van*). When students hear the /w/ sound, they wave.

Extra activities: see page TB127 (if time)

12   **Listen and act.**

Animal sounds

13 **Listen and say.**

A wolf in the water. A white whale with a wheel.

→ Workbook page 79

Functional language: *Would you like to come to my party?*
Pronunciation: *w, wh* **97**

What do **farmers** do?

1 CD3 31 Listen and say.

plant seeds   turn soil   water plants   harvest plants

2 Watch the video.

3 Look and say.

Number 1. He turns soil.   Yes!

Guess What!

Project

4 Draw how farmers grow our food.

Lesson aims Students learn vocabulary for things that farmers do.

New language *What do farmers do? plant seeds, turn (the) soil, water plants, harvest plants, A farmer/ He/She (plants seeds / turns the soil / waters plants / harvests plants / feeds the chickens / milks the cows / drives a tractor / rides a horse)*

Recycled language farm animals and places, *take care of, animals, food, water*

Materials CD3 | DVD (optional) | Flashcards: 83–91

Warmer

- Review the farm words with the flashcards. Play *Reading race* (see page xviii). Example sentences: *A duck can swim and fly. A barn is a house for animals.*

Student's Book page 98

What do farmers do?

- Say *Open your books to page 98, please.* Ask questions about the photograph, e.g., *What can you see? (A farm/fields/trees/a tractor.) Can you see animals? (No, birds.) What are the birds doing? (Flying. / Following the tractor.) What's the farmer doing?* Students guess in their first language.
- Then ask the opening question *What do farmers do?* Explain the meaning of the question. Students may be able to suggest *take care of plants/animals, feed animals* in English.

Student's Book page 99

1 Listen and say.

- Say *Now look at page 99, please.* Use the photographs to present the things farmers do.
- Say *Listen and say.* Play the recording. Students listen and repeat the phrases.
- Students look at the photograph on page 98 again. Ask *What's this farmer doing? (Turning the soil.)* Talk briefly about why farmers need to turn the soil (to bury the remains of old crops, to bring nutrients to the surface for the seeds, and to put air into the soil).

CD3:31

1 plant seeds **2** turn soil **3** water plants **4** harvest plants

2 Watch the video.

- Play the video.
- If you don't have the video, ask students to think about the farms close to their hometown / in their region. Ask, e.g., *What do farmers do in* (students' region)*? Do they have plants or animals? Do they plant seeds? When do they harvest plants?* Ask students what kind of work they usually see farmers doing (maybe they harvest fruit or feed animals). If you wish, teach names for the different kinds of farms in the region (e.g., *fruit farm, pig farm, chicken farm, cattle farm, wheat farm*).

Video 08 : see page TB132

3 Look and say.

- Students work in pairs. They look at the photographs and say what the farmer does in each one. They use the speech bubbles to help them. Point out that they need to add an "s" to the verb because they are talking about the farmer.
- Check the activity by saying the number of the photograph. Students make a sentence, e.g., *He plants seeds.*

Key: 2 He plants seeds. **3** He waters plants. **4** He harvests plants.

Guess What!

- Students look at the swirled image and guess what it is. Check by asking *What does the farmer do? (He plants seeds. / Plant seeds.)*

Key: *He plants seeds (photograph 2, activity 3).*

Workbook page 80

1 Look and number the pictures.

- Students look at the photographs and number them in the correct order.

Key: a 4   b 2   c 3

2 Look at Activity 1 and write the letter.

- Students read the sentences. They look at the photographs in activity 1 again and write the letter.

Key: 2 d   3 c   4 a

Ending the lesson

- Ask students to stand up. Say *Let's play farmers! Drive your tractor.* Mime driving a tractor. Students copy. Continue with different jobs a farmer does (students can also suggest jobs and do mimes, as they get the idea), e.g., *Plant seeds.* (Mime sowing seeds by hand.) *Drive your tractor. Harvest fruit.* (Mime picking fruit from a tree.) *Drive your tractor. Milk the cows.* (Mime milking by hand.) *Drive your tractor. Feed the chickens. Drive your tractor. Go home. Open the door. Sit down!*

Extra activities: see page TB127 (if time)

Lesson aims Students draw a diagram to show how food is produced by farmers. They also complete the Evaluation in the Workbook.

New language *how farmers grow our food*

Recycled language farm animals and places, *A farmer (drives a tractor / milks cows, etc.)* | Students review all unit vocabulary and grammar in the evaluation.

Materials CD3 | A piece of blank paper and colored markers/pencils for each student

Warmer

- Play *Correct my mistakes* (see page xv), saying false sentences about what farmers do, e.g., *A farmer drives a bus. (No. A farmer drives a tractor.) A farmer plants sausages. (No. A farmer plants seeds.) A farmer milks horses. (No. A farmer milks cows.)*

Student's Book page 99

4 Draw how farmers grow our food.

- Say *Open your books to page 99, please.* Point to the picture in activity 4 and say *Look. This is how farmers grow our food.* Explain the meaning of *how farmers grow our food.* Elicit a sentence for each picture, beginning *A farmer …* Point out that the different things have to happen in the right order (turning the soil first, then planting, then watering, and finally harvesting). Ask what happens after harvesting (plants are transported to be processed (e.g., wheat into flour) or sold (e.g., potatoes, carrots, fruit)).

- Say *Draw how farmers grow our food.* Students work individually. Give each student a large piece of blank paper. Show students how to divide the paper into four and number the sections 1 through 4, as in the example on page 99. Alternatively, students can work in groups of four, with each student drawing one picture in the farming process.

- Each student decides which kind of crop to show in their pictures. Elicit some examples (e.g., rice, cereal, vegetables, apples). They draw the different stages of turning soil, planting, watering, and harvesting. Circulate, help, and ask, e.g., *What's the farmer doing? What's this?*

- Display the drawings in the classroom and give students time to look at their classmates' work.

Workbook page 81 – Evaluation

1 Write the words and find.

- Students label the pictures. Then they circle the words in the word search puzzle.

Key: 2 donkey **3** field **4** pond **5** sheep **6** barn

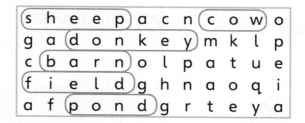

2 What's your favorite part? Use your stickers.

- Students choose their favorite part of the unit – the story, the song, or the video – and put a sticker under their chosen preference.

3 What's different? Circle and write. Then go to page 93 and write the letters.

- Students circle the picture that doesn't belong and write the name of the animal. They then go to page 93 and write the letters in the puzzle.

Key: goat, letters for the puzzle – g, t

Ending the lesson

- Students repeat their favorite activity from the unit.

Extra activities: see page TB127 (if time)

Review Units 7 and 8

1 Look and say the words.

Number 1. Café.

2 CD3 32 Listen and say the name.

Grace

Lola

Kento

Dan

Lesson aims Students reinforce the language of Units 7 and 8.

New language *hay*

Recycled language places in town, farm animals and places, *farm, next to, in front of, behind, between, The (school) is (next to) the (movie theater). Is there a (toy store) (behind) the (school)? Yes, there is. / No, there isn't. What's he/she doing? He's/She's (drinking). I'm (jumping). sleeping, flying, eating, running, riding, feeding the goat*

Materials CD3 | Flashcards: 73–91 | Pictures of vocabulary items from Level 2 (e.g., from the Internet, magazines, or catalogs) cut up into pieces to make simple jigsaws (one puzzle piece for each student) OR a slip of paper for each student and a box or bag (optional)

Warmer

● Ask *What can you remember from Units 7 and 8? Let's find out.* Allow students time to look through the units and at any work displayed in class. Encourage them to say what is easy or difficult. Ask *What's your favorite activity?*

Student's Book page 100

1 Look and say the words.

● Say *Open your books to page 100, please.* Students look at the close-up photographs and guess the animals/places. Check the activity by saying the picture number, e.g., *Number 1.* Students say the word: *Café.* Alternatively, check the activity by asking *What's number (1)? / What's this (place/animal)?* Elicit *It's a (café).*

● If you have time, provide further review by asking questions related to the photographs, e.g., *Number 1. What's the name of a café in our town?* (Students' own answers.) *Where is it?* (e.g., *It's next to the movie theater.*) *Is there a bookstore behind the supermarket?* (*Yes, there is. / No, there isn't.*) *Can ducks swim?* (*Yes, they can.*)

Key: 2 duck **3** pond **4** playground **5** cow **6** bookstore **7** sheep **8** movie theater

2 Listen and say the name.

● Say *Look at the children in the photographs.* Point to each photograph and ask *What's his/her name? Where is he/she? What's he/she doing?* Explain that students will hear the children talking and that they have to choose the correct photograph each time.

● Say *Listen and say the name.*

● Play the recording, pausing after each section. Students listen and guess which person is speaking. Explain the meaning of *hay* if necessary.

● Depending on time available, ask students further questions about the children, e.g., *Where's the hay? (In the field, next to the barn.) What's Grace drinking? (She's drinking orange juice.) What's Kento's favorite animal? (A donkey.)*

Key: Dan, Lola, Grace, Kento

CD3:32

Dan: This is me on the farm. I'm feeding the goat.
Lola: I'm on the farm. I'm jumping on the hay. The hay is in the field next to the barn.
Grace: This is me in a café. I'm drinking juice. I like orange juice. Do you like juice?
Kento: I'm on the farm. I'm riding my favorite animal. It's a donkey! Can you ride a donkey?

Workbook page 82

1 Look and write the word. Then draw Number 11.

● Students look at the pictures and complete the words in the puzzle grid. They work out the answer for number 11 by reading the word spelled by the shaded letters in the grid. Then they draw the missing item and write the word.

Key: 2 clothing store **3** barn **4** toy store **5** goat **6** horse **7** bookstore **8** duck **9** pond **10** donkey **11** playground

Ending the lesson

● Play *Last one standing* (see page xvi), making sentences from Units 1 through 8, e.g., *My family has a white car. I don't have a pet cat. I'm wearing shoes. There's a closet in my bedroom. I like cereal for breakfast. I don't like playing tennis. There isn't a playground next to my house. I like donkeys.*

Extra activities: see page TB127 (if time)

Lesson aims   Students play a game and continue reinforcing the language of Units 7 and 8.

New language   Stop! Wait for the green light.

Recycled language   places in town, farm animals and places, Is there a (supermarket) next to the (playground)? Yes, there is. / No, there isn't. What's between the (bookstore) and the (café)? What's the (duck) doing? It's (eat)ing. Is he/she (sleep)ing? Yes, he/she is. / No, he/she isn't. What's he/she doing? He's/She's (runn)ing. Look left and right. It's safe now. Let's cross/go. Would you like to (take photographs at the park with me)? I'd love to.

Materials   CD3 | Flashcards: 73–91 | A classroom object / item of food / small toy wrapped in layers of paper (to play Pass the present), a music CD, a timer or bell (optional)

Warmer

- Play *Pass the present* (see page xviii). When the music stops, ask students a variety of questions from *Guess What!* Level 2, e.g., *How do you spell your name? Do you like computer games? Is a baby young or old? Are you wearing pants? How many cabinets are there in the classroom? Do you like toast for breakfast? Do you like playing field hockey? Is there a toy store in our town?*

Student's Book page 101

3 Ask and answer.

- This is an observation game. The aim is to answer corrrectly as many of the questions below the picture as possible.
- Say *Look at the picture. What's this place? (A park.) What can you see? (A pond, a playground, a goat,* etc.*) Where's the (café)? It's next to the (toy store).* Point to different people and animals in the picture and ask *What's he/she/it doing? (She's dancing.) Is he/she/it (sleep)ing? (Yes, he/she/it is. / No, he/she/it isn't.)*
- Students play in pairs. They read the questions and write answers in a numbered list in their notebooks. Circulate and check comprehension of the questions.
- Pairs swap answers with another pair. Elicit answers to the questions. Invite volunteers to point to the parts of the picture that helped with the answer. Elicit correct sentences for the "no" answers.
- Students check the other pairs' answers and give them a score out of ten. The partners with the highest score are the winners. **Note:** Alternatively, this can be played as a memory game. Ask students to look at the picture and remember where people and things are and what the people and animals are doing. Set a timer for two minutes or ring a bell when the time is up. Say *Now cover the picture.* Students cover the picture, e.g., with a book, but with the questions below showing. They answer the questions individually and swap their list of answers with a partner. Check answers as before. The student with the highest score in the pair wins.

Key: 1 No, there isn't. **2** A toy store. **3** Yes, there is. **4** It's eating. **5** No, it isn't. (It's swimming.) **6** It's eating (an apple). **7** No, she isn't. (She's eating a burger.) **8** He's jumping. **9** No, she isn't. (She's running.) **10** He's sleeping.

Workbook page 83

2 Look, read, and write the answers.

- Students look at the pictures and answer the questions.

Key: 2 No, there isn't. **3** Yes, it is. **4** It's sleeping/sitting.

3 Listen and check ✓.

- Students listen and check the correct picture in each pair. Confirm the meaning of *Stop!* and *Wait for the green light.* if necessary.

Key: 1 picture 1 **2** picture 1

CD3:33

1 Boy: Would you like to come to my house?
  Girl: Yes, please. I'd love to.
  Boy: OK. Let's go.
  Girl: Stop, Sam!
  Boy: What's the matter?
  Girl: Wait for the green light. Look left and right.
  Boy: It's safe now.
  Girl: Let's cross.
2 Girl: Do you like taking photographs?
  Boy: Yes, I do. Would you like to take photographs at the park with me?
  Girl: I'd love to. Let's go. Oh, no!
  Boy: What's the matter?
  Girl: I don't have my camera.
  Boy: Here you are. You can use my camera.
  Girl: Thanks.

Ending the lesson

- Students close their books. Make sentences about the picture on Student's Book page 101 (e.g., *There's a toy store in the park. (true) Four children are dancing in the picture. (false) There's a cow in the field. (false) The goat is black. (false) A man is sleeping. (true)*). Students wave or give a thumbs-up if the sentence is true or do nothing / give a thumbs-down if the sentence is false. Elicit correct sentences for the false sentences. Alternatively, play this as a team game. Make a true or false sentence for each team. Students confer with their teammates and give their answer. Keep score on the board.

Extra activities: see page TB127 (if time)

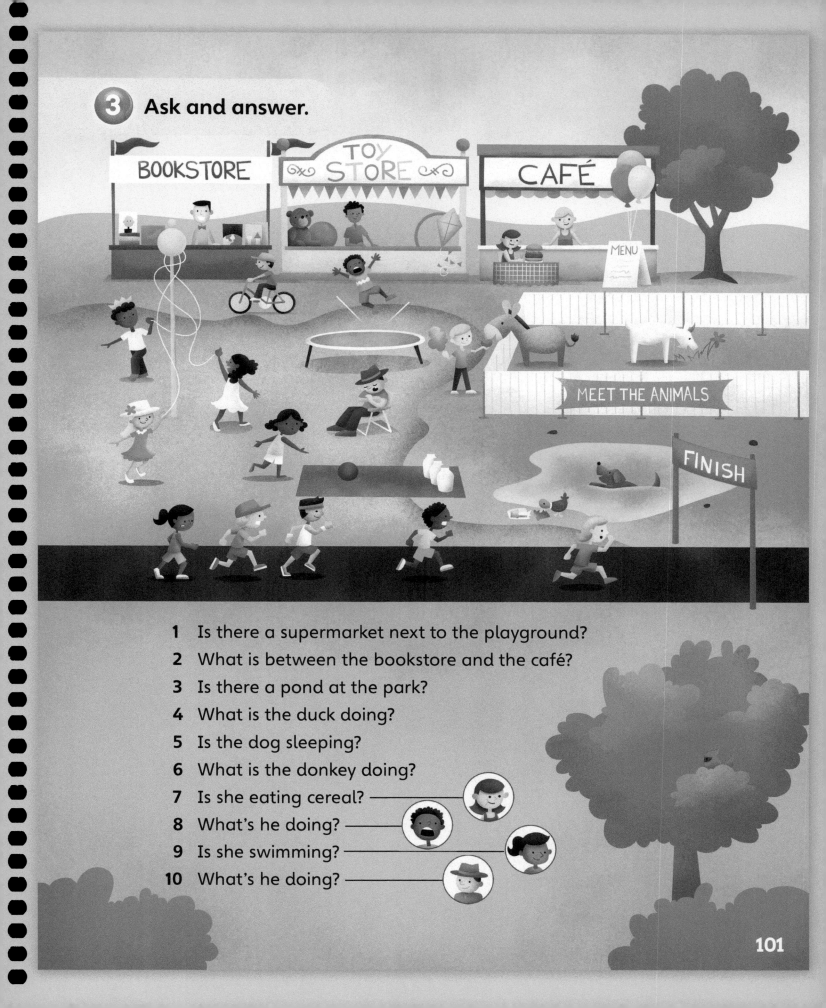

3 Ask and answer.

1 Is there a supermarket next to the playground?
2 What is between the bookstore and the café?
3 Is there a pond at the park?
4 What is the duck doing?
5 Is the dog sleeping?
6 What is the donkey doing?
7 Is she eating cereal?
8 What's he doing?
9 Is she swimming?
10 What's he doing?

My sounds

lion • rabbit

gorilla • hippo

fox • vulture

jakal • yak

meerkat • newt

seal • zebra

camel • kangaroo

queen bee • ox

wolf • whale

Songs and chants

Hello again! (page 4)

Guess What!
Come and see.
Guess What!
Come and play.
Guess What!
What can we learn today?

Guess What!
Come and see.
Guess What!
Come and play.
Guess What!
It's time to learn today!

Guess What!

Hello again! (page 7)

This is my sister.
Her name's Olivia.
How old is she?
She's eight.

This is my brother.
His name's David.
How old is he?
He's seven.

This is my friend.
Her name's Tina.
How old is she?
She's seven.

This is my friend.
His name's Ben.
How old is he?
He's eight.

Hello again! (page 8)

A, B, C, D, E, F, G
A, B, C, D, E, F, G
Happy, happy, look and see
We can sing our ABCs.

H, I, J, K, L, M, N, O, P
H, I, J, K, L, M, N, O, P

Happy, happy, look and see
We can sing our ABCs.

Q, R, S, T, U, V
Q, R, S, T, U, V
Happy, happy, look and see
We can sing our ABCs.

W, X, Y, and Z.
W, X, Y, and Z.
Happy, happy, look and see
We can sing our ABC.

Unit 1 (page 17)

This is my car,
It's a big, red car.
This is my car,
And it goes like this.
Vroom! Vroom!
Vroom! Vroom!

This is my bike,
It's a big, pink bike.
This is my bike,
And it goes like this.
Ding! Ding!
Ding! Ding!
Ding! Ding!

This is my train,
It's a big green train.
This is my train,
And it goes like this.
Toot! Toot!
Toot! Toot!
Toot! Toot!

This is my boat,
It's a big, blue boat.
This is my boat,
And it goes like this.
Honk! Honk!
Honk! Honk!
Honk! Honk!

Unit 1 (page 18)

I have a truck,
You have a train.
He has a motorcycle,
And she has a plane.

Let's play together.
Let's share our toys.
Let's play together.

All the girls and boys.

I have a teddy bear,
You have a doll.
He has a robot,
And she has a ball.

Let's play together.
Let's share our toys.
Let's play together.
All the girls and boys.

I have a helicopter,
You have a kite.
He has a tractor,
And she has a bike.

Let's play together.
Let's share our toys.
Let's play together.
All the girls and boys.

Unit 2 (page 27)

One frog, two frogs,
Big and small.
Come on now, let's count them all.
One, two, three.
Three green frogs.

One dog, two dogs,
Big and small.
Come on now, let's count them all.
One, two, three, four.
Four brown dogs.

One fish, two fish,
Big and small.
Come on now, let's count them all.
One, two, three, four, five.
Five orange fish.

One mouse, two mice,
Big and small.
Come on now, let's count them all.
One, two, three, four, five, six,
seven!
Seven white mice!

Unit 2 (page 29)

I'm at the pet store.
I'm at the pet store.
Can you guess which pets are my
favorites?

Is it small? No, it isn't.
Is it big? Yes, it is.
Is it beautiful? No, it isn't.
Is it ugly? Yes, it is.
It's big and ugly.
Let me guess
Let me guess – Oh yes.
It's a fish!
It's a fish!

I'm at the pet store.
I'm at the pet store.
Can you guess which pets are my favorites?

Are they old? No, they aren't.
Are they young? Yes, they are.
Are they sad? No, they aren't.
Are they happy? Yes, they are.
They're young and happy.
Let me guess
Let me guess – Oh yes!
They're dogs!
They're dogs!

Unit 3 (page 39)

Here's your jacket,
Your favorite red jacket.
Put on your jacket,
Let's go out and play.

Here are your shoes,
Your favorite purple shoes.
Put on your shoes,
Let's go out and play.

Here's your T-shirt,
Your favorite green T-shirt.
Put on your T-shirt,
Let's go out and play.

Unit 3 (page 40)

What are you wearing?
What are you wearing?
What are you wearing today?
What are you wearing?
What are you wearing?
What are you wearing today?

I'm wearing red pants,
And a green skirt
I'm wearing a blue jacket
And a yellow T-shirt.
I look great today!

What are you wearing?
What are you wearing?
are you wearing today?
What are you wearing?
What are you wearing?
are you wearing today?

I'm wearing an orange skirt
And a purple sock.
I'm wearing blue shoes
And a green dress.
I look great today!

What are you wearing?
What are you wearing?
are you wearing today?
What are you wearing?
What are you wearing?
are you wearing today?

Unit 4 (page 49)

Is the lamp on the table?
Yes, it is. Yes, it is.
The lamp's on the table.

Are the books in the bookcase?
Yes, they are. Yes, they are.
The books are in the bookcase.

Is the clock on the table?
Yes, it is. Yes, it is.
The clock's on the table.

Are the clothes in the closet?
Yes, they are. Yes, they are.
The clothes are in the closet.

Unit 4 (page 50)

It's moving day, it's moving day
And everything's wrong on
moving day.
It's moving day, it's moving day
And everything's wrong on
moving day.

There's a couch in the bathroom.
There's a table in the hallway.
There's a closet in the kitchen.
And I can't find my ball today.

It's moving day, it's moving day
And everything's wrong on
moving day.
It's moving day, it's moving day
And everything's wrong on
moving day.

There are four lamps in the yard
There are two mirrors on my bed.
There are three clocks on the
couch.
And where is baby Fred?!

It's moving day, it's moving day
And everything's wrong on
moving day.
It's moving day, it's moving day
And everything's wrong on
moving day.

Unit 5 (page 61)

Do you like toast for breakfast?
Do you like cereal, too?
Toast and cereal for breakfast?
Yum! Yes, I do.

Do you like sausages for lunch?
Do you like carrots, too?
Sausages and carrots for lunch?
Yum! Yes, I do.

Do you like fish for dinner?
Do you like potatoes, too?
Fish and potatoes for dinner?
Yum! Yes, I do.

Unit 5 (page 62)

My friend Sammy likes meat for
lunch.
He doesn't like potatoes
And he doesn't like peas.
He likes beans and carrots.
And he likes cheese.

Munch, Sammy.
Munch your lunch!
Munch your lunch!
Munch your lunch!
Munch your lunch!

My friend Sally likes fish for lunch.
She doesn't like cheese.
And she doesn't like meat.
She likes beans and carrots.
And potatoes and peas.

Munch, Sally.
Munch your lunch!
Munch your lunch!
Munch your lunch!
Munch your lunch!

Unit 6 (page 71)

I can play tennis.
I can't play field hockey.
Let's play tennis!
Good idea!

I can play basketball.
I can't play baseball.
Let's play basketball!
Good idea.

I can fly a kite.
I can't ride a horse.
Let's fly a kite!
Good idea!

I can take photographs.
I can't roller-skate.
Let's take photographs.
Good idea!

Unit 6 (page 73)

Do you like flying a kite?
No, I don't. No, I don't.
Do you like riding a bike?
Yes, I do. Yes, I do.
I like riding a bike.

Does he like flying a kite?
No, he doesn't. No, he doesn't.
Does he like riding a bike?
Yes, he does. Yes, he does.
He likes riding a bike.

Do you like playing tennis?
No, I don't. No, I don't.
Do you like playing soccer?
Yes, I do. Yes, I do.
I like playing soccer.

Does she like playing tennis?
No, she doesn't. No, she doesn't.
Does she like playing soccer?
Yes, she does. Yes, she does.
She likes playing soccer.

Unit 7 (page 83)

Come with me and look around.
Who's in the café in the town?
It's my sister! She's in the café.
She's in the café in the town!

Come with me and look around.
Who's in the toy store in the town?
It's my brother! He's in the toy store.
He's in the toy store in the town!

Come with me and look around.
Who's in the bookstore in the town?
It's my mom! She's in the bookstore.
She's in the bookstore in the town!

Come with me and look around.
Who's in the movie theater in the town?
It's my dad! He's in the movie theater.
He's in the movie theater in the town!

Unit 7 (page 84)

Come and visit my town,
My friendly little town.
It's nice to be in my town,
My little town.

There's a toy store and a clothing store.
There's a bookstore and a movie theater.
There's a café and there's a supermarket.
In my little town.

And the toy store is behind the clothing store.
And the bookstore is in front of the clothing store.
And the clothing store is between the bookstore and the toy store!
In my little town.

And the movie theater is next to the café.
And the café is next to the supermarket.
And the café is between the supermarket and the movie theater.
Come and visit my town.

Come and visit my town,
My friendly little town.
It's nice to be in my town,
My little town.
My little town.

Unit 8 (page 93)

Where's the donkey?
It's in the barn.
It's in the barn on the farm!

Where are the goats?
They're in the field.
They're in the field on the farm!

Where's the cow?
It's in the barn.
It's in the barn on the farm!

Where are the ducks?
They're in the pond.
They're in the pond on the farm!

Unit 8 (page 94)

Field and pond, house and barn,
Look at the animals on the farm.
Field and pond, house and barn,
Look at the animals.

What's the duck doing?
It's swimming. It's swimming. It's swimming
What's the duck doing?
It's swimming in the pond.

Field and pond, house and barn,
Look at the animals on the farm.
Field and pond, house and barn,
Look at the animals.

What's the horse doing?
It's running. It's running. It's running.
What's the horse doing?
It's running in the field.

Field and pond, house and barn,
Look at the animals on the farm.
Field and pond, house and barn,
Look at the animals.

What's the cat doing?
It's sleeping. It's sleeping. It's sleeping.
What's the cat doing?
It's sleeping in the house.

Field and pond, house and barn,
Look at the animals on the farm.
Field and pond, house and barn,
Look at the animals.

What's the cow doing?
It's eating. It's eating. It's eating.
What's the cow doing?
It's eating in the barn.

Field and pond, house and barn,
Look at the animals on the farm.
Field and pond, house and barn,
Look at the animals.
Look at the animals on the farm.

Hello again! word cards

one	two
three	four
five	six
seven	eight
nine	ten

PHOTOCOPIABLE © Cambridge University Press 2016

Unit 1 word cards

boat	bus	car
helicopter	motorcycle	plane
tractor	train	truck

PHOTOCOPIABLE © Cambridge University Press 2016

Unit 2 word cards

✂

baby	**boy**
cat	**dog**
fish	**frog**
girl	**man**
mouse	**woman**

PHOTOCOPIABLE © Cambridge University Press 2016

Unit 3 word cards

dress	jacket	jeans
pants	shirt	shoes
skirt	socks	T-shirt

PHOTOCOPIABLE © Cambridge University Press 2016

Unit 4 word cards

bookcase	cabinet
clock	closet
couch	lamp
mirror	phone
table	TV

PHOTOCOPIABLE © Cambridge University Press 2016

Unit 5 word cards

beans	carrots
cereal	fish
meat	peas
potatoes	rice
sausages	toast

PHOTOCOPIABLE © Cambridge University Press 2016

Unit 6 word cards

fly a kite	play baseball
play basketball	play field hockey
play tennis	ride a horse
roller-skate	take photographs

PHOTOCOPIABLE © Cambridge University Press 2016

Unit 7 word cards

bookstore	café
clothing store	movie theater
park	playground
school	street
supermarket	toy store

PHOTOCOPIABLE © Cambridge University Press 2016

Unit 8 word cards

✂

barn	cow	donkey
duck	field	goat
horse	pond	sheep

PHOTOCOPIABLE © Cambridge University Press 2016

Extra activities

Hello again! Page TB6

- **Reinforcement activity:** Play *Meet and greet* (see page xvii).
- **Extension activity:** Write some or all of the following prompts on the board: *I'm … (name and age). My favorite color is … I like … (food). I can … .* Students copy and complete the sentences. Circulate and help with language. When students have finished writing, tell them to change places and sit next to someone they don't know very well. Students work in pairs. They exchange information by asking and answering questions. Elicit the questions they need and write them on the board: *What's your name? How old are you? What's your favorite color? Do you like apples? Can you swim?*

Hello again! TB7

- **Reinforcement activity:** Play *Count and collect* (see page xv). Review names of classroom objects before beginning the game (*book, pencil, pencil case, eraser, pen*).
- **Extension activity:** Review members of the family. Students draw a picture of their family (mom, dad, brothers or sisters, aunts, uncles and cousins). They show their picture to a partner and introduce each person, giving as much information as they can, e.g., *This is my uncle. His name's Teo.*
- **Home-school link:** Students find a photograph of a friend (not in their English class) or sibling. They show it to a partner and say, e.g., *This is my sister. Her name's Ursula. She's ten.* Provide help with numbers above ten as necessary. Students change partners and repeat.

Hello again! TB8

- **Reinforcement activity:** Play *Bingo* (see page xiv) with letters of the alphabet.
- **Extension activity:** Draw a simple family tree on the board (parents and siblings or cousins) or show a photograph of your family. Say *This is my family. Listen and write their names.* Point and say, e.g., *This is my mom. Her name's Christine. How do you spell Christine? It's C-H-R-I-S-T-I-N-E.*
- **Home-school link:** Students make a list of the names of their close family – mom, dad and siblings, or cousins. They exchange information in pairs (without showing each other their lists), e.g., Student A: *My mom's name is Ximena.* Student B: *How do you spell Ximena? Student A: It's X-I-M-E-N-A.*

Hello again! TB9

- **Reinforcement activity:** Play *What's in the bag?* (see page xix) with classroom objects or small toys (sometimes with just one object in the bag and sometimes more than one).
- **Extension activity:** Students work in pairs. They move around the classroom and take turns asking each other about furniture/items, e.g., *What's this? It's a window. What are these? They're books.* Circulate and check/help with language.

Hello again! TB10

- **Reinforcement activity:** Students look at the story in the Student's Book. Mime an action from one of the frames (e.g., climbing the ladder to get to the tree house in frame 1). Students say the number of the frame and the name of the character(s) (e.g., *1, Tina*). Other possible mimes: carrying a ball (1, Ben), looking surprised but happy (3, Ben), kneeling down painting (4, Ben, David), calming someone down (5, Olivia), looking very worried/scared (5, Ben), pointing to a picture on the wall (6, David). When students have the idea, they can play this game in pairs.
- **Extension activity:** Students work in groups of four or five. Give each group a game to play together (e.g., dominoes, ludo, happy families, snakes and ladders). Students play together. Encourage them to say the numbers/colors/family members in their game in English, as appropriate, and to take turns (help students say *It's my/your turn*).
- **Home-school link:** Students think of games they usually play together with their friends. They write a list of games and bring it to the next class. Which game can be played by the most people at the same time? Which games can only be played with other people (not alone)?

Hello again! TB11

- **Reinforcement activity:** Play *Listen and do* (see page xvi) with r and l words. Students run on the spot (like the rabbit) when they hear words which start with the sound /r/ and pretend to be asleep (like the lion) when they hear words which start with the sound /l/.
- **Extension activity:** Students play *Me too!* (see page xvi).

- **Home-school link:** Students draw a picture of themselves and a friend playing with their favorite toy or game (it has to be a game they usually play with someone else). In the next lesson, provide the name in English. Students write *I like …* and the name of the game. They show their pictures to a partner and ask *Do you like … ?* Encourage students to respond with short answers and the student asking the question to add *So do I*, where appropriate. Make a class display with the pictures, entitled *Let's play*.

Hello again! TB12

- **Reinforcement activity:** Students practice talking about the photographs on Student's Book pages 12 and 13 in pairs. Student A points to a photograph and asks *What's this?* Student B replies, e.g., *It's a drawing*. Students can continue the conversation with more questions, e.g., *Do you like it? What color is it? Can you draw?*
- **Extension activity:** Students make a kind of art from the lesson (not a sculpture – see Project in the next lesson), e.g., a painting, drawing, or (if cameras are available) a photograph. They choose which kind of art to make and the topic. Alternatively, provide a still life of objects (e.g., a kite and a ball on a chair, or some fruit in a bowl) for students to represent using their chosen kind of art. They complete their artwork in class or at home. Circulate and ask questions about what they are making. Display the artwork in a future lesson, as if in a gallery, in different sections with signs (photography, painting, drawing, collage).
- **Home-school link:** Students look around their house and see what kinds of art they have on the walls/decorating the rooms. They make a list or take photographs and write the name of the artist and the title of each artwork (they ask their parents for this information). In the next lesson they make sentences in small groups, e.g., *In the living room there's a painting. In my bedroom there are photographs.* Circulate and ask questions about the titles and artists of the works.

Hello again! TB13

- **Reinforcement activity:** Play *Alphabetical order* (see page xiv) with the character names (Leo, Tina, David, Olivia, Ben) and five slips of paper per student.
- **Extension activity:** Play *Hangman* (see page xvi) with character names, colors and kinds of art from the unit.

Unit 1 TB16

- **Reinforcement activity:** Play *Does it match?* (see page xv) with the transportation flashcards and word cards.
- **Extension activity:** Students work in pairs. They look at the picture on Student's Book page 16. Student A makes a true or false sentence about the picture, e.g., *I can see a black truck.* Student B says *Yes/No, it's blue.* Then they swap roles.
- **Home-school link:** Students draw a picture or take a photograph of the method of transportation they use to get to school and bring it to the next class (e.g., a car, a bus or themselves walking to school).

Unit 1 TB17

- **Reinforcement activity:** Play *Pass the flashcards* (see page xvii). When the music stops, students with a flashcard show their picture and say, e.g., *This is my train. It's long and red. (It goes Toot, Toot!)*.
- **Extension activity:** Move students to a large space, if possible. Explain that you are all going to travel on the same method of transportation. Say *Look, listen and copy me. This is my bus. It's a big, red bus.* Mime being the driver and invite students to mime lining up and getting on the bus. Say *Let's go!* Students mime moving up and down as the bus moves along. Then say *Let's change!* Students get off the bus. Repeat for train, boat, plane and helicopter. Once students have the idea, they can play the game in groups, taking turns to be the "driver" (if you have a large class, you may want to divide the class into groups at the beginning and give each group different instructions).
- **Home-school link:** Students talk about the pictures of their/their family's vehicles (see notes for page 16), e.g., *This is my family's car. It's big and blue./This is my bike. It's purple and yellow.*

Unit 1 TB18

- **Reinforcement activity:** Play *Who has it?* (see page xix) with the transportation flashcards and/or the toy flashcards from Level 1.
- **Extension activity:** Give each student a blank piece of paper. Ask them to draw one of the vehicles or toys from the lesson on it and color it a known color (or two colors). Set a time limit for the drawing and coloring. Divide the class into two. Half the class stand up with their notebooks and a pen and walk around writing sentences about what the other students have, e.g., *Marta has a yellow boat. Yoris has a green robot.* Tell them they have only five minutes to write and they have to write as many sentences as they can. When the time is up, the students swap over, so that the other half of the class write sentences. After another five minutes, see who has written the most correct sentences. He/She is the winner. Elicit more sentences from the rest of the class.
- **Home-school link:** Students think about the vehicles and toys from the lesson and which people in their family/friends have each thing. They write four or five sentences, e.g., *My mom has a purple bike. My uncle has a red motorcycle. My sister has a pink doll. My cousin has a robot.*

Unit 1 TB19

- **Reinforcement activity:** Draw a stick man on the board. Stick three or four flashcards on the board near the man (methods of transportation and/or classroom objects, toys and food from Level 1 (if available). Draw a stick woman on the other side of the board. Stick three or four flashcards near the woman. Ask questions about the man, e.g., *Does he have a truck?* Students reply *Yes, he does./No, he doesn't.* Repeat for the woman. Students do the activity again in pairs. Circulate and check language.

- **Extension activity:** Play *Questions tic-tac-toe* (see page xviii) with the transportation flashcards. Students ask *Does he/she have a … ?* or use the names of students in the class, e.g., *Does Cristina have a car?*

Unit 1 TB20

- **Reinforcement activity:** Divide the class into groups of three or four. Give each group a toy. One student in the group plays with the toy. The others take turns throwing a dice. Whoever gets a six says *Can I have a turn, please?* to the first student. He/She replies *Yes, of course* and hands over the toy. This student then joins the rest of the group taking turns throwing the dice. The next student who gets a six has the chance to say *Can I have a turn, please?* The game continues in this way. Encourage students to say the numbers on the dice in English.

- **Extension activity:** Put slips of paper or card with "yes" or "no" written on them in a bag or box. Make sure there are enough for students to have one each. If possible, ask students to sit in a circle. Put a toy, game or floor-sized jigsaw puzzle in the center of the circle. Give the bag to the first student. He/She pulls out a slip of paper. If the paper has "yes" on it, that student goes into the middle of the circle and starts playing with the game. The slip of paper goes back in the bag and it is passed on. If the paper says "no" he/she passes the bag to the next student in the circle. The student in the center continues playing until another student gets a "yes" slip from the bag. This student then comes to the center of the circle and asks *Can I have a turn, please?* The student who is playing stops and says *Yes, of course*, returning to his/her place in the circle.

- **Home-school link:** Ask students to think of situations when they need to take turns. They make a list. Elicit examples in the next class (e.g., using a computer or a favorite toy at home, using play equipment (swings, slides) at the park, using classroom equipment (scissors, glue) at school, speaking in class or in a conversation (not interrupting)).

Unit 1 TB21

- **Reinforcement activity:** Play *Listen and do* (see page xvi) with the following words: *go, get, help, green, how, head, great, hair, grandma, give, helicopter*. Students face you and wave as if saying "hello" for the /h/ words and wave then turn away from you as if saying "goodbye" for the /g/ words.

- **Extension activity:** Move your class to an empty classroom or clear a space at one end of your classroom. Stick pictures of flowers and trees on one wall or in one corner. Point and say *This is the yard*. Stick pictures of windows and a door on another wall/corner. Point and say/elicit. *This is the house*. Students wait in a group. Say a word beginning with the sound /h/ or /g/. Students run to the correct wall/corner of the room. Repeat with another word (if it has the same sound as the last word, they stay where they are). If you have a large class, divide them into groups and say a word to each group

in turn so that only one group is moving at one time (e.g., *Group 1, helicopter*). If you don't have space for students to move, then point to the correct place.

Unit 1 TB22

- **Reinforcement activity:** Play *Traffic lights* (see page xix) giving instructions such as *Run, Jump, Sing, Swim, Play soccer, Play a computer game, Dance, Paint, Ride a bike, Climb*. Students mime as appropriate until you show a red traffic light.

- **Extension activity:** Set up a large water tray or provide small water trays for each group of four or five students. Show students an object or give an object to each group and ask them to guess if it will float or sink (teach the words *float* and *sink*). Call a volunteer to put the object in the water tray and see what happens. Encourage students to say *Yes, it floats* or *No, it doesn't float*. Students could write the results in a simple table, with the objects numbered 1 to 6 and a check if it floats or an X if it sinks. Possible objects: a toy boat, a paper boat, a piece of wood, a cardboard tube, a toy car, a plastic yogurt pot.

Unit 1 TB23

- **Reinforcement activity:** Play *Mime and match* (see page xvii) with the transportation flashcards and word cards.

- **Extension activity:** Teach students a traditional song related to the topic of transportation, e.g., *The wheels on the bus, A sailor went to sea* or *Row, row, row your boat*.

Unit 2 TB26

- **Reinforcement activity:** Students work in pairs. They both look at the picture on Student's Book page 26. Student A acts being one of the people or pets in the picture (e.g., holding a dog lead). Their partner guesses, points to the person or animal on the page and says the word (e.g., *Girl!*). Then they swap roles.

- **Extension activity:** Students play *Guess what?* (see page xvi) in pairs. They use the picture on Student's Book page 26. Make sure they know the words *pet* and *person* before they begin.

- **Home-school link:** Students draw a picture or take a photograph of their pet or the pet of a member of their family. They write the kind of animal and its name. If no one in their family has a pet, they can draw the pet they would like to have. In the next lesson, students show their pictures in small groups or to the whole class and say, e.g., *This is Carlos. He's my cat.* Help students to express themselves if the pet is owned by a different member of the family (e.g., *He's my grandma's cat.*).

Unit 2 TB27

- **Reinforcement activity:** Say *Listen and write*. Say a word from the lesson. Students have to write the plural form, e.g., *child (children)*. Include: *mouse (mice), baby (babies), boy (boys), girl (girls), child (children), woman (women), fish (fish), man (men), frog (frogs)*.

- **Extension activity:** Teach students the following rhyme (or sing it to the tune of *Ten green bottles*):

Five green frogs,	*Where it's nice and cool.*
Sitting on a log.	*Then there are four*
Five green frogs,	*green frogs*
Sitting on a log.	*Sitting on a log!*
One jumps into the pool,	*Four green frogs …*

The number of frogs decreases in each verse until there are no frogs left (*Then there are no green and yellow frogs! Glug, glug, glug!*).

- **Home-school link:** Tell students to think about the people who live in their house. Ask *How many men? How many women? How many children? How many babies?* Write a list on the board as a model, e.g., *In my house: 2 women, 1 man, 3 children (2 girls, 1 boy).* Students write a similar list, with their parents' help, at home. In the next lesson they compare in pairs or small groups and explain who each person is (e.g., *Two women – my mom and my grandma. One man – my dad. Two girls – me and my sister. One baby – my brother.*)

Unit 2 TB28

- **Reinforcement activity:** Choose a volunteer and say *Find something small.* The student finds and names something small – either of their own belongings, or in the classroom near them and puts in on your desk, e.g., an eraser. Repeat with other students and the adjectives *big, beautiful, ugly* and *old* until you have about eight items on your desk. Ask students to name the items, (e.g., *It's an eraser. It's small. It's a book. It's beautiful,* etc.). Then say *Close your eyes.* Take an item away and say *Now open your eyes. What's missing?* Students look at the items on your desk and try to remember the missing one. Repeat the activity a few times.

- **Extension activity:** Give each student a blank piece of paper. Ask them to draw one of the pets from the unit (or another known animal, e.g., a snake or a spider) and color it a known color (or two colors). Tell students to draw their animal to show whether it is big or small/beautiful or ugly/happy or sad. Set a time limit for the drawing and coloring.

- Students work in pairs. Student A shows his/her picture and Student B makes two or three sentences about it, e.g., *It's a dog. It's big. It's happy. It's black and white.* Student A helps if necessary. Then they swap roles. Say *Change!* Students change partners (taking their pictures with them) and repeat the activity. Do this several times.

Unit 2 TB29

- **Reinforcement activity:** Draw or stick the following pictures on the board: an ugly spider or snake, two or more beautiful animals (e.g., birds, fish), some elephants or other big animals, two or more small animals (e.g., mice/frogs), a happy child/some happy children, a sad person, an old person/group of old people, a baby/some babies.

- Use homemade word cards of the eight adjectives (*big, small, happy, sad, old, young, ugly, beautiful*) to play a version of *Does it match?* (see page xv). Call eight students to the front instead of four. Ask questions with the words on the word cards, e.g., *Are they big?* not *Does it match?* Make sure students guess the describing words, not the animals names (e.g., *Young!* not *Babies!*).

- **Extension activity:** Draw three or four large circles and three or four rectangles (to be animal enclosures and tanks) on the board and say *Look! This is our pet store.* Ask students *Which animals are in our pet store?* Draw animals in each of the enclosures/tanks, according to students' suggestions, e.g., if a student says *Spiders!* ask more yes/no questions and draw what students decide, e.g., *OK. We have spiders. Juan Manuel, how many spiders? (Three.) Nieves, are they big? (Yes, they are.) Alba, are they ugly? (Yes, they are.) Iñigo, are they sad? (No, they aren't.)*

Unit 2 TB30

- **Reinforcement activity:** Students work in pairs. Student A puts five or six of his/her possessions on the desk, e.g., an eraser, a pen, a pencil, a book, a bag. He/She says what there is to Student A, e.g., *I have an eraser, a pen …* then Student A closes his/her eyes. Student B removes one of the items. Student A then opens his/her eyes and looks sad. Student B asks *Can I help?* Student B says *Yes, please. I can't find my* (the name of the object Student B removed). Student B "finds" it and gives it back. Student A says *Thank you!* Encourage Student B to reply *You're welcome!* Demonstrate the game with a volunteer first.

- **Extension activity:** Students work in groups to make a poster with the title *Be helpful!* Each group things of a way to be helpful at school (provide ideas, if necessary, e.g., *Share your things./Remember your books./Listen to the teacher./Help your friends./Clean up the classroom./ Don't shout out.*) They draw pictures to show their idea and write a caption (provide new language, as necessary). Display the posters around the class.

- **Home-school link:** Ask students to think of things they can do to be helpful at home. They make a list, with the help of their parents/carers. Elicit examples in the next class (e.g., cleaning their bedroom, making their bed, helping in the yard, playing with their younger brother/sister, helping to make breakfast).

Unit 2 TB31

- **Reinforcement activity:** Play *Sound bingo* (see page xviii) with the students writing words beginning with the sound /f/ in their bingo grid.

- **Extension activity:** Divide the class into two groups. Name them *Frogs* and *Vultures*. Tell the students to listen carefully. If they hear the sound for their group (/f/ for frogs and /v/ for vultures) they have to mime being the animal. If they don't hear it they do nothing. Say a list of words with the two sounds (they don't have to be words students know). Students respond by doing actions, in their groups. Possible words: *van, Friday, fat, viper, fast, foot, vote, visit, from, first, vow.*

Unit 2 TB32

- **Reinforcement activity:** Stick pictures of different kinds of animal food, forms of water and shelter animals might use on the board. Write the three headings water, shelter, food on the board. Invite volunteers to come to the board, choose a picture and put it under the correct heading, saying, e.g., *This is shelter.*
- **Extension activity:** Tell students to think of an animal they can name in English. They draw water, food and shelter for that animal (without drawing the animal). Students work in pairs. Student A shows his/her pictures, points and say *This is food, This is water, This is shelter.* Student B guesses the animal, e.g., *(Is it a) rabbit?* Then they swap roles.

Unit 2 TB33

- **Reinforcement activity:** Play *Categories* (see page xv) with the pet and people flashcards (and the headings *pets* and *people*). You could also play the game with the pet flashcards and pictures of wild animals (or flashcards from Level 1, Unit 8, 83–91), using the headings *pets* and *wild animals*.
- **Extension activity:** Describe animals for students to guess, using as much language from the unit as you can, for example, *This animal is a pet and a wild animal. It's small. It's ugly. It's green. It can jump. Its food is insects. Its shelter is water. (Frog.) This is a wild animal. It's big. It's beautiful. Its food is trees. It's black and white. It has a long, black tail. (Zebra.)* Students can repeat the activity in pairs.

Review Units 1 and 2 TB34

- **Reinforcement activity:** Make teams for a spelling game. Students play in teams of no more than five. Stick a selection of six to eight flashcards from the first three units on the board. Say *How do you spell these words? Write the words.* Students work together in their teams to write the words on a piece of paper. Make sure they keep their books closed. Set a time limit for the writing if you wish (e.g., two minutes). Teams swap their papers. Elicit the spellings by asking, e.g., *How do you spell train?* Students spell out the word letter by letter. Stick the word card on the board for confirmation or write the word. Teams get a point for each correct word. The team with the most correct spellings is the winner.
- **Extension activity:** Ask students questions from the Welcome unit to Unit 2, e.g., *How do you spell your name? Does your dad have a motorcycle? What's this/What are these? Is it a (mouse)? Are they (boys)? Is it (big)? Are they (happy)?* Then play *Test the teacher* (see page xviii), with students asking you these questions.

Review Units 1 and 2 TB35

- **Reinforcement activity:** Play *Stand in order* (see page xviii) with flashcards from the first three units.
- **Extension activity:** Students work in pairs. They both look at the game board on Student's Book page 35. Student A describes one of the things, people or animals on the board, e.g., *They're green and blue. They're on land. They aren't animals.* Student B says the color and number of the square and the name of the item (e.g., *Red, two – cars*). Student A says *Yes* or *No.* They can also keep score.

Unit 3 TB36

- **Reinforcement activity:** Play *Anagrams* (see page xiv) with the clothes words.
- **Extension activity:** Play *Reading race* (see page xviii) with the clothes flashcards.
- **Home-school link:** Students draw a picture of themselves wearing their favorite outfit. They label the items of clothing and/or write sentences, e.g., *These are my favorite pants. They're brown. I like this T-shirt. It's yellow and green.*

Unit 3 TB37

- **Reinforcement activity:** Students work in groups of three (A, B and C). Student A describes Student B's clothes, but making mistakes with the colors, e.g., *His pants are black. His T-shirt is green. His shoes are purple.* Student C corrects the mistakes, e.g., *His pants aren't black. They're blue. His T-shirt isn't green. It's red and blue. His shoes aren't purple. They're black.* Then they swap roles (e.g., Student B describes Student C's clothes and Student A corrects).
- **Extension activity:** Hand out clothes catalogs/magazines. Students find a picture they like, cut it out and stick it on a piece of paper. They talk about their pictures in pairs or write sentences describing the clothes, e.g., *Her skirt is green. It's long. Her jacket is brown.* Provide new vocabulary as necessary (e.g., *boots, top, shorts*).
- **Home-school link:** Students draw a picture or find a photograph of at least two people in their family, there must be at least one male and at least one female in the picture (e.g., their mom and dad or their brother and sister). They write sentences describing the colors of the clothes or talk about their pictures in the next lesson, e.g., *This is my dad. His jeans are blue. His jacket is black. His shoes are brown. This is my mom. Her skirt is purple. Her T-shirt is white. Her shoes are black.*

Unit 3 TB38

- **Reinforcement activity:** Play *Pass the ball* (see page xvii). When the music stops, choose a volunteer to ask the student with the ball *What are you wearing today?* The student describes what he/she is wearing in as much detail as he/she can (e.g., *I'm wearing a blue skirt and a purple and white T-shirt. I have a picture of a cat on the T-shirt. I'm wearing white socks. They're short. I'm wearing black shoes.*). Prompt with questions about color, length etc., if necessary.
- **Extension activity:** Show the flashcards and the homemade cards and ask *What's this?/What are these?* for each one. Then put the cards face down in three piles – one pile for T-shirts, jackets and dresses, one pile for skirts and pants, one pile for shoes and socks. Call a volunteer to the front. Say *Take three cards.* Show him/

her how to take a card from each pile. He/She sticks the cards on the board. Ask *What are you wearing today?* The student imagines he/she is wearing the cards on the board and says, e.g., *I'm wearing an orange T-shirt, purple pants and yellow socks.* Encourage him/her to say *I look great today!* Repeat with different volunteers.

If you have made sets of cards, students can play the same game in groups. Suggested cards (15 in each set): an orange jacket, a green T-shirt, a red T-shirt, a pink shirt, a green shirt, blue pants, pink pants, a purple skirt, a white skirt, a brown dress, a black dress, yellow socks, blue socks, purple shoes, orange shoes. Students can help color in the cards before they play.

Unit 3 TB39

- **Reinforcement activity:** Students work in pairs. They look at the picture on Student's Book page 38. Student A imagines he/she is one of the people in the picture. Student B has to guess who by asking yes/no questions about clothes, e.g., *Are you wearing a green skirt? (No, I'm not.) Are you wearing a white T-shirt? (No, I'm not). Are you wearing shoes? (No, I'm not). You're Ben!*
- **Extension activity:** Play a version of *Blindfold game* (see page xvi). The blindfolded student has to guess the name of the student he/she stops, as well as an item of clothing he/she is wearing (by asking, e.g., *Are you wearing black shoes?*).

Unit 3 TB40

- **Reinforcement activity:** Play *Match the pictures and words* (page xvi) with the clothes flashcards and word cards.
- **Extension activity:** Students draw a picture of themselves wearing a fancy dress costume. They write about what they are wearing in the picture (e.g., *I'm wearing a big hat, brown pants and a white shirt. I have a horse.*) and write about who they are (e.g., *I'm a cowboy*). Supply new language as necessary.
- **Home-school link**: Ask students to find a photograph of themselves or someone else in their family wearing a fancy dress costume. They write a description or talk about the costume in the next class.

Unit 3 TB41

- **Reinforcement activity:** Play *Listen and do* (see page xvi). Ask students to jump when they hear the sound /ʤ/. Example words: *just, giraffe, Gina, yes, young, grandma, jacket, jeans, great.*
- **Extension activity:** Prepare a selection of clothes (jackets, hats, skirts, boots) which make up fancy dress costumes (e.g., a pirate hat which goes with some pirate pants or a toy parrot, a fairy skirt with a matching top and hat, cowboy pants and a matching jacket). Hand out the items of clothing to different children around the class (one item each, not a complete costume). Call a student who has one item of clothing to the front. He/She shows the item, puts it on and says, e.g., *I'm wearing a hat.* He/She looks around the class for another

item to add to the costume. When he/she sees an item he/she wants, he/she says, e.g., *I don't have a pink skirt.* The student with the correct item offers to share it, saying *Here you are. You can use this one.* He/She brings the item to the front. The first student says *Thank you* and puts it on. Repeat with another student who has some clothes, until all the costumes are complete. Repeat the game, with different students, if time.

Unit 3 TB42

- **Reinforcement activity:** Play *Find something (red/plastic)* (see page xvi), using materials from the lesson and from Level 1 (wood/plastic/metal/glass). Students point to or pick up items and clothes in the classroom.
- **Extension activity:** Students look at their own clothes and think about what they are made from. They check the labels inside if necessary. Teach new materials (e.g., *nylon, acrylic*) as necessary. Students write a sentence about each item, e.g., *I'm wearing a cotton shirt. I'm wearing nylon pants. They're made of nylon. I'm wearing leather shoes.*
- **Home-school link:** Students bring an item of clothing made from one of the materials in the lesson to the next class. If possible, ask them to bring an item they/someone in their family wears on a special occasion (e.g., for dancing/for a regional feast day or as part of a traditional national costume). They show the item of clothing, say what it's called and what it's made of. Students can then draw pictures or take photographs of the items and make a class display.

Unit 3 TB43

- **Reinforcement activity:** Play a game of *Simon Says* (see page xviii), giving instructions with the clothes and material words (e.g., *Put on your jacket. Touch your T-shirt. Touch something made of cotton.*)
- **Extension activity:** Students play *Mirror game* (see page xvii) in pairs. Review parts of the body before they begin.

Unit 4 TB48

- **Reinforcement activity:** Play *Act and guess* (see page xiv). You/the students mime using one of the furnishing items (e.g., switching on a lamp, looking in a mirror, opening a closet and taking out an item of clothing on a hanger).
- **Extension activity:** Give students two minutes to look at and remember the picture on Student's Book page 48. Books closed. Divide the class into two or more teams. Ask questions to each team in turn, e.g., *Who's under the bed? (Tina) Where's Leo? (Under the couch) What color is the book on the table? (It's red.) What's on the bookcase? (The phone.) What's in the closet? (A red jacket.) Who has a video camera? (Ben.) Where's the TV? (On the cabinet.) What color is Tina's T-shirt? (Green.) Where's David? (In the cabinet.) What color is the mirror? (It's blue.)* Keep score on the board. The team with the most correct answers wins. Alternatively, students can play a similar game in pairs.

- **Home-school link:** Students draw a picture of their house/flat or bring a photograph to the next class. They show their pictures and talk about the different rooms in the house in pairs/small groups (e.g., *My house has a living room, a kitchen, a bathroom and three bedrooms. It has a yard. It doesn't have a balcony.*)

Unit 4 TB49

- **Reinforcement activity:** Play *Where's the (lamp)?* (see page xix).
- **Extension activity:** Play a version of *Describe and draw* (see page xv). Draw a simple bedroom on the board with a bed, table, cabinet (with one door open), closet (with one door open), chair and bookcase. Students copy the picture. Then tell students to choose five things and draw them in/on or under the furniture in the room. They can choose items from the unit (*phone, TV*, etc.) and/or other items they know in English (e.g., *book, pencil case, teddy bear, robot*). Note that when they describe what's in their picture to their partner, students need to say, e.g., *I have a teddy bear. It's on the bed.*
- **Home-school link:** Students draw a simple picture of their living room at home, showing the position of the phone, TV, bookcase, clock, mirror, table, couch, etc. as well as members of the family. They compare pictures in pairs in the next lesson and describe where things are (e.g., *My dad's on the couch.*). Alternatively, write a list of five items on the board (e.g., *mirror, TV, phone, toys, shoes*). Students copy the list and at home, find each item and write one or two sentences about where it is (e.g., *The mirror is in the hallway. The toys are in my bedroom. They're in the cabinet.*). Help with new language as necessary.

Unit 4 TB50

- **Reinforcement activity:** Choose a volunteer. He/She stands at the front and puts on a blindfold. Make true/false sentences about the position/color/number of items in the classroom, e.g., *There's a black lamp on the bookcase./There are five books on my table.* The blindfolded student has to remember and say *Yes* or *No*. When the student gets an answer wrong, he/she takes off the blindfold and swaps with a different volunteer. When students get the idea, the rest of the class can make the true/false sentences.
- **Extension activity:** Put six to eight objects (both singular and plural) in a bag. These can be items of clothing, pieces of food, toys, classroom objects or flashcards from Units 1 to 3. Take each thing out and show it to the class, making a sentence with *There's/There are*, e.g., *There's a ball in my bag. There are three pens in my bag.* Give students time to look at the items and then put them back in the bag. The students have to remember what's in the bag (you can also ask them the color/number), e.g., *There's an orange ball in your bag.* You can make this game competitive – students score a point when they guess correctly, you get a point if they make a wrong guess.

Unit 4 TB51

- **Reinforcement activity:** Play *Circle it!* (see page xv) with numbers between 1 and 20.
- **Extension activity:** Students work in pairs. Each student writes a list of ten numbers between 1 and 20. Student A then dictates his/her numbers for Student B to write (in figures, not words). They check to see how many Student B has written correctly. Then Student B dictates his/her numbers.

Unit 4 TB52

- **Reinforcement activity:** Play *Alphabetical order* (page xiv) with the furnishing words.
- **Extension activity:** Stick the flashcards for closet, cabinet and bookcase on the board, at a height your students can reach, but with plenty of space around each one. Have a selection of 8 to 10 flashcards or pictures ready of toys (e.g., teddy bear, doll, computer game, camera) and clothes (e.g., T-shirt, jacket, pants, skirt) and several pictures of books, comics and magazines.
- Show the flashcards and elicit the words. Teach *comic/magazine*, if necessary. Stick the words in a large group at the bottom of the board. Say *Look at these things. What a mess! Let's clean up.* Take one of the clothes flashcards and say, e.g., *Let's put the skirt in the closet.* Move the flashcard next to the closet. Invite volunteers to come forward one by one, choose a flashcard, move it and make a similar sentence, deciding whether to put the flashcard in the closet, cabinet or bookcase.
- **Home-school link:** Ask students to clean their bedroom at home and then draw pictures of their closet, cabinet and/or bookcase, showing the things inside. They can write sentences about what is in each place, e.g., *There are books in the bookcase. There's a jacket in the closet.*

Unit 4 TB53

- **Reinforcement activity:** Move your class into a large empty room. Make three or four teams and give them names, e.g., colors. Stick the flashcards of closet, cabinet and bookcase on three different walls of the room. Put a pile of real items in the center of the room (clothes, toys, books, magazines, etc.). Teams stand in lines at one side of the space, with one student at the front of each, ready to play. Say *What a mess! Let's clean up!* Encourage students to join in.

Give instructions to each team in turn, e.g., *Green team. Let's put a T-shirt in the closet.* The student at the front of the named team finds the item in the pile, picks it up and puts it in the correct place in the room (e.g., next to the wall with the closet flashcard). He/She repeats your sentence *Let's put …* at the same time. He/She gets a point for putting the correct item in the correct place. Continue in this way until all the items have been cleaned up. The team with the most points wins.

Alternatively, give an instruction to all the teams (e.g., *Let's put a T-shirt in the closet*), the students at the front of each team come to the pile of things at the same time and race to be the first to find the correct item and put it in the correct place. They score a point for their team if they are first.

- Extension activity: Play *Sound pairs* (see page xviii), using words with the sounds /j/, /dʒ/, /m/ and /n/ (e.g., *yak, yellow, juice, giraffe, mom, monkey, nine, nice*).

Unit 4 TB54

- **Reinforcement activity:** Play *Stand in order* (see page xviii) with ten number cards, each with a number from 11 to 20 on it (in figures). Say the numbers (together with the rest of the class) in ascending order from 11. Students with cards stand in order. Then mix the cards up and hand them to ten different students. Repeat, this time starting at 20 and saying the numbers in descending order. Students with cards stand in order. You can also call students with cards to stand forward, or hold up their card, e.g., *13, 15 and 17*.
- **Extension activity:** Draw a simple table on the board, with four columns, headed *streetlights, bus stops, mailboxes, traffic lights*. Students copy the table on a blank piece of paper. Give each student a clipboard, if possible. Take students out on a walk around their local area. They count how many of each item of street furniture they see and make a mark in the correct column of their table. When you return to class, elicit a total for each item (ask, e.g., *How many streetlights are there?*) and write them on the board for students to check. Students will use this information to make a bar chart in the next lesson.
- **Home-school link:** Students draw a picture or take a photograph of the street outside their house. They write the name of their street and label any items of street furniture. They talk about their pictures and write sentences in the next class, e.g., *There are three streetlights. There isn't a post box. There's a bus stop. It's green and white.* Help with new language as necessary.

Unit 4 TB55

- **Reinforcement activity:** Play *Bingo* (see page xiv), with numbers between 1 and 20 (students write the numbers as figures).
- **Extension activity:** Students play *Who has it?* (see page xix) with the furnishings flashcards or *Traffic lights* (see page xix), with students miming using the different pieces of furniture.

Review Units 3 and 4 TB56

- **Reinforcement activity:** Play *Tic-tac-toe* (see page xvii) with flashcards of word cards from Units 3 and 4.
- **Extension activity:** Play *Follow my instructions* (see page xvi) using the furniture and furnishings from Unit 4, as well as clothes from Unit 3 (e.g., *Put your jacket on the bookcase.*).

Review Units 3 and 4 TB57

- **Reinforcement activity:** Play *Memory pairs* (see page xvii) with a selection of flashcards and word cards from Units 3 and 4.
- **Extension activity:** Play *True or false* (see page xix), making sentences about what is in the classroom/school and what students are wearing, e.g., *There's a closet in the classroom. Fran is wearing a brown jacket.* Students can repeat the game in pairs or small groups.

Unit 5 TB60

- **Reinforcement activity:** Play *Class survey* (see page xv) using the food flashcards.
- **Extension activity:** Play *Pass the flashcards* (see page xvii). When the music stops, students with food flashcards say whether they like or dislike the item (e.g., *I don't like sausages.*).
- **Home-school link:** Draw a table with six columns and four rows. Tell students to write six foods from the lesson in columns 2 to 7 as column headings. Tell them to write *Me* in the second row of the table and then the names of two other people in their family in rows 3 and 4 (e.g., *My sister. My brother*). They complete the "Me" row of the table by checking the foods they like and putting an X for the foods they don't like. Then they complete rows 3 and 4 at home by asking the other two people whether they like each of the five foods in turn (e.g., *Do you like peas?*). They compare results in the next lesson. Help them to write sentences, e.g., *Three people in my family like peas.*

Unit 5 TB61

- **Reinforcement activity:** Ask students *What do you like for breakfast? What do you like for lunch? What do you like for dinner?* They write a sentence about each meal, e.g., *I like milk and cookies for breakfast. I like meat and rice for lunch. I like fish and bread for dinner.* Circulate and help with new language.
- **Extension activity:** Play *Reading race* (see page xviii). Use sentences including food and meals, e.g., *I like carrots for lunch. I don't like cereal for breakfast.*
- **Home-school link:** Students keep a note of what they eat for the three main meals in one day at the weekend (e.g., Sunday). They write notes, e.g., *breakfast: orange juice, cereal, milk; lunch: bread, soup, banana; dinner: potatoes, chicken, beans, orange.* They use their notes to draw pictures of what they ate at each meal. They can either draw pictures of three plates at home, or hand out three paper plates to each student and have them draw the food onto the plates. They label the foods. You can use the plates to make a classroom display with three sections. The display can have a large heading *What we like for …* and smaller headings for the three sections: *breakfast, lunch, dinner*.

Unit 5 TB62

- **Reinforcement activity:** Draw a picture of a friend of yours on the board or show a photograph. Talk about what the friend is wearing in the photograph and his/her likes and dislikes, e.g., *This is Cristina. She's wearing a green skirt. She likes One Direction. She likes cereal for breakfast. She doesn't like meat.* Students describe a friend of theirs in the same way, in pairs.

- **Extension activity:** Using the information from the pairwork in Student's Book Activity 8, students draw a Venn diagram (two overlapping circles) showing how their own food tastes overlap with those of their friend. On the left they draw a picture of themselves inside a circle, with pictures of the foods only they like. On the right they draw a picture of their friend, with a circle which overlaps with the first circle. In the left part of the circle the draw the foods only their friend likes. In the central space, where the circles overlap, they draw food both they and their friend like. Below the diagram they write sentences, e.g., *I like potatoes. José Luís doesn't like potatoes. I like peas. José Luís doesn't like peas. He likes meat. I don't like meat.*

  Help students to write about the foods they both like by writing a model sentence on the board, e.g., *We both like rice and beans.*

- **Home-school link:** Students write about what a member of their family likes to eat for each meal and two things they dislike, e.g., *My dad likes toast and coffee for breakfast. He doesn't like milk. He likes fish and rice for lunch. He doesn't like potatoes. He likes meat and pasta for dinner.* At the end of the next class, students can work in pairs and ask each other about the person they wrote about, e.g., *What does your dad like for breakfast/lunch/dinner? Does he like (toast) for breakfast?*

Unit 5 TB63

- **Reinforcement activity:** Students work in pairs. They take turns asking questions about members of their family's likes and dislikes, e.g., *Does your brother like meat? Does your dad like peas?*

- **Extension activity:** Hand out the unit flashcards at random. Students with flashcards stand up, show them to the class and say whether they like or dislike the food, e.g., *I don't like sausages.* Tell the students with flashcards to show a "thumbs up" if they said they like the food and thumbs down if they said they don't like it. Give students two minutes to look at the flashcards and remember who likes which food. Then the students with flashcards put their hands down.

  Ask the class about one of the students with a flashcard, e.g., *Does Nina like sausages?* Students say, *Yes, she does* or *No, she doesn't.* The student with the flashcard confirms by saying *That's right. I don't like sausages* and gives the flashcard back to you or says *No. That's wrong,* and keeps the flashcard.

  When students have the idea, repeat, but this time students with flashcards hide their cards after they have spoken about them. Volunteers can try to say where all the cards are and whether the students like or dislike the foods by making sentences, e.g., *Nina doesn't like sausages. Renata likes bread.* etc. You can make the game competitive by giving a point for each correct sentence or guess.

Unit 5 TB64

- **Reinforcement activity:** Stick pictures of healthy and unhealthy foods on the board. Elicit the words. Label any new items (e.g., *cookies, chips*). Draw a table with two columns on the board, the first column headed *healthy* and the second *unhealthy*. Students copy the table in their notebooks. Then they work in pairs to decide which foods are healthy and which are unhealthy and write the names of the foods in their table. Elicit answers and move the pictures on the board into the two groups.

- **Extension activity:** Draw two large plates on the board, one with the heading *healthy food* and one with the heading *unhealthy food*. Students copy the plates in their notebooks. Tell them the plates need to be large enough to write four or five words inside. Dictate a series of eight to ten foods, around half healthy and half unhealthy, e.g., *oranges, apples, cake, cereal, hamburger, peas, cola, carrots.* Students write each word on the correct plate (in pencil). They compare answers in pairs. Elicit the words in their groups and write them on the board for students to check their answers and spelling.

Unit 5 TB65

- **Reinforcement activity:** Play *Listen and do* (see page xvi). If students hear a word with the sound /z/ they lie down or sit with their heads on their desks, being *lazy*. If they hear a word with the sound /s/ they *stand* up. Possible words: *snake, seven, zoo, zip, swim, Zorro, see, sun, zap, swim.*

- **Extension activity:** Play *Messages* (see page xvii) with students writing offers on the slips of paper (e.g., *Would you like (sausages) for breakfast?*).

Unit 5 TB66

- **Reinforcement activity:** If possible, move your class to a larger space. Give out food flashcards from Levels 1 and 2 and / or pictures of food at random, so that each student in the class has a picture or a flashcard (some foods can be repeated). Write the five food groups: *fruit, vegetables, meat and fish, dairy, grains and cereal* on the board. Students look at their card and work out which food group they belong in. Tell students to find other members of the same food group and then all stand together. Circulate and help. When students are in their five groups, give instructions to each group in turn, e.g., *Fruit, touch your head! Meat and fish, jump!*

- **Extension activity:** Draw a food pyramid on the board, as shown below:

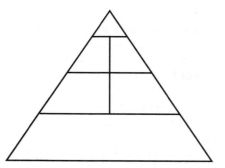

Number the sections 1 to 6, from top to bottom. Write the food groups *dairy, grains and cereals, sugars, meat, fruit, vegetables* on the board. Explain the meaning of sugars and ask students which part of the pyramid shows sugar and why (number 1 – the top section, because we need less food with sugar than any other kind of food). Students guess which numbered sections represent the other food groups (make sure they understand how the diagram works – the largest section at the bottom shows the kind of food we need to eat lots of). Discuss with the class and number the sections on the board, then label them with the group names. Students can copy the diagram in their notebooks.

Key: 1 sugars, 2 dairy, 3 meat, 4 fruit, 5 vegetables, 6 grains and cereals

- **Home-school link:** Students write the names of the five food groups in a column in their notebooks (*fruit, vegetables, meat, grains, dairy*). They find an example of each kind of food at home (not a food they have already learned in class), find out the name in English, if they can, and write it next to the food group name in their notebook. If they can't find the English word they write the word in L1. Students compare the foods they found in the next lesson. Provide new language as necessary.

Unit 5 TB67

- **Reinforcement activity:** Play *Categories* (see page xv) with the food flashcards and extra pictures of foods from the different groups. The category headings will be the names of the food groups.
- **Extension activity:** Play *Can I have?* (see page xv), with the food flashcards, either using the names of the foods (e.g., *Can I have some toast, please?*) or the names of food groups (e.g., *Can I have a vegetable, please?*)

Unit 6 TB70

- **Reinforcement activity:** Play *Act and guess* (see page xiv) using the activity flashcards.
- **Extension activity:** Play *Action treasure hunt* (see page xiv) with the new activities from the lesson and, if appropriate, actions from *Guess What! Level 1* (*paint, draw, run, jump, sing, climb, swim, ride a bike, play soccer, dance*).
- **Home-school link:** Students write a list of four or five people in their family in a column in their notebooks (e.g., *my dad, my mom, my brother, my cousin*). They

write an activity the person can do next to each name. In the next class, help students make sentences about each person, e.g., *My mom can ride a horse. My dad can play soccer.*

Unit 6 TB71

- **Reinforcement activity:** Play *Last one standing* (see page xvi), making sentences with *I can/can't* … Students who agree (i.e., they can or can't do the same thing as you) stay standing. Those who don't agree sit down. Ask the students who are sitting down and standing up *Can you (roller-skate)? (Yes, I can./No, I can't.)* to check they have responded in the correct way.
- **Extension activity:** Give each student a piece of paper and tell them to draw a line down the center to divide it into two sections. In the left section, students draw a picture of the equipment they need to do their favorite activity/an activity they are good at. They write a caption with *I can* … (e.g., *I can play basketball.*). In the right section, students draw equipment for an activity they can't do. They write a caption with *I can't* … (e.g., *I can't ride a horse*). They compare their pictures in pairs. If you wish, encourage students to respond to their partner's pictures by saying *Me, too* or *Me, neither.*
- **Home-school link:** Draw a table on the board as shown below:

Activities	me		
play soccer			
dance			
roller-skate			
ride a bike			
ride a horse			
swim			

Students copy the table and write the names of two members of their family at the top of columns 3 and 4. They complete column 2 with checks and Xs to show what they can/can't do. Ask them to complete the rest of the table by asking their relatives *Can you (play soccer)?* In the next lesson they compare their tables in pairs/small groups.

Unit 6 TB72

- **Reinforcement activity:** Students work in pairs. Student A Students describes a member of their family to a partner, talking about what the person likes to eat and what he/she likes doing. Student B draws pictures of the food and the equipment needed to do the activities the person likes. Then they swap over.
- **Extension activity:** Play a version of *Who has it?* (see page xix). Students with flashcards make a sentence with I like/don't like and the activity on the card (e.g., I like taking photographs.) The rest of the class have to remember who has which flashcard and whether they like the activity or not. You/the students guess by saying, e.g., *Alessandra likes taking photographs.*
- **Home-school link:** Students choose one member of their family and write about the things he/she likes/doesn't

like doing, e.g., *My brother Lucas likes playing computer games and roller-skating. He doesn't like playing basketball. He likes riding his bike and playing soccer.* They can also draw a picture of the person or include a photograph.

Unit 6 TB73

- **Reinforcement activity:** Students play *Find a partner* (see page xv). They start by writing a sentence about something they like doing (e.g., *I like roller-skating*). They find a partner by asking around the class *Do you like roller-skating?* When they have found a partner they stand together. Check by eliciting sentences from one of the students in the pair, e.g., *I like roller-skating and Ruslan likes roller-skating, too.*

- **Extension activity:** Students work in pairs. In secret, they write four sentences about what they think their partner likes/doesn't like doing, e.g., *Carolina likes playing tennis. She likes taking photographs. She doesn't like playing field hockey. She doesn't like dancing.* Then they take turns asking each other questions to find out if they have written the correct information, e.g., *Do you like playing tennis? Do you like taking photographs?* They check sentences which are correct and put an X next to sentences which are incorrect. Then they compare. Find out who knows their partner best – did any students get four checks? Elicit example sentences and interesting information from volunteers about their partner.

Unit 6 TB74

- **Reinforcement activity:** Students work in pairs or small groups. Show a series of balls used for different sports (e.g., a basketball ball, a soccer, a tennis ball, a baseball ball, a rugby ball, a table tennis ball, a field hockey ball, a volleyball ball), for each ball say, e.g., *This is ball number 1.* Students guess the name of the sport the ball is used for. They confer in their pairs/groups and write the answer down but don't say it. You could write the name of the sports on the board in random order for students to choose from. At the end of the game, elicit the sport for each ball. Students check their answer. See if any pairs/groups guessed all the sports correctly.

- **Extension activity:** Play *Whisper down the line* (see page xix) with the activity words and/or phrases from the story. Make sure students play nicely and say *That's not fair!* or *Play nicely.* during the game, when appropriate. Encourage the losing teams to say *Good job!* to the winners at the end.

- **Home-school link:** Students draw a picture or find a picture of their favorite sports team (if they don't have a favorite team, they choose a team liked by a member of their family). They write two sentences about the name of the team, the sport they play and what they wear, e.g., *My favorite soccer team is Spartak Moscow. They have red and white shirts.*

Unit 6 TB75

- **Reinforcement activity:** Play *Sound bingo* (see page xviii). Students write four words with the sound /k/ (spelled either with a "c", a "k" or both letters together). Read a list of words spelled with "c" and "k", but mix in some words in which these letters make a different sound, (e.g., *cheese, cereal, know*).

- **Extension activity:** Play *Word race* (see page xx) with words with the letters "c" and "k", e.g., *kitchen, snake, climb, field hockey, truck, jacket, socks, bookcase, rice, kite*.

Unit 6 TB76

- **Reinforcement activity:** Describe a sport or activity, e.g., *It's a team sport. You need a ball. You don't need sticks or a bat. There are eleven players in team. You can't touch the ball. (soccer)* Students guess the sport. You can make the game competitive by making teams and giving four points if a team guess after the first clue, three points if they guess after the second clue, and so on.

- **Other examples:** *You can play this sport with two people or four people. You need a racket and a ball. (tennis) One person can do this activity. You don't need a racket or a ball. You need a kind of transportation. You don't need an animal. You need a bike. (ride a bike) One person can do this activity. You don't need a ball. You need special clothes. You need a hat. You need water. (swimming)*

- **Extension activity:** Students play *Me, too!* (see page xvi) in pairs. Tell them to include sentences about activities they like/dislike doing (e.g., *I like playing field hockey. I don't like roller-skating.*). After they have found out what they have in common, call on volunteers to tell you about their partner, e.g., *Melinda likes playing field hockey. Me, too!*

- **Home-school link:** Students draw pictures or make a list of the sports equipment they/their family have at home. They compare in pairs or small groups in the next lesson. Provide new vocabulary, as necessary.

Unit 6 TB77

- **Reinforcement activity:** Play *Pass the actions* (see page xvii) with the activity word cards and word cards from Level 1 Unit 7.

- **Extension activity:** Play the *Yes/No* game (see page xx) with the activities from the unit and from Level 1. Students can ask you questions with *like*, e.g., *Do you like (basketball)?* or questions about the teams and equipment needed for an activity, e.g., *Do you need a racket?/Is it a team sport?*

Review Units 5 and 6 TB78

- **Reinforcement activity:** Play *Memory 1 through 10* (see page xvii) with a selection of flashcards from Units 5 and 6.

- **Extension activity:** Play *Class survey* (see page xv) with the activities flashcards from Unit 6. You can either carry out a survey of the class, with you asking the questions (e.g., *Do you like playing baseball?*) or students can work in groups and do their own survey of their friends, using a table to record the answers. After the survey, ask questions about the results, e.g., *How many children like playing baseball? What's our favorite activity?*

Review Units 5 and 6 TB79

- **Reinforcement activity:** Play *Categories* (see page xv) with flashcards or word cards from Units 1 to 6.
- **Extension activity:** Students work in pairs with someone they don't usually work with. They write four sentences they guess are true about what their partner likes/doesn't like to eat/doing (e.g., *Ainhoa likes fish. She doesn't like peas. Ainhoa likes playing basketball. She doesn't like playing tennis.*) Then they ask their partner questions to find out whether they guessed correctly, e.g., *Do you like fish/playing basketball, Ainhoa?* They check the sentences which were true. Circulate and ask students to feed back (e.g., *Ainhoa doesn't like fish. She doesn't like peas.*)

Unit 7 TB82

- **Reinforcement activity:** Play *What's missing?* (see page xix) using the flashcards.
- **Extension activity:** Play *Alphabetical order* (see page xiv) with the town words. Students may need to work in pairs, as they need to look at the second letter in some of the words to be able to put them in order correctly (e.g., *school, street, supermarket*).
- **Home-school link:** Students draw a picture or take a photograph of their favorite place in their hometown. They write one or two sentences, e.g., *My favorite place in* (name of town) *is the toy store. It's in* (name) *street.* They compare pictures in the next lesson and read their sentences in small groups. You can also use their work to make a class display with the title *Our favorite places.*

Unit 7 TB83

- **Reinforcement activity:** Students play *I can see* (see page xvi) in pairs, using the large picture on Student's Book page 82.
- **Extension activity:** Play *Anagrams* (see page xiv) with the town words.
- **Home-school link:** Students choose a person in their family. They draw a picture of that person in their favorite place in town. They compare pictures in the next lesson and say, e.g., *This is my brother. He's in the movie theater.*

Unit 7 TB84

- **Reinforcement activity:** Draw a horizontal line on the board to represent a street. Check four or five flashcards of places along the line (e.g., clothing store, bookstore, café, supermarket). Stick three or four more flashcards behind the places, (e.g., park, school, movie theater), making sure the positions of the second group of flashcards show *behind/in front of*. Point to the flashcards and elicit sentences about where things are, e.g., *The clothing store is next to the bookstore. The café is between the bookstore and the supermarket. The park is behind the supermarket.* Then make false sentences (e.g., *The school is next to the clothing store*). Students correct you (e.g., *No, it isn't. The school is in front of the park.*)

- **Extension activity:** Students work in pairs. Student A makes a sentence about the position of two or three places in their hometown, e.g., *The ABC movie theater is between the café and the supermarket.* Student B says *True* or *False*. He/She corrects the false sentences. Then they swap roles.
- **Home-school link:** Students choose a famous or favorite place in their town and draw a simple map to show which buildings/places are next to/in front of/behind it. Then they write two sentences, e.g., *This is an old bookstore in my town. It's next to a café.*

Unit 7 TB85

- **Reinforcement activity:** Students work in pairs. Student A looks at the picture on Student's Book page 82. Student B keeps his/her book closed. Student A asks a question with *Is there … ?* e.g., *Is there a café next to the supermarket?* Student B tries to remember and answers *Yes, there is/ No, there isn't.* Then they swap roles. They can make the game competitive by keeping score.
- **Extension activity:** Give each student two pieces of blank paper. Draw a simple pictorial map on the board, in the same style as the map on Student's Book page 85 (a street at the bottom of the map with two other streets behind this main street). Draw places on the map. Students copy the basic map, but add places where they wish. Circulate and help/check. Students work in pairs to play *Describe and draw* (see page xv) with their pictures. They ask questions to help in the drawing phase, e.g., *Is there a playground behind the school? Is there a bookstore? Where is it?*

Unit 7 TB86

- **Reinforcement activity:** Move your class to a large space (e.g., an empty classroom). Stick flashcards of five or six places in town on the walls on opposite sides of the room (e.g., three on one wall, two on the opposite wall). If possible, stick some black and white stripes made of cardboard on the floor (or draw stripes) to make a crosswalk from one side of the room to the other.
- Students stand at one end of the space, next to each other or in one or more rows, so that everyone can walk around easily. Give instructions, e.g., *Let's go to the supermarket. Stop! Let's go to the crosswalk. Stop! Press the button. Wait for the green man! The man is green. Is it safe? Look right and left. It's safe now! Let's cross. … Let's go to the movie theater. Get the tickets… .* Students move around, following your instructions/miming as if they were walking around an imaginary town. Get them to cross from side to side of the room, using the crosswalk each time.
- **Extension activity:** Students draw two pictures of a typical light from a crosswalk in their country – one showing the light when they have to wait (e.g., a red light/a person standing still) and one showing the light when they can walk (e.g., a green light/a person

walking). They write captions: for the first light *Be careful!/You need to wait*, and for the second light *It's safe now./Let's cross*. You can make a class display of the pictures, with the title *Be safe!*

Unit 7 TB87

- **Reinforcement activity:** Teach students the tongue twisters *A quick kiss* and *Six boxes*. Students practice saying them in pairs, as fast as they can.
- Extension activity: Play *Match the pictures and the words* (see page xvi) with the unit flashcards and word cards.

Unit 7 TB88

- **Reinforcement activity:** Play *Circle it!* (see page xv) with the flashcards and pictures of a police station, fire station, sports center and hospital (if available).
- **Extension activity:** Give each student a piece of paper with two grids of 15 squares, lettered A to E along the bottom and 1 to 3 along the left-hand side (like the grid on Student's Book page 89). Write a list of places from the unit on the board. Students work in pairs. They decide where to put the places on the board in their grid, and write the name of the place or draw a picture in each square, e.g., in A1 they draw an X to represent the hospital.

  Students then work in groups of four (two pairs together). They take turns saying where they put the places on the map, e.g., First pair of students: *We have the school in B7.* Second pair of students: *We have the school in C3.* Each pair uses the second (blank) grid to draw the positions of the other pairs' buildings/places. Circulate and help/check. See if any of the pairs' buildings are in the same place.

Unit 7 TB89

- **Reinforcement activity:** Play *Question tic-tac-toe* (see page xviii), encouraging students to ask different kinds of question from the unit (e.g., *Where's the toy store?/Is there a toy store?/Is there a toy store behind the school?*)
- **Extension activity:** Students make a video about their hometown, similar to the one the characters were making on Student's Book page 82. Assign places to each pair/group of students (e.g., the hospital, the police station, the park, a café). They think about where their place is (which street it is in and what is next to/behind/in front of it) and any interesting fact they would like to say. Circulate and help with language. Tell students to imagine they are introducing the place to a tourist and write a short script, e.g., *This is the park. It's in King Street. It's next to the station. I love roller-skating here with my friends.* Encourage them to memorize the script, taking turns to say the lines.

  Film the pairs/groups in turn, if possible standing in front of or holding a picture/photograph of their place. You could show the resulting "tour" of the students' hometown to the students' parents/another class at your school.

Unit 8 TB92

- **Reinforcement activity:** Play *Drawing game* (see page xv), with the animals and places from the lesson.
- **Extension activity:** Play *Bingo* (see page xiv) with the farm words.

Unit 8 TB93

- **Reinforcement activity:** Play *Word race* (see page xx) with the farm word cards.
- **Extension activity:** Students play a memory game using the picture on Student's Book page 92. They work in pairs. Student A looks at the picture and asks, e.g., *Where's Ben?* Student B has his/her book closed and tries to remember (e.g., *He's next to the barn.*) Then they swap roles. They can also ask about numbers (e.g., *How many ducks are there?*) and colors (e.g., *What color is the cow?*). They can make the game competitive by scoring a point for each correct answer.
- **Home-school link:** Students think about the question *What farm animals are there in your country?* at home (they can ask parents/carers). Ask them to draw a picture or find a photograph of a farm animal from their country and write the name. Use the pictures to make a class poster in the next lesson, with the title *Farm animals in* (name of students' home country).

Unit 8 TB94

- **Reinforcement activity:** Play *True or false* (see page xix) with the photographs in Student's Book page 94 Activity 8 (e.g., *The goat is sleeping. (false) The duck is swimming. (true)*). Students can repeat the game in pairs.
- **Extension activity:** Play *Action treasure hunt* (see page xiv) with verbs from the lesson and activities from Unit 6. Encourage students to describe what others are doing using the present continuous, e.g., *He's sleeping.*
- **Home-school link:** Students find a photograph of an animal (if possible their family pet). They write two sentences, e.g., *This is my cat. It's sleeping.* They compare pictures in pairs or small groups in the next lesson and ask each other *What's that? What's it doing?*

Unit 8 TB95

- **Reinforcement activity:** Call six volunteers to the front of the class. Hand each volunteer a slip of paper with an action on it (e.g., *run*). Use actions from this unit (*run, jump, swim, eat, sleep*) and from Level 1 and Unit 6: *paint, draw, climb, ride a bike/horse, play soccer/tennis/basketball/ field hockey, dance, take photographs, fly a kite, roller-skate*). The volunteers all mime their actions at the same time. Ask the rest of the class questions about what they are doing, e.g., *Is Emma running? (Yes, she is./No, she isn't.)* Repeat with six different volunteers and new actions.
- **Extension activity:** Call six volunteers to the front of the class and give each one a farm animal flashcard. The volunteers look at the cards but don't show the rest of the class. If possible, tape the flashcards to the

volunteers' backs. Then tell each volunteer to mime doing an action their animal might do, e.g., if they have donkey, they mime running. The rest of the class guess the animal and the action for each student by asking, e.g., *Is the donkey running?* When they guess correctly the volunteer turns to show the flashcard and says *Yes, it is.*

Unit 8 TB96

- **Reinforcement activity:** Ask students to look through all the episodes of the story in the book. They work in pairs to choose their favorite episode and their favorite picture from that story. They practice saying the dialog for their favorite picture and try to memorize it. Ask volunteer pairs to perform their dialog for the class.

- **Extension activity:** Ask students to draw a picture of their home. It can be the outside of their home or their favorite room inside. They can write two or three sentences about what they like best about their home, e.g., *I love my home. This is my favorite room. It's the kitchen.*

Unit 8 TB97

- **Reinforcement activity:** Play *Sound bingo* (see page xviii). Students write four words with starting with *w* or *wh*.

- **Extension activity:** Play *Pass the ball* (see page xvii). When the music stops, the student with the ball has to invite the person next to him/her to a party (*Would you like to come to a party?*) The student replies *Yes, please/ thanks. I'd love to.*

Unit 8 TB98

- **Reinforcement activity:** Play *The last word* (see page xviii) with sentences about what farmers do, e.g., *A farmer drives a … (tractor). A farmer turns the … (soil). A farmer plants … (seeds). A farmer waters … (plants). A farmer harvests … (plants). A farmer feeds the … (chickens/animals). A farmer milks the … (cows). A farmer rides a … (horse).* Students can play the same game in pairs, with one student looking at the sentences on Workbook page 80 and the other with his/her book closed.

- **Extension activity:** Tell students to imagine they are farmers. Write the following questions on the board for them to copy and answer:

  1 What's your name?   Farmer _____
  2 How old are you?   I'm _____
  3 Where is your farm?   My farm is _____
  4 What animals or plants
     do you have?   I have _____
  5 What do you like doing
     on the farm?   I like _____ing _____

Students can also draw a picture of themselves doing one of the jobs a farmer does. Help students write a sentence in the present progressive describing what they are doing in the picture (e.g., *I'm feeding the chickens./ I'm driving the tractor.*)

Unit 8 TB99

- **Reinforcement activity:** Play *Odd one out* (see page xvii), with groups of flashcards from the course (suggestions: *cow, baby, horse, sheep (baby – It isn't a farm animal.), boat, motorcycle, bus, car (boat – Boats are on water, not the street.), pants, shoes, jacket, skirt (skirt – Men don't wear skirts.), clothing store, movie theater, barn, supermarket (barn – It isn't in town.), potatoes, carrots, beans, fish (fish – It isn't a vegetable./ Farmers don't grow it.), dog, cat, cow, mouse (sheep – It isn't a pet/It's big.)*)

- **Extension activity:** Tell students to think about what a farmer does in a normal day and the order he does things. Brainstorm and write some phrases on the board to help, e.g., *eat breakfast, milk the cows, feed the chickens, take care of the cows, eat lunch, drive the tractor, turn the soil, go home, eat dinner.* Assign one of the phrases to each student/pair of students and ask them to draw a picture and write a caption, e.g., *The farmer eats breakfast.* Circulate and help with language (students will need to use the third person). Use the pictures to make a class poster about a farmer's day, with the title *A day on the farm.* If you wish, add a picture of the rising sun near the morning activities, a sun at the top of the sky for afternoon jobs and a setting sun at the end of the day, to show that the farmer's day is in line with the rhythms of nature.

Review Units 7 and 8 TB100

- **Reinforcement activity:** Play *Jigsaw matching* (see page xvi) with pictures of items from all units of *Guess What!* Level 2.

- **Extension activity:** Play *Messages* (see page xvii). Tell students to write a factual question (e.g., *Is there a café next to the movie theater? Do you like cows? What are you wearing? How many table are there in the classroom?*) or an invitation/request (e.g., *Would you like to come to a party? Would you like some juice?*)

Review Units 7 and 8 TB101

- **Reinforcement activity:** Play *Stand up and sit down* (see page xviii), making sentences from Units 1 to 8 or *Sound pairs* (see page xviii), revising sounds from Units 1 to 8.

- **Extension activity:** *End of course quiz.* In groups, students make up questions for another group or the rest of the class to answer. Encourage them to use different question kinds from all units of *Guess What!* Level 2.

Guess What! Level 2 Video

Introduction

Before the video

- Use the opening question on the first CLIL page in the Student's Book and activity 1 on the second page to discuss what students already know about the topic and teach new key CLIL vocabulary.
- Ask students to guess what the video is going to be about.

During the video

- Play the whole video in the first instance. Students watch to see if they've guessed correctly what some or all of the video is going to be about.
- Congratulate any students who guessed the content of the video correctly.
- Then play the video again, this time encouraging students to interact with the video more fully, using one of the following techniques:
  - Pause the video to ask questions or elicit new vocabulary.
  - Show the video with the sound off, pausing for students to guess what the presenter is saying.
  - Use homemade flashcards of the CLIL vocabulary shown in the audio and ask students to put them in order.
  - Write questions on the board for students to answer while they are watching.

After the video

- Check students' answers to any questions you have asked.
- Then use activity 3 in the Student's Book for students to reinforce understanding of the CLIL question. The project provides an opportunity for students to produce their ideas about the CLIL topic in words and pictures. There is further practice provided in the Workbook.

Hello again!

Unit Topic: Hello again!

Topic: Art – kinds of art

Question: What kind of art is it?

Learning objective: Children should:
- be able to identify 4 different kinds of art
- understand that we can use different techniques in art work

Video 00

Hi. Welcome to *Guess What!*
Today we're asking,
What kind of art is it?
Let's find out.

drawing

This kind of art is called drawing.
People draw with pencils.
People draw with colored pencils,
and people draw with pens, too.

painting

Look at this kind of art. It's called painting.
Painting is fun! Artists paint with different kinds of paints.
Painters paint on wood,
and painters paint on windows, too.
Look! Face painting!

photography

Photography is a kind of art, too.
People take photographs with a camera.
Some photographs are black and white.
Look at this photographer.
Look at her photograph.
Now, look at this photographer.
Look at his photograph.
Some photographs are in color.
Look at this photographer.
Look at his photograph.
Now, look at this photographer.
Look at his photograph.

sculpture

This kind of art is called sculpture. Look at these two animal sculptures!
We can make sculptures from a lot of different materials.
Look at this sculpture. The material is wood.
And the material of this sculpture is metal.
Look at this sculpture. It's a sand sculpture,
and this is an ice sculpture.

What do you know?

What kind of art is it?
It's a painting.
It's a drawing.
It's a sculpture.

Good job!

See you next time on *Guess What!* Bye!

Unit 1

Unit Topic: Transportation

Topic: Science – kinds of transportation

Question: Where is the transportation?

Learning objective: Children should:
• be able to identify 3 places transportation goes
• understand that transportation moves on land, on water, and in the air

Video 01

Hi again. Welcome back to *Guess What!*
Today we're asking,
Where's the transportation?
Let's find out.

on land

These kinds of transportation are on land.
Look at the bus,
the long train,
the bicycles,
and the trucks and cars.
Look at all the different kinds of transportation on land.
Can you see the motorcycles and cars?

on water

These kinds of transportation are on water.
Look at the big ship in the ocean,
the small boats on the canal,
and the boats on the river.
And look! This boat is like a bus on water! It's called a ferry.

in the air

These kinds of transportation are in the air.
Look at this helicopter. It's in the air.
This helicopter is in the air, too. It's above the trees.
Look at this plane. It's big. Now, it's in the air.
And look at this plane. It's small. It's on water!
Now it's in the air.

What do you know?

Where's the transportation?
It's on water.
It's on land.
It's in the air.

Good job!

See you next time on *Guess What!* Bye!

Unit 2

Unit Topic: Pets

Topic: Science – needs of animals

Question: What do animals need?

Learning objective: Children should:
• be able to identify 3 basic needs of living things - animals
• understand that animals need water, food, and shelter as basic needs

Video 02

Hi again. Welcome back to *Guess What!*
Today we're asking,
What do animals need?
Let's find out.

water

All animals need water.
Look at these zebras. They all have water.
The cow has water, too.
Look at these small birds. They need water.
The cats need water, too.

food

All animals need food.
Look at the elephant. It has food.
Look at the monkey. It has food, too.
Look at the sheep. It needs food.
Look at the small birds. They need food, too.

shelter

All animals need shelter.
Big animals need shelter. Look at the lion. It has shelter.
And the sheep have shelter, too.
Small animals need shelter. Look! The frog has shelter.
The rabbits need shelter, too.

What do you know?

What do animals need?
They need water.
They need food.
They need shelter.

Good job!

See you next time on *Guess What!* Bye!

Unit 3

Unit Topic: Clothes

Topic: Science – kinds of materials for clothes

Question: What are clothes made of?

Learning objective: Children should:
- be able to identify 4 different kinds of materials for clothes
- understand that we can use different materials for making clothes

Video 03

Hi again. Welcome back to *Guess What!*
Today we're asking,
What are clothes made of?
Let's find out.

cotton

Some clothes are made of cotton.
Cotton is a plant.
Look at the men! They're making cotton fabric for clothes.
Look. This baby is wearing a cotton dress.
And the boy and the girl are wearing cotton pants and T-shirts.

silk

Some clothes are made of silk.
Silkworms make silk.
The woman is making silk fabric for clothes.
Silk is beautiful. Look. The men are wearing silk pants and shirts.
And this man is wearing a silk jacket.

wool

Some clothes are made of wool.
Wool is from animals, like sheep.
Look at this woman. She's making a wool sweater.
We wear clothes made of wool in cold places.
This woman is wearing a sweater. It's made of wool.
And this woman is wearing socks. They're made of wool, too.

leather

Some clothes are made of leather.
Leather is from animals, like cows.
Look! The machine is painting the leather.
And this woman is cutting the leather for a jacket.
Look! This boy is wearing a leather jacket,
and this woman is wearing leather shoes.

What do you know?

What are clothes made of?

wool.
leather.
cotton.

Good job!

See you next time on *Guess What!* Bye!

Unit 4

Unit Topic: Rooms

Topic: Math – counting and interpreting data on a bar chart

Question: How many are there?

Learning objective: Children should:
- be able to use the math symbols + and - then add and subtract numbers between 0 and 20
- understand that + means add and - means minus

Video 04

Hi again. Welcome back to *Guess What!*
Today we're asking,
How many are there?
Let's find out.

This is a bar chart.

streetlights

There are many kinds of streetlights.
Some streetlights are modern,
and some streetlights are not modern.
Lots of streetlights. How many are there?
Fourteen.
Look how we show the number of streetlights in a bar chart!
Fourteen streetlights.

bus stops

There are many kinds of bus stops. Look at these bus stops!
These bus stops are in Asia,
and these bus stops are in Europe.
Lots of bus stops. How many are there?
Eleven.
Look how we show the number of bus stops in a bar chart!
Eleven bus stops.

mailboxes

Look at these mailboxes! They are all different.
This mailbox is white,
and these mailboxes are gray.
These mailboxes are big, and they're red and yellow.
Lots of mailboxes. How many are there?
Seven.
Look how we show the number of mailboxes in a bar chart!
Seven mailboxes.

traffic lights

There are many kinds of traffic lights.
These traffic lights have three colors – green, orange, and red.
This traffic light has four lights.
Look! This traffic light is for bikes.
Lots of traffic lights. How many are there?
Sixteen.
Look how we show the number of traffic lights in a bar chart!
Sixteen traffic lights.

What do you know?

How many are there?
Fourteen streetlights.
Eleven bus stops.
Seven mailboxes.
Sixteen traffic lights.

Good job!

See you next time on *Guess What!* Bye!

Unit 5

Unit Topic: Meals

Topic: Science – food groups

Question: What kind of food is it?

Learning objective: Children should:
- be able to identify 4 different food groups and classify examples of food into those groups
- understand that food is classified into different groups

Video 05

Hi again. Welcome back to *Guess What!*
Today we're asking,
What kind of food is it?
Let's find out.

fruit

Fruit is a kind of food.
Apples, oranges, and bananas are fruit. They're healthy food.
We can eat fruit for breakfast, lunch, and dinner!

vegetables

Vegetables are a kind of food.
Beans are vegetables,
and carrots and peas are vegetables, too.
Look at this family! They like vegetables for dinner.

meat

Meat is a kind of food.
Chicken is a kind of meat.
Beef is a kind of meat, too.
We can eat meat for breakfast, lunch, or dinner.

grains

Grains are a kind of food.
Bread is made from grains. Look at all the different kinds of bread.
Look at the girls! Their cereal is made from grains.
We can eat cereal and toast for breakfast. Toast is made from grains.

dairy

Dairy is a kind of food, too.
Dairy food is made from milk.
Look! Cheese is made from milk.
We all need some dairy food. It's healthy.
Fruit, vegetables, grains, dairy, and meat are all kinds of food we eat.

What do you know?

What kind of food is it?
fruit
dairy
grains

Good job!

See you next time on *Guess What!* Bye!

Unit 6

Unit Topic: Activities

Topic: Physical education – sports equipment

Question: What equipment do we need?

Learning objective: Children should:
- be able to identify 4 kinds of equipment used when playing different sports
- understand that there are different kinds of sports equipment we need

Video 06

Hi again. Welcome back to *Guess What!*
Today we're asking,
What equipment do we need?
Let's find out.

a ball

We need a ball for playing some sports. We need a ball for playing basketball.
We need a ball for playing soccer, too.

a racket and a ball

We need a racket and a ball for playing tennis.

a stick and a ball

We need a stick and a ball for playing field hockey
and for playing golf.
We need a stick and a ball for playing this sport on horses.
It's called polo.

a bat and a ball

We need a bat and a ball for playing baseball,
and for playing softball.
We need a bat and a ball for playing cricket, too.

We don't need equipment for some sports.
We don't need equipment for swimming,
and we don't need equipment for running!

What do you know?

What equipment do we need?
We need a bat.
We need a ball.
We need a racket.

Good job!

See you next time on *Guess What!* Bye!

Unit 7

Unit Topic: In town

Topic: Geography – reading basic map references

Question: Where are the places?

Learning objective: Children should:
- be able to read a basic grid reference and identify places/building on it
- understand that a grid reference is used to read where places/buildings are on a map

Video 07

Hi again. Welcome back to *Guess What!*
Today we're asking,
Where are the places?
Let's find out.

fire station

These are fire stations.
This fire station is in North America. Look at the fire truck.
This fire station is in Europe. Look! The two fire trucks are next to each other.
This fire station is in South America. The fire trucks are in front of the fire station.
And look at the long ladder!
Look how we find the fire station on the map! It's in square B4.

hospital

These are hospitals.
This hospital is in Europe. It's between two buildings.
Can you see the word *hospital* on the wall?
This hospital is in Europe, too. It's very beautiful.
This hospital is in Australia. It's very big. Look! There's an ambulance!
Look how we find the hospital on the map! It's in square C1.

sports center

These are sports centers.
This sports center is round.
This sports center is round, too.
Look at this sports center. It's red and yellow!
Look how we find the sports center on the map! It's in square D5.

police station

These are police stations.
This police station is very big. It's in North America.
And look! There's a police car.
This police station is in North America, too. It's small.
This police station is very big. It's in Asia. Can you see the word *police*?
Look how we find the police station on the map! It's in square E3.

What do you know?

Where are the places?
The police station is in E3.
The hospital is in C1.
The sports center is in D5.
The fire station is in B4.

Good job!

See you next time on *Guess What!* Bye!

Unit 8

Unit Topic: On the farm

Topic: Science – farming process for growing crops

Question: What do farmers do?

Learning objective: Children should:
- be able to explain the steps in the process of growing food on a farm
- understand a farmer's role in the process of growing food

Video 08

Hi again. Welcome back to *Guess What!*
Today we're asking,
What do farmers do?
Let's find out.

turn soil

These farmers are turning the soil in their fields.
This farmer has an animal to help him.
This farmer has a machine to help him.
This farmer doesn't have an animal or a machine to help him. He's turning the soil by hand.

plant seeds

These farmers are planting seeds.
Some farmers plant seeds by hand. This farmer is a man, and this farmer is a woman.
Some farmers have machines to plant their seeds.

water plants

The seeds are now small plants. Farmers need to water the plants.
Some farmers water the plants by hand.
Some farmers have machines to water their plants. This is a small machine,
and this is a big machine.

harvest plants

These farmers are harvesting their plants.
This farmer is harvesting her rice plants by hand.
This farmer is harvesting the fruit from his coffee plant by hand.
This farmer has a very big machine to harvest his grain.

What do you know?

What do farmers do?
They plant seeds.
They water plants.
They harvest plants.

Good job!

Bye!